The Annual of Scientific Discovery: Or, Year-Book of Facts in Science and Art
by David Ames Wells

Benjamin Peirce

ANNUAL

OF

SCIENTIFIC DISCOVERY:

OR,

YEAR-BOOK OF FACTS IN SCIENCE AND ART

FOR 1871,

EXHIBITING THE MOST IMPORTANT DISCOVERIES AND IMPROVEMENTS IN MECHANICS, USEFUL ARTS, NATURAL PHILOSOPHY, CHEMISTRY, ASTRONOMY, GEOLOGY, BIOLOGY, BOTANY, MINERALOGY, METEOROLOGY, GEOGRAPHY, ANTIQUITIES, ETC.

TOGETHER WITH

NOTES ON THE PROGRESS OF SCIENCE DURING THE YEAR 1870; A LIST OF RECENT SCIENTIFIC PUBLICATIONS; OBITUARIES OF EMINENT SCIENTIFIC MEN, ETC.

EDITED BY

JOHN TROWBRIDGE

ASSISTED BY

SAMUEL KNEELAND, M.D., A.M.,

PROFESSOR OF ZOOLOGY AND PHYSIOLOGY IN THE INSTITUTE,

AND

W. R. NICHOLS,

GRADUATE OF THE INSTITUTE.

BOSTON:

GOULD AND LINCOLN,

59 WASHINGTON STREET.

NEW YORK, SHELDON AND COMPANY.

LONDON: TRÜBNER & CO.

1871.

ANNUAL

OF

SCIENTIFIC DISCOVERY:

OR,

YEAR-BOOK OF FACTS IN SCIENCE AND ART,

FOR 1870,

EXHIBITING THE

MOST IMPORTANT DISCOVERIES AND IMPROVEMENTS

IN

MECHANICS, USEFUL ARTS, NATURAL PHILOSOPHY, CHEMISTRY,
ASTRONOMY, GEOLOGY, BIOLOGY, BOTANY, MINERALOGY,
METEOROLOGY, GEOGRAPHY, ANTIQUITIES, ETC.,

TOGETHER WITH

NOTES ON THE PROGRESS OF SCIENCE DURING THE YEAR 1869; A LIST
OF RECENT SCIENTIFIC PUBLICATIONS; OBITUARIES OF
EMINENT SCIENTIFIC MEN, ETC.

EDITED BY

JOHN TROWBRIDGE, S.B.,

ASSISTANT PROFESSOR OF PHYSICS IN THE MASSACHUSETTS INSTITUTE OF TECHNOLOGY;

AIDED BY

SAMUEL KNEELAND, M.D.,

PROFESSOR OF ZOÖLOGY AND PHYSIOLOGY IN THE INSTITUTE;

AND

W. R. NICHOLS,

GRADUATE OF THE INSTITUTE.

BOSTON:

GOULD AND LINCOLN,

59 WASHINGTON STREET.

NEW YORK: SHELDON AND COMPANY.

LONDON: TRÜBNER & CO.

1871.

NOTES BY THE EDITOR,

ON THE

PROGRESS OF SCIENCE FOR THE YEAR 1869.

THE opening of the Pacific Railway and of the Suez Canal, and the completion of the laying of the French Cable, are tempting subjects to dwell upon.

It is not fitting to indulge in national boasting, at the completion of our line to the Pacific, before we learn the exact condition of the road, and the thoroughness of the work; although the rapidity of its execution, and its magnitude, might excuse any display of national egotism. The opening, however, of our great territories to the enterprise of both Atlantic and Pacific coasts, and to the cheap labor of Asia, is a result clearly to be seen.

We shall soon be called upon to chronicle other Pacific Railways; a northern, and possibly a southern one. As in the case of the French Atlantic Cable, the success of later attempts will be received as a matter of course, and the Pacific Railroad, whose completion we note to-day, will lose its prestige among the coming number of routes to the Pacific. In the present volume will be found accounts of the coal-fields of the territories. Apprehensions of lack of fuel for our great railway, by the discovery of these deposits, are seen to be ill-founded. It is felt that the Pacific Railway, with all its great realities and possibilities, is inadequate as a means of communication between our lines of coast, and attention has been redirected to the Darien Ship Canal. An appropriation has been made by Congress to pay the expenses of a new survey for this work, and an expedition has already sailed.

The completion of the Suez Canal undoubtedly had its share in directing public attention in the United States to the possibility of this enterprise. This canal has been opened with impressive

III

ceremonies; the reports are somewhat contradictory in regard to the work.

Shallow iron steam-ships are being built on the Tyne, for the navigation of the canal. Mr. Ashbury, who sailed through the canal in his yacht, Cambria, writes that after taking careful soundings, he is of the opinion that no vessel drawing over nineteen feet of water can pass through the canal.

The "New York Tribune" states: "Two of the steamers of the Messageries Imperiales (French Company), of 2,400 tons burden, have safely passed through the Suez Canal. Steamers drawing fifteen feet can navigate the canal from Port Said to Suez, with ease, in fifteen hours. The water does not wash away the banks as much as apprehended. The complete success of the great work exceeds all expectations."

The Suez Canal Company has issued regulations for the navigation of the canal. Article I. states that the navigation of the Suez Maritime Canal will be open to all ships without distinction of nationality, provided their draught of water does not exceed 7½ metres, the depth of the canal being 8 metres, equal to 26 English feet.

To-day we witness a return to old routes of commerce. In early times, the track of commerce between the West and the East was by the way of Egypt and the Red Sea; from this commerce Alexandria rose to opulence, and Venice became a first-rate power. Afterwards, by the discovery of the Cape route, trade was diverted into new channels, and Venice and Alexandria sank in wealth and importance. The opening of the Suez Canal brings commerce back into its old channel.

We are called upon to chronicle the successful laying of the French Atlantic Cable.

A project to extend telegraphic communication from Cuba (already in connection with Florida) by Porto Rico, through the West India Island, is favorably entertained. Prussia, too, we hear, is beginning to think of securing more direct communication with America. It has been suggested that if a cable were laid from a point on her seaboard round by the north of Scotland, and by the western shore of Ireland, to join the Anglo-American cables at Valentia, Prussia would send all the North of Europe messages by this route.

It is understood that the Prussian Government have had the subject recently before them, and that a concession has been granted to carry out an Atlantic cable, having North Germany for its terminus. The old project of the North Atlantic is being again mooted. That route was to go by Iceland, Greenland, and so on to Canada and the United States, Denmark being the assumed starting-point. The cable to India by the Red Sea is going on satisfactorily, and an auxiliary line, one between Marseilles and Malta, is spoken of.

All these projects indicate increased convenience and gain to the public. At present the use of the ocean telegraph is confined to the commercial community; but ere long, when the tariff is reduced from Europe to America, and to India, the general public will send messages as freely as they do by the land wires. We may reasonably hope, too, that the cost of submarine cables will be reduced by and by, and this will do more to cheapen messages than anything else.

In Northern Russia the construction of a land line is far advanced to connect St. Petersburg with the mouth of the Amour River, on completion of which only a submarine link will be wanting to complete the telegraphic girdle round the earth.

Electricity and steam are the great agents of civilization. The introduction of telegraphic lines and railways in Russia and Asia is destined to revolutionize this part of the globe. We Americans are apt to think ourselves the most progressive nation, and point with especial pride to our Pacific Railway. Russia, however, is making great strides; and the English railways in India compete in difficulty of execution and magnitude with the Pacific Railway.

During the past year several improvements in railway carriages have been brought before the public.

Mr. Robert F. Fairlie has invented a steam carriage which will round curves of 50 feet radius at 20 miles an hour, with, it is alleged, perfect safety. The carriage, instead of seating the usual complement of 100 passengers (English car), seats only 66. The English papers are enthusiastic in regard to this carriage.

The Portmadoc and Festiniog Railway, in Wales, has also attracted much attention, from the narrowness of its gauge, — two feet only. The Fairlie carriage and the narrow-gauge railway will undoubtedly come into play in difficult countries.

We are certainly far from perfection in the construction of our railways in America. The fearful catastrophes that have taken place from cars taking fire have reawakened an interest in new methods of heating them. No method has yet been devised to meet the difficulty satisfactorily. In this volume will be found

1*

the description of an electro-heating apparatus. The introduction of steel rails promises to make accidents from defective rails rarer.

The English have lately turned their attention to the American system of constructing railroads. They have found, to their surprise, that in India they must adopt American ideas. Notwithstanding its defects, it has been found that our system is likely to prove the best for their colonies. A commission of English engineers are now investigating our system with a view to the railways of India.

The brake power on several of the French and Spanish railways has been greatly increased by an ingenious arrangement conceived by Monsieur Chatelier, of applying what has been termed "contre vapeur" to the engine, converting it, for the time being, into a pump forcing steam and water into the boiler.

At a meeting of the American Academy of Arts and Sciences, held in Boston, U. S., the Rumford medals were presented to Mr. George H. Corliss, of Providence, R. I., for his improvements in the steam-engine. The presentation was made by Dr. Asa Gray, the President of the Academy. We make the following extract from his remarks :—

"It appears that within the twenty years since this machinery was perfected, more than 1,000 engines of the kind have been built in the United States, and several hundred in other countries, giving an aggregate of not less than 250,000 horse-power; that as to economy of fuel, evidence has been afforded to the Rumford Committee, showing a saving over older forms of engines of about one-third. As to its other crowning excellence, uniformity of velocity, the purchasers of one of the engines, now in its eighteenth year of service, certify that, with the power varying from 60 to 360 horse-power within a minute, the speed of the engine is not perceptibly affected."

While we chronicle the great works in engineering, the improvements of the past year in making steel promise still greater achievements. The Bessemer process has already done much; the later discovery of Bessemer, the high-pressure furnace, by which the melting of ores is accomplished much more speedily and economically than by the old processes, is destined, it is thought, to further cheapen steel. It is stated that Bessemer was led to this discovery by meditation on the cause of the heat of the sun, and the influence that the force of gravity, 27 times greater than that upon our earth, must have upon the intensity of that heat.

The Siemens regenerating furnaces are being rapidly introduced into this country.

These processes tend towards cheapening a very first-class material, which will undoubtedly supersede iron for almost all structural purposes. Engineers hesitate at present to use this material, since no adequate experiments have been made in regard to the limits to which steel structures can be loaded with safety. Experimental researches have been carried on for some time in England, at Woolwich, under a committee appointed by the Institution of Civil Engineers, which promise to supply this want.

The results of Mr. Whitworth's experiments, tending to supersede the hammer and rolls by forcing cast steel, while in a semifluid state, into strong iron moulds by hydraulic pressure, are regarded with great interest.

The use of pulverized fuel, experiments on which are now being conducted, promises, by surrounding each particle with just the amount of oxygen which it needs for perfect combustion, to utilize fuel to greater advantage.

"The Bulletin of the American Iron and Steel Association" states that 65 new blast furnaces have been erected in this country during the last 18 months. It adds that it has a record of 58 more in contemplation, the greater number at the West, nearly all of which will be built the coming year, if those engaged can be assured of the stability of the tariff.

The "Bulletin" computes the total product of Pig Iron in this country during 1869 at more than 1,900,000 tons. In 1865 (the first year after the war), it was but 931,000 tons, — an increase without a parallel in the history of any country.

Steel rails are being largely adopted both at home and abroad. The results of the experiments made are not merely satisfactory in regard to the increased durability of the new material. They demonstrate that the section might be materially reduced. The Northern Railway Company, of Austria, was one of the earliest to experiment upon rails of Bessemer steel, and exhibited specimens of its rails at the exposition of 1867. With a weight per yard of only 45 pounds, the company obtained a steel rail having double the strength of the iron rails of a larger section previously employed by them; the cost to the company per ton of iron rails having been from 60 dollars to 70 dollars, and that of steel rails being from 90 dollars to 100 dollars. The expense per running mile is still kept nearly within its original limits, with a very great improvement in regard to strength and durability.

The French Railway Companies are also extensively introducing rails of Bessemer steel upon their roads. These rails, as manufactured at the principal French works, cost from 60 to 70 dollars per ton.

There is a growing feeling among engineers and steel makers, that the compound rail, made wholly or partly of steel, will prove more safe and economical than any solid rail, for, if the same durability of track can be obtained with a steel cap as with an all-steel rail, the first cost will be greatly decreased. A rail made in two or three continuous parts, breaking joints, is also a practical insurance against disaster from broken rails.

It is estimated that in the United States from 40,000 to 50,000 tons of steel rails are in use on our various railways.

The Lehigh and Susquehannah is entirely built of steel. Other railways are using them largely, the Hudson River, Erie, and Pennsylvania Railways using 10,000 tons or more each. The last report of the New Jersey Railway and Transportation Company says: "It is probable that steel rails will be gradually laid the entire length of the road, the greater durability of these rails overcoming the objection to their increased cost."

The use of steel rails will guarantee greater safety of life and limb, and their introduction, therefore, should be hailed with delight, for the term American rails has become a synonym for the cheapest and least durable rails manufactured.

Our late war taught us much in regard to ordnance and iron ships. The great advances in the manufacture of steel, and the discovery of new explosives, are destined to materially further our knowledge.

The most noteworthy improvement of this year in fortifications is Captain Moncrief's system. By an ingenious device he lowers his gun upon its rocking carriage after firing, and thereby does away with embrasures (the weak places in protecting works), while he gains the advantage of reloading his gun in comparative of safety.

What influence the new explosives, picrates, dynamite, and ammonia powder will have on warlike operations, remains to be seen.

Attention has lately been turned to gas as a calorific agent. Profs. Silliman and Wurtz, by their researches, promise to increase our knowledge of its illuminating power. Articles will be found on page 90 bearing upon this subject.

Prof. Tyndall says that the superiority of gas for light-houses over oil is rendered very manifest by the experiments lately instituted at Howth Baily and Wicklow Head.

One cannot fail to notice the impulse which the completion of the Pacific Railway, the Suez Canal, and the French Atlantic Cable have given to the desire implanted in the human breast to overcome natural obstacles. M. Lesseps advocates flooding the desert of Sahara by means of a canal, and thus afford communication with the interior of Africa.

Among the projects that have been re-agitated the past year, are the project of a canal around the Falls of Niagara; a re-enlargement of the Erie for vessels of 1,000 tons; one across the Alleghanies in Virginia; one through the Isthmus of Darien, the expedition for surveying which has already started, and one from Huron to Ontario. In tunnels we have that of Mt. Cenis, 8 miles, and the Hoosac, 5 miles, in length, both in rapid progress; one of wrought-iron tubes at London, and another at Chicago; tunnels proposed under the East and North Rivers at New York; under the Ganges at Calcutta, and under the Straits of Dover.

In view of past achievements, it is not safe to pronounce any of these projects not feasible.

In physical science, Tyndall commenced the year with a picturesque account of a discovery of the peculiar action of light upon vapors.

In electricity we have no startling discoveries to chronicle. M. Jamin, it is said, has ascertained that magnetism can be condensed for a short period in the same way as electricity. Prof. LeRoy Cooley, of Albany, has discovered a way of registering vibrations by means of electricity. His method will be found on page 162.

He dispenses with the sirene, and obtains a direct registration, the vibrating body itself opening and closing a circuit.

We have about the usual number of new batteries to chronicle. The combination of elements to produce currents seems unlimited.

The energies, however, of most of our physicists, both at home and abroad, have been directed to the field of spectrum analysis.

The late eclipse undoubtedly awakened greater interest in this new branch of science.

Prof. Magnus has lately published a research upon heat spectra.

Angström and Thalen have also lately published laborious and accurate tables of the wave lengths of the different metals.

Roscoe's work on Spectrum Analysis, published this year, presents the subject in a very lucid manner.

We incorporate herewith the notes of Mr. Nichols on the progress in the field of chemistry.

In Chemistry no startling discovery has been made during the past year. Yet each year marks progress, especially in the contributions to the history of the compounds of carbon, and each year adds to the number of those complex bodies which, a short time ago, were found only in the bodies of animals or in plants, but which now can be prepared at will, in the laboratory. Especial attention may be called to the production during the past year, by artificial means, of *alizarine*, the coloring matter of the madder root (vide p. 205). Such discoveries extend our views of the domain of chemistry and cause us to have less apprehension in regard to the limited supply of many substances, the demand for which is continually increasing.

The publication by Professor Bunsen, of Heidelberg, of a paper on the "Washing of Precipitates" (vide p. 210), has wrought a great change in the manner of conducting in the laboratory an operation of constant occurrence, that of filtration. By his method, as contrasted with that formerly employed, the saving of time amounts in certain cases to many hundred per cent., — an advantage which, at the present day, we cannot afford to overlook.

The researches of Graham (vide p. 194) on the metallic character of hydrogen as deduced from the deportment of the alloys of palladium and hydrogen show how close is the relation between mechanical force and chemical affinity. It seems as if he were "led not only to manifest the metallic character of hydrogen, but also to seize the very moment at which the phenomenon of the mechanical condensation of a gas by a porous body changes into a truly chemical combination." [*]

The council of the Chemical Society (London) having determined to found an annual lectureship in honor of Faraday, the inaugural lecture was delivered this year (June 18) by the French

---

[*] Dumas. Faraday Lecture.

chemist, Dumas, who was eminently fitted to perform this duty, not only on account of his having been an intimate friend of Faraday, but also on account of his great eloquence, and on account of his eminent position among the chemists of his own country. He began with an admirable eulogy of him whom his discourse commemorated, and then reviewed, from the stand-point of the present day, the progress of chemistry from its first beginnings.

He paid tribute to the labors of Lavoisier, Dalton, and Prout, and, pointing out the analogies existing between the elements of mineral chemistry and the compound radicals of organic chemistry (so called), and at the same time the relations between the atomic weights of those bodies which are now accepted as elements, he argued the probability of their being themselves proved to be complex.

The limits of chemistry he defines in these words: "The existing chemistry is, therefore, all powerful in the circle of mineral nature, even when its processes are carried on in the heart of the tissues of plants or of animals and at their expense; and she has advanced no further than the chemistry of the ancients in the knowledge of life and in the exact study of living matter; like them she is ignorant of the mode of generation.

"The ancients were mistaken when they confounded, under the name of *organic matter*, sugar and alcohol, which have never lived with the living tissue of plants, or in the flesh of animals. Sugar and alcohol have no more share of life than bone-earth, or salts contained in the various liquids. The chemist has never manufactured anything which, near or distant, was susceptible even of the appearance of life. Everything he has made in his laboratories belongs to ' brute' matter; as soon as he approaches life and organization, he is disarmed."

The medal which accompanies the Faraday lectureship is struck in palladium, and, in addition to this medal, Dumas carries back to France with him a medal struck in the alloy of palladium and hydrogen to commemorate the discovery of the alloy by Graham.

The subject of the disposal of the sewage of towns becomes daily of more importance. At the meeting of the British Association at Exeter, a report was presented, in which were collected statistics showing the various methods adopted in towns and cities on the continent for utilizing the sewage, and that committee has issued circulars to the town authorities throughout England asking for aid in collecting information and in making experiments in regard to this matter. The earth-closet is finding favor, and, no doubt, will eventually supersede the water-closet in rural districts, and in towns where a supply of water cannot readily be obtained. The fact that it has been made the subject of a patent adds to its cost, and will retard somewhat its adoption in this country, but now that attention has been called to the matter, use will be made, and with advantage in a sanitary aspect, of the principle which is involved in it, — the disinfecting power of dry earth.

"Like some other valuable discoveries, it seems surprising that nobody thought of it or applied it before. But the simple fact is, that the privy may be made as inoffensive as the corn-barn by the application of about a pint and a half of *dry earth* every time it is used. There are one or two things about it important to remember: (1.) It should be *earth* (not sand or gravel), and should be thoroughly dried by exposure to the sun or otherwise; (2.) The privy-vault should be kept free from rain, from slops, and from excessive moisture of any sort. The more fluid thrown in, the more dry earth required to absorb it. How often it happens that a country hotel or boarding-house, crowded with people, becomes late in the season disgusting and unhealthy from decomposing material when a few shovelsful of dried earth thrown into the privy once a day would remove all offence." *

It has been proposed for dried earth to substitute charcoal, which would be regenerated by burning. It is stated that one hundred weight of charcoal per month would be sufficient for a closet used by six persons daily. It is not likely, however, that this modification will find extensive adoption, except in localities peculiarly situated."

We incorporate herewith the notes of Dr. Kneeland on the progress in biology: —

"The theory of Darwin is steadily progressing in the estimation of naturalists; indeed it may be said to be no longer simply a theory, as it has been demonstrated, in a few instances at least, both in the vegetable and animal kingdom, that 'natural selection,' or the survival of the fittest, is one of the causes of the existing varieties and so-called species among animals and plants. No naturalist can now presume to sneer at or ignore this and kindred theories, when such men as Lyell, Hooker, Huxley, and Owen reject utterly the doctrine of innumerable special acts of creation, and accept in variously modified forms the development

* Report of Massachusetts State Board of Health, 1870.

of living things by the operation of laws impressed upon them at the beginning. The 'derivative hypothesis' of Owen, detailed on pp. 267–270, apparently meets the approval of naturalists more generally than any other; this maintains the incessant new development of living beings out of non-living material, and sees the grandeur of creative power, not in the exceptional miracle of one or few original forms of life, but in the daily and hourly calling into existence many forms by conversion of chemical and physical into vital modes of force; his conclusion is that, from the magnet which chooses between steel and zinc, to the philosopher who chooses between good and evil, the difference is one of degree, not of kind, and that there is no need of assuming a special miracle to account for mental phenomena. 'Natural selection' also is operative in the case of men, among whom there is a perpetual survival of the fittest; in the most barbarous conditions of mankind the struggle is almost entirely between individuals; in proportion as civilization has increased among men, it is easy to trace the transference of a great part of the struggle, little by little, from individuals to tribes, nations, leagues, guilds, corporations, societies, and similar combinations; and accompanying this transference has been undeniably the development of the moral qualities and of social virtues.

"The Social Science Associations are actively working out the great problems of moral and physical evils incident to civilization, especially those pertaining to hygienic or sanitary reform. The first step in the moral elevation of a community has been found to be the diffusion of knowledge of sanitary laws; cleanliness and good health are recognized as the best foundations of public prosperity. Hence science is constantly progressing in attempts to secure for the masses of the people cheap and wholesome food, pure air and pure water, ventilation of public buildings and the crowded dwellings of the poor; the removal of sewage, so as not only not to contaminate the earth, air, and water, but to convert it, even in our own houses, into an inodorous and valuable fertilizer, has been successfully accomplished. Fire-extinguishing and life-saving apparatus, both on land and sea, have reached a high degree of efficiency; man is gradually obtaining the mastery over the epidemic diseases which have for ages decimated the human race; and the return from human to vaccine lymph direct from the cow will restore the wavering faith of the public in the efficacy of vaccination, and eventually put a stop to the ravages of small-pox.

The recent successful employment of chloral as an anæsthetic,

2

by the stomach instead of the lungs, and its undoubted efficacy as a sedative in nervous diseases and insanity, has drawn the attention of physiological chemists to the nearly unexplored field of the action of medicines by decomposition within the inmost recesses of the body.

Deep-sea dredgings have revealed an extensive and varied range of life at depths heretofore deemed untenanted, and have proved that there is a band of organisms encircling the globe at the bottom of the ocean, — these organisms, too, resembling those found in the immensely remote cretaceous epoch. The amœba, described on p. 294, seems to be one of the links which connect the inorganic with the organic world, its organless tissue being capable of combining physical forces so as to assume organic functions."

Great advances have been made in celestial chemistry during the year, through the medium of spectrum analysis.

The observations of Huggins by means of this delicate method have proved that the star Sirius is receding from the earth at the rate of 29.4 miles per second; the observations of Huggins have been confirmed by Father Secchi, made at Rome. It is thought that the results of these and similar observations may one day lead to a determination of the motion of the solar system in space. By the same method of analysis, traces of aqueous vapor have been discovered in some of the planets.

The President of the British Association, in his address at Exeter, thus details Lockyer's discovery: —

"After having observed the remarkable spectrum of the prominences during the total eclipse, it occurred to M. Janssen that the same method might allow the prominences to be detected at any time; and on trial he succeeded in detecting them the very day after the eclipse. The results of his observations were sent by post, and were received shortly after the account of Mr. Lockyer's discovery had been communicated by Mr. De La Rue to the French Academy. In the way hitherto described a prominence is not seen as a whole, but the observer knows when its image is intercepted by the slit; and by varying a little the position of the slit, a series of sections of the prominence are obtained, by putting which together the form of the prominence is deduced. Shortly after Mr. Lockyer's communication of his discovery, Mr. Huggins, who had been independently engaged in the attempt to render the prominences visible by the aid of the spectroscope, succeeded in seeing a prominence as a whole by somewhat widening the slit, and using a red glass to diminish the glare of the light, admitted by the slit, the prominence being seen by means of the C line in the red. Mr. Lockyer had a design for seeing the prominences as a whole by giving the slit a rapid motion of small extent, but this proved to be superfluous, and they are now habitually seen with their actual forms. Nor is our power of observing them restricted to those which are so situated that they are seen by projection outside the sun's limb; such is the power of the spectroscopic method of observation, that it has enabled Mr. Lockyer and others to observe them right on the disc of the sun, — an important step for connecting them with other solar phenomena. One of the most striking results of the habitual study of these promi-nences is the evidence they afford of the stupendous changes which are going on in the central body of our system. Prominences, the heights of which are to be measured by thou-sands and tens of thousands of miles, appear and disappear in the course of some minutes. And a study of certain minute changes of position in the bright line F, which receive a simple and natural explanation by referring them to proper motion in the glowing gas by which that line is produced, and which we see no other way of accounting for, have led Mr. Lockyer to conclude that the gas in question is sometimes travelling with velocities comparable with that of the earth in its orbit. Moreover, these exhibitions of intense action are frequently found to be intimately connected with the spots, and can hardly fail to throw light on the disputed question of their formation. Nor are chemical composi-tion and proper motion the only physical conditions of the gas which are accessible to spectral analysis. By comparing the breadth of the bright bands (for though narrow they are not mere lines) seen in the prominences, with those observed in the spectrum of hydrogen, rendered incandescent under different physical conditions, Dr. Frankland and Mr. Lockyer have deduced conclusions respecting the pressure to which the gas is subject in the neighborhood of the sun."

Since the discovery of Lockyer's, Janssen's, and Huggins' method of viewing the prominences, Zöllner has discovered a way of seeing them as a whole. His method will be found on page 322; Prof. Young's method will be also found in detail on page 315. He makes use also of the C line, and likens it to looking at the sun-set sky through a chink in the window. It is thought that this method may be used to advantage in the coming transit of Venus. The total eclipse of August 7th, 1869, was very fully observed.

The "American Journal of Arts and Sciences" thus speaks of the arrangements made for observing the phenomenon:—

"Few astronomical phenomena have probably ever called out a more thoroughly organized system of observation than that arranged for the recent eclipse. The line of total obscuration crossed the North American continent diagonally, entering the territory of the United States at Behring's Straits, in about the 65th degree of latitude, and longitude 90° west of Washington, while it left our shore at the latitude of 34° and the meridian of Washington itself. It traversed a central belt of well-populated territory, yet there seems to have been scarcely a town of any considerable magnitude along the entire line which was not garrisoned by observers having some special astronomical problem in view.

An appropriation was made by Congress, at its last session, for carrying out a series of observations under the direction of the Superintendent of the Nautical Almanac, and Prof. Coffin has succeeded, by the liberal aid of the Navy Department, and the very generous and extensive facilities contributed by some of the principal railroads, in providing for an amount of work which for magnitude, variety, and thoroughness, seems large beyond all proportion to the sum placed at his disposal. Three cities in Iowa, Burlington, Mount Pleasant, and Ottumwa, were occupied by astronomical, photographic, and physical observers under his direction, and special observers, provided with telescopes and instruments for determining geographical position, were sent by him to the North and South, to fix the limits of the belt of total obscuration.

The Navy Department, besides making other provisions, sent observers to the western shore of Behring's Straits; and the War Department detailed Dr. Curtis to make special photographic observations at Des Moines, Iowa.

The Coast Survey established parties on the Yaken River, in Alaska, at Des Moines in Iowa, Springfield in Illinois, and Abingdon in West Virginia, and perhaps at still other stations,— that at Springfield being amply provided with photographic observers and apparatus. Most of the principal observatories likewise organized expeditions of greater or less magnitude. From Washington, the several observers arranged independent series of investigations, stellar, spectroscopic, physical, and meteorological. From Cambridge, a large party went to Shelbyville, Ky., with large photographic outfit, and spectroscopic equipments.

From Albany, a similar party went to Mattoon, Illinois; others, from Clinton and Chicago, went to Des Moines, from Cincinnati to Sioux City; and the number of private astronomers who established themselves along the central line with telescopes and other apparatus of investigation must have been exceedingly large.

The beginning and end of the eclipse seem to have been observed a few seconds later, and the beginning and end of the totality about fifteen seconds later than the predictions of the American Nautical Almanac. As regards the exact position of the central line, and of the limits of the total belt, we have as yet insufficient information to determine the degree of accordance with computation. There can be no doubt that materials have been collected capable of improving the adopted values of the moon's diameter and horizontal parallax. One of the most interesting results is the introduction of a new and accurate method of determining the time of first contact, by observing with a spectroscope the gradual occultation of the bright lines of the chromosphere. This we owe to Prof. Young, of Dartmouth College, who formed one of Prof. Coffin's Nautical Almanac party at Burlington. By keeping the centre of the slit directed to the point at which the contact is to take place, the observer is forewarned of the approach of the moon's limb, by the shortening of the bright lines belonging to the chromosphere. The line C is well adapted to this purpose, and is seen to grow steadily shorter, until it is totally extinguished. The moment of disappearance of the last bright ray is of course that of the first contact, which is thus observed with the same care and accuracy as any other appulsive phenomenon.* Although the first contact, as determined in this way by Prof. Young, was noted some five seconds before its recognition by any other observer, it was subsequently found by Prof. Mayer to accord within a small fraction of a second with the time as determined by measurement of a series of photographs taken during the first minute.

Prof. Harkness, of Washington Observatory, observed at Des Moines the spectra of five protuberances, no two of which gave the same lines. In the corona spectrum he found no absorptive lines, and but one bright line. Measures of the protuberances were made by Prof. Rogers, at Des Moines, who found the largest to be nearly a minute and a half high, and observed a peculiar honeycombed or cellular appearance in all of them. Special search was made for intra-mercurial planets by Prof. Newcomb, at Des Moines, according to the plan suggested by

2*

him in the April number of the "American Journal of Science and Arts," with two 6-inch object-glasses, having a field of about 20° each, and previously clamped to the desired position. A similar scrutiny of the ecliptic near the sun was made by Dr. Gould, at Burlington, in connection with Prof. Coffin's party, using a Tolles' telescope of five inches' aperture and a field of nearly 2°, provided with occulting discs at the focus. But neither of these observers, nor any others engaged in similar research, found any indications of planets nearer than Mercury.

Dr. Gould says in a letter to Prof. Morton: "An examination of the beautiful photographs made at Burlington and Ottumwa, by the section of your party in charge of Professors Mayer and Himes, and a comparison of them with my sketches of the corona, have led me to the conviction that the radiance around the moon, in the pictures made during totality, is not the corona at all, but is actually the image of what Lockyer has called the chromosphere."

Prof. Pickering, of the Massachusetts Institute of Technology, who observed at Mt. Pleasant, Iowa, concludes his report as follows : —

"An increase of heat and actinic power is observed in the beginning of the eclipse, caused by an increased brightness of the sun's disc near the moon's limb. The spectrum of the corona appears to be free from dark lines, but may contain two or three bright ones. Its striæ are spiral rather than radial, and its light is unpolarized. The sky adjoining it, however, reflecting light from the earth, shows strong signs of polarization."

From Prof. Winlock's report we learn that "The chromosphere was carefully examined both before and after the eclipse. Only three lines could be seen, C, one near D, and F. During totality only, the brightest protuberance on the lower limb of the sun was examined carefully. In the short time occupied in getting into this, nothing was seen but a faint continuous spectrum ; but since the observing telescope took in only a small part of the spectrum at once, nothing conclusive can be inferred from the observation as to the non-existence of bright lines in the corona.

"During totality, eleven bright lines were seen. Besides the three described above, there was a short line at or very near E ; the three lines of B were bright and very sharp, and there were four lines above F. Although these lines were very bright on a dark ground, all of them but the three seen before the eclipse disappeared instantly on the first burst of sunlight, and the same point in the sun's disc was examined with great care after totality without finding any of the lines but those above described.

"The photograph of the corona, taken at Shelbyville, shows a flattening at the extremities of the sun's axis, and an elevation about the equatorial region. The appearance can be explained by the hypothesis that it is a photographic view of the sun's atmosphere, and the form is that which it would assume from the sun's rotation about its axis with its upper surface disturbed by the protuberances or planes below, and by large waves which are to be expected in such an atmosphere."

The report of Com. B. F. Sands, U. S. N., Superintendent of the U. S. Naval Observatory, on the late eclipse, just published, is an exhaustive one, and compares favorably with the best efforts of a similar nature on the other side of the Atlantic.

Prof. Kirkwood, of Bloomington, Indiana, has lately published two able papers; one upon the periodicity of the solar spots, and another on comets and meteors. In the first-named paper he discusses the disturbing action of the planets on the sun's envelope, and suggests the hypothesis that a particular portion of the sun's surface is more favorable to spot formation than other portions. From his discussions he concludes : —

1. A connection between the behavior of sun-spots and the configuration of certain planets has been placed beyond reasonable doubt.

2. The theory, however, of spot formation by planetary influence is encumbered with anomalies and even inconsistencies, unless we admit the co-operation of a modifying cause.

3. The hypothesis that a particular part of the solar surface is more susceptible than others to planetary disturbance is rendered probable by the observations of different astronomers.

4. The 11-year cycle of spot variation is mainly dependent on the influence of Mercury.

5. The marked irregularity of this period from 1822 to 1867 is in a great measure due to the disturbing action of Venus.

6. Wolf's 56-year cycle is determined by the joint action of Mercury and the earth; and, finally, the hypothesis proposed accounts for all the well-defined cycles of spot-variations.

In the paper on comets and meteors, Prof. Kirkwood considers the probable consequences of the sun's motion through regions of space in which cosmical matter is widely diffused, and compares these theoretical deductions with the observed phenomena of comets, aerolites, and falling stars.

From the variation in the number of observed comets and the periodicity of shooting stars, it is concluded that during the interval from 700 to 1200 the solar system was passing through, or near, a meteoric cloud of very great extent; that from 1200 to 1700 it was traversing a region comparatively destitute of such matter; and that about the commencement of the 18th century it again entered a similar nebula of unknown extent.

The present Earl of Rosse has been engaged upon the determination of the radiation of heat from the moon. It appears from his research that the greater part of the moon's heat which reaches the earth appears to have been first absorbed by the lunar surface. The amount of lunar heat appears to indicate an elevation of temperature for the moon's surface at full moon of 500° F.

Full arrangements have been made in France and England to observe the coming transit of Venus. Some constants in astronomical science will be tested by these observations.

The new facts in geography may be thus summarized : —

The explorations and discoveries in South-eastern and East Equatorial Africa.

The additional and conclusive evidence now brought to light of a climate in the ice-bound region of the Arctic, at a past and remote period of time, resembling that of the countries lying near the equator.

The marvellous results of the deep-sea dredgings of Profs. Thompson and Carpenter, revealing the existence of animal life at immense depths in the ocean, where it has been supposed to have been impossible.

The very general disturbance throughout this year of the earth's surface by earthquakes, distinguishable not so much for the effects in particular localities as for the wide distribution of the phenomena over the globe, and its appearance in parts of the world where such disturbances have never been previously witnessed within the memory of man.

The attractive power of mountains, discovered in the pendulum experiments made during the past year at the observing stations upon the Himalayas, in India.

The discovery of trees of enormous size in Australia, one of which was found to be 69 feet in circumference; of great deposits of valuable coal throughout the whole of New Zealand, and the finding of coal upon the borders of the Caspian, verifying in the last particular a prediction of Humboldt, made forty years ago;

both of which discoveries are of the highest importance to commerce.

The anthropological researches in Europe, Asia, and Africa, revealing the structure, mode of life, and customs of the earliest inhabitants of the earth.

The assembling at Copenhagen, last August, of the International Congress of Prehistoric Archæology, under the auspices of the King of Denmark, interesting in the circumstance that it brought into communication with each other learned men from all parts of Europe, and for the valuable information the papers and descriptions elicited in respect to the three successive periods of man's early history, known as the stone, the bronze, and the iron.

The return of Capt. Hall from the Arctic regions with valuable information respecting that mysterious country.

The exploration by Dr. Hayes of the remains of the early settlements made on the south-eastern shore of Greenland. The return of captain Adams and his men from the exploration of the Colorado and its tributaries.

The completion of the French explorations of the river Cambodia to the province of Tunan in China, the official details of which have not yet appeared.

The expedition of Sir Samuel Baker into the interior of Africa, which started last October.

The escape of Captain Livingston, of the American ship Congress, through a cyclone of extraordinary intensity and force, and the gaining of valuable information thereby.

The expedition of the Russian Merchant Soidorow, in his own steamer, around the coast of Norway, and through the polar ocean, to the mouth of the Pitschora.

A dispatch from Bombay, Oct. 6, states: A letter has just been received here from Dr. Livingstone, the great African traveller. He was at Lake Bangweolo at time of writing (in July, 1868), and was in excellent health and spirits. He mentioned that he believed he had at last found the true source of the Nile.

A caravan arrived at Zanzibar, Oct. 14, 1869, bringing the news that Dr. Livingstone had arrived at Nigi alive and well.

A later report, at our time of writing, Feb. 5th, 1870, states that he has been burnt as a wizard, by a native chief; it is trusted that time will contradict this.

In a letter to the Earl of Clarendon, he says: "I think that I may safely assert that the chief sources of the Nile arise between 10° and 12° south latitude, or nearly in the position assigned to them by Ptolemy.

" The springs of the Nile have hitherto been searched for very much too far to the north. They rise some 400 miles south of the most southerly portion of the Victoria Nyanza, and, indeed, south of all the lakes except Bangweolo.

An International Exhibition of select works of fine and industrial art, and scientific inventions, is to be held in 1871, at South Kensington, England. This is the first of a series of annual exhibitions.

The movement which established the South Kensington Museum is having its parallel in Massachusetts and New York. It is proposed to establish a museum of the fine arts in New York and Boston. At the last session of the Legislature of Massachusetts, the following resolve was passed : —

" *Resolved*, That the Board of Education be directed to consider the expediency of making provision by law for giving free instruction to men, women, and children, in mechanical drawing, either in existing schools, or in those to be established for that purpose, in all the towns in the Commonwealth having more than five thousand inhabitants, and report a definite plan therefor to the next General Court. [Approved June 12, 1869.]"

It is felt that our common schools do not give the right training to the industrial classes, and that if we are to have skilled mechanics, we must educate them. In view of the great natural advantages of the West, we at the East can hold our ground only by skilled labor ; and the proper education of the lower classes has become a question of vital importance.

We present the readers of the ANNUAL OF SCIENTIFIC DISCOVERY for 1870, with a fine portrait of BENJAMIN PIERCE, LL. D., Professor of Mathematics, in Harvard College, and Superintendent of the United States Coast Survey.

THE

ANNUAL OF SCIENTIFIC DISCOVERY.

MECHANICS AND USEFUL ARTS.

PACIFIC RAILROAD TIME TABLE.

THE following statement of time and distances is given by the "Western Railroad Gazette":—

	Miles.	Hours.
New York to Chicago, Ill.,	911	36½
Chicago to Omaha, Nebraska,	491	24½
Omaha to Bryan,	858	43
Bryan to Ogden, Utah,	233	10½
Ogden to Elko, Nevada, via Central Pacific R. R.,	278	12½
Elko to Sacramento, Cal., via Central Pacific R. R.,	465	31
Sacramento to San Francisco, via Western Pacific R. R.,	117	3½
	3,353	161½

Thus a total distance of 3,353 miles is made, according to the present schedule time, in 6 days and 17½ hours, actual time, by a traveller's watch, from which we deduct 3½ hours, difference of time, when going West, leaving the apparent time consumed in making the trip 6 days and 14 hours.

At San Francisco the mails will connect with the various steamship lines running on the Pacific, and may be landed at Honolulu in 9 days from that city, or 15½ days from New York. They can reach Japan in 19 days from San Francisco, or 25½ days from New York, or 33 to 34 days from Great Britain — thus beating the British mails sent via Suez, 3 to 4 weeks. The trip between Yokohama, Japan, and either Hong Kong or Shanghai, is readily accomplished by the Pacific Mail steamships in from 5 to 6 days, which, added to the time in reaching Japan, will give the through time necessary to reach either of the above-named ports of China.

The mails for Australia, it is thought, will hereafter go via

San Francisco, as the Australian and New Zealand Steamship Company intend transferring the terminus of their line, which has been running from Sydney to Panama, so as hereafter to run from Australia to Taluti, thence to Honolulu, and thence to San Francisco, making 28 days, schedule time, which will give us monthly mail to Australia in 34 or 35 days through time.

THE RAILWAYS OF INDIA.

A great deal has been said and written respecting the completion of the Pacific Railway across the American continent; and much praise has been very justly bestowed upon the energy of the American character which has brought the work to its present position. While, however, we are lavish in our expressions of admiration for the great qualities which have thus been called into existence, we ought not to lose sight of the still greater works which have been accomplished in India, in the matter of railways. A vast work has been carried on silently and unobtrusively, and under difficulties even greater than any which have been experienced in regard to the Pacific Railroad, and we claim for those by whom these great works have been achieved some share of that admiration which is given so freely and so fairly to our American cousins. The Pacific line, including as it does the two separate schemes of the Union Pacific and the Central Pacific, is about 1,700 miles in length. Two of our leading Indian lines, namely, The East Indian and the Great Indian Peninsula, at present in work, have a joint mileage of 2,230 miles, and when completed it will be 2,768 miles, greater by more than one-half of the whole length of the Pacific road. Like the Pacific these lines cross our Indian empire from east to west, and connect Bombay and Calcutta, just as the Pacific forms the connecting link between San Francisco and New York. By means of the East Indian a railway connects Calcutta with Delhi, more than 1,000 miles distant from each other; in the south, Madras and Baypore are connected by a line crossing Southern India; Nagpore, in Central India, is connected with the port of Bombay by means of the flotilla and Punjaub line; Lahore in the north-west and Kurrachee in the Indus are brought into direct connection with each other. There are now actually completed and at work in India, 3,942 miles of railway, or about 600 more than the whole mileage between New York and San Francisco, and there remain to be completed of lines already sanctioned 1,665 miles. This great extent of railway has been constructed in a country many thousands of miles distant from England, where, with a trifling exception, the whole of the capital was provided. For the construction of these works there was required to be shipped from this country 3,529,000 tons of goods, of the value of 23,252,000 pounds, and which was conveyed in 5,339 ships. In America no such difficulty as this was experienced. The road, as it was formed, was enabled to carry the iron and timber required for the construction. The contractors worked from an already organized base of railways at home; the material for the Indian lines had to be borne over thousands of miles of a sea voyage. The construction of the Indian railways has presented difficulties of a much more formidable character than those which have been met with on the Pacific line. It is true that this railway has been carried over vast plains and mountain ranges of which little was known, and in the face of the attacks of hostile Indian tribes. In India, the works were carried out in the face of difficulties connected with the oppressive heat of the climate; through forests and jungles which were the resort of savage animals, and the people employed were natives of the country, speaking a language unknown to those by whom they were employed, and whose habits and modes of life unfitted them for labor such as that on which they were engaged. Great works such as those of the Bhore Ghaut and Thull Ghaut inclines presented difficulties equal to, if not greater, than any experienced in the crossing over the Rocky Mountains. Streams wider and more rapid than met with between Omaha and San Francisco have been successfully bridged, and present some of the greatest triumphs of modern engineering science. — *Engineering.*

ON ROADS AND RAILWAYS IN NORTHERN INDIA AS AFFECTED BY THE ABRADING AND TRANSPORTING POWER OF WATER.

Mr. Login, at the meeting of the British Association, commenced by stating general conclusions he had arrived at, to the effect that the abrading and transporting power of water was increased directly as the velocity and inversely as the depth; also, that when flowing water had once got its proper load of solid matter in suspension all erosive action ceased. In short, that it was like a balance, the load being always equal to the power, which power, somehow or other, increased as the velocity became greater, and decreased as the depth of a stream increased, Nature always adjusting the load to the various circumstances. He then gave a short description of the plains and rivers of Northern India, and, by the aid of diagrams, went on to argue that rivers flowing through alluvial plains were raising rather than lowering their beds, and, though this silting-up process may be very slow, yet it was satisfactory to the engineer to know that the foundations of his bridges would be as safe, if not safer, a hundred years hence, as they are now. In speaking of the changes of the course of rivers, he said that there was more or less a constant cutting going on, on the concave banks of a river, with a tilting-up process on the opposite side. The next subject referred to was the denudation of the high level plains of Northern India called "Doabs" (two waters), and locally known by the name of "Bhanger" land, in contradistinction to the term "Khadir," or low valley lands, through which the large rivers, fed by the melting snows, now meander. Mr. Login said that the higher ridges, or "back bones," of these Doabs were not caused by any upheavals, but were formed by the denudation of these high level

2*

plains; and, as the rainfall was three or four times as great in the valley of the Ganges as that of the Indus, these back bones in the plains of the Punjaub disappeared, as well as all defined drainage lines some 50 miles below the hills, for the simple reason that the water spread over these plains and was absorbed. To this peculiarity in the Punjaub particular attention was drawn; for Mr. Login argued that, if standing crops and grass could permit, without receiving injury, the rain which fell higher up to flow through rather than over those standing crops, surely the same water could flow *over* an iron rail at very slow velocities, seldom, if ever, rising to such a height as to interfere with a locomotive passing over the line; however, if it did, the obstruction could only last for not more than one day in a whole year. By acting on this principle, Mr. Login believed that hundreds of thousands of pounds can be saved in the construction of railways in Upper India, as no embankments or masonry culverts and bridges would be required in crossing such high level plains as the Bechna doabs, which he had surveyed; while, by pounding back those flood-waters by embankments, and forcing it to find an escape through culverts, was more costly and dangerous, for it increased the abrading and transporting power of the water, at the very point where alone it could do injury, namely, where it crossed the rail. In support of his arguments he quoted actual occurrences. He urged that deep foundations for bridges was the proper mode for spanning the large rivers of India, and that only the opening for both the main stream and the inundation water should be provided, while any little water that might be left behind in the swamps, or low ground which is below the level of the main river, should be drained off by what he calls " spoon-mouthed syphons." Speaking of the minor torrents, he briefly referred to another description of bridge, resting on " inverts," with deep, massive curtain walls, which may, with economy, be introduced in some instances; and concluded by stating that once the abrading and transporting power of water was more fully investigated, the engineer could proceed with all descriptions of works affected by flowing water with greater confidence and economy, instancing harbors on the Madras coast, which province, from being at present a financial loss to the State, would soon become profitable, both to India and England, by increased commerce.

COMMUNICATION BETWEEN GUARD, DRIVER, AND PASSENGERS.

Mr. S. Varley, at the meeting of the British Association, read a paper "On a System of Communication between Guards and Passengers on Railway Trains when in Motion." The system was applied in 1866, and is now in use on the Royal train, and it has since been adopted in other trains. He believed electricity to be the best agent for signalling on rolling stock, and the difficulty in applying it, he believed, was more with reference to the mechanical parts than the electrical. Three electrical systems had been applied to railway travelling: one used by Mr. Preece, on the

South-Western Railway; one by Mr. C. V. Walker, on the Great Eastern Railway, applied to trains which run 20 miles without stopping; and one by Mr. Martin on the North-Western Railway; and this was the one which formed the subject of this paper. Insulated wire is run underneath the carriages, and the iron works, the coupling bars, and the wheels are connected electrically together. Two insulated wires (one of which is connected with the wire underneath the carriages, the other to the iron work) are led up to each compartment, and when these two wires are brought in contact the telegraphic circuit is closed, and the alarum set ringing. The carriages are connected together by means of flexible conductors, and these are also laterally connected with the insulated wire underneath the vehicles. The apparatus in the guard's van consists of a battery placed in a box, and an electric alarum, and on the engine is another alarum. By moving a handle in any of the carriages the alarums are set going. The action of moving the handle sets free a spring, and the handle is locked, and cannot be put in its original position until the spring or lock is opened, which is done by means of a key in the possession of the guard. No electrical knowledge is needed to work or keep in order the apparatus; the maintenance of it is not costly, and the alarums, batteries, etc., can be easily shifted from one train to another. At the request of the Board of Trade, in 1866 a train was fitted up with this apparatus, which had travelled 250 miles each day, and been started and stopped by its means. Mr. H. Palmer, M.P., said that, in the House of Commons, Mr. Bright said the rope system — merely a rope running above the door of the carriage, with no communication with the inside — was the best, and at the same time simplest and cheapest system, but it had been adopted on the North-Eastern Railway, and had been found to be very inefficient. He wished to know what investigations the various systems had undergone by the Board of Trade, and whether this system was actually in use on the railway. Mr. Parkes agreed as to the inefficiency of the rope system. Mr. Varley, in reply, said the various plans were tried at York. The cord system failed, inasmuch as it was not detective of the person giving the alarm. His apparatus had been tested daily for two years, the train being started with it, and it had worked regularly. As a practical proof of the uselessness of the cord communication, he might state that it was attached to the train that took them to Plymouth, when it was pulled but failed to attract attention. He believed it was only adopted to satisfy public opinion.

THE CHANNEL RAILWAY.

J. F. Bateman, F.R.S., at the meeting of the British Association, read a paper on "The Channel Railway." He referred at some length to the advantages which would accrue from a continuous railway communication between England and France, and to the various proposals for effecting that object by a tunnel to be driven beneath the bed of the sea; by submerged roadways and tubes; by large ferry-boats carrying trains on board; and by bridges to be carried on piers formed on islands to be sunk in the Straits. A ferry-boat, large enough to receive a whole ordinary train on board, would be a material improvement on the present means of conveyance. Such boats cannot, however, be employed, except by the construction of special harbors on each coast. With reference to a tunnel, it has been proposed to drive one of ordinary size for a double line of railway, which shall descend by a gradient of one in 60 on each side of the channel to a depth of about 270 feet below the bed of the sea. The total length of the tunnel would be 30 miles, of which 22 would be beneath the sea. A special commission, appointed by the Emperor of the French, recently reported in favor of a submarine tunnel. We propose to lay a tube of cast iron on the bottom of the sea, between coast and coast, to be commenced on one side of the channel, and to be built up within the inside of a horizontal cylinder, or bell, or chamber, which shall be constantly pushed forward as the building up of the tube proceeds. The bell or chamber within which the tube is to be constructed will be about 80 feet in length, 18 feet internal diameter, and composed of cast-iron rings 8 inches thick, securely bolted together. The interior of the bell will be bored out to a true cylindrical surface, like the inside of a steam cylinder. The tube to be constructed within it will consist of cast-iron plates, in segments 4 inches in thickness, connected by flanges, bolted together inside the tube, leaving a clear diameter of 13 feet. Surrounding this tube, and forming part of it, will be constructed annular discs or diaphragms, the outside circumference of which will accurately fit the interior of the bell. These diaphragms will be furnished with arrangements for making perfectly water-tight joints, for the purpose of excluding sea-water and securing a dry chamber, within which the various operations for building up the tube, and for pressing forward the bell as each ring of the tube is added, will be performed. There will always be 3 and generally 4 of these water-tight joints contained within the bell. A clear space between the end of the tube and the end or projecting part of the bell of 36 feet will be left as a chamber for the various operations. Within this chamber, powerful hydraulic presses, using the built and completed portion of the tube as a fulcrum, will, as each ring is completed, push forward the bell to a sufficient distance to admit the addition of another ring to the tube. The bell will slide over the water-tight joints described, one of which will be left behind as the bell is projected forward, leaving 3 always in operation against the sea. The weight of the bell and of the machinery within it will be a little in excess of the weight of water displaced, and therefore the only resistance to be overcome by the hydraulic presses when pushing forward the bell is the friction due to the slight difference in weight and the head or column of water pressing upon the sectional area of the bell against its forward motion. In like manner, the specific gravity of the tube will be a little in excess of the weight of water which it displaces; and in order to obtain a firm footing upon the bottom of the sea, the tube will be weighted by a lining of brick in cement, and for further protection will be tied to the ground by screw piles, which will pass through stuffing-boxes in the bottom of the tube. These piles will, during the construction of the tube within the bell-chamber, be introduced in the annular space between the outside of the tube and the inside of the bell, and will be screwed into the ground as they are left behind by the progression of the bell. The hydraulic presses, and the other hydraulic machinery which will be employed for lifting and fixing the various segments of the tube, will be supplied with the power required for working them from accumulators on shore, on Sir William Armstrong's system, and the supply of fresh air required for the sustenance of the workmen employed within the bell and within the tube will be insured also by steam power on shore. As the tube is completed, the rails will be laid within it for the trains of wagons to be employed in bringing up segments of the rings as they may be required for the construction of the tube, and for taking back the waste water from the hydraulic presses, or any water from leakage during the construction. The tube will be formed of rings of 10 feet in length, each ring consisting of 6 segments, all precisely alike, turned and faced at the flanges or joints, and fitted together on shore previously to being taken into the bell, so that on their arrival the segments may, with perfect certainty and precision, be attached to each other. The tube when laid will be secure from all dangers arising from anchors, or wrecks, or submarine currents. The building of the tube will be commenced on dry land above the level of the sea, and will be gradually submerged as the tube lengthens. The first half mile will test the feasibility of construction, for that will have to be built both above and under water. When once fairly under water, the progress should be rapid, and it is estimated that the whole undertaking may be easily completed in 5 years. The precise line to be taken will probably be between a point in close proximity to Dover, and a point in close proximity to Cape Grisnez, on the French coast, where the sea bed on this line appears to be the most uniform in level, and, while free from hard rocks and broken ground, to consist of coarse sand, gravel, and clay. The average depth of water is about 110 feet, the maximum about 200 feet. On the line suggested the water increases in depth on both sides more rapidly than elsewhere, although in no instance will the gradient be more than about one in 100. The tube, when completed, will occupy about 16 feet in depth above the present bottom of the sea. Up to the point on each shore at which the depth of water above the depth of the tube would reach, say 30 feet at low water, an open pier, or other protection, would have to be constructed for the purpose of pointing out its position, and of preventing vessels striking against the tube. The tube at each end would gradually emerge from the water, and on arriving above the level of the sea would be connected with the existing railway systems. The distance across the Channel on the line chosen is about 22 miles.

The tube as proposed is large enough for the passage of carriages of the present ordinary construction, and to avoid the objections to the use of locomotives in a tube of so great a length, it is proposed to work the traffic by pneumatic pressure. The air will be exhausted on one side of the train and forced in on the other, and so the required difference of pressure will be given for carrying the train through at any determined speed. Powerful steam-engines, for exhausting and forcing the air into the tube, will be erected on shore at each end. This system of working the traffic will secure a constant supply of the purest air. By this system of working there would scarcely exist the chance of accident — no collision could take place. There would never be foul air within the tube. The pneumatic system can be as cheaply worked, and be in every way preferable to locomotive power. Combined goods and passenger trains might be sent through the tube at 20 miles an hour, with occasional express trains at 30 miles an hour. The estimated cost of the whole undertaking is 8,000,000 pounds. Mr. Chalmers estimates the total annual revenue at 1,300,000 pounds. The working expenses would be amply covered by 150,000 pounds, leaving about 14 or 15 per cent. dividend.

Mr. Bidder remarked that this subject had not been without interest to him, as it would be recollected that he made a few remarks on it when presiding over the section at Norwich last year. The atmospheric system, which was a very old subject, and which had been tried to a very great extent in this neighborhood, failed on account of using a small tube with a large pressure, but it was different with a large tube. He believed the pneumatic principle was the only one that could be adopted to work the tunnel. He thought there would be a difficulty in getting the united actions of the two governments to carry out the work. Unless the tunnel was worked pneumatically, he would rather cross in the present boats. Until an experiment had been made to test this plan, and the probable cost, it would be more reasonable to construct a huge breakwater, and build vessels that should be adapted to cross, except on special occasions, with certainty and dispatch.

Mr. C. Vignoles believed that if ever there was to be a tunnel to Calais it must be on this principle. The real cause of the failure of the atmospheric system was not as Mr. Bidder put it, but from an accumulation of heat in the air-pumps. It would never pay as a commercial undertaking, as there was not sufficient traffic; but it might be done by the governments. They, as engineers, considered the scheme a practical one; but he was afraid it must be left to the next generation to carry out.

Mr. Bateman, in reply, contended that the cost would not exceed his estimate.

MT. WASHINGTON RAILWAY.

The depot is 2,685 feet above the level of the sea, or 1,117 feet above the White Mountain House. This leaves a grade of 3,600 feet to be overcome, as the height of the mountain is 6,285 feet above the level of the sea. The length of the road is two miles and thirteen-sixteenths.

The heaviest grade is 13 inches to the yard, and the very lightest, one inch to the foot. A part of the course is over "Jacob's Ladder," the zigzag portion of the old bridle-path lying just above the point where the trees are left behind. The railroad takes a generally straight line, however, curving slightly, only to maintain a direct course.

The locomotive pushes the car before it up the incline, and both run upon three rails, the centre one being a cog rail. The engine and car are kept upon the track by friction rollers under the side of the cog rail, and the appliances for stopping the descent are ample. By means of atmospheric brakes either the car or engine could be sent down alone at any given rate, fast or slow, and there are also hand brakes operating with equal directness upon the central wheels, together with other means of governing the machinery of locomotion. Every competent person who has examined the road and the running machinery pronounces both as safe as they could possibly be made. The landing-place at the top of the mountain is directly in the rear of the telegraph office, and but a few rods from the door of the Tip-Top House.

ELECTRICITY AND RAILROADS.

On the railroads in France electricity is taking the place of human watchfulness. On many lines there are contrivances where the passing of a train is automatically announced to neighboring stations. The cars pass over connecting wires, and the train records itself before and behind, so that its progress and appearance are alike indicated.

WHY DO RAILWAY CARRIAGES OSCILLATE?

There is so prevalent an idea that the unpleasant, and, to the nervous, injurious oscillation of railway coaches is due to the axles being too wide for the line, that the following explanation given in the "Times," by Mr. Charles Fox, is of much importance, both to the public and the "companies:"—

"The oscillation of railway trains, more especially at high velocities, producing what is ordinarily called 'gauge concussion,' is a very serious source of wear to the permanent way and rolling stock of railways, and as a consequence, of great expense, to say nothing of the discomfort it occasions to passengers, and is, in my opinion, caused, in very great measure, by the use of wheels the tires of which are portions of cones instead of cylinders.

"It is well known to engineers that the tires of railway-wheels are generally coned to an inclination of one in 20. It is considered that these were first introduced by Mr. George Stephenson, in the expectation of facilitating the passage of vehicles round curves, by their adapting themselves, through their various diameters, to the different lengths of the two rails on which they were running. This, however, is not the case in practice, as any one will find upon carefully investigating the matter, inasmuch as, in a vehicle passing round a curve, the flange of the off fore wheel will be found close up to the outer rail, while that of the aft near wheel will be found running with its flange close up to the inner one, so that no benefit whatever accrues from the use of the cone, even in going round curves.

" The question of passing with steadiness over straight lines seems to have been altogether overlooked in the introduction of coned wheels, for it will be obvious that with the inch 'play' allowed between the tires and the rails, unless one-half of such play be constantly preserved on each side of the way, two wheels staked upon the same axle will be running upon different diameters, and, consequently, a struggle arises which cannot fail to result in oscillation, inasmuch as the moment one of the flanges touches a rail, that wheel, becoming larger than the opposite one, turns it off from the rail, only to make the opposite one perform, in its turn, the same operation, when serious oscillation is the result.

" As I have already stated, no advantage is found to arise in the use of conical wheels in passing round curves, and as much evil results therefrom, on straight lines, I have constructed upward of 250 miles of railway abroad, in the rolling stock of which I have departed from the usual form of wheel, and have used only cylindrical ones, and have, as I expected, been gratified with the satisfactory reports I have received of the steadiness of trains supplied with them.

" Now that main-line companies are running their express trains at such high velocities, this oscillation is becoming a very serious matter, not only as a question of safety, but also one of great discomfort to the passengers, to say nothing of the enormous cost occasioned by this destructive action. I would, therefore, venture to recommend, that should any one desire to test the correctness of the principles here stated, he should select a carriage known to be most subject to oscillation, and place under it 4 cylindrical instead of conical wheels, and let this carriage run in an express train, care being taken to avoid the oscillation of the two adjoining carriages with conical wheels being communicated to it, which would be effected by the introduction of two coupling links, say 10 feet long, instead of the shorter ones in general use, and he will at once perceive the advantage of using cylindrical wheels."

THE USE OF COUNTER-PRESSURE STEAM IN THE LOCOMOTIVE ENGINE AS A BRAKE.

M. L. De Chatelier gives the history of the improvement as follows : —

" About the middle of 1865, when first I thought of organizing a system of experiments for removing the difficulties of reversing the steam, I began by trying whether it would be possible to work the engine for any considerable time by means of the compressed-air apparatus of M. de Bergue. I soon convinced myself that the heating of the cylinders went on so rapidly that this system was inapplicable for any length of run. It was then that I drew up a complete programme of experiments, the sum and substance of which was to establish a communication between the boiler and the lower end of the exhaust-pipe, in order to supply there a jet of steam or of water, and to force into the boiler the elastic fluids, — steam or gases discharged from the cylinders by the return stroke of the piston. I pointed out three combinations to be experimented on in succession, according to the greater or less difficulty found in completely cooling the cylinders.

" 1st. Injection of steam mixed with air.

" 2d. Injection of steam in sufficient excess to prevent the entrance of air.

" 3d. Injection of water, instead of steam.

" At first I supposed that the steam would carry along with it a sufficient quantity of water to absorb the heat produced, and that it would be condensed before reaching the cylinders. This idea was incorrect. During the working with steam reversed, the water ceases to be in a state of violent ebullition, and is only carried over in small quantities; and, besides, when the steam expands in issuing from the boiler, it dries, and the small quantity of water brought with it is almost entirely converted into steam.

" The first experiment with a mixture of steam and gases drawn into the cylinders did not give favorable results. With the injection of an excess of steam — a system which I characterized as an *inverted steam engine* — more satisfactory results were obtained, and it was found possible to work with a moderate admission of steam with light loads on moderate gradients, without burning the packings, and without injuring the rubbing surfaces. We have in France the example of a railway on which 200 engines have only a cock for the injection of steam, and the substitution of this for the gases drawn from the smoke-box has proved sufficient to render the counter-pressure steam applicable for stopping and shunting in stations, and for moderating the speed in the descent of goods trains on gradients of one in 260. Indeed, the injection of steam alone has been effectually applied to light trains on a short incline of one in 22.

" But experience soon showed that the only general and complete solution of the question is found in the injection of water. To complete the absorption of the heat produced by the compression in the cylinders, to force back the steam into the boiler, and to render the reversal of the steam an absolutely innocuous operation, water is the only appliance.

" When we speak of injecting water issuing from the boiler into the cylinders of a locomotive engine, it must be borne in mind that it is not water in the state in which it would flow from a fountain; it is at a high temperature when it issues from the boiler, and rushes into space at atmospheric pressure. It enters at once into ebullition, and becomes steam at 100° C., in quantity corresponding to the heat employed.

3

" The new system of reversing steam has been, until recently, limited to the use of a mixture of steam and water. The engineers to whom I had entrusted the task of making the first trials followed my instructions with some apprehension, endeavoring as much as possible to avoid the injection of water into the cylinders. The result has been that, even now, in Spain, where these first trials were made, the use of counter-pressure steam has not had the success which it has had elsewhere. In France, the part played by the water was better understood; it has been abundantly injected, and the results have been most satisfactory; but up to the moment when I had an opportunity of personally experimenting, in order to verify the correctness of my first conceptions, steam was universally considered as a necessary agent, and was used in a greater or less proportion. It was supposed that its function was to fill the cylinders during the period of aspiration, and that it served as the vehicle for the water which was shut in with it, behind the piston, at the moment the period of cushioning and forcing back commenced. It was supposed that the water led from the boiler was applied directly to the absorption of heat.

" I have shown that the water is converted into steam from the moment that it enters the cylinder, even during the period of aspiration, and the conclusion is that not only is it not required to take steam directly from the boiler, but that the addition of steam to the water, beyond a certain limit, might become prejudicial.

" In every case the substitution of steam for, or the addition of steam to, water results in a discharge of a less moist steam from the cylinders into the boiler, and it is the same with the steam in the exhaust-pipe used for aspiration. The rubbing surfaces are therefore drier, and the friction greater. The more the proportion of steam is increased, the more these effects become sensible. At last the steam actually diverts the water indispensable for the absorption of the heat, although large quantities of steam escape by the funnel, and although no gases from the smoke-box get into the cylinders.

" The intervention of steam during the working with inverse admission, unless required for some particular purpose, which I shall point out presently, is always more or less prejudicial. The rule, in fact, should be, to add the least possible quantity of steam to the water. The wet steam, on the water issuing from the boiler, gives this minimum proportion.

" The apparatus to be fitted to the locomotive, to admit of working counter-pressure steam as a brake, is as simple as the principle itself. It consists of a tube of an inch to an inch and a quarter in diameter, — one inch diameter is very convenient, — which communicates between the boiler and the exhaust-pipe, and a distributing cock by which the driver regulates the supply. If, as I advise, although it is not indispensable, it is desired to have the power of injecting water and steam alternately or simultaneously, a second cock is placed, with a short tube as a branch from the first, at a short distance from its origin. The one tube enters the boiler below the lowest level of the water, the other above the highest, so that steam only shall pass through the latter.

"When the engines have external cylinders, the exhaust-pipe divides into two branches. The injection-tube must therefore have also two branches; one going to the under side of each branch of the exhaust-pipe. The bifurcation should be perfectly symmetrical, so that the water held in suspension in the steam may not take the line of steepest descent, and that the distribution to each cylinder may be equal."

CAR-WHEELS.

From Auchincloss' Report of the Paris Exhibition we extract the following : —

" The practice of nations seems much divided on the subject of the proper material for car-wheels. The wrought-iron wheel is almost exclusively adhered to in England, France, and Prussia ; while Holland and Austria discover features worthy of attention in the cast iron. The general properties of the cast-iron spoke wheel are familiar to all. The society of Providence (limited), whose office is at 208 Quai Jemmapes, Paris, display specimens of rolled wrought-iron wheel centres, without weld, whose radial section is similar to an I-beam. Upon such centres the tire is held with 4 seven-eighth inch rivets.

" The Society of Mines and Steel Works, Bochum, Prussia, exhibits a remarkable cast of wheels. It was formed by stacking the flasks 22 wheels high, with the hubs in contact, and then pouring in crucible steel through a side-runner. Although this cast was made more as a matter of curiosity, it is quite customary with this company to arrange them in tiers of 6 wheels each, and thus save the numerous side-runners required when cast singly. One swinging of the set in the lathe answers for facing up all the treads and flanges. These wheels have a single plate, and are 40 inches in diameter. The Austrian exhibitions are by A. Ganz, of Ofen, Hungary, and Mr. Derno, of the same section of country. The former gentleman is the most extensive manufacturer in Austria, and makes a double-plated wheel, similar in design to that known in America as the ' Snow Patent.' He exhibited a wheel 38 inches in diameter, cast in 1856, which has served under a 10 ton four-wheeled wagon for the past 11 years. The tread of this wheel appears in excellent condition, the metal close-grained without signs of honey-combing.

" The director-general of the Austrian I. R. P. State Railway Society certifies to the fact of this wheel having run 50,000 miles. The road on which these wheels are used is 419 miles in length, and pursues a south-easterly course from Vienna through Hungary. In respect to climate the trial is most severe. Its merits are certainly appreciated or the shop number would not extend as high as 84,981, which was noticed on a wheel cast during the present year. The wheels, as usual, have 3 core-holes in the back. The only peculiarity about these holes is a V-groove cast near the opening, into which, when the core is removed, an eighth of an inch sheet-iron disk is sprung. This method is employed on wheels designed specially for passenger coaches, and prevents the entrance of stones, which, rattling within a wheel of so large diameter, become a source of much annoyance."·

WOODEN WHEELS.

The directors of the New York and New Haven Railroad have decided, as an experiment, to use wooden wheels on some of the cars upon their road. Quite a number of these wheels have been purchased, and will be substituted for the present iron ones on some of the new cars. They are understood to cost nearly treble the price of iron wheels, but are considered quite as cheap in the end. They are made of elm or teak wood, and bound with steel tires. Besides being less liable to break by the action of frost, they make less noise.

SLIDING OF CAR-WHEELS.

An experiment has been made at Munich for the purpose of determining if a railway-carriage wheel rolls regularly without sliding, so that by recording the number of revolutions of a wheel, the circumference of which is known, the distance accomplished could be accurately ascertained. The difference between the measurement by mathematical instruments and that obtained by noting the revolutions of the wheel was found to be no more than one sixty-eight thousandth of the whole.

A NEW ALARM-BELL FOR LOCOMOTIVES.

A new alarm-bell was tested on the Detroit and Milwaukie Railroad lately. The invention consists of an ordinary bell, weighing about 100 pounds, placed on the platform of the locomotive, immediately over the cow-catcher. A rod attached to the eccentric shaft causes a clapper to strike the bell each turn of the driving-wheel. The bell is suspended loosely, and revolves from the force of the stroke it receives, so that all parts of the surface are equally exposed to wear. The advantages of this arrangement are a continuous sound, slow or rapid in proportion to the speed of the engine, each 15 feet producing a stroke of the bell. In case of an accident, the railroad company can always prove that their bell was ringing according to law; and owing to the position in which this bell is placed, the sound can be distinctly heard about 3 miles in daytime, and by night 4 miles or more, the ground and the continuous rail, both excellent conductors of sound, assisting in carrying the vibrations. The Detroit and Milwaukie Railroad have 24 of these alarms already in use, and intend to provide all their passenger-engines with them.

IMPROVED TRACTION UPON STEEL RAILS AND STEEL-HEADED RAILS.

It has been too much the practice of railway managers to consider only the increased durability of steel. A less striking, but perhaps equally important advantage, is that it has double the strength and more than double the stiffness of iron. Some 3 years since, Mr. George Berkley made, in England, above 600 tests of the stiffness of steel and iron rails of equal section. The rails were supported on 5-feet bearings, and loaded with dead pressure at the middle. The first rails tried weighed 68 pounds per yard, and loads respectively of 20 tons and 30 tons were applied. The average of 427 tests of the Ebbw Vale Co.'s and two other standard makers of iron rails, gave, with 20 tons, a deflection of five-eighths inch and a permanent set of one-half inch. With 30 tons the deflection was two and one-fifth inch and the permanent set two and one-sixteenth inch. With Brown's steel rails, 45 tests gave an average deflection of but five-sixteenths inch and permanent set of one-eighth inch. With heavier rails and loads, the comparative stiffness of steel was still more marked. The great and constant resistance of traction, and the wear and tear of track wheels and running gear, due to the deflection of rails between the sleepers and the perpetual series of resulting concussions, may be much reduced, or practically avoided, by the use of rails of twice the ordinary stiffness; in such a case, however, reasonably good ballasting and sleepers would be essential. When a whole series of sleepers sinks bodily into the mud, the consideration of deflection between the sleepers is a premature refinement. If the weight of steel rails is decreased in proportion to their strength, these advantages of cheaper traction and maintenance will not, of course, be realized. The best practice, here and abroad, is to use the same weight for steel as had been formerly employed for iron.

Many attempts have been made in England, on the Continent, and in this country, to produce a good steel-headed rail, and not without success. Puddled steel-heads have all the structural defects of wrought iron, as they are not formed from a cast, and hence homogeneous mass, but are made by the wrought-iron process, and are, in fact, a " high," steely wrought iron. They are, however, a great improvement upon ordinary iron, although probably little cheaper than cast-steel heads. Rolling a plain cast-steel slab upon an iron pile has not proved successful. The weld cannot be perfected, on so large a scale, and the steel peels off under the action of car-wheels. Forming the steel slab with grooves, into which the iron would dovetail when the pile was rolled into a rail, has been quite successful. The greater part of some 500 tons of such rails, made in this country, and put down where they would be severely tested, about 4 years ago, have outworn some 3 iron rails. Others failed in the iron stem, which was too light, after a shorter service. Rolling small bars of steel into the head of an iron pile has been recently commenced

3 *

at various mills in this country and in England. No conclusions are yet warranted by the short trial of these rails.

There is a growing feeling among engineers and steel-makers that the compound rail, made wholly or partly of steel, will prove more safe and economical than any solid rail, and that the defects of the old compound iron rail, largely used in this State some years since, may be avoided, since these defects were chiefly due to the nature of the material. The experiments in this direction will be watched with great interest by railway managers, for if the same durability of track can be obtained with a steel cap as with an all-steel rail, the first cost will be greatly decreased. A rail made in two or three continuous parts, breaking joints, is also a practical insurance against disaster from broken rails. — *State Engineer's Report on Railroads.*

NARROW GAUGE RAILWAY.

The Portmadoc and Festiniog Railway, Wales, is now attracting much attention from railroad men. This is a little line in North Wales, which was originally constructed for the purpose of acting as a tramway for slate and stone from the hills of Merionethshire to the sea-shore. It is now being used as a regular goods and passenger line. The chief peculiarity in its construction is that the gauge is only two feet broad. Hence, though the line runs through a very difficult country, the expenses of construction and working are so small that the traffic yields the enormous revenue of 30 per cent. The reason is simple enough. It is because the proportion between the dead weight and paying weight is so much less than upon other railways. The engine and tender upon this line weigh about 10 tons, against 40 tons upon the wider gauge of other lines. Instead of a first-class carriage, weighing $7\frac{1}{2}$ tons, to carry 32 passengers, and representing nearly 5 cwt. of dead weight for each passenger, the carriages on the Festiniog weigh only 30 cwt. for 12 passengers, or two and a half cwt. for each person carried.

STEEL RAILS. — THEIR DURABILITY.

The annual report of the State Engineer of New York, prepared by S. H. Sweet, Deputy Engineer, contains the following regarding steel rails: " Bessemer steel rails have been in regular and extensive use abroad over 10 years. For some 5 years large trial lots have been laid on various American roads having heavy traffic, and during the last two years importations have largely increased. The manufacture of steel rails has also been commenced at four large establishments in this country, and some 7,000 tons of home manufacture have been produced and laid down. It is estimated that from 40,000 to 50,000 tons of steel rails are in use on our various railways. Among the users of steel rails are the Hudson River, Erie, and Pennsylvania Railway, — 10,000 tons or more each; the Lehigh and Susquehannah (entirely built of steel) ; also the Philadelphia and Baltimore ; Camden and Amboy line ; Lehigh Valley ; New York Central ; New York and New Haven ; Naugatuck ; Morris and Essex ; Cumberland Valley ; South Carolina ; Chicago and North-western ; Chicago and Rock Island ; Chicago and Alton ; Michigan Central ; Lake Shore line ; Chicago, Burlington, and Quincy ; Pittsburgh, Fort Wayne, and Chicago ; also the Boston and Providence, Boston and Worcester, Boston and Maine, Boston and Albany, Eastern, Connecticut River, and other lines in New England.

" *The Wear of Steel Rails.* — As no steel rails are reported to have worn out on our roads, the comparative durability of steel and iron cannot be absolutely determined. The president of the Philadelphia and Baltimore Railway states (in the letter before quoted) that the use of steel commenced in 1864, that the rails (25 miles in all) were laid on the most trying parts of the line ; that none have been taken up on account of breakage, wear, or defect ; that upon the portion of the line near Philadelphia the first steel rail imported had already worn out 16 iron rails ; and that none of the steel rails have shown any imperfection, but are all wearing smoothly and truly.

" On the Pennsylvania Railway, the report of the Chief Engineer for 1868 states that 11,494 tons of steel rails had been purchased, and 9,656 tons laid. The first were laid in 1864. They are all wearing smoothly, showing no change except the slight diminution of section to be reasonably expected from the heavy traffic. No steel rails have yet worn out. The report of the superintendent (Feb., 1869) says : ' The use of steel rails continues with satisfactory results, and 4,544 tons of this material have been laid since date of last report.' It is officially reported that on the Camden and Amboy line some of the steel rails laid 3 years ago are now good in places where iron lasted but a few months.

" The last report of the Engineer of the Lehigh Valley Railway says : ' Another year's wear has made no perceptible impression upon the 200 tons (of steel rails), the first of which was laid in May, 1864, none of which has broken or given out since last report. These rails have had a severe test, being in those places in the track where they are subject to the greatest wear, laid with a chair, which is much inferior to the most approved joint now in use. There is no longer any possible doubt as to the superiority of steel over iron in economy, as in every other respect.'

" Unofficial reports from the Erie, Hudson River, and other roads, show that the above statements represent the average quality of steel rails. The last report of the New York and New Haven Railway states that ' the subject of steel rails has received special attention, and after a careful investigation of all the points involved, it has been determined hereafter to make all renewals of track with steel rails only ; 2,900 tons of Bessemer steel rails have been contracted for on account of renewals for the present year.' The report of the Morris and Essex Railway for 1868 says : ' During the last year one track through the tunnel has been relaid with steel,' — also some 150 tons of steel laid elsewhere.

' The wear of steel shows conclusively that economy will require its use on all heavy grades and sharp curves.'   The last report of the New Jersey Railway and Transportation Company says : ' It is probable that steel rails will be gradually laid the entire length of the road, the greater durability of these rails overcoming the objection to their increased cost.' " — *Railway Times.*

STEEL-CAPPED RAILS.

" The invention by J. L. Booth, of Rochester, N. Y., of a process for capping iron rails with a solid cap of steel about one-half or five-eighths of an inch in thickness, in the opinion of the most experienced railroad men who have examined it, meets the requirements of safety and durability.   The rail consists of an iron base with a steel cap, united to the base not by bolts, screws, rivets, or welding, but simply by clamping.   The iron bar is rolled of the required form and weight, after which it is passed through the compressing machine, which clenches powerfully upon it the heavy steel cap.   The subsequent action of weight upon it, as the passage over it of heavy trains, is to grip the iron more and more firmly, until the base and the cap become as firmly united as if they were a single piece of metal.   Over the experimental rails laid down two years ago near the depot in Buffalo have passed 40,000 engines and 500,000 cars.   The iron rails adjoining opposite them have, in the interval, been six times renewed.   No change is as yet observable in the steel-capped rails, and to all appearance they bid fair to wear out 20 successive sets of the ordinary sort.

" Two of the rails were also laid on the New York Central Railroad, at Rochester, N. Y., June 7, 1867.   On one the cap was loose and even rattling ; on the other it was firm.   They were laid continuously, and with the old style of chairs.   They were placed where 70 engines and trains daily passed over them on the main line, and where the track was used constantly for switching and making-up of trains.   The rate of speed over them varies.   The through freight trains are frequently joined at this point, three or four in one, to ascend an up-grade.   They pass over these rails often at the rate of 25 or 30 miles an hour. The loose cap rail became tight in a very short time, and both are now in perfect order.   Four sets of iron rails have been completely worn out, and new sets replaced, on the opposite side of the track, during the period of time these duplex rails have been down."

TESTS OF STEEL RAILS.

Messrs. John A. Griswold & Co.'s circular thus describes their method of testing steel rails : 1st. A test ingot from each 5-ton ladleful of liquid steel is hammered into a bar, and tested for malleability and hardness, and especially for *toughness,* by bending it double cold.   In case any test bar falls below the standard established as suitable for rails, all the ingots cast from that ladleful of steel are laid aside for other uses. 2d. All the ingots, and each rail rolled from them, are stamped with the number of the charge or ladleful. A piece is cut from one rail in each charge, and tested by placing it on iron supports a foot apart, and dropping a weight of 5 tons upon the middle of it, from a height proportioned to the pattern of rail. A blow equivalent to a ton weight falling 10 to 15 feet is considered a severe test. We use a 5-ton weight falling from a less height, believing that it more nearly represents in kind (although it of course exaggerates in severity) the test of actual service in the track. In case a test rail does not stand the blow deemed proper and agreed upon, the whole of the rails made from that charge or ladleful of steel are marked No. 2, and sold for use in sidings, where their possible breaking would do no great harm, and where their greater hardness and resistance to wear would be specially valuable. In addition to this double test, the rails are rigidly inspected for surface imperfections. We believe that these tests render it practically impossible for us to send out rails of inferior quality. We farther invite railway companies to send inspectors to our works to witness the tests mentioned, and other tests and inspections agreed upon.— *Van Nostrand's Eng. Mag., Oct.*, 1869.

AMERICAN RAILS.

The term American rails has become a synonym for the cheapest and least durable rails manufactured. They are usually about 10 shillings per ton cheaper than the ordinary rails made for English and Continental companies. In the case of American rails the quality of the material and the construction of the rail pile are left entirely to the manufacturer, the rails not being made according to any specification; and hence there is not the slightest guaranty that a good, serviceable, or safe rail will be obtained; the one great desideratum being, apparently, that the price be low. Hence, the maker's chief study is, naturally enough, to produce the cheapest possible article, and to devise means of manufacturing at a low price what is, to all appearances, a clean-looking rail; to do this, he carefully studies the character of his iron, and so manipulates it as to obtain a well-finished and salable rail, regardless of its brittleness, — so long, indeed, as it does not break previously to delivery and payment, — and indifferent whether it is likely to last one year or ten. Fortunately for him, the section for American rails is one very easy to roll, — low, heavy, and without angles, — so that almost any quality of iron, and any construction of pile, will not interfere with the one object he has in view. When, however, the iron is very red-short (or liable, through the presence of sulphur, to crack in rolling), a top-slab of a better class of iron (No. 2) must be used in the pile, to serve as the wearing surface of the rail. This wearing surface may, however, vary considerably in thickness, forming either the entire head of the rail, or only a portion more or less thick. Even when the iron is not red-short, the pile is often composed of puddled bars only, and rolled out into rails, at the lowest possible heat, so as to economize iron and fuel, but regardless of insuring a perfect weld; and hence, lamination and failure rapidly follow after a few months' wear.   So much for the durability of the ordinary American rail.   Now as regards its safety: Just as the presence of sulphur in iron renders the metal redshort, as previously explained, so the presence of phosphorus causes the iron to become brittle and cold-short.   It is, therefore, of great importance, in producing a good and serviceable rail from such inferior materials, that the hard, cold-short iron should form the top, or wearing portion, of the rail, while the redshort, or tough and fibrous iron, should be used for the flange; as the character of the ores distributed through the principal railmaking districts of this country is such that cold-short iron is produced in one district, and red-short in another, it is necessary that the two kinds of metal should be brought together, and used in association, as previously described, if they are to produce a truly serviceable rail.   But as the cost of transport from one district to another becomes an important item, it will evidently be to the interest of the manufacturer, if not restricted, to use the unmixed home material, whether cold-short or red-short.   Under such circumstances, a rail is produced either too brittle, and therefore dangerous, or too pliable, and therefore less capable of enduring the wear and tear of traffic.   There are, perhaps, few countries that of late have suffered more from fracture of rails than America.   This has led some railway administrations, in that country, to require that the rails should be tested; but whereas they were formerly too careless in this respect, they now seem inclined to err on the other side by specifying too severe a test for the rail, and thus compelling the maker to use too soft an iron.   For instance, it is often required that a weight of one ton should fall upon the rail from a height of 10 feet, when half such a test would insure breakage of the rail in any climate.   I may now briefly refer to the method adopted in making rails for the English and Continental companies.   There are but few of these railway administrations which, when inviting tenders for a supply of rail, do not specify distinctly that the top slab, constituting the wearing surface of the rail, must be of the very best material, and at least two inches in thickness, thus giving a wearing surface of one-half inch in the head of the rail; and, further, that the rail should stand a test half as severe as that previously mentioned as applied to American rails.   From what has now been advanced respecting the different modes of manufacturing American and European rails, I leave the respective American railway administrations to judge whether they would not best consult their own interests by adopting the English and Continental system of well-defined specification and tests, instead of looking merely to the small saving effected by always accepting the lowest tender —— E."——*Journal of the Franklin Institute, March*, 1869.

WOODEN WHEELS.

Mansells' patent wheels for railway carriages are fast coming into general use. They have already been adopted by the London, and North-Western, Great Western, Midland, Great Northern, Great Eastern, Metropolitan, and other English lines, and the Imperial Government has sanctioned their adoption on all the railways of Russia. It may not be generally known that Mansells' original patent was for securing the tire to the wheel by retaining rings, the fillets of which are turned to fit into corresponding grooves in the tires. The whole is secured by nuts and bolts. Between the tire and the boss spokes are dispensed with by the insertion of stout, close-fitting panels of East India teakwood, the oily nature of which preserves from oxidation the iron passing through it. For this purpose teak is superior to any other wood, and it has further the advantage of never shrinking. The superiority of these wheels over iron ones is well known to all observant travellers, their special merits being absence of jarring, and also of noise. — *Van Nostrand's Magazine, Sept.*, 1869.

NEW RAIL-LEVELLING DEVICE.

The ordinary lever-bar used for lifting rails and sleepers in constructing and repairing the permanent way of railways involves in its operation the labor of several men. To obviate this, an English engineer, Mr. De Bergue, has constructed a simple and compact tool, composed of a kind of shoe combined with a bar pivoted at one end, and at the other furnished with a screw by which it may be raised relatively to the shoe. The instrument with its bar depressed is thrust under the rail or sleeper to be raised, and the screw is turned until the bar has been forced upwards sufficiently to bring the superincumbent parts to the required position. Those portions of the apparatus subjected to heavy strains are made of steel, and the working surfaces are hardened so that it cannot easily get out of repair. — *Van Nostrand's Eclectic Engineering Magazine.*

THE FAIRLIE STEAM CARRIAGE.

The name of Mr. Robert F. Fairlie has for some time past been brought prominently before the public in connection with the economical working of railways. A trial of this carriage was made July 15, at the Hatcham Iron Works, which successfully demonstrated the practicability of working the system upon railways with curves of only 50 feet radius. The steam carriage exhibited, and which was not quite completed, was designed to work on a metropolitan railway, at the terminal stations of which sufficient space could not be given for laying down rails on a curve of 25 feet radius for the standard carriage to run itself round; consequently the standard carriage had to be altered in dimensions to allow of its being turned on an ordinary 40-feet turn-table.   Hence, instead of seating, as is intended, the 100 passengers in the standard carriage, the carriage under trial only gave seating space for 16 first-class and 50 second-class, in all 66 passengers.   The accommodation per passenger is as good as is given on the best lines, and infinitely superior to the stock usually worked on branch lines.   The length of the carriage is 43 feet, including a compartment near the engine for the guard.   The engine, carriage, and framing all complete, in working order, but exclusive of passengers, weighs under 13½ tons, and including its full load of passengers, 18½ tons only.   The carriage when finished complete will have a broad step or platform on each side, extending its entire length; this step is protected by a hand-rail on the outside, with an arrangement for lifting it on the platform side at the doors to allow the passengers to get in and out.   The object of this platform is to enable the guard to pass completely round the train at all times, and while doing so he is perfectly safe from any accident.   Passengers can also pass along the platform to the guard, so that in this manner there is an easy and perfect mode of communication between passengers and guard.   It is intended, however, in the standard steam-carriage to provide a central passage inside, the entire length of the carriage, leading direct from and to the guard's compartment; thus there is the most direct means of communication between the passengers and guard.   The compartments in the carriages will be quite as separate and distinct as they are at present, or as the most fastidious could desire.   The guard passes through the carriage at pleasure. Those in the higher classes can pass to the lower, but the lower cannot get to the higher, while all can pass to the guard when required.   The standard carriage will have two compartments first-class, to seat 16 persons; 3 compartments second-class, to seat 30 persons; and 4½ compartments, third-class, to seat 54 persons —in all, 100 passengers.   The machine complete, in working order, will weigh about 14 tons, and, with 100 passengers, from 20 tons to 21 tons.   These carriages will convey their full complement of passengers at 40 miles per hour up gradients of one in 100, and, as demonstrated, will pass round curves of 50 feet radius at 20 miles an hour with perfect safety. — *Mechanics' Magazine.*

LIGHT ROLLING STOCK.

It has now been indisputably established that it is possible to construct a combined engine and carriage capable of accommodating 66 passengers, of both classes, the whole weight of which, fully loaded, shall not exceed, if it do not fall short of, 20 tons, while the adhesion weight is nearly half as much, or 10 tons, and the average steam tractive force at least half a ton.   The resistance of such a carriage at 20 miles an hour, upon a level, would not exceed 300 or 400 pounds, nor upon a gradient of one in 60 more than from 1,050 pounds to 1,150 pounds, the whole actual work done being, say 25 horse-power in the one case, and 75 in the other, or supposing the speed to be diminished on the gradient to 17 miles an hour, to but 50 horse-power. The carriage is not of the omnibus kind, but has 7 compartments, and guards-van, in all respects in conformity with the standard rolling stock of the English lines. The weight being in no case greater than two and one-half tons per wheel, lines of corresponding lightness would serve as well as heavy lines now serve for heavy engines, loaded as they are from 5, 6, 7, and even 8 tons upon each driving-wheel. If even half filled with passengers, such a carriage at ordinary fares would earn about 5s. per mile, and if filled about twice as much. The whole cost of working would be small. When working upon moderately easy gradients, the consumption of coal would run but from 6 to 8 lbs. per mile, the wages of stoker, driver, and guard making 100 miles a day, to 1¾d. per mile, including all train charges. Permanent way, station expenses, and general expenses might carry the whole to 1s., or 1s. 3d.; but even at twice the last-named cost, there would be a high proportion of profit on the work. The motion of the carriage is easier than that of an ordinary train; the total wheel-base being so much longer and yet so much easier from being formed upon swivelling bogies. It is almost impossible to imagine that if branch-line and other short traffic passengers were allowed to use this carriage, they would not universally pronounce in its favor. Mr. Fairlee, the designer, having worked out his system upon the great scale, and with the most perfect success, — as the experiments at Hatcham have abundantly shown, — is not only to be congratulated, but is entitled to the warmest thanks of the whole railway body politic. — *Engineering*

DURABILITY OF ENGLISH LOCOMOTIVES.

The life of a locomotive boiler has been found to be about 350,000 train miles; but this may probably on some lines go up to 400,000, or even 500,000 miles, as its wear and tear would depend greatly on local circumstances, and particularly on the chemical qualities of the water employed. Assuming that the life of the engine is determined by the endurance of the boiler, and that if, under favorable circumstances, it will last 500,000 miles, then during that time the fire-box will probably require to be renewed at least 3 times; the tires of the wheels, 5 or perhaps 6 times; the crank-axles, 3 or 4 times; and the tubes probably from 7 to 10 times. — *Van Nostrand's Engineering Magazine*, *Sept.*, 1869.

PEAT FOR LOCOMOTIVE FUEL.

The State-Line Bavarian Railway has been worked with turf since 1847, or for above 20 years, rather from necessity than choice. The peat is got from the bogs of Haspelmoos. The method of its preparation is that of M. Exeter, whose statement is that he can produce 10,000 cubic metres of prepared turf per annum, at a cost of 2.80 francs per metre. The turf, as dug or dredged, appears loaded with much admixed earthy matter; from this it is separated by grinding up. large dilution with water, and decantation of the water bearing the light peat particles still in suspension from the heavier earthy matter which has deposited. This is left to dry in layers exposed to the air like "hand-turf," and compressed in moulds by power. From other sources of information on the subject of artificially prepared peat, we conclude that these results admit of being contested. As a locomotive fuel, turf, at the best, is a bad and troublesome one; it gives much smoke and sparks, leaves an evil smell after it, experienced in the train, and is so bulky as often to need supplementary wagons to feed the tender on a long run. There is also great waste by the broken particles passing through the fire-bars. As to comparative heating powers (not theoretic, but taking into account all these circumstances), the result of 9 years' working on the Bavarian State Line indicate that 100 cubic feet, or 2.486 cubic metres, of the prepared turf of average quality and dryness, are equivalent to 312.5 kilograms of coke, or to 3.135 cubic metres of white firewood, that is, of wood principally of birch, beech, and alder. Thus, during this interval of working, the cost of firing with turf was about half that of coke *in Bavaria*, and two-thirds that of wood. By taking everything into account, as derived from the accounts of the line for 1861–62, it may be shown that even this is too favorable, for that the fuel account per kilometre per engines stands thus : —

	Fired with Coal.	Fired with Peat.
Passenger Engines, ...	0.166 f.	0.172 f.
Luggage Engines, ...	0.249 f.	0.207 f.

It is thus, though rather cheaper than coal for slow traffic, a trifle dearer than coal for fast, and that even in Bavaria, where coal was then exceptionally dear. — *Van Nostrand's Eng. Mag.*, *Oct.*, 1869.

BRIQUETTES.

The general use on the Continent of "Briquettes" as fuel for locomotives is a matter of deep interest to our railway companies, both as respects economy of consumption and room required for storage. They are composed of finely powdered, washed coals, cemented with a material which forms the refuse of starch factories, or with coal tar. The mixture is subjected to the pressure of a piston in a cylindrical or polygonal case, and then exposed to a current of hot air in a kiln for about 3 hours. The resulting blocks weigh on an average 8 pounds, and burn with a residue of from 4 to 7 per cent. of ashes. The experience of the Austrian railways is, that they evaporate 7.2 pounds of water per pound of coal.

NAPHTHA AS FUEL FOR LOCOMOTIVE ENGINES.

M. Portski, a Russian engineer, has run a railway train successfully for a distance of 53.6 English miles, the only fuel applied being raw commercial naphtha, instead of coal, coke, or wood. — *Les Mondes.*

AERO-STEAM ENGINES. STORM'S EXPERIMENTS.

During a period of several years, dating from about 1851, Wm. Mount Storm, an inventor and engineer of considerable note, made a series of experiments with air and gases in connection with steam, with a view to promote economy in fuel used for generating motive power. An engine, called the "Cloud Engine," was exhibited by him at the Fair of the American Institute, in 1855. The engine was named as above from the fact that the air, which was mingled in the cylinder with the steam, changed the latter into a vesicular condition, resembling fog. The inventor claimed 33 per cent.; and those who saw it state that, at times, it did actually make a gain of even more than this.

Its operation was, however, fitful and unreliable, and it finally was withdrawn from public attention, and nothing more has been heard from it.

None of these experiments, however, seems to have been made on the same principles as those of Mr. George Warsop, of Nottingham, whose object is to attain to a method whereby the expansive force of heated air may be used in an engine without the difficulties attending the use of heated air alone in the cylinder, and which are met with in the engines of Ericsson, and others employing only heated airs.

In Warsop's experiments the object seems to have been to make steam assist in applying the expansive force of air.

Warsop, however, has found that a maximum effect from mixed air and steam depends upon the proper proportion of the two gaseous bodies, — a conclusion which might have been theoretically drawn from a consideration of the relative capacities of air and steam for heat. Still such an inference would scarcely have warranted great hopes of economy from this source without extended experiment, and although extraordinary results — stated in a former article — are claimed, we shall not be surprised to hear that some offset to these claims has ere long been discovered.

Incidental to the results sought by Warsop is of course a better circulation in the boiler employed to generate the steam used in the experiments, from which some gain might be expected, though nothing like what is claimed.

AERO-STEAM ENGINES.

To the mechanical engineer, the paper bearing the above title, read before the British Association, at Exeter, will be one of the most interesting of any of the able and valuable contributions to the transactions of that distinguished body.

The first part of the paper was devoted to a review of the data by which it has been satisfactorily established that not more than one-tenth of the entire heat of coal is on the average utilized by steam engines.

The author, Mr. Richard Eaton, of Nottingham, England, then discusses the practical difficulties encountered in the effort to substitute heated air for steam, the principal of which is, as our readers are already aware, the effect of highly heated air upon such metals as may be economically employed in the construction of machines.

He then proceeds to give a brief history of the new aerosteam motor, which avails itself of air expansion, using at the same time steam, which removes the difficulty above mentioned.

In the first attempts at practically carrying out the system, the arrangement adopted was an ordinary high-pressure engine with vertical boiler as used where fuel is cheap. An air-pump is added, which is put in operation by the action of the steam engine.

Thus, cold air is taken in by the air-pump, and is forced on in its compressed state through an air-pipe, which, in the case before us, is conducted first within the exhaust, then in a coiled form down the funnel of the boiler, then past the fire, and finally past a self-acting clack-valve at the bottom of the boiler into the boiling water itself; rising naturally through the water, the air is intercepted and subdivided by diaphragms of metal gauge. Thus a twofold service is rendered by the contact of the elements, the water becoming aerified and deprived of its cohesion and prompted to a free ebullition, while the air on rising above the water is saturated by the steam, and the two together pass on to their duty in the cylinder where saturation assists lubrication. The agitation of the water prevents scaling.

In this form of the apparatus the power obtained by the increased volume of the air forced in by the pump did not compensate for that consumed in forcing it into the boiler. At the same time there were encouraging indications which led to further experiment. One of the air-pumps being discarded, experiments were made with waste-holes in the barrel of the other pump, to ascertain what proportion of air admitted to the boiler compensated for compression. It was found that about 10 per cent. of the effective consumption of fluid in the working cylinder gave much better results. At the same time the cam motions were discarded and the pumps left to their own unaided action. In this form it is claimed that a gain in work done by the combined air and steam engine was made of 42.5 per cent.

Here, although a very remarkable relative economy was apparent, it became obvious on consideration that danger of mistake would arise in assuming this economy as absolute, inasmuch as the duty performed, when contrasted with that obtained from engines of standard types, actuated by steam was manifestly low, and it seemed probable that, as, by judicious improvement in details, the duty was made to approximate more closely to fair steam-engine duty, this relative economy might fall off considerably, inasmuch as there would be less margin to economize upon.

With a view of testing this point, and also for the satisfaction of railway engineers, of conducting experiments at locomotive pressures, a thorough remodelling of the whole apparatus was effected. The tappet motions were thrown aside in favor of the usual slide-valve arrangement, working with a moderate amount of expansive action. The former wasteful vertical boiler was discarded in favor of a more economical one of the compound or Cornish multi-tubular description, so as to obtain a better evaporative duty from the coal consumed. The radiating surfaces of the cylinder-pipes were reclothed, and the feed water heated by the exhaust steam. Instead of exposing the air-pipe to the direct heat of the furnace, as in the former case, the air became thoroughly heated on its passage from the pump to the boiler at a temperature of from 500° to 600° Fah., by being conducted through suitable coils and pipes through the exhaust steam in the heater, and the waste heat in the boiler flues and uptake.

When these changes were made a gain of 47 per cent. over steam only, was claimed on an even-pressure trial, and a gain of nearly 30 per cent. on an open-valve trial, a step in advance so huge that it staggers belief.

AMMONIACAL GAS ENGINE. BY F. A. P. BARNARD, LL.D., COMMISSIONER TO THE LATE FRENCH EXPOSITION.

If hot-air engines and inflammable gas engines fail as yet to furnish power comparable to that which steam affords, without a very disproportionate increase of bulk, and for high powers fail to furnish it at all, the same objection will not hold in regard to the new motors now beginning to make their appearance, in which the motive power is derived from ammoniacal gas. The gas, which is an incidental and abundant product in certain manufactures, especially that of coal gas, and which makes its appearance in the destructive distillation of all animal substances, is found in commerce chiefly in the form of the aqueous solution. It is the most soluble in water of all known gases, being absorbed, at the temperature of freezing, to the extent of more than 1000 volumes of gas to one of water, and at the temperature of 50° F. of more than 800 to one. What is most remarkable in regard to this property is, that, at low temperatures, the solution is sensibly instantaneous. This may be strikingly illustrated by transferring a bell-glass filled with the gas to a vessel containing water, and managing the transfer so that the water may not come into contact with the gas until after the mouth of the bell is fully submerged. The water will enter the bell with a violent rush, precisely as into a vacuum, and if the gas be quite free from mixture with any other gas insoluble in water, the bell will inevitably be broken. The presence of a bubble of air may break the force of the shock and save the bell.

This gas cannot, of course, be collected over water. In the experiment just described, the bell is filled by means of a pneumatic trough containing mercury. It is transferred by passing

4*

beneath it a shallow vessel, which takes up not only the bell-glass, but also a sufficient quantity of mercury to keep the gas imprisoned until the arrangements for the experiment are completed.

The extreme solubility of ammoniacal gas is, therefore, a property of which advantage may be taken for creating a vacuum, exactly as the same object is accomplished by the condensation of steam. As, on the other hand, the pressure which it is capable of exerting at given temperatures is much higher than that which steam affords at the same temperatures; and as, conversely, this gas requires a temperature considerably lower to produce a given pressure than is required by steam, it seems to possess a combination of properties favorable to the production of an economical motive power.

Ammonia, like several other of the gases called permanent, may be liquefied by cold and pressure. At a temperature of 38.5° C., it becomes liquid at the pressure of the atmosphere. At the boiling-point of water it requires more than 61 atmospheres of pressure to reduce it to liquefaction. The same effect is produced at the freezing-point of water by a pressure of 5 atmospheres, at 21° C. (70° F.) by a pressure of 9, and at 38° C. (100° F.) by a pressure of 14.

If a refrigerator could be created having a constant temperature of 0° C., or lower, liquid ammonia would furnish a motive power of great energy, without the use of any artificial heat. The heat necessary to its evaporation might be supplied by placing the vessel containing it in a water-bath, fed, at least during summer, from any natural stream. Such a condenser could not be economically maintained. A condenser at 21° C., however, and an artificial temperature in the boiler of 38° C., would furnish a differential pressure of 5 atmospheres, with a maximum pressure of 14. By carrying the heat as high as 50° C. (122° F.), a differential pressure of 11 atmospheres could be obtained, with an absolute pressure of 20.

These pressures are too high to be desirable or safe. Moreover, condensation is more easily effected by solution than by simple refrigeration, and hence, in the ammoniacal gas engines thus far constructed, the motive power has been derived, not from the liquefied gas, but from the aqueous solution. The gas is expelled from the solution by elevation of temperature. At 50° C. (122° F.) the pressure of the liberated gas is equal to that of the atmosphere. At 80° C. (176° F.) it amounts to 5 atmospheres, and at 100° C. (212° F.) to 7½. At lower temperatures the gas is redissolved, and the pressure correspondingly reduced.

In the ammoniacal engine, therefore, the expulsion and resolution of the gas take the place of vaporization and condensation of vapor in the steam engine. The manner of operation of the two descriptions of machine is indeed so entirely similar, that but for the necessity of providing against the loss of the ammonia they might be used interchangeably. The ammonia engine can always be worked as a steam engine, and the steam engine can be driven by ammonia, provided the ammonia be permitted to escape after use. The advantage of the one over the other results from the lower temperature required in the case of ammonia to produce a given pressure, or from the higher pressure obtainable at a given temperature. These circumstances are favorable to the economical action of the machine in two ways. In the first place they considerably diminish the great waste of heat which always takes place in the furnace of every engine driven by heat; the waste, that is, which occurs through the chimney without contributing in any manner to the operation of the machine. This waste will be necessarily greater in proportion as the fire is more strongly urged; and it will be necessary to urge the fire in proportion as the temperature is higher at which the boiler, or vessel containing the elastic medium which furnishes the power, has to be maintained. In the second place, that great loss of power to which the steam engine is subject, in consequence of the high temperature at which the steam is discharged into the air, or into a condenser, is very materially diminished in the engine driven by ammoniacal gas.

For instance, steam formed at the temperature of 150° C. (302° F.) has a pressure of nearly 5 atmospheres (4.8). If worked expansively, its pressure will fall to one atmosphere, and its temperature to 100° C. (212° F.), after an increase of volume as one to 4. If, now, it is discharged into a condenser, there is an abrupt fall of temperature of 50°, 60°, or 70°, without any corresponding advantage. If it is discharged into the air, this heat is just as much thrown away. In point of fact, when steam of 5 atmospheres is discharged into the air at the pressure of one, considerably more than half the power which it is theoretically capable of exerting is lost; and when, at the same pressure, it is discharged into a condenser, more than one quarter of the power is in like manner thrown away. And as the expansion given to steam is usually less than is here supposed, the loss habitually suffered is materially greater.

The ammoniacal solution affords a pressure of 5 atmospheres at 80° C. (176° F.), and in dilating to 4 times its bulk, if it were a perfectly dry gas, its temperature would fall below 0° C. But as some vapor of water necessarily accompanies it, this is condensed as the temperature falls, and its latent heat is liberated. The water formed by condensation dissolves also a portion of the gas, and this solution produces additional heat. In this manner an extreme depression of temperature is prevented, but it is practicable, at the same time, to maintain a lower temperature in the condenser than exists in that of the steam engine. It must be observed, however, that owing to the very low boiling-point of the solution it is not generally practicable to reduce the pressure in the condenser below half an atmosphere.

The advantages here attributed to ammoniacal gas belong also, more or less, to the vapors of many liquids more volatile than water; as, for instance, ether and chloroform. Engines have therefore been constructed in which these vapors have been employed to produce motion by being used alone, or in combination with steam. The economy of using the heat of exhaust steam in vaporizing the more volatile liquid is obvious. But all these vapors are highly inflammable, and in mixture with atmospheric air they are explosive. The dangers attendant on their use are therefore very great. Ammonia is neither inflammable nor explosive, and if, by the rupture of a tube or other accident, the solution should be lost, the engine will still operate with water alone.

The action of ammonia upon brass is injurious; but it preserves iron from corrosion indefinitely. It contributes, therefore, materially to the durability of boilers. A steam engine may be converted into an ammonia engine by replacing with iron or steel the parts constructed of brass, and by modifying to some extent the apparatus of condensation.

ELECTRO-HEATING APPARATUS.

This invention, patented March 12, 1869, is based upon the well-known fact that electricity, in passing through a conductor of insufficient capacity (such, for instance, as a wire of very small diameter), evolves or develops heat. It is also well known that a wire of any great length, and of sufficiently small size to evolve considerable heat, will not conduct a strong current of electricity without difficulty and loss, and that as the wire becomes heated, its non-conductivity is increased, and that, in consequence, the heat becomes so great that the wire will be fused.

The object of the invention is to obviate this difficulty, by enabling a strong current of electricity to pass through a heat-evolving apparatus of any length; and to this end it consists in providing an electrical conducting coil, or chain, with intervals of small conducting power, in traversing which the electricity will be caused to evolve heat; and further, in interposing between said obstructing intervals free conductors of much larger size, which constitute reservoirs of electricity and radiators of heat, and will effectually obviate the difficulty experienced in a continuous length of conductor of insufficient capacity.

In this application of the invention, namely, for railway carriages or cars, it is proposed to employ magneto-electric machines, constructed especially for this purpose, for producing the requisite current, placed, if necessary, under the car, and to obtain the power to operate them from the axle of the car, — thus taking advantage of a motive power which already exists, but of which, heretofore, no use has been made.

A machine capable of heating to incandescence one foot of platinum wire one-tenth of an inch diameter, will heat 100 feet one-hundredth of an inch; 200 feet, two-hundredths of an inch, etc.; the law being that the lengths of the wires vary inversely in proportion to the squares of their diameters. Now, to reduce this to practice, it will be seen that a machine or battery of the power above referred to will heat a length of coil or chain, in which the aggregate length of the small wire of one-hundredth of an inch diameter, forming the obstructions, is 100 feet; and 200 feet, if their diameters are reduced one half, etc. In other words, having a machine of a certain power, and a certain degree of heat is required, the diameters of the obstructing media may be reduced or increased in order to accommodate them to the power of the machine.

In order to warm an American car upon this plan, allowing for a tray placed in the floor of the car, in front of each seat, it is estimated it would require an entire length of the chain or coil of about 360 feet, and in which the obstructing media form an aggregate length of about 70 feet; so that to accomplish this it would require a machine to heat this latter number of feet of small wire.

Although this may be a new application of electricity, and no machines can now be obtained already organized, and of sufficient power to be applied for this purpose, English electricians have made estimates of machines which come within all the requirements, as to power, space occupied, weight, power to operate them, etc., to make the invention practical and economical. Even with machines constructed for light-house purposes, 18 feet of number 20 iron wire can be melted instantly; and the fact is well known to electricians, if the same machine were organized for producing a current of *quantity*, the heating power would be greatly increased.

The inventor is not aware of any chemical battery by means of which this invention may be economically applied. In this case, the law of equivalents is in the way; and there must be a destruction of the battery corresponding to the amount of heat produced. In the course of time, however, chemical batteries may be constructed so as to be applied advantageously, as, for instance, those having large metallic surfaces exposed to a weak chemical action; or earth currents may be accumulated and utilized for this purpose; but for the present he relies entirely upon the magneto-electric machine. Advantage may be taken of a train of cars going down grade, when usually the steam is cut off and the brakes put down, without taxing the locomotive at all; whereas, in case of combustion of coal, the loss is the same whether going up or down grade. Among some of the advantages claimed for this method of heating railroad cars are the following : —

First, its economy; second, its safety; and third, its comfort. Concerning its economy, the trays may be constructed of hard wood, and covered by any metal, but copper would be best, on account of its absorbing heat more rapidly and retaining it longer. As regards the cost of magnet machines, this would be materially reduced if they were made by machinery and in large numbers, instead of by hand. There would be but little wear and tear of them except at certain points; and in case the magnets should in time become weakened, they could be easily taken apart and recharged. There being no strain or wear and tear upon the coil, being protected from injury by the plate covering it, and, besides, there being no possibility of its becoming oxidized by the degree of heat it would be subjected to, — say 120 or 140 degrees, — it is supposed it would last for an indefinite period. It is to be borne in mind, also, that by dispensing with stoves, 8 seats in each car are gained, and, consequently, a train of 7 cars would accommodate the same number of passengers, which, with stoves, would require 8 cars. In short, the percentage upon the original outlay would not compare to the annual expense of warming cars upon the plans now in use.

BRIDGES.

The East River Bridge. — The plan of the East River Bridge, as proposed by Mr. Roebling, has met with the approval of the Board of U. S. Engineers, appointed to examine it, and of the Government, and has been fully adopted by the Board of Consulting Engineers, consisting of Horatio Allen, Wm. J. McAlpine, J. J. Serrell, Benj. H. Lathrop, James P. Kirkwood, and J. Dutton Steele, who have made to the Directors of the Bridge Company their final report, of which the following is the substance : The plans, including foundations, towers, and superstructure, have been laid before the board by Mr. Roebling at various times between February 16 and April 26, and from him they have received the fullest information touching all the details. Having completed the examination of the plans, and the investigation of the combinations and proportions proposed, the board deemed it an appropriate part of their duty to examine the structures of the same general character erected by Mr. Roebling across the Monongahela and Alleghany, at Pittsburgh, in 1846 and 1860; across the Niagara Falls in 1850, and across the Ohio, at Cincinnati, in 1860. They have thus had an opportunity of learning the successive steps in bridge-building, which, beginning with a span of 822 in 1854, and one of 1,057 feet in 1867, all standing this day, are a practical demonstration of the soundness of the principles and proportions on which these structures have been erected, and rendering unnecessary, at least for spans of 1,000 feet, any other demonstration, and affording the best source of information as to the practicability of taking another step in a span of 1,600 feet. The bridge proposed by Mr. Roebling, a steel wire cable suspension bridge, 1,600 feet between the towers, 135 feet above the water, will be, in the opinion of the board, a durable structure, of a strength sufficient to withstand six times the strain to which it can under any circumstances be subjected; that it will bear the action of the greatest storm of which we have any knowledge, and that the method of joining the parts cannot be surpassed for simplicity and security in the result.

In the United States, the most remarkable suspension bridges are Ellet's Wheeling bridge, over the Ohio, with a span of 1,010 feet; erected in 1848, and blown down in 1854. The Lewiston bridge, 7 miles below Niagara Falls, built by E. W. Serrel, spanned 1,040 feet. Roebling's bridge, at the Falls, spans 821 feet. McAlpine's new Niagara bridge has a span of 1,264 feet, and the proposed bridge to connect New York and Brooklyn is to have a span of 1,600 feet.

Suspension Bridge over the Missouri River. — To Kansas City belongs the honor of building the pioneer bridge over the Missouri. On the south or west side of the river the Pacific Railroad (of Missouri) extends from St. Louis to the State line at Kansas City; the Kansas Pacific Railway, late Union Pacific Eastern Division, is now in operation 405 miles west from the same point of the boundary. The Missouri River Railroad, now operated in connection with the Missouri Pacific, continues that line up the river to Leavenworth; and the Missouri River, Fort Scott, and Gulf Railroad, running at present to Paola, 40 miles south, is being pushed rapidly to the Indian Territory, and will become the great route from the North to the South-west. On the opposite river bank the North Missouri Railroad forms a second line to St. Louis; the Missouri Valley Railroad runs northward to St. Joseph; and the Kansas City and Cameron Railroad, forming part of the Hannibal and St. Joseph Railroad line, opens a direct route to Chicago. The bridge, now completed, was built by the last-named road, and will enable the seven roads to unite at common points within the city.

The location of the bridge is opposite the town, and immediately below a bend in the river. It was begun in January, 1867. In February, Mr. Chanute, the chief engineer, took charge of the works. In the spring the enterprise was interrupted by a high flood, and it was not until August that work could be resumed. The south abutment of the bridge was placed 80 feet back from the face of the bluff, and from it a 66-foot span extends over a street and the track of the Missouri Pacific Railroad to a pair of pillars standing near the edge of the rock face; a span of 133 feet reaches from them to pier No. 1, the first river pier. A pivot-draw of two spans, each 160 feet in the clear, and 363 feet long over all, from centre to centre of piers Nos. 1 and 3, turns upon pier No. 2, which is placed as nearly as possible in the centre of the channel. Pier No. 4 was located 250 feet beyond No. 3; No. 5, 200 feet further north, on the edge of the sand-bar; and two spans, 200 and 177 feet respectively, cover the distance remaining to pier No. 7, which stands on the edge of the wooded shore, taking the place of a north abutment. The railroad is then carried over the bottom land on 2,360 feet of trestle-work, descending one foot in 100 to an embankment. The carriage-way is carried down on a heavier grade by a side trestle.

The difficulties attending the building of this bridge were wholly in the foundations. The length of the structure is one mile.

The masonry of all the piers is of limestone, quarried in the neighborhood, the facing being of ashlar, and the backing of heavy rubble. The ashlar of the upper courses, above the ice-breaker, is of a good blue-stone, of uniform color, and the stones used below are of a grayish tint. The piers finish 11 feet higher than the great flood of 1844, and 48 feet above the lowest water observed. The total height of pier No. 4, from rock to coping, is 89 feet. The pivot pier is circular in form, and 29 feet in diameter, finishing 32 feet on top.

The entire structure was completed by July 3, 1869.

The Mississippi Bridge at St. Louis. — Work on the Mississippi bridge at St. Louis is rapidly being pushed forward. The shore pier on the St. Louis side has been completed to a point above low-water mark, and the dredge-boats are now employed in sinking a caisson for the second pier, which will be located about 300 or 400 feet from the shore. The bed rock has been sounded. In order to hasten the completion of the bridge, a large body of workmen is engaged on the Illinois side, digging for the final completion of the pier, and within two or three weeks the second pier in the water and the fourth pier on the Illinois side will be under way. The most difficult pier to construct is the third, near the centre of the stream, owing to the rapidity of the current, and the sloping character of the rock's bed. Engineering skill will, however, overcome all these obstacles, and so soon as the second pier is under way, the caisson will be sunk for the central one. The levee for several squares is covered with stone, brick and lumber, which are being prepared for their respective positions. The estimated final cost of the structure is 7,000,000 dollars, 4,000,000 dollars of which have already been raised. As the work progresses, the legislature, city council, and the county court will undoubtedly send sufficient aid to complete the work at an early day. The rapid currents, quicksands, and other difficulties incidental to spanning a great stream like the Mississippi, will necessarily prolong the work, but that within three years, at the farthest, the bridge will be duly inaugurated, there can be but little doubt. Captain Eads is laboring with great energy; he is the chief engineer. While in Europe he visited all the bridges of note, and secured translations of the various reports of civil engineers on the subject of bridge-building, with a view of employing in the construction of the bridge the most approved plans, so as to secure a work that will be not only a model of beauty, but durable as well. Associated with him is Henry Fladd, — a man who ranks deservedly high among practical and scientific engineers. Both are confident of completing the bridge in three years at the longest, and even talk of two years as the most probable time. The work of tunnelling Washington Avenue, St. Louis, will not prove as difficult a task as many suppose, and it is believed that it can be accomplished without disturbing even the sewer-water or gas-mains. Should this operation prove too hazardous, then an elevated railway will be constructed. In either event the road will terminate in a grand union depot near Fourteenth Street, forming a direct communication with the Pacific and other roads. — *St. Louis Times.*

The Dusseldorf Bridge. — The great railway bridge over the Rhine, near the village of Hamm, a little above Dusseldorf, is progressing rapidly, and will probably be completed before the end of November. The bridge is to consist of 4 arches, the upper part of which will be made of iron. The iron work of each arch will weigh 14,000 centners. The bridge is united to the main line on the left bank by a viaduct, consisting of 15 stone arches, but this viaduct does not immediately join the bridge; it is separated from it by a revolving drawbridge, so that the line can be rendered impassable at any moment. On the right bank a fort is being built, which will command the bridge.

Bridge at Omaha, U. S.—One of the most important works on the Union Pacific Railroad—the construction of a bridge across the Missouri River, at Omaha, 400 miles west of Chicago—is about to be commenced by General G. M. Dodge, engineer of the Union Pacific Railway. The bridge is about 2,800 feet long, and is divided into 11 spans of 250 feet each, the piers being cylinders of cast iron, 8 feet 6 inches in diameter, and filled with concrete. The treacherous bottom of the Missouri River presents more than ordinary difficulties in obtaining a reliable foundation, from the great depth of the shifting sand, which is constantly filling up old channels, and opening fresh ones, so that the section of the bed is ever varying. Where it is possible, the cylinders will be lowered on to the rock, and elsewhere, to a depth of 70 feet below low water, in the sand, the bases being enlarged from 8 feet 6 inches to 12 feet in diameter, to spread the bearing surface, which will also be increased by flat bars projecting from the foot of the cylinder into the surrounding sand. Foundations of this class have been successfully employed by the Hon. W. J. McAlpine, in various bridges he has constructed. The length of the cylinders, from low water to the underside of the girders, will be 69 feet, making a total height of the main columns of 139 feet. The 10 piers, each with two cylinders, will be braced transversely, and protected up stream with ice-breakers attached to columns 5 feet diameter, and placed 20 feet in advance of the piers. The faces will be of cast-iron plates, meeting at an angle of 45 degrees, in front of the columns to which they are braced with oak timber, the intermediate spaces being filled with rubble and concrete. From below low water to the highest flood levels, the cylinders will be cased by plates, and the enclosed space will be enclosed with concrete, to prevent any accumulation of ice, or other obstructions, which may be carried down the stream, from getting between the cylinders, and straining them on the intermediate bracing. The girders of the superstructure will be trusses made of wrought iron, with the exception of a cast upper chord. The approaches to the bridge on both shores will be on a gradient of one in 30, made in embankment on the eastern side to a height of 40 feet above the ground, the remainder being a viaduct of trestle-work. The total length of the whole, including the river crossing, will be about 3½ miles.—*Journal of the Franklin Institute, March,* 1869.

Concrete Bridge.—The tests applied to the experimental bridge of concrete, set in cement, erected over that branch of the Metropolitan District Railway which forms one of the junctions between the circular line and the West London Extension, prove conclusively the reliable character of concrete exposed to compressive strains. The structure experimented upon spans the open cutting between Gloucester-Road Station and Earle's Court Road. It is a flat arch of 75 feet span, and 7 feet 6 inches rise in the centre, where the concrete is 3 feet 6 inches in thickness, increasing towards the

5

haunches, which abut upon the concrete skewbacks. The material of which the bridge is made is formed of gravel and Portland cement, blended in the proportions of six to one, carefully laid in mass upon close boarding set upon the centring, and enclosed at the sides. In testing the bridge, rails were laid upon sleepers over the arch, which brought a load of two seventy-fifths of a ton per foot run upon the structure. Seven trucks, weighing, together with their loads, 49 tons, were formed into a train, having a wheel-base of 57 feet; hence the rolling load amounted to forty-nine-fifty-sevenths of a ton per foot run. The deflection produced by the passage to and fro of this train four times was noted upon a standard, cemented to the side of the arch, at a distance of one-third the span from the abutments. When one side of the bridge was loaded, the extreme rise of the branch on the opposite side was about one-sixteenth of an inch, which was produced by a maximum strain of 10 tons 14 cwt. per square foot. At a subsequent trial, a mass of gravel, 10 feet wide and 3 feet thick at the crown, and 6 feet deep at the haunches, was laid over the bridge, and upon this, ballast was placed the permanent way. After an interval of a few days, the trucks, loaded as before, were passed over the bridge, at first in pairs, and finally all together. In this test the strain upon the concrete was as follows: —

The weight of the arch, as before,	. . . . .	7 tons 17 cwt.
170 tons of ballast,	. . . .	4 tons 8 cwt.
Strain per square foot from dead load,	. . . .	12 tons 5 cwt.
Strain per square foot from passing load,	. . .	2 tons 17 cwt.
Total strain per foot,	. . . .	15 tons 2 cwt.

After repeated transit, the load was left upon the bridge all night, and the arch, upon examination, showed no signs of failure or distress under the severe strains to which it had been exposed. From these trials it is fair to assume, that a thoroughly well-constructed arch of concrete is absolutely stronger than a similar one of brick; but in practice the danger arises that it would be difficult to ensure so high a quality of concrete as that employed in the present instance, and the proper supervision of the contractor's work by the engineer would be almost impossible in structures of this material, whilst the inspection of brick-work is an easy matter. The utter uselessness of inferior concrete was shown by the failure of the bridge which was previously erected on the site of the present one, which yielded under its own load when the centres were struck.

Blackfriars New Bridge. — Blackfriars bridge is altogether formed of wrought iron, so far as the main structure is concerned, the embellishment only being of cast metal. Preparatory to the actual commencement of this important undertaking, the erection of a temporary wooden substitute, as well as the demolition of the old bridge, was necessary. The first piles, for the requisite gantry, —one-third of which is now removed,— were driven in June, 1864. As it is generally considered in the London district that the London clay must be reached to obtain a sure foundation for large buildings, this course was here followed, involving 3 or 4 months of incessant daily and nightly anxiety and labor, on account of the tides. For our part, however, we coincide with the opinion of some eminent practical engineers, that there is no absolute necessity for going to this clay, and that, consequently, in doing so, much needless expenditure of time and money is incurred. The bridge consists of 5 arches, namely, two of 155 feet span each, two of 175 feet, and one of 185 feet. The height of rise in the centre arch is 17 feet, and in the others 16 feet and 12 feet respectively. Instead of regularly framed centring, piles were driven down to support the ribs where required, which doubtless saved the contractor much expense both in erection and demolition. The ribs were then wedged up to the soffit of the arch; these wedges or slacks are now removed, so that each arch rests on its own skewbacks, and the piles can be taken away at once. Mallet's patent buckled plates, which, as most of our readers know, are made of about one-quarter inch plates of iron placed heated over a mould, and stamped by hydraulic pressure into the shape of a groined arch, are bolted to the roadway bearers by five-eighths inch rivets, and form an immensely strong platform. On this is put one inch thick of asphalte; over this again — an addition to and improvement on the usual practice — a layer of broken stones and asphalte, from 9 inches to 12 inches in thickness, is placed; and lastly, on top of all, is granite-pitching as ordinarily laid on roads. The total length of the bridge is 1,272 feet; its width, including the roadway of 45 feet, and two footpaths of 15 feet each, is 75 feet. The gradient is one in 40. There are 8 polished red granite columns, between which there are parapets 3 feet 9 inches in height. Over each column there are recesses in which there are seats capable of resting ten or a dozen weary pedestrians. A handsome row of lamps will be placed along each pathway, a little back from the curb, — a plan not adopted on any other of the Thames bridges, — and they will be so arranged as to facilitate the navigator after dark. The balustrades are Venetian-Gothic in design. — *Van Nostrand's Eng. Mag.*, Sept., 1869.

The Cincinnati and Newport Bridge. — All preliminary arrangements and work have now been begun upon this bridge, which is to connect Butler Street, in Cincinnati, with Saratoga Street, in Newport, Kentucky. The stone-work of all the piers is to be of the best limestone, up to the line of high water, and freestone above that, excepting the two piers of the middle, or long span, which will be entirely limestone. Much of the stone for the piers has already been quarried. George A. Smith, of Cincinnati, has the contract for the stone-work. The bridge proper will be of the best wrought iron, in lower and upper chords, uprights, braces, etc. No timber will be used save in the flooring. The train, as seen, will be about 100 feet above low water. This span is planned at a length of 420 feet; the one next south is 240 feet, and the others as near 200 feet each as the division of distance will admit. There will be 7 spans in all, with the 8 piers. Beyond the front streets of both Newport and Cincinnati, the grade to the cities will increase, that of the wagon tracks being much sharper than the longer and easier one of the railroad. The bridge will be 41 or 42 feet in width, with 13 feet in the middle, for trains, one way on either side for cattle and vehicles, and on the outside of these still the passages for foot-passengers.

The East River Bridge. — "The work is assuming shape. The caisson for the great tower on the Brooklyn shore has been contracted for. Operations are to be commenced at once. The wood-work at the oil-docks and piers will be torn up and everything down to low-water mark will be removed. The bottom of the river will be excavated to a depth of 22 feet below high tide. The space to be cleared and levelled is 170 feet long by 102 feet, extending out into the river. Divers will be employed to remove the obstructions at the bottom, and blasting will have to be resorted to.

"The caisson is like a large scow, or flat-bottomed boat, turned upside down; nothing more. Then, if one imagines its being sunk to the bottom of the river on a level space prepared for it; that the water is forced out of the boat, or 'air-chamber,' as it is called, by means of compressed air; that workmen are sent down into the air-chamber in a shaft, cut through the top of the caisson (bottom of the boat), who, with the aid of calcium lights, dig out the material beneath them, which is hoisted up to the world above; that they continue excavating until the proper depth is reached, the caisson sinking, and, of course, on a perfect level as the work progresses, and that the 'air-chamber' is last of all filled up with cement, a general idea can be formed of the way in which the foundation of the tower will be laid.

"Experiments which have been made on the quicksand bed of the East River while excavating a dry dock prove its bearing power to be 10 tons per square foot. By Mr. Roebling's plan, it is proposed to rest upon this bed a weight of only 4 tons per square foot. The weight of each tower is to be somewhat over 75 tons.

"To distribute this vast weight so that no part of the pressure on the base shall be over 4 tons per foot, it has been decided that the area of the foundation shall be 170 feet long by 102 feet broad. This area will be composed of huge timbers resting on the sand, and bearing the masonry-work of the tower upon it. The timber will be 20 feet thick, and this vast mass of 20 feet by 170 by 102 will be securely bolted into one solid frame, so that the weight of the tower above can never deflect in the slightest degree at any point.

"The board unanimously hold that 300 feet high of a masonry structure could be safely and unyieldingly erected on such a timber foundation as proposed by Mr. Roebling, and that the superstructure thereon, if properly built, would easily bear the weight of the bridge, and all the weight that could be put on the bridge.

"The bridge company have purchased about 4,000,000 feet, broad measure, of yellow Georgia pine, the greater part of which is now on hand. Before the contract with the builders was made, proposals to construct the caisson were invited from all the ship-builders in this vicinity, and their bid proved to be the lowest. A more than ordinary depth of water in front of the yard was required, — not less than 23 feet, as, when launched, the caisson will draw fully 17 feet of water. It is to be 170 feet long, 102 feet wide, — as already stated, — and 15 feet deep, with a top 5 feet thick, and sides of a thickness tapering from 9 feet at the top to a foot below. The time required to build it will be about 4 months. As soon as it has been set afloat it will sink to within 18 inches of the surface of the water; and when the proper time arrives it will be towed-down to the ferry and placed in position ready for being submerged. This is to be accomplished by building on the top of the caisson successive layers of timber and concrete to a height of 20 feet. The weight of the caisson, with this 20 feet of timber and cement above the 'air-chamber,' will be 11,000 tons.

"The material excavated is hoisted from the 'air-chamber' through two water-shafts by means of dredges, and as it is raised the caisson sinks, being uniform-undermined round the 4 edges and throughout its whole extent. As the caisson thus gradually sinks, the mason-work, enclosed in a coffer-dam, is in progress on the top of the timber, thus adding the necessary weight. Access is had to the 'air-chamber' by means of two air-shafts 3 feet in diameter. The depth to which it will be probably necessary to go into the bed of the river will be about 55 feet below high-water mark, so that all the timber of the foundation will be enclosed in the sand and other material through which an excavation has been made." — *Journal of Gas Lighting.*

Beginning with a span of 822 in 1854, one of 1,057 in 1867, the bridge proposed for the East river by Mr. Roebling, a steel-wire suspension bridge, is to have a span of 1,600 feet between the towers, 135 feet above the water; it is calculated to bear six times the strain which can, under any circumstances, be brought to bear on it.

Bridge over the Schuylkill.—The plans of Mr. Kneats have been adopted for an iron bridge over the Schuylkill, at South Street, Philadelphia. The centre and river piles will be of iron sunk by the pneumatic process; the length of the bridge will be 2,488 feet, and the clear height 32 feet above high water.

The Kansas City Bridge was formally opened July 3d, with appropriate ceremonies; the municipal authorities of Chicago and St. Louis and an immense concourse of people participating.

The bridge consists of combination wood and iron trusses for spans 130 feet, 177 feet, 200 feet, and 250 feet, an iron span 70 feet, and a Linville & Piper patent wrought-iron pivot span 360 feet in length. The superstructure was erected by the Keystone Bridge Company, of Pittsburgh.

Missouri Iron Bridge. — The draw spans 363 feet long, and weighs 360 tons. The spans are respectively 200, 250, 200, and 117 feet in length. — *Engineering and Mining Journal, July 20.*

Bridge at Louisville. — The largest span of any truss bridge in the United States is that of the great bridge across the Ohio

River at Louisville, which is destined to connect the Kentucky and Indiana shores. The bridge itself will be, when finished (and the engineer in charge expects to turn over his contract for the building some time in November), one of the most splendid structures of the kind in this or any other country. The last span covers 370 feet, and is a marvel of engineering skill.

Bridge over Cape Fear River. — The new iron bridge over the Cape Fear River, to connect all the railroad lines centring in Wilmington, North Carolina, was opened on the 28th of August.

ENGINEERING ITEMS.

Resistance of Roads to Traction. — The following results of the experiments of Sir John McNeill, in regard to traction on roads of different kinds, are pretty generally accepted as accurate:

Resistance in pounds per ton on different roads: —

Iron floor,	8 lbs. per ton.
Stone tramway,	20 lbs. per ton.
Paved road,	33 lbs. per ton.
Macadamized road,	44 to 67 lbs. per ton.
Gravel,	150 lbs. per ton.
Soft, sandy and gravelly soil,	210 lbs. per ton.

—*Van Nostrand's Eng. Mag., Oct.,* 1869.

House-lifting. — In the work of straightening and widening some of the crooked streets in Boston, Mass., it became necessary to move a huge building known as "Hotel Pelham." This building is of freestone, 96 feet high, and weighs 10,000 tons. It was moved 14 feet in 3 days, by means of rollers and screws, a portion of the sidewalk being also moved with it. So carefully and well was the work done that not a crack was made in the building, and nothing in it was disturbed. The fastest time accomplished was two inches in four minutes. A great number of screws 21 inches long were employed.

The French Cable. — Length between Brest and St. Pierre, 2,595 nautical miles, a length that makes this the longest cable ever laid.

Heavy Blast. — A great blast was lately made at Clitheroe, Eng. A tunnel, 28 yards in length, was bored, and 6,000 lbs. of powder walled in it. The mass of stone, 60 feet in length, was thrown upwards in a vertical direction, and at least 50,000 tons of limestone displaced.

An immense Gasometer. — The Manhattan Gas Company are building, at the foot of Eleventh Street, in this city, a new gasometer of unusually large dimensions. The basin is 225 feet in diameter, and 38 feet deep. The circular wall is 7 feet thick, arranged upon which are 16 elegant guiding columns, each 72 feet high, of wrought iron, united at the top by ornamental girders. This will be one of the largest gasometers in the country.

Fog-whistle. — We learn that a fog-whistle, to be worked by a 10-horse power engine, is being constructed for Thatcher's Island, off Salem, Mass. It will be ready by the first of June. This will be the largest and most powerful fog-whistle in the world.

Forty-two ton Hammer. — In England a huge steam-hammer, weighing 1,000 tons, is being made for the Russian government. The hammer-head weighs 42 tons, the anvil-block 500 tons, and it is to be used in forging steel guns. — *Van Nostrand's Eng. Mag., Oct.*, 1869.

Steel-headed Rails. — Steel-headed rails are made at the Trenton (N. J.) Rolling Mills by the following process: The steel which is to form the head of the rail is first welded to a quite thin piece of iron. The combined bar is then beaten and rolled down until the iron is very thin and the steel reduced to about half its former bulk. After this operation is completed, the whole quantity of iron requisite to complete the bulk of the rail is added to the bottom of the combined bar and welded to the thin layer of iron. This process, it is asserted, doubles the strength of the weld between the iron and the steel, — always a difficult operation to perform. The old process consists in welding the relative thickness of iron and steel at one operation, but the new method is reported to furnish better rails. — *Van Nostrand's Eng. Mag., Oct.*, 1869.

Centrifugal Pumps. — The great Appold centrifugal pump to be worked in connection with Mr. Hawkshaw's important work, the Amsterdam Ship Canal, is to lift 2,000 cubic metres, or, say, 440,000 gallons of water per minute. The lift is not great, but for each foot of lift, the actual duty, irrespective of all losses of effect, is $133\frac{1}{2}$ horse-power. — *Engineering.*

Inverted Siphon. — An iron-pipe, 11 inches in diameter, and 8,800 feet (one and two-thirds miles) long, has been laid in Tuolumne County, California. It runs down a mountain, under a creek, and up the ascent on the opposite side, under a perpendicular pressure at the lowest point of 684 feet. — *Journal Franklin Inst.*

A rapid Change of Gauge. — In Missouri, the Missouri Pacific Railway — a road nearly 200 miles long — changed its line from the broad to the narrow gauge. Nearly 1,400 men were engaged in the work; and they labored with such celerity, that the task was accomplished in 12 hours, and without interrupting the business of the road.

Large Blast. — The operation of blasting off the rocky headland of Lime Point, opposite Fort Point, and forming the northern entrance to St. Francisco Bay, for a heavy water-battery, has been conducted under the direction of Col. G. H. Mendell, U. S. Engineers corps. Two blasts have already been made; one with about 10,000 lbs. of powder and a second with 24,000. This second blast is supposed to be the largest ever used in military engineering, and moved about 80,000 lbs. of rock. At the point a tunnel had been run in a north-westerly direction into the base of the hill, a distance of about 30 feet, where a chamber was formed on the right to contain 3,000 lbs. of powder; thence the tunnel ran in a direction south of west 31 feet, where a chamber was formed on the left for 6,000 lbs. of powder, thence on the same line 45 feet, where the third chamber was formed to contain 7,500 lbs. These chambers were about 5 feet by 7 feet, to contain from 125 to 130 cubic feet. When all were chambered out, a board partition was put up in front of each chamber to hold the powder. The greatest care was used in placing the powder in the chambers; the men wore the French sabots, or bandaged their feet in bagging; the barrel of powder was opened at the mouth of the tunnel, and carried into the chamber in sacks, the men groping their way into the dark tunnel, and delivering their dangerous burden to the foreman, who emptied it into one immense bin in the chamber. At a certain stage of the filling up, 8 cartridges were distributed at different points in the mass, each cartridge having an electric wire leading to the central wire connected with the machine outside. As fast as these chambers were filled, they were sealed up with clay and the tunnel tamped with the same material, the wires for firing the mass leading through a small box at the bottom of the tunnel. These wires, two in number, were of copper, one an insulated wire to convey the electricity to the mass of powder, and the other a plain wire for the return current; one connected with the positive, and the other with the negative pole of a powerful "Beardslee" magnetico-electric machine, located in a secure place outside, and several feet distant. On connecting the poles, the explosion took place with a heavy, dull sound, and an immense mass of earth and rock was thrown into the air about 70 feet, and the whole face of the cliff came crashing down to the base and tumbled into the sea. The cliff has been blasted off for about 200 feet along its base and tumbled into the sea, and about 175 feet in height with an average depth of about 60 feet. — *San Francisco paper.*

THE NEW THAMES TUNNEL.

The way the tube tunnel is built is by means of 3 segments of a circle of cast iron, each weighing 4 cwt., with a centre key-piece at the top, weighing one cwt. Each segment or ring when bolted together is only 18 inches long, but no fewer than 6 of these rings are bolted on in every 24 hours, so the tunnel is advancing at the rate of 9 feet a day. As the shield, which is 7 feet 3 inches in diameter, is pushed on for a length of 18 inches, it leaves within the tube or rim a space one inch greater all round than that occupied by its own tube on the outside. This, therefore, leaves ample room to fit in the segments of the tunnel-tube easily. This is done very rapidly. The bottom segment is laid in its place, and the two side segments above it, and between these at the top the key-piece is slid in. Between the long horizontal flanges a layer of white pine is placed before they are screwed close up. The spaces between the circular flanges of each segment are regularly calked in with tow and cement. Still, the shield on the cap is one inch wider all round than the diameter of the tunnel tube within it, which comes afterward to occupy it, leaving an opening of that space between the clay and iron. This interstice, when the segment ring is fixed, is closed by pumping in blue lias cement, which, as it quickly sets, forms a ring of stone-work, preventing the action of the water on the iron tube. The tube is to be fitted with a tramway of 2 feet 6 inches gauge, on which is to run a light iron omnibus of 10½ feet long, 5 feet 3 inches wide, and 5 feet 11 inches high. This will accommodate 14 people with ease. Ordinary lifts will take them down and up the shafts at either end, and at the end of the shaft the omnibus will be waiting. For the first hundred feet or so the omnibus will be pulled by a rope fixed to a stationary engine; after that it will descend by its own velocity down the incline and up the incline on the other side to the foot of the shaft. The whole transit, including time for descent and ascent, is calculated not to exceed 3 minutes. — *The Artisan.*

THE MONT CENIS TUNNEL.

During the past year an advancement of 1,320.15 metres has been made at the Mont Cenis Tunnel, of which 638.60 was driven on the Italian side, at Bardonnêche, and 681.55 metres on the French at Modane. This gives an average advancement of 110 metres per month, or 53.20 on the Italian side, and 56.80 on the French; and at this rate of progress the time necessary for the completion of the tunnel would be 28 months, or about April, 1871, and for opening the railway about 6 months more, or in less than 3 years from the present time.

THE SUTRO TUNNEL.

There is a mountain in Nevada which miners and some geologists believe to contain more than 500,000,000 dollars' worth of silver. Unluckily the veins run through the centre rather than along the slopes of the mountain; and the mines which have been sunk on the great Comstock lode, as it is called, have already reached such a depth that to pump them out and ventilate them is too costly, while no means exist to drain them.

Mr. Adolph Sutro has proposed that a tunnel shall be run into the mountain, which would cut the veins of ore, and serve to drain the mines and open the whole deposit. Here is his present scheme : —

" Let 3,000 laboring men pay in an average of 10 dollars per month, which gives you 30,000 dollars per month, or 360,000 per annum, and insures the construction of the tunnel, carrying with it the ownership of the mines. That amounts to 33 cents per day ! Who is there among you so poor as to miss it ? How many of you expend that much every day in stimulants, cigars, and other luxuries ? Put that money into the tunnel; it is laying up something for a rainy day. The money will be expended directly again in labor among yourselves, under your own direction, and from dependents you will become masters."

It is reported that the miners are responding to this appeal, and that Mr. Sutro is not unlikely to get the money. This would be a gigantic co-operative enterprise; one worthy of the age, and of the energetic and determined men who have developed the mining

regions of the far West. An act of Congress has given to the
Sutro Tunnel Company the ownership of all freshly discovered
and unworked deposits of ores which may be cut by the tunnel.
If Mr. Sutro's theory is correct, of which he at least entertains no
doubt, the tunnel would open a mass of silver sufficient to make
independent the whole 3,000 miners, from whom he asks 30 cents
a day. — *Evening Post, Oct.* 29.

THE PROPOSED TUNNEL UNDER THE BRITISH CHANNEL.

The conditions on which the success of this enterprise depend
are comparatively few and simple. The first condition relates to
the geological formation in which the work would have to be done.

It has frequently been pointed out, and there appears to be no
difference of opinion on the subject, that there are to be found, on
opposite sides of the Channel, tracts of coast presenting geological features almost identical. The English coast between Deal
and Folkestone, for instance, corresponds in every particular with
3 miles of the French coast, a little to the westward of Calais.
That the same formations continue under the bed of the sea is a
probability that has been noticed in a report to the Geological
Society on " The Chalk Ridges which extend parallel to the Cliffs
on each side of the Channel tending towards the North Sea," by
Captain J. B. Martin, in 1839. Careful geological investigation
has been made with a view to discovery whether the chalk formations obtaining on each coast continue unbroken for the whole
distance dividing them; and there appears no reasonable cause
of doubt that this is the case.

Impressed by these facts, Mr. William Low, an engineer who
for many years had been confident of the feasibility of connecting
the English and French railway systems by means of a sub-
channel tunnel, set himself earnestly to examine for himself the
geological formations of the two shores. After most careful examination, Mr. Low became satisfied that the deductions of the
geologists were correct. His examination of the borings for several artesian wells on both sides of the Channel strengthened his
opinion as to the regularity of the strata. It became his firm conviction that along a certain line, about half a mile west of the
South Foreland, and 4 miles west of Calais, the tunnel could be
made entirely through the lower, or gray, chalk, which, owing to
its comparative freedom from water, and other qualities, would
be a most desirable stratum in which to work. With the result
of these investigations, and with plans of the tunnels he projected, Mr. Low, in 1867, betook himself to the Emperor of the
French, who, giving the English projector a cordial reception,
desired him further to organize his plans, and to come again
when he might be prepared to submit definite proposals.

In 1856, M. Thomé de Gamond, a French engineer of repute,
who had for many years been advocating the construction of a
tunnel between England and France, obtained, by order of the
emperor, an investigation of his plans at the hands of a scientific
commission. This body, satisfied with the substantial accuracy

of M. de Gamond's geological conclusions, recommended that his investigations should be practically tested by sinking pits on the two coasts, and driving a few short headings under the sea at the expense of the two governments. Owing possibly to the backwardness of the Great British Circumlocution Office, this recommendation does not appear to have had any practical result. In 1857, M. de Gamond published the upshot of his researches, and the report of the commission; and at the Paris Exposition of 1867, he publicly exhibited his plans. It was very natural that Mr. Low, after his interview with the emperor, should put himself in communication with M. Thomé de Gamond. This gentleman unreservedly placed his experience at Mr. Low's disposal, and, after a time, the results of their joint labors were laid before Mr. James Brunlees. He, after careful examination, consented to co-operate with the two engineers in the prosecution of the work. A committee of French and English gentlemen of influence and position was, by desire of the emperor, formed to further the project; and it is by the executive committee of this body, under the chairmanship of Lord Richard Grosvenor, that the matter is now practically brought before the public.

But the opinions of Messrs. Low and Brunlees, and of M. Thomé de Gamond, received further confirmation.

Mr. John Hawkshaw, whose name is well known to the public at large and to the engineering world, was induced to test the question, and to ascertain, by elaborate independent investigation, the possibility of a sub-channel tunnel. With characteristic care and caution he took nothing for granted, but went himself over the whole ground already traversed by Mr. Low and by M. de Gamond. His geological researches led him to the same conclusions, and his expression of opinion in favor of the gray chalk was very decided. Not even satisfied with the theoretical results of these investigations, carefully though they were made, Mr. Hawkshaw held it necessary to make borings on each coast, at the precise points at which the ends of the tunnel would be situated. Thus Mr. Hawkshaw and the French commission came to the same decision. Now, the well at Calais, from which a considerable part of the geological inferences had been drawn, was at some distance from the spot where it was proposed to begin the tunnel on the French side, and possibly the strata might, in the precise place indicated, not run as anticipated.

This did not, however, turn out to be the case. The actual borings conclusively proved the correctness of the views entertained.

The boring on the English coast was commenced at St. Margaret's Bay, near the South Foreland, in the beginning of 1866, and was satisfactorily completed in 1867. It was carried completely through the chalk and into the green sand, which was reached at a depth of 540 feet below high water. The boring on the French coast, 3 miles westward of Calais, was carried to a depth of 520 feet below high water. It was intended to pass through the chalk as on the English side, but accident frustrated this design.

Simultaneously with these borings the bottom of the Channel was carefully examined, by means of a steamer provided with all suitable apparatus.   The main useful results established by these experiments appear to be, that on the English coast the depth of chalk is 470 feet below high water, of which 295 feet are of the gray formation, in which it is proposed to work; that on the French coast, the depth of chalk is 750 feet, 480 being gray; and that there appears to be no room to doubt the regularity of the strata between the two shores along the line proposed.

So, it would seem, first, that the chief condition is satisfactorily insured, and the geological formation of the sea's bed is such as to admit of the excavation of a tunnel through the lower gray chalk; and, secondly, that it is not necessary to go to a depth unsuitable for railway traffic.   It is calculated that the approaches to the tunnel can be constructed at gradients not exceeding one foot in 80.

The next point of paramount importance to the travelling public is the question of the safety of the tunnel when made.   The dangers most carefully to be guarded against are two: any possible irruption of water from the sea, or from unexpected land-springs; and any deficiency in ventilation.

Engineers are of the opinion that these dangers can all be provided against.   Recent borings on either side of the Channel have proved that there need be no fear of land water, and the impermeability of chalk, and the depth below the bottom of the sea, at which the tunnel will be placed, being in no case less than 100 feet, it is maintained that there would be no danger from incursions of the sea-water.   The submarine excavations in the Cornish mines are an existing demonstration of the safety of the proposed tunnel.

Ventilation will be secured by means of powerful steam engines, and attempts to raise the necessary funds are wisely to be postponed until two small headings, or galleries, are driven from each country, connected by transverse driftways.   Ventilation would thus be secured in the manner customary in coal mines and works of a similar nature, and the feasibility or otherwise of connecting England and France by a tunnel can be demonstrated.

CANALS.

The great ship canal which is to connect Amsterdam with the North Sea is now once more in progress, the government of the Netherlands having relieved the contractors of certain difficulties which for a time hindered the work.   The canal will be about 15 miles in length.   The Zuyder Zee is to be shut out from Amsterdam, and the Pampus dam, by which this is to be effected, is already half finished, and the locks and sluices connected with it are in progress.

A ship canal is to be constructed through Schleswig-Holstein to connect the Baltic and the North Seas.   The preliminary surveys have been completed.   It is thought the Prussian Government will undertake the work of building.

M. de Lesseps, the Suez Canal engineer, having sent some surveyors to examine the desert of Sahara, has, it is said, become convinced that the desert is at its nearest limit 27 metres below the level of the Red Sea, and that the depression continues increasing toward the interior. He therefore thinks that he can make the desert the bed of a large inland sea, by a canal of 75 miles in length, bringing the water from the Red Sea. Besides climatic changes, an easy method of intercourse with Central Africa would be effected if this project could be accomplished.

Mr. Lange, the London representative of the Suez Canal Company, has made some experiments on the canal with a corvette carrying ten Armstrong guns, and driven by engines of 300 horsepower. He has ascertained the following important points: First, the speed necessary to be maintained on a vessel of the dimensions of the ship experimented with, in order to enable a straight course to be steered, is from 3.2 to 3.7 knots an hour. Second, the embankments suffered no injury while the vessel was going at a rate of 5.4 or 6.4 knots an hour. Third, it was found that the loss of speed incurred by the vessel navigating the canal when compared with the rate on the open sea in smooth water, amounted to one-fourth, the same power being employed in both cases.

STEAM POWER ON CANALS.

A successful application of the principle of low speeds seems to have been made by Mr. Edward Backus, of Rochester. If the result of the several trials made are correctly stated by the inventor of this novel mode of steam propulsion, then the cost of transportation may be reduced about 32 per cent.

The following extract from a letter written by Gen. Quimby, U.S.A., who witnessed two trials of this boat, will convey an idea of the character of this new mode of propulsion: —

"In this boat the motive power, steam, causes a wheel located near the centre of the boat to roll on the bottom of the canal, and thus drive the boat in the same manner that the locomotive is propelled by its driving-wheels. The wheel, placed at one end of a lever frame, readily adjusts itself to the varying depths of the water, and its weight, together with the cog-like projections distributed over its circumference, prevents slipping and consequent loss of traction. It has been found that in the whole extent of the Erie Canal there are not to exceed 20 miles in which the depth of the water is too great for the wheel to work well. For very deep water, a screw-propeller wheel is used, and the motive power is changed from the ground wheel to it with the utmost ease and expedition."

PASSAGE THROUGH THE SUEZ CANAL.

The Rob Roy and English merchant-vessel recently passed through the Suez Canal, and the captain writes to the "London Times" the following account of the present condition of this great undertaking, after 13 years have been spent in its construction:

3

" The canal, as designed, is about 100 miles long. Of this length, about half is sufficiently advanced for the sea-water to reach 50 miles, — that is, into the middle of the isthmus. It is finished to its full breadth, which is 100 yards, or the width of a considerable river, but not to the intended depth of 26 feet. The remaining 50 miles not yet penetrated by the sea-water are in various states of progress; parts are excavated, parts are under water, parts will have to be laid under water which is to be supplied from a great lake not yet filled, while a good many miles have to wait for blasting operations. To English ears it must sound promising that a good deal of clay has to be cut through; for nothing can be dealt with so successfully in this country as that material. The completion of the southern half of the canal would look like a very long work, but for the fact of the immense subsiding works being completed, and a vast mass of appliances being on the spot. The service canal, from the Nile to the mid-point of the salt canal, and branching thence to either extremity, is an immense work, not less than 150 miles long, and in full use for the supply of fresh water for navigation, and for otherwise assisting the work to be done. The port at the Mediterranean end is an immense work, already available. The sea-channel at the Suez end has difficulties, but only such as engineers are familiar with. Forty enormous and costly dredging-machines are at work on different parts of the canal, — chiefly, we conclude, the northern half, — discharging mountains of mud, sand, and clay over the banks or into barges. The rate of expenditure is put at 200,000 pounds per month, or 2,500,000 pounds a year. Our informant calculates that a driving wind, after blowing a month together, will send into the canal, when finished, 500 tons of sand a day, or 15,000 tons a month. This, however, is no more than a single dredging-machine would be able to keep down at a certain moderate cost in coal. The difficulty of keeping up the banks of the canal, exposed as they will be to the wash of the steamers, and to a surface often agitated by the wind, is a more serious matter, but one which does not enter into the present question. Upon the whole, it does seem a moral certainty that at least in two or 3 years — for one year seems out of the question — this great undertaking, worthy of a heroic age, will be brought to what we may fairly call an actual completion. In the course of the year 1871 we may probably see the sea-water of one ocean flowing into the other."

SUEZ CANAL.

The following figures show the condition of the work on the canal on 1st January, 1869, also the progress made during the past year. The two exhibits, taken together, may give us the data for calculating the time when the entire work will be completed. The estimates of quantities are given in *cubic metres*, to which 37 per cent. should be added to show the results in *cubic yards*. The aggregate amount of earth to be moved, to dig the canal according to the plans adopted, was 74,112,130 cubic metres; of this there remained on 1st January, 1868, 40,000,000 cubic metres yet to be done. The time now named by Mons. Laralley for the entire completion of the work is 1st October next, and there seems to be no reason to doubt his ability to make good this prediction. The success of the dredging-machines has been even beyond the anticipations of their strongest advocates. One machine is credited with 108,000 cubic metres of excavation, in a single month; another with 88,889; another with 78,056 cubic metres within a like period. They have double gangs of men, and work night and day. Six dredges in November, in the Port Said division of the canal, raised 313,628 cubic metres; three other machines, at Ras-el-Ech, raised 214,042 cubic metres. The last new dredge of the contractors was put at work in December; and now their entire force, 60 machines, is being driven to its utmost capacity, in order that the canal in its full dimensions may be opened to the commerce of the world with the least possible delay. The piers or jetties at Port Said are entirely finished. The western pier was completed on the 8th September, and the making of the concrete blocks was stopped the same day. On 15th December, there remained but 316 blocks to be sunk to finish the eastern pier; and these could easily be handled in 10 days. The harbor and basins at Port Said have been dredged to a depth throughout of 23 feet; and now the French, Russian, Austrian and Egyptian steamers touch there regularly. No difficulty is experienced in running into this harbor at any time of day, or in any weather; whereas at Alexandria no vessel drawing 15 feet ever attempts to enter except by day; and, in heavy weather, steamers have been obliged to wait outside the bar for two and three days, on account of the narrow, shallow entrance to the harbor. During the first 6 months of last year 813 vessels entered at Port Said, landing 3,282 passengers, and 105,832 tons of merchandise. The Viceroy of Egypt has ordered the line of railway between Cairo and Suez to be abandoned; and a new line of railroad has been constructed from Alexandria and Cairo to Suez, by way of Lagazig and Ismailia. This new route was opened in November last; and henceforth Ismailia will be the stopping-place on the Isthmus for passengers between Europe and India, while waiting for their steamers either in the Red Sea or the Mediterranean.

SMELTING, CARBURIZING, AND PURIFYING IRON.

Mr. Isham Baggs, of High Holborn, has patented some processes by means of which the smelting, carburization, and purification of iron are greatly facilitated. In charging the furnace, the coal or coke usually thought necessary for smelting is in a great measure dispensed with, and in its place Mr. Baggs burns in the smelting-furnace coal gas, hydrogen, carbonic oxide, or other combustible gas or gases, and also the vapor of petroleum, naphtha, and other hydrocarbons under pressure, and in combination with a blast of hot or cold air. In the case of the inflammable hydrocarbon vapors, the same may be forced into the furnace under the pressure of their own atmospheres, or by means of mechanical appliances. The gases and vapors which are employed for the purposes of this invention may be previously mixed with the air furnished by the blast, or may be caused to meet the air in the furnace or at the tuyeres. The proportions of the mixture, when a combination of gas or vapor and air is employed, are subject to constant regulation by valves. One very convenient mode of obtaining combustible gases for the purposes of this invention is to generate coal gas in the usual way, and then carbonic oxide, and to blow air or carbonic oxide gas under pressure through the retort containing the residual coke. For the purpose of carburizing the iron, whether in or out of the furnace, as may be desirable, coal gas or other carbides, or other materials containing carbon, are blown through the furnace, or brought into contact with the molten metal by blowing them through it. Carbon in any suitable form or combination may also be directly introduced into the furnace for the purpose of carburization, and although generally for smelting purposes it is desirable to exclude all solid mineral fuel from the furnace as part of the charge, yet where a suspension of operations is necessary, such a charge of coal, coke, or other fuel may be introduced into the furnace as will prevent the materials, on renewal of work, from falling through the crucible or any iron remaining therein or below it from being permanently solidified. When purification is required, hydrofluoric acid is blown through the molten metal in its way from the furnaces, the gases being mixed with common air, or with some gaseous diluent. — *Mechanics' Magazine*, Sept., 1869.

BESSEMER ON THE HEATON STEEL PROCESS.

Mr. Henry Bessemer, the inventor of the Pneumatic process, addresses a letter to the "London Times," under date of Dec. 1, in reply to an article in that paper, to the effect that by the Bessemer process no good malleable iron or steel can be produced from inferior pig, while, by the Heaton process, steel is produced from very inferior pig iron, and steel of the first class, The exception taken by Mr. Bessemer in his letter is, that the steel produced by Mr. Heaton is not homogeneous or cast steel, but has the general nature of puddled steel; that is, is laminated and fibrous in form, besides appearing in the shape of porous steel sponge, similar to the iron sponge produced from a Swedish furnace. Heaton's result, Mr. Bessemer says, can only be converted into cast steel by the old Sheffield crucible process, at a cost of from 5 to 6 pounds sterling per ton. The nitrate of soda (270 pounds) necessary to reduce a ton of pig by the Heaton process, costs 6 pounds sterling on the average; so that while the inferior pig used by the Heaton costs 5 pounds less per ton than that used by the Bessemer process, the cost of the nitrate overbalances this gain on the ton by one pound sterling. The result is, that laminated steel, which must be remelted at a cost of 5 or 6 pounds to the ton to produce cast steel, costs a pound more to the ton by the Heaton process than good homogeneous steel from the best Cumberland pig costs by that of Bessemer.

Mr. Bessemer concludes that there can be no competition between his process and Heaton's.

BESSEMER'S HIGH-PRESSURE FURNACE.

Theoretically the total quantity of heat required to raise from an ordinary temperature and fuse a ton of steel does not exceed by more than 30 per cent. that requisite to melt the same weight of cast iron; but practically, the amount of fuel is 30 times as great in the former as in the latter operation. This waste is due to the fact that the temperature required for the fusion of the metal comes very near the maximum temperature which can be obtained in the furnace, and the heat is communicated to the metal much more slowly than if a greater difference of temperature were available. The production of a very intense heat on a large scale is, practically, very difficult, as it is necessary to guard against radiation and too great access of air, and to secure the complete conversion of carbon into carbonic acid; the systems of Mr. Siemens and Mr. Schinz, using as fuel carbonic oxide wholly or in part, have remedied the evils in a high degree. Mr. Bessemer's system may be employed as readily for the combustion of heated air and gases as for solid fuel with a cold blast. Mr. Bessemer, while meditating the construction of a large lens, 20 feet in diameter, to be mounted equatorially, to collect the rays of the sun from an immense surface for hours together, was led to inquire why the solar heat was so intense; and the solution was that the great intensity of the solar heat was due to the fact that the combustion of the solar gases took place under great pressure, the force of gravity being at the sun's surface 27.6 times as great as it is at the surface of the earth. He therefore constructed a small cupola furnace, in which the products of combustion could not freely escape, but were maintained under a pressure of 15 to 18 pounds per square inch above the atmosphere. With this moderate pressure, steel and wrought iron may be melted more readily than cast iron in an ordinary cupola; 3 cwt. of wrought-iron scrap, introduced cold into a small furnace, was run off completely fluid in 15 minutes. This process, which marks an epoch in the application of heat for metallurgical purposes, is fully described and illustrated in the London "Engineering," for Sept. 17, 1869.

THE OXYHYDROGEN LIGHT.

The Oxyhydrogen Light scheme has now taken a definite shape in Paris. A company has been formed, the capital necessary has been raised, and application has been made for permission to lay down pipes to carry oxygen and hydrogen over about a fourth of the city. It is not very likely that the permission will be granted, and the promoters will have to confine themselves to supplying individuals with compressed gases, as was originally proposed.

The prospectus of the company enlarges upon the cheapness and purity of the light, the complete combustion, and the absence of all deleterious matters in the products of the combination; but is quite silent as to the danger of introducing into a house two gases not possessing any smell, and which, consequently, may escape without observation, and the mixture of which forms an explosive compound of far greater power than any mixture of coal gas and air. To any danger of this kind, continental engineers appear to shut their eyes. We saw, a short time ago, a patent taken out in Belgium for making a mixture of coal gas and air, storing it in gas-holders, and distributing it over the city of Brussels for heating purposes. The engineering details given showed a complete knowledge of the subject of the manufacture and distribution of gas, but there seemed to be no recognition of the risk, imminent enough, of blowing up the whole concern. A consideration of this kind, some years ago, stood in the way of a scheme of the kind projected for Birmingham, and will, no doubt, prevent the Oxyhydrogen Light Company from getting permission to lay down their pipes over Paris. — *Journal Franklin Institute.*

NORWEGIAN BOXES OF FELT FOR COOKING.

Prof. Joy, of Columbia College, describes the contrivance and its use in the following terms : —

"Another adaptation of well-known scientific principles is to be found in the use of Norwegian felted boxes for cooking food. There are few devices more simple or more valuable than this. From an economical point of view, such contrivances pay for themselves a thousand-fold, and in a sanitary direction there is no estimating their value to the poor laborers, as well as to the rich consumers of half-cooked food.

"It is curious how little these boxes are known; but, thanks to the Paris Exhibition, this ignorance bids fair to be of short duration. The whole thing is so absurdly simple that that is probably one reason why so little attention has been paid to the subject. We will attempt a description of the apparatus. Take a box a foot square, line it with successive layers of felt, leaving a round space in the centre large enough to hold the kettle customarily used for cooking food. Have a thick cap to cover up the kettle after it is introduced, so that it is in the middle of the box surrounded by a thick layer of non-conducting material. When it is required to boil meat, it is only necessary to heat the kettle for a few minutes up to the requisite temperature, and then to put it into the snug place prepared for it. Here the cooking will go on by itself as long as may be desirable, up to certain limits; and the meat will remain warm for 5 or 6 hours. By having a series of these boxes, the dinner can be prepared at no expense, save the original cost of starting the fire. A little experience will enable the cook to determine the length of time to leave the kettles in the boxes. It is easy to be inferred that the same arrangement will serve to keep ice-cream from melting, or substances from growing warm which have been previously cooled in ice. The value of the felted boxes from a sanitary point of view is to be found in the possibility of providing poor mechanics and laborers with warm food. By portable contrivances it will be easy to keep food warm for some hours, and the advantages to poor workmen cannot be overestimated. To the rich it also insures thoroughly cooked food, while even by them the economy will not be despised. At the Paris Exhibition of 1867 these felted boxes in the Norwegian department attracted a good deal of attention. They were shown in actual operation, and an opportunity was afforded of tasting food that had been kept in them for some hours."

CAST-IRON STOVES.

At a recent meeting of the French Academy of Science, a report was presented from the committee appointed to inquire into the alleged insalubrity attending the use of cast-iron stoves. Extensive experiments had been made, and the results arrived at were, first, that all heating apparatus made of metal, and all stoves made of cast iron, give off, while in use, a large quantity of carbonic acid; second, that the quantity of that gas given off from stoves of plate iron was often insignificantly small; third, that the carbonic acid contained in the air was readily converted into carbonic oxide, by coming into contact with thoroughly red-hot stoves; and, fourth, that the oxide of carbon thus generated may, especially in confined localities, become very injurious to health. To obviate all bad effects, the committee recommend that cast-iron stoves be lined inside with fire-brick, and enveloped outside with a casing of sheet iron, so arranged as to leave space for free circulation of air in communication with a well-drawing chimney.

BARON LIEBIG "ON A NEW METHOD OF BREAD-MAKING."

Baron Liebig has just made some important researches on a new method of bread-making. He remarks on the stationary character of this art, which remains to the present day much in the state in which it was thousands of years ago. He dwells upon the sanitary importance of the mineral constituents of grain, and the necessity of a sufficiently abundant supply of them in bread. These are best found in certain kinds of black and brown bread, which are, therefore, more wholesome than the white bread that is nevertheless preferred by most people (especially by the lower orders), on account of its better appearance and superior palatableness. The problem has hence arisen, how to provide a beautiful white bread which shall contain all the essential mineral constituents of black bread. These mineral constituents (phosphate of potash, lime, magnesia, and iron) are introduced into the bread by the use of the baking-powder invented by Professor Horsford, of Cambridge, in North America. This baking powder consists of two powders, — the one acid, the other alkaline. The acid powder is phosphoric acid in combination with lime and magnesia; the alkaline powder is bicarbonate of soda. Two measures made of tinned iron, the larger one for the acid powder and the smaller one for the alkali, are employed.   When bread is required to be made, every pound of flour is mixed with a measure of the acid powder and a measure of the alkali powder, and sufficient water added to make dough, which is presently made into loaves and baked.   In one and a half to two hours bread may be made by this process.   The chemical change which takes place will be easily intelligible ; carbonic acid is generated and phosphate of the alkali is formed at the same time. The essential feature in Horsford's invention is the economical getting of phosphoric acid in the shape of a dry, white powder. This is done by taking bones, burning them, and then treating the well-burnt bone-earth (which consists of phosphate of lime and magnesia) with a certain quantity of sulphuric acid, so as to remove two-thirds of the lime, and leave a soluble superphosphate of lime.   The sulphate of lime which results from the action of the sulphuric acid is separated from the rest by filtration, and the solution subsequently concentrated by evaporation, and, when it becomes very concentrated, mixed with a certain quantity of flour, and dried up.   The mixture of flour with the superphosphate admits of being reduced to the finest powder, and constitutes the acid powder just referred to.   It will be observed that the alkali powder contains soda, whereas potash is required, in order to furnish the right.kind of mineral salts.   Liebig proposes to rectify this defect by using a certain quantity of chloride of potassium along with the alkali.   Chloride of potassium is now tolerably cheap, owing to the finding of immense quantities of it at Stassfurt. — *British Medical Journal.*

TELEICONOGRAPHY.

M. Revoil, an architect well known in France, from having the charge of the restoration of the Roman remains at Montpellier, Toulan, Nîmes, has recently been engaged in a special study of the early architecture of the southern provinces of the ancient kingdom.   In the course of his attempts to arrive at exactitude of definition, by the aid, at one time, of the camera lucida, and at another, of the telescope, he has been induced to make experiments as to the combination of the principles of the two instruments.   The result of this effort M. Revoil has called the *Téléiconograph.*

The principle of this instrument is that of allowing the image transmitted by the object-glass of a telescope to pass through a prism connected with the eye-piece.   The rays of light that would, in the ordinary use of the telescope, be transmitted direct to the eye, are refracted by this prism, and thrown down upon a table placed below the eye-piece.   The distance between the prism and the table determines the size of the image projected on the latter, and it is easy for the observer to trace on a paper placed on this sketching-table the actual outlines indicated by the refracted light.

The idea once grasped, it is easy to work out the details.   The telescope is placed on a stand with screws and clamps, allowing of both horizontal and vertical motion, as it may often be necessary to give traverse to the instrument in order to make a connected drawing of a larger area than can be included in the object-glass at one view. In fact, an entire panorama can be traced, if the relative position of the axis of the telescope and the surface of the sketching-table are undisturbed.

We see no reason to doubt that M. Revoil's eye-piece might be adapted to the ordinary theodolite, so that any person who possesses one of these instruments may, at a small expense, obtain a good sketching apparatus.

The advantages possessed by the téléiconograph over the camera lucida are manifest. The size of the image may be determined at will by the person who uses the former, without any diminution of accuracy. We have before us a lithograph of the summit of one of the towers of Notre Dame de Paris. The "croquis" was taken by means of the instrument of M. Revoil, at the distance of about 300 metres. It is 12 inches long. A sketch, taken by the aid of a camera lucida, is drawn alongside, and is only one inch in length, or one-twelfth part of the linear measure of the bold outline of the teleiconogram (as we suppose the new likeness will be called.) Two mountain-peaks, in Provence, sketched by aid of the same apparatus, show how admirably it can be applied to the sketching of country. For the purpose of military surveying its services promise to be of the utmost value.

The teleiconograph insures certitude in drawing, but it does not draw. It is an aid to the artist, not a self-acting substitute for his eye and hand. The sharp, bold touch of a master of the art of drawing will be as distinct from the feeble peddling of an inferior workman, when the refracting prism is used, as when freehand sketching is resorted to. The division of attention between the object and the copy, which is often so painful, will be entirely avoided by the use of this instrument. In the hands of a true artist the result will be every way admirable, — exact as a photograph, without the distortion of all those parts of the field which are distant from the centre, and at the same time marked by all the peculiarity of touch proper to the master. The camera lucida, from its greater portability, will still hold its own; but we shall hope to see M. Revoil's instrument brought into familiar use in this country, to meet circumstances for which it is peculiarly adapted. — *Builder, July* 17.

METHOD OF DETECTING POISONOUS GASES. THE GASOPHANER.

The "Pioneer," England, states that a discovery has been made by an officer, which, if the results on a large scale are at all commensurate with the experiments made on a small one, may prove of great value in giving a timely indication of the approach or presence of that poisonous state of the atmosphere which is generally believed to precede cholera and other epidemic diseases.

The gasophaners, or poisonous gas indicators, as the discoverer calls them, are easily and cheaply made. A piece of fused boracic acid, the size of a walnut, from which the water of crystallization has been expelled, is heated to redness in chlorine, or has dissolved in it while hot a small quantity of common salt, care being taken that there is not sufficient soda—16 per cent.—to convert the boracic acid into borax, which would spoil the effect. The red-hot lump of boracic acid thus charged is blown with a common glass-blower's tube into a thin glass ball or bulb, about the size of a small hand-lamp shade, and the gasophaner is ready for use. When first made, the glass is clear, with beautiful irridescent colors, due partly to the thinness of its sides; but left for a time, shorter or longer, according to the amount of moisture in the atmosphere, in normal breathing air, it becomes covered or clouded with a light-blue film (due chiefly to the carbonic acid gas of atmosphere), which, combined with the irridescent colors beneath, has an opaline or pearly lustre. On bringing the clouded gasophaner carefully to the flame of a spirit-lamp, this film instantaneously vanishes, leaving the glass of that part again clear and shining. The delicacy of this test is so great that, although by breathing on the newly-made gas the film may be much more rapidly formed than by mere exposure to the atmosphere, an approach to the spirit-lamp flame will no longer drive off the carbonated compound formed, on account of the impure gases contained in breath. At the same time, carbonates thus formed from the breath of a child, or of an extremely healthy person, vanish precisely as the aerial ones do on application of gentle heat. Held over a solution of ammonia, the air carbonate will not form, except on the upper part, where the ammoniacal gas has less action; but if held so that the breath may mix with the ammoniacal gas, a thick white cloud of carbonate of ammonia without opaline lustre covers the gasophaner. This cannot be driven off by heat, but froths up on an approach being made to the lamp flame. But the most remarkable indication given by the gasophaner is when it is held over a solution of sulphuretted hydrogen. The gasophaner immediately becomes pitted, as it were, with small-pox on the surface next the gas; and these spots, on being examined with a microscope, are found to be round, radiated crystals, the centre or nucleus of which soon bursts into a hole. They are white by transmitted, and dark brown by reflected, light. Nitride of boron gave exactly similar crystals as the chloride, and so did pure boracic acid. These crystals, therefore, are presumed to indicate a combination of boron with hydrogen, a fact hitherto unknown to chemists. The gasophaner can be reheated and reblown as often as required.

UNIFORMITY OF WEIGHTS AND COINS.

Professor Leone Levi, at the meeting of the British Association, read the report of the committee on "Uniformity of Weights and Coins in the interest of Science." The report commenced by stating that considerable progress has been made during the year in the assimilation of weights, measures, and coins in different countries. The North German Confederation of 1868 adopted the metre as the basis of measures and weights, and resolved to take as the primary standard measure of length the platinum bar in possession of the Prussian government. This bar is equal to 1.000.0301 metre at the temperature of melting ice. Metre weights and measures are made legal in the United States, and are employed in post-office exchanges with foreign countries. It were much to be desired that our post office would follow the good example. Still greater progress had been made in the introduction of the metrical system into India, — with regard to which the report entered into particulars. Efforts had been made to promote the adoption of the same system in the colonies. The second report of the royal commission had lately recommended the removal of every difficulty, and the full and legal introduction of the metric system. Chambers of Agriculture and Commerce (including the Barnstable Farmers' Club) had petitioned Parliament in favor of a uniform system of weights and measures. With respect to international coinage no further step had been taken since the report of the royal commission. The Chancellor of the Exchequer had, however, recently enunciated his views in favor of imposing a seignorage of about one per cent. for coining gold into sovereigns. This was a difficult question, and the committee contented themselves with echoing the recommendation of the royal commission, that another international congress be speedily held to consider the scheme. In conclusion, the report recommended the reappointment of the committee for the purpose of further stimulating the early realization of a uniform system of weights, measures, and coins in all countries.

NEW OXYGEN PROCESS.

Oxygen procured cheaply and easily, is, as we have often said, a very desirable thing. The numerous applications that could be made of it are so evident that we need not stop to mention them, but we lay before our readers yet another plan; and this time an ingenious one, for obtaining it. The mineral sources of oxygen being comparatively expensive, MM. Montmagnon and Delaire have betaken themselves to that cheap reservoir, our atmosphere, and have further availed themselves of the discriminative action of wood charcoal and water, or certain saline solutions. We give here, it must be understood, the figures of the authors named, without checking them by a reference to the figures of Dr. Angus Smith, who has made most careful experiments on the absorptive action of charcoal. According, then, to our authors, 100 litres of fresh wood-charcoal will, when exposed to atmospheric air, occlude 925 litres of oxygen, but only 705 litres of nitrogen. Now, it would appear that when the charcoal so saturated with gas is thoroughly saturated with water, there will be expelled 650 litres of nitrogen, but only 350 litres of oxygen. Thus we have now left in the pores of the charcoal 575 litres of oxygen, and only 45 litres of nitrogen, that is, oxygen practically pure for industrial purposes. To extract the gases, the authors employ a pump, and they tell us that if again exposed to charcoal, the oxygen will be obtained almost pure. There can be no doubt of it. They give no account of the cost of oxygen; but it is clear that it will be represented chiefly by the cost of the machinery and cost of working it. — *Mec. Mag.*

THE SEWAGE QUESTION.

Among the best of the labored articles upon this subject we have perused is one entitled "A Chemist's view of the Sewage Question," by Edward C. C. Stamford, F.C.S., published in the *Chemical News*. Mr. Stamford clearly shows in his essay that the problem cannot be solved upon merely mechanical data. He says: "The present water-closet system, with all its boasted advantages, is the worst that can be generally adopted, briefly because it is a most extravagant method of converting a molehill into a mountain. It merely removes the bulk of our excreta from our houses, to choke our rivers with foul deposits and rot at our neighbors' doors. It increases the death rate, as well as all other rates, and introduces into our houses a most deadly enemy, in the shape of sewer gases."

Mr. Stamford predicts that the water-closet will be ultimately doomed to oblivion. He reviews the process of Mr. Chapman, one of the latest proposed methods of dealing with town sewage, which is briefly a process of distillation, after treatment with lime and thorough putrefaction, points out important defects, and decides that its effectiveness is to say the least problematical. The process of Mr. Glassford, evaporation with sulphuric acid, he deems far more certain. But both these methods are connected with the water system, and this Mr. Stamford considers a radical defect.

The dry-earth system of Moule he considers the most hopeful of any yet proposed. The question of removal of sewage is not the only one that is to be considered; what to do with it after it is removed is the most puzzling part of the problem, and is strictly a chemical question.

The Moule earth system is the only one that has taken into full account the chemical bearings of the question and has dealt with it in a simple and practical manner. It at once provides for disposal and removal, making the former the prime object.

Mr. Stamford, in order to obviate a difficulty which seems to us purely imaginary, namely, the difficulty of obtaining a sufficient supply of pure dry earth, proposes to substitute seaweed charcoal, a powerful absorbent.

Now, so far as this is concerned we believe there will ultimately be no difficulty in obtaining earth for the purpose, but if the system should become general, the privilege of furnishing earth and taking away the resulting compost will be so valued as to make it a subject of solicitation; perhaps even a commercial value will become fixed to the compost, and we may live to see the time when it will be found quoted in commercial price lists with guano and other fertilizers.

The amount of earth required is only $3\frac{1}{2}$ times the weight of the excreta, and as seaweed charcoal, though only one-fourth as much would be required, would certainly cost more than earth, the latter could never compete with the former except on shipboard, or in cases where large bodies of earth must be transported, unless the charcoal could be in some way renovated and its absorbent power restored.

As charcoal can be used over several times, and then redistilled with the mixed excreta, the whole ammonia product being recovered, and the charcoal thus renovated recovers its absorbent power, it may be that the system of Mr. Stamford will be found to possess some advantages.

Mr. Stamford has made some interesting researches on the products of the distillation of the mixed charcoal and excreta. These products are, he finds, remarkably similar in composition to the distillates from bones, in manufacturing boneblack. Ammonia, acetic acid, butyric acid, acetone, and pyrol are the most marked products, and the charcoal produced is, he asserts, second only in value to that of bones. The redistilled seaweed charcoal, and the charcoal resulting from the destructive distillation of the excreta, will give an increased weight of charcoal, so that, if this process were adopted, the product for the city of Glasgow alone, it is estimated, would be 19 tons per day.

The uses to which this charcoal might be applied are various. The system seems to have been the result of much study and close thought, but we doubt whether its merits will ever prove so great as to supersede the dry-earth method. — *Scientific American.*

SALINE SOLUTIONS FOR STREET-WATERING.

The superintendent of street cleansing, etc., of Liverpool, has just issued his report to the Health Committee upon the trials made during the past season of Mr. Cooper's street-watering salts. The main thoroughfare along Lord, Church, and Bold Streets, chiefly macadamized, is considered to have afforded as severe a test as possible from the heavy traffic over it during the hottest period of summer. It is stated in the report that the use of these salts has been entirely successful, and beyond comparison superior to plain water. In practical results, two water-carts with the weak solution were found equal to seven under the old system upon the macadamized road; but in paved streets one may be expected to do the work of five where the traffic is only ordinary. Financially, notwithstanding the saving of horses and carts, it appears that, at the price of 8 pounds per ton, hitherto charged for the salts, no economy can be effected; but then the supply has been so far in experimental quantities, and it should be stated that the patentee is now prepared to deliver in quantity at 40 shillings. It is further considered that a reduction of 70 per cent.

would be effected in water wasted in the streets, and that there is the collateral advantage of the surface of the roadways being maintained in superior condition, a saving of 20 per cent. in the cleansing being due to this effect. The system has also been tested in Greenock, and is reported upon equally favorably by Mr. Barr, C.E., the master of the works.

PEAT MANUFACTURE IN OHIO.

According to a writer in "Putnam's Monthly," for November, the following is the method employed in the manufacture of peat, near Ravenna, Ohio: —

"The peat is dug to a depth of from 8 to 15 feet with shovels and slanes, the latter being a kind of spade, with a wing at the side bent at right angles with the blade, so as to form two sides of a square, and loaded into dump cars, which are drawn up an inclined plane upon iron rails by friction gearing, and the contents rapidly emptied into an immense hopper containing 150 tons of crude peat. At the bottom of the hopper is a large elevating belt, running over drums, upon which the peat is thrown and rapidly carried into the condensing and moulding machine. Two men are all that are required to keep the machine full. The condensing and manipulating machine is run by steam power. It receives the crude peat from the elevating belt in a wet or moist state, and delivers it in a smooth, homogeneous condition, through 10 oval-shaped dies, each $3\frac{1}{4}$ inches by $4\frac{1}{4}$ inches in area, from which it is delivered on drying racks, passing horizontally under the machine. Each rack is 26 by 72 inches, constructed of light pine, holding 5 bars or canes of peat, which, when dry, will yield, to each rack, from 30 to 60 pounds of fuel, according to the density of the peat. The racks are carried from the machine on an inclined tramway made of light friction wheels, so that the racks will almost glide from their own gravity. These racks are taken from the tramway, and set up like an inverted V, on the drying-ground, where, being exposed to the sun, and the air circulating freely around and between the bars, they dry in from 10 to 12 days, and are ready to be loaded into cars for shipment and use. The distance between the legs or base of the V being the same as their length, the drying ground is greatly economized. An acre will hold about 5,000 of these racks, from 15,000 to 20,000 being a requisite complement for the machinery. Sixteen men and 10 boys on the rackway will make 80 tons of prepared fuel per diem, — indeed, there is hardly a limit to the capacity of the machinery, if labor enough is employed. With 37 men digging and clearing off the racks from the tramway, 150 tons of dried fuel can be made per day. This fuel can be delivered at a less price than the best coal, and the cost of preparing it for market is lighter than that required in coal-mining. It can be afforded as low as 4 dollars 50 cents per ton, and even lower, within a reasonable distance from the bogs, and it is more economical than coal.

"An analysis of the surface peat of this bog gives the following result: carbon, 68 per cent.; oxygen, 18; water, 16; and ash 3.68 per cent. It also contains ammonia, acetate of lime, fixed and volatile oils. The deeper the peat found, the richer is it in carbon, and there are portions of the bog which will yield 70 to 75 per cent. of carbon. The average amount of carbon, thus far ascertained by analysis of the various peat bogs of the United States, equals 50 per cent."

HEAT IN MINES.

The "Virginia City (Nev.) Enterprise" says: "The increase in the heat of our mines is now beginning to give many of our mining companies more trouble, and is proving a greater obstacle to mining operations in those levels lying below a depth of 1,000 feet, than any veins or 'pocket' deposits of water yet encountered. A number of the leading companies on the Comstock are now engaged in putting in engines to be used expressly for driving fans for furnishing air to the lower levels, forcing it through large tubes of galvanized iron. With this great increase of heat in our mines comes a great decrease of water; in fact, in our deepest mine — the Bullion, which has attained the depth of 1,200 feet — not a drop of water is to be seen; it is as dry as a lime-kiln and as hot as an oven.

" In the lower workings of the Chollar-Potosi mine, which are at a perpendicular depth of 1,100 feet below the surface, the thermometer now stands at 100 degrees, — a frightful heat to be endured by a human being engaged in a kind of labor calling for severe muscular exertion. Here, also, we find the water to have decreased till there is at the present time a very insignificant amount, it being necessary to run the pump but 4 hours out of the 24.

" We might give other instances illustrative and corroborative of what we have stated, but deem the evidence afforded by two of our deepest mines, situated some considerable distance apart, sufficient. Does it not appear likely, judging from the present situation in the deepest levels of our mines, that the great Sutro tunnel, if ever constructed, is more likely to be found useful as a means of entrance for fresh air than of exit for water? The 'situation,' if we may so call it, so changes in our mines that we hardly know one month ahead what would be of advantage to us. Some months since we supposed we were to be drowned out of the lower levels of our mines, or rather prevented from ever attaining any very great depth, by a tremendous influx of water. Now we find no water at all — or at best a trifling quantity — but in its place hot air. No doubt this is a change for the better. It will be much easier to force a column of light and elastic air 1,000 feet downward than to lift a column of water the same distance.

" Should it prove a fact, as now seems probable, that the water in our mines is confined to certain strata at no great depth from the surface, say between the depths of 400 and 900 feet, and should it be found practicable to ventilate the deep workings of our mines by forcing down air, some of our leading companies are likely to reach a depth much below the point where the Sutro tunnel will tap the lead before it is completed, even though work upon it should be at once commenced. Should the Chollar-Potosi Company continue downward with their shafts at the same rate of speed that has distinguished their progress for some months past, they would, in less than two years, attain a point below that of the intersection of the Sutro tunnel with the Comstock lead. Whether another water stratum exists in the 800 to 1,000 feet of hot, unexplored region of rock lying between our present lower levels and that point on the lead which would be cut by the Sutro tunnel, no man can know."

VENTILATION OF MINES.

It having been asserted that the sole cause of the recent frightful destruction of life at Avondale, in Pennsylvania, was the use of a furnace for ventilating the mine instead of mechanical apparatus, we give some extracts from a paper which was recently read before the Institution of Mechanical Engineers, at Newcastle, England, by Mr. William Cochrane, and published in The "Engineer:" —

"It is considered a fair estimate of the economic value of the average conditions in which furnaces are worked that only one fifth of the heat due to the combustion of the coal is utilized. There are many objections, besides the small useful effect, to the use of a furnace, which cannot be overcome, and which form a constant source of cost attendant upon it, namely, the necessity of cleaning the flues and the consequent suspension of the active ventilation of the mine; the inconvenience, and in some cases the impossibility, of using a shaft highly heated, and often full of smoke, for any other purpose than as a ventilating shaft; and the serious damage done by the products of combustion to cast-iron tubing, timber, pumps, or wire ropes, where winding is carried on in the upcast shaft, especially where the shaft is damp. If the conditions are unfavorable for the use of a furnace, such as shallow shafts and heavy resistances to be overcome, the furnace then is quite unable to compete with a good mechanical ventilator in economical effect. In a table compiled by Mr. J. J. Atkinson, Government Inspector for the Durham coal-field, has been shown the depth at which the furnaces are estimated to be equal to ventilating machines in point of economy of fuel, assuming that the sources of loss are of the same extent in each case, that is, the loss of fuel in furnaces by cooling in the upcast, and in ventilating machines utilized 60 per cent. of the engine-power. A recent calculation by M. Guibal, of Mons, deduces the following comparison: That if a furnace in a 12-feet shaft, 400 yards deep, circulate 53,000 cubic feet of air per minute under the total resistances represented by $3\frac{1}{4}$ inch water-gauge, and an average excess of upcast temperature of 108° above the downcast, with a duty of 31 lbs. of coal per horse-power in the air estimated on the total resistances, then a mechanical ventilator, utilizing 60 per cent. of the power employed, would, under the same conditions, have a duty of 11 lbs. of coal per horse-power on the air, being a saving of 64 per cent. At a depth of 550 yards to circulate the same volume, the duty of the furnace being 22 lbs. of coal, that of the mechanical ventilator would be 11 lbs., being a saving of 50 per cent."

While on this subject we may also state that a machine has been invented for the purpose of proper ventilation of mines, a description of which we take from the "London Mining Journal:" —

"This subject has of late occupied the attention of mining and mechanical engineers, as well as that of others who have been startled into activity by the many appalling accidents which of late have occurred in consequence of the explosive gases being allowed to accumulate in mines. The question is, no doubt, one of great importance, and they who shall succeed, either by mechanical or other contrivance, in keeping up a constant supply of good wholesome air in all parts of a mine, will have conferred an incalculable boon upon mining science. Hitherto, little provision beyond the natural condition of things, or by adding a fire in the shaft or bottom of the shaft, has been adopted; and these, no doubt, in small shafts, and in mines of very limited extent, have been sufficient in determining a current by effecting thermometrical variations. There is a degree of uncertainty about it, however, in consequence of the varying conditions of the external atmosphere, changing as it does throughout the year. Hence machines have been invented for the purpose of blowing fresh air in and of exhausting foul air out of mines, some working by means of pumps, and others effecting the same object by means of centrifugal action. Mr. Lloyd, the able engineer of the Lilleshall Company, has been turning his attention to this, and he has succeeded in inventing a machine of ingenious construction, which the company has patented. The success of the plan appears to depend upon the peculiar construction and disposition of the fans, which beat the air out of the shaft, depending upon the well-known elasticity of the atmosphere to supply its place.

This he does by means of a centrifugal fan, driven by an engine. The one we saw was a beautifully executed model, with fan 18 inches in diameter and 6 inches wide over the blades, which, measured by the aerometer, produced exhaustion at the rate of 2,500 feet per minute, with a water-gauge of one-quarter inch. But the company are erecting a larger one, to be worked by a small horizontal, direct-action engine, which shall be described when in operation. It may be stated that the success which has hitherto attended the trials made surpasses all expectation, and the effects produced appear incredible. He first made a two-feet 3-inch fan, which exhausted 2,500 feet of air per minute; and another, with a 5-feet fan, one foot 10 inches broad, which exhausted 25,196 cubic feet per minute, with a water-gauge of two and three-eighths inches. Indeed, the effects were such as to be incredible to the inventor until after repeated measure-

ments, in the course of which several aerometers were torn to
pieces by the force of the current of air created."

THE MODERN ICE MACHINE.

The amount of ice produced by an ice machine, worked by
means of an exhaust or condensing air-pump, driven by steam-
power, is easily determined, theoretically, from the amount of
coal burned in the furnace of the steam boiler. It has been
proved that the combustion of one pound of anthracite coal produces, in round numbers, 14,000 units of heat, and that in order
to freeze water of 72° F., it is necessary to abstract, besides 40°
of sensible heat, 140° of latent heat — together 180° — which, for
one pound of water, is, of course, equivalent to 180 units of heat.
As this number of units is the eightieth part of the 14,000 units
produced by the combustion of one pound of coal, it is clear that
the heat produced by the combustion of one ton of coal is equivalent to the heat to be abstracted from 80 tons of water of 72°, in
order to change it to ice.

But in practice we find here exactly the same state of affairs as
is the case with the steam engine. Theoretically, a steam engine
ought to produce at least 700 units of force (foot-pounds) for
every unit of heat consumed; in practice, good machinery only
produces from about 70 to 100 foot-pounds, from about one-tenth
to one-seventh part of the theoretical amount. In the best ice
machines, thus far constructed, instead of freezing 80 tons of
water for every ton of coal consumed, only from about 8 to 11
tons of ice are produced, also from one-tenth to one-seventh part
of the theoretical amount; proving, thus, the remarkable fact, that
in both the steam engine and the ice machine exactly the same
relation exists between the theoretically calculated effects and the
practical results.

As, however, all the best ice machines accomplish the conversion of the heat of the fuel into the freezing operation by the intervention of a steam engine, the fact that they practically produce only from one-tenth to one-seventh of the amount of the
cold they theoretically should produce, is solely due to the other
fact, that the steam engine, itself, practically produces only from
one-tenth to one-seventh of the amount of power which would be
strictly equivalent to the number of heat units consumed. It must
not be lost sight of that it is only the power of the steam engine
which generates the cold in the freezing machines, and that,
therefore, improvements in the steam engine, which bring its
practical results nearer to the theoretical standard, will at once
exert their influence on the amount of ice the ice machines can
produce, and, consequently, also on the cost of the ice manufactured in these machines.

Moreover, it appears that the kind of freezing machines in
question, which convert power into cold, notwithstanding they
are yet in their infancy, have already attained such a degree of
excellence, that they are ahead of that class of machines which

convert heat into power, either by steam, hot air, or any other possible means, as it is proved that they produce the full theoretical equivalent of cold (negative heat) for the number of foot-pounds employed; namely, cooling one pound of water one degree for a power equivalent to 700 pounds descending one foot, which, expressed in the adopted scientific manner, is one unit of negative heat for every 700 foot-pounds consumed.

SOLAR HEAT AS A MOTIVE POWER.

M. Mouchot, in a contribution to the "Comptes Rendus," thus speaks of some of his results: —

"According to my experiments, it is easy to collect, at a cheap rate, more than three-fifths of the solar heat arriving at the surface of the globe. The intensity of this calorific source, so feeble in appearance, was revealed by Pouillet, more than 30 years ago. At Paris, a surface of one square metre, normally exposed to the sun's rays, receives, at least, whatever may be the season, during the greater part of a fine day, 10 heat-units (calories) per minute. [The unit of heat adopted by most physicists is the quantity necessary to raise one pound of water from 0° to 1° C. We suppose M. Mouchot adopts the same standard.] To appreciate such an amount of heat, it is sufficient to observe that it will boil, in 10 minutes, one litre of water, taken at the temperature of melting ice, and it is almost equal to the theoretical power of a one-horse steam engine. Under the same conditions, a superficies of one 'are' (119.603 square yards) would receive, during 10 hours of insolation, as much heat as results from the combustion of 120 kilogrammes (321,507 pounds troy) of ordinary oil. These numbers are eloquent; they should, if not dispel, at least weaken the serious fears entertained by some, in consequence of the rapid exhaustion of coal mines, and the necessity of going to increasingly greater depths, disputing with the subterranean water this precious-combustible. The intensity of the calorific radiation of the sun is, moreover, much less at Paris than in intertropical regions, or upon the elevated plains. It is, therefore, probable, that the invention of 'sun-receivers' will, some day, enable industry to establish works in the desert, where the sky remains very clear for a long time, just as the hydraulic engines have enabled them to be established by the side of water-courses.

"Although I have not been able to operate under very favorable circumstances, since my experiments have only been made with the sun of Alençon, Tours, and Paris, I proved, as far back as 1861, the possibility of maintaining a hot-air engine in motion, with the help of the sun's rays. More lately I have succeeded in boiling, tolerably quickly, several litres of water submitted to insolation. In short, having satisfied myself that it was sufficient to have a silver reflector, with a surface of one square metre, to vaporize, in 100 minutes, one litre of water (0.88 quarts), taken at the ordinary temperature, or, in other words, to produce 17 litres of vapor a minute, I tried to work a small steam engine by solar heat, and my efforts were crowned with success in June, 1866. In the mean time I have been able, by very simple apparatus, to obtain some remarkable effects from insolation, such as the distillation of alcohol, the fusion of sulphur, perfect cooking of meat, bread, etc. None of these experiments, particularly the application of the sun's heat to machinery, have been tried upon a sufficiently large scale. It would, therefore, be useful to repeat them in tropical countries, with 'sun-receivers' of suitable dimensions. We would measure the volume and the tension of steam produced in an hour by a given insolated surface, the pressure developed by the sun in a considerable mass of confined air, and the temperature which might be obtained by vast reflectors, formed of a framework of wood covered with plates of silver, etc."

IMPROVED MARINER'S COMPASS.

The Earl of Caithness is the inventor of a new mode of suspending ships' compasses, which for efficiency and simplicity is said to surpass anything yet produced. Instead of the two concentric brass rings having their axles at right angles, known as gimbals, Lord Caithness employs a pendulum and ball, which ball works in a socket in the centre of the bottom of the compass bowl. The compass works, therefore, on one bearing on the ball-and-socket principle, and thus maintains its parallelism with the horizon in the heaviest weather. If we may credit the published reports of the trials, the simplicity of this invention is not more striking than its efficiency. It is stated that it has already stood the most trying tests, and the oscillation of compasses to which it is applied, as compared with the oscillation of the gimbal compass, is as degrees to points.

TO MEASURE HEIGHTS.

A very compact and useful instrument, called the "apomecometer," that can be carried in the waistcoat-pocket, for ascertaining the vertical heights of towers, spires, and other buildings, has been invented in England. It cannot be better explained than by quoting the description given by Mr. Millar, the inventor: "The 'apomecometer' is constructed in accordance with the principles which govern the sextant, namely, as the angles of incidence and reflection are always equal, the rays of an object being thrown on the plane of one mirror are from that reflected to the plane of another mirror, thereby making both extremes of the vertical height coincide exactly at the same point on the horizon glass; so that, by measuring the base line, we obtain a result equal to the altitude."

RESEARCHES ON MATERIALS FIT FOR RESISTING VERY HIGH TEMPERATURES.

M. Audouin. — (*Cosmos.*) — While engaged with other studies on geology in the southern parts of France, the author found that between Tarascon and Antibes there exists a very valuable and extensive bed of *bauxite* (hydrate of alumina), which is occasionally applied for the manufacture of sulphate of alumina. This material has been applied, at the suggestion of Audouin, for the manufacture of crucibles and fire-bricks; and on having been tested in comparison with the best products of the kind from France, England, and Germany, it was found that even best fire-bricks might be melted in bauxite-made crucibles heated by mineral oils and a blast.

SILVER EXTRACTION — ELECTRO-CHEMICAL TREATMENT.

To do away with the tedious and expensive process of amalgamation in the production of pure silver is a feat which Becquerel, Sen., of the French Academy of Sciences, asserts he has recently accomplished, after having experimented on this subject since the year 1835.

The experiment was tried successfully on 40,000 lbs. of silver ores from Peru, Mexico, and Chili, etc.

A powerful battery, with double liquid voltaic elements separated by porous diaphragms, was made to act on the prepared ore, from which the pure silver was thus obtained at once in a finely divided state and in a crystalline form. Messrs. Wolf and Pioche are at present, it is said, preparing for a trial of this system in California. — *Scientific American.*

ON THE GLASS USED FOR LIGHT-HOUSES.

The special composition of the crown-glass used for the light apparatus for light-houses was, until quite recently, kept a secret by the manufacturers of Saint Gobain, in France, and some firms in Birmingham, which had the monopoly of this branch of trade.

From the researches of David M. Henderson, C.E., published in "Dingler's Journal," we are able to furnish the recipes for both of these.

The French glass is composed of: —

Silicic acid,	72.1 parts.
Soda,	12.2 "
Lime,	15.7 "

Alumina and oxide of iron, traces.

In Birmingham it is made from the following mixture: —

	cwts.	qrs.	lbs.
French sand,	5	—	—
Carbonate of soda,	1	3	7
Lime,	0	2	7
Nitrate of soda,	0	1	0
Arsenious acid,	0	0	3

The best qualities of this glass are at present produced in the Siemens furnace.

CUTTING GLASS WITH STEEL.   THE MAGIC DIAMOND.

The cutting of glass with steel has been demonstrated to be possible, provided its point is ground into the form of a common glazier's diamond. But while hard steel of this form will cut glass, it is difficult to bring a steel point to the required shape, and it also soon wears out and becomes worthless, until reground. Many efforts have been made to make a tool of steel that would compete at least approximately with the real diamond for this purpose. It has been discovered that a small cylindrical point of steel, when made to rotate upon glass in such a manner that its longitudinal axis shall make an angle of 45 degrees with the surface of the glass, approaches in effect so nearly to that of the real diamond that it is a very cheap and effective substitute.

HEAVY MODERN MACHINERY.

A mass of metal of a ton weight was unknown before the Christian era. Now those in cast iron up to 150 tons, in wrought iron to 40 tons, and in steel or bronze to 25 tons, are made in any desired form, and turned or bored with the most perfect accuracy. Two years ago I saw the largest lathe in England, which swings 22 feet, and will take in a shaft 45 feet long. Six months ago I saw one in this country which swings 30 feet, and will take in a shaft of 50 feet. There are planers which will plane iron 50 feet in length; others of 18 feet in width; others of 14 feet in height, taking off metal shavings of two and a half inches in width and a quarter thick. — *W. J. McAlpine.*

NEWEST COLORING MATTERS.

A lecture has been given by Mr. W. H. Perkin, at the Royal Institution, "On the Newest Coloring Matters." Among the many interesting facts then put forward was the discovery of a beautiful blue color, by a German chemist, on treating rosaline with sulphuric acid. Unfortunately, it was not a "fast color." A dyer made many trials therewith, in the hope of turning it to account, but all in vain. He happened to mention his difficulty to a photographer, who, knowing that hyposulphite of sodium would fix a photograph, recommended the dyer to try that. The trial was made; when mixed with the hyposulphite, the blue became a beautiful green, and, better still, a "fast color." This was the origin of that brilliant dye commonly known as "Night green," because of its remaining unmistakably green in appearance when seen by artificial light. Let it be remembered that nearly all the new colors are extracted in some way from coal tar; that the first was discovered not more than 13 years ago, and that the annual value now manufactured is 1,250,000 pounds, and it will be seen that in the industry created by these new products there is an admirable example of the results of scientific investigation. The best of it is that the field is inexhaustible; for many years to come it will yield a rich harvest of discoveries.

REFINING VEGETABLE OILS.

Mr. C. Michaud, of Honfleur, has discovered a new method of refining oil, which will probably eclipse all those in general use at the present day. This method has just been communicated by M. Chevallier to the Société d'Encouragement. While sulphuric acid is introduced into the oil in minute numerous streamlets, air is blown into the oil so as to produce a great commotion in the liquid and to fill it with air-bubbles. The mucilage contained in the crude oil, being acted on by the acid, soon forms with the air a voluminous layer of scum at the surface, which is skimmed off as it forms. This insufflation of air is repeated several times in succession, and the scums cleared off every time until the oil is clarified. At this point of the operation it still retains free sulphuric acid. It is now run into a copper vessel, and steam is forced through it until the oil has reached a temperature of 100° C. The steam is then allowed to bubble through for half an hour or an hour longer. After the oil has cooled down some 20° or 30° C., which may be done artificially, it is run through an ordinary filter. Two large refineries have lately been put up on the "Michaud" plan, and the oil produced by them is so pure, that the wick of a lamp burning it will not carbonize after many days' usage.

ON THE PENETRATION OF ARMOR-PLATES BY SHELLS WITH HEAVY BURSTING CHARGES, FIRED OBLIQUELY. BY JOSEPH WHITWORTH, LL.D., F.R.S.

At the meeting of the British Association last year, Mr. Whitworth contributed a paper "On the Proper Form of Projectiles for Penetration through Water," wherein he claimed for the flat-fronted form of projectile made of his metal three points of superiority over the Palliser projectiles. First: Its power of penetrating armor-plates even when striking at extreme angles. Secondly: Its large internal capacity as a shell. Third: Its capability of passing undeflected through water, and of penetrating armor below the water line. He illustrated the penetrative power of long projectiles, with the flat front fired at extreme angles against iron plates, by the projectiles actually fired and the plates they penetrated. The gun from which all the projectiles were fired was a 3-pounder; it weighs 315 lbs., and the maximum diameter of its bore is 1.85 inches. The charge of powder used was 10 ounces, and the weight of the 6-inch diameter projectiles is 6 lbs. He considered he had established the superiority of the flat-fronted projectiles made of his metal, and that the Palliser projectiles fail to penetrate when striking at an angle, solely on account of the form of the head. The results obtained with the small calibre of the rifle closely agree with those of the 3-pounder gun. He had always found that what he could do with the smaller calibres could be reproduced in the larger sizes, and could be repeated on a proportionate scale with his 9-inch gun, or the 11-inch guns his firm are now engaged in constructing. The 9-inch guns weigh 15 tons each, and are capable of firing powder charges of 50 lbs. A 9-inch armor shell, 5 diameters long, weighs 535 lbs., and will contain a bursting charge of 25 lbs. These projectiles would pierce the side of a ship plated with armor at a distance of 2,000 yards, and at some depth below the water line. The 11-inch guns will weigh 27 tons, and will be capable of firing 90 lbs. powder charges. The 11-inch shells, 5 diameters long, will weigh 965 lbs., and will contain bursting charges of 45 lbs., and would pierce a side of the ship "Hercules," plated with 9-inch armor, at a distance of 2,000 yards. He had named these long projectiles the "anti-war" shell. Four guns of 12 inches bore have lately been put on board the "Monarch;" they weigh 25 tons each, and fire charges of 50 lbs. and 67 lbs., and projectiles of 600 lbs. weight; but the weight of these guns was in proportion to their bore; and if the material were the best that could be supplied, they ought to fire 117 lbs. of powder and projectiles 1,450 lbs. weight.

LIFE OF AMERICAN VESSELS.

At the meeting of the American Association, at Salem, Professor E. B. Elliott, of Washington, gave a Life Table of American Sea-Going Sailing Vessels, derived from the career of 26,737 vessels, of which 4,165 were known to be extant. The table shows that out of 1,000 vessels 584.4 survive 10 years, 219.5 20 years, 57.2 30 years, 11.1 40 years, and none 50 years. The average duration of ships is 13.8 years; of those which have been built 10 years, 9.3 years longer; built 20 years, 7.2; 30 years, 6.2; 40 years, 2.7.

Professor Pierce expressed his interest in the paper, and a desire that a similar table might be made for English vessels, to see if the superior education of British sea-captains would be evinced.

Professor Elliott also gave the values of the standard Monetary Units in which United States securities are quoted in the commercial centres of Europe. In London, the 54 pence sterling, at which a dollar is rated, are really equivalent to 1.095 dollar; the Frankfort standard, two and one-half silver gulden, to 1.0144 dollar; at Paris, 1.09645 dollar; Antwerp, 1.0226 dollar; Bremen, 1.0989 dollar; Amsterdam, 1.0065 dollar; Berlin, 1.0059 dollar; Hamburg, 1.0771 dollar.

SEA-GOING SHIPS.

Mr. C. W. Merrifield, F.R.S., at the meeting of the British Association, read extracts from the report of the committee on the state of knowledge of stability and sea-going qualities of ships. The report treated at considerable length on the rolling of ships in still water, followed by an account of the mechanism of waves and an abridgment of what is known on the subject of the rolling of ships in wave water. The report itself being, in reality, a very condensed abstract of our existing knowledge, it would be difficult to make a useful selection for reading. Meanwhile, it may be stated in general terms that the rolling of a ship in still water, and her behavior in a seaway, although interdependent, involve very divergent conditions. It seems that the chief point to attend to, to secure easy rolling, is that the natural period of the ship's oscillation should not coincide, or nearly coincide, with the period of the waves; and there seems reason to suppose that we already know how, in a rough way, to influence the natural periodic time of the ship, so as to be able to predict nearly in what waves she will and in what waves she will not roll through excessive angles and with excessive quickness. But our knowledge is exceedingly crude and deficient in detail, and even our known means of observation of the height and form of waves are very unsatisfactory.

SHIPS' LIGHTS.

M. Tronsens has made a communication to the Paris Academy of Sciences, in which he suggests a new arrangement of ships' lights to prevent collision at sea. He proposes the use of 3 lights, arranged in the form of a right-angled triangle, one side of which is vertical, and another parallel, with the medial line of the vessel, and towards the head, and placed in the highest possible position. The light of the summit is to be of a different color from the other two, and the distance between the lights to be about 18 feet. Observation of the two lights in a vertical line will, says the author, furnish the approximate distance from the approaching ship, and by comparing the apparent distance of the two lights on the horizontal side with that of the two on the vertical side, an idea of the ships' route may be obtained; at any rate the relative distances will show whether that course is to the right or left of the line of observation, which is the main fact to be ascertained, and that without any instrument. — *Mech. Mag.*, *July 2, 1869.*

8

BRONZES.

The production of a fine patina on our bronze statues, instead of a coating of dust and soot, is, especially in our large cities, a thing to be desired. In Poggendorff's Annalen for April, we find the report of a series of experiments which were made by the direction of the Berlin Verein zur Reforderung des Gerwerbfleisses, to examine into the causes determining the formation of this *vert antique* patina on bronze statues.

The experiments while in progress led the observers to suppose that grease had much to do with the formation of the finest patina. Four busts were therefore placed in a part of the town which was very unfavorable. One of them was rinsed every day, with the exception of rainy days, and was painted once a month with bone oil, which was rubbed off with woollen cloths at once. Another bust was washed daily, but not oiled. A third was cleaned daily, but oiled only twice a year. The fourth was not touched at all. These experiments have been continued for 4 or 5 years; the result is that the bust which has been oiled once a month possesses a dark-green patina, which is considered very beautiful by connoisseurs; the bust which has been rubbed twice a year does not look so well; the others have no patina. The bust which has been washed regularly is the usual dark bronze color; the other is quite dull and black. The final result of those who have been engaged in the experiments is: this use of oil justifies the hope that for the future we may retain beautifully patinated monuments, even in large towns. Where coal is the only combustible they will not be bright, but dark-green, and perhaps black; but they will have the other beautiful condition of the patina, the peculiar transparent property of the surface. — *Quarterly Journal of Science, July.*

ELECTRIC ORGAN.

A new electric organ action has been patented by Mr. Hillborne L. Roosevelt, of New York. The object of this new electric action, as well as the means employed, are very simple. In the first place it is necessary to mention, for the benefit of those who are not familiar with the usual mode of building a large church-organ, that, as a general rule, it is a great advantage for the organist to be placed at a considerable distance from the sounding body of the instrument. To accomplish this purpose, the key-board, at which the performer sits, is often placed on the floor of the church, while the organ itself is aloft in the gallery; and this arrangement enables the organist to form a better judgment of the effect of his performance, and also accommodate the choir. But, of course, it is indispensable to connect the key-board with the main body of the organ, in order that the keys under the touch of the player may promptly open the valves or pallets under the distant organ-pipes; and this formerly required a complicated system of wooden rods, wires, and squares, running under the floor from the key-board up to the gallery. The machinery, under the old system, was subject to great friction and constant derangement, and was affected by changes of weather, and the former action was often so stiff and capricious that the organist found his duty extremely laborious; while the organ-builder was often called in to make expensive repairs.

Under these circumstances a difficult problem was to be solved. Any improvement on the old action must be simple in itself and easily kept in order, and must of course be free from the effects of friction or atmospheric changes, so as to insure a light touch on the keys, and an instantaneous response from the organ-pipes at any practical distance from the key-board. The new electric organ action, it is believed, will fully comply with all those requirements. When actually and practically applied it is found that the touch is always as light as that of the piano, and the action is literally as quick as lightning, while any one of ordinary intelligence having charge of the building in which the organ may stand can keep it in running order, so far as the battery, which is the motive power, is concerned. It is based, in a word, on the well-known principles of the electric telegraph, as well as the electric burglar alarm, the hotel annunciators, the electric clocks and police telegraphs; all of which are in successful daily operation. The new organ, now building by Messrs. Hall, Labagh, & Co., is intended to be a powerful instrument, considering its size, of about 9 stops, including the pedal bass; and, although necessarily limited by want of space, will fairly exhibit the principles involved.

The key-board will be detached from the organ at a distance of about 25 feet, though it might as well be removed to the distance of 25 miles, excepting for the necessity of the organist hearing his own performance, since we know, from recent scientific investigations, that the electric current will travel a mile in a fraction of a second. The only connection between the key-board and the body of the organ is a bundle or rope of flexible, insulated copper wires, which may be carried in any direction without injury, and there is no pull or strain on these wires, as they are merely the passive means of conducting the electric current.

The source of the electric current is an ordinary "single fluid" battery, placed in any convenient position, composed of a series of jars containing a mixture of sulphuric acid and water, and in each jar is suspended a plate of carbon, in company with two plates of zinc, connected in the usual way by copper wires. From one end of this series of jars, a copper wire proceeds to the key-board; and, if we take the case of a single key, for example, when it is pressed down by the finger of the player, we shall find this wire so connected that it forms an unbroken circuit and proceeds from the key-board onward to the body of the organ, where it is coiled around a soft piece of iron shaped like a horse-shoe, and thence returns from the organ to the other end of the battery. When a wire is connected with both poles or ends of a battery the current passes, and the piece of soft iron becomes a powerful magnet; but the moment the current is broken, by disconnecting the copper wire, there is an instant loss of power. When the key of the organ is not touched, the wire is not connected and the current does not pass; but on pressing down the key a metallic contact is formed, the electricity darts along the circuit, and the electro-magnet, becoming at once excited, pulls down the pallet, or opens the valve in the wind-chest, admitting air to the organ-pipes and with lightning speed causing them to speak.

The couplers are applied and the stops drawn upon the same principle. It has been stated that a more expensive and less simple arrangement has been successfully applied in England and France.

THE AMERICAN STEREOSCOPE.

The following is an abstract of a paper in the "Philadelphia Photographer" of January, 1869, by Dr. Oliver Wendell Holmes, the inventor of the American stereoscope: —

"'The British Journal of Photography' had two articles lately, the first dated Oct. 16, 1868, and the second the following week, relating to the 'American Stereoscope,' as I see it is called in England. The figure they give in the second of these papers, though not of the best model, yet shows that the instrument referred to is a copy of the one which was first made in Boston, and of which I shaped the primitive pattern with my own hands.

"This simple stereoscope was not constructed by accident, but was the carrying out of a plan to reduce the instrument to its simplest terms. Two lenses were necessary, and a frame to hold them. I procured two of the best quality, and cut a square frame for them out of a solid piece of wood. A strip of wood at right angles to this was required to hold the pictures. I shaped one, narrow in the middle, broad at both ends; at one end to support the lenses, at the other to hold the stereographs, which were inserted in slots cut with a saw at different distances. A partition was necessary, which I made short, but wedge-shaped, widening as it receded from the eye. A handle was indispensable, and I made a small brad-awl answer the purpose, taking care that it was placed so far back as to give the proper balance to the instrument. A hood for the eyes was needed, for comfort, at least, and I fitted one, cut out of pasteboard, to my own forehead. This primeval machine, parent of the multitudes I see all around me, is in my left hand as I write, and I have just tried it, and found it excellent. . . . . . I contrived another form of stereoscope like the first, but with a gilded, slanting diaphragm with two oval openings, so that the effect was that of seeing the stereograph through a round window, with a golden light on it reflected from the slanting surface of the diaphragm. This I showed also to various dealers, as a form of stereoscope that might please certain exceptional amateurs. Some time after showing it, I found the so-called 'Bellevue' stereoscope in the market, which I had good reason to consider an imperfect attempt at a reproduction of the pattern I had somewhat freely exhibited. The effect referred to, of cutting off all the borderings of the picture, and throwing (by means of the slanted and gilded diaphragm) a Claude Lorraine light on the stereograph, is, in many cases, very striking, but, for common use, the simple form is preferable."

PRACTICAL APPLICATION OF SENSITIVE FLAMES.

An apparatus has been invented by Barrett for making practical use of sensitive flames. It consists of two perpendicular copper rods, one of which, on its upper end, holds a metallic ribbon, which is composed of thin leaves of gold, silver, or platinum, welded together. Such a ribbon expands unequally under the influence of heat; it bends toward one side, and, in doing so, comes in contact with a fine platinum wire attached to a galvanic battery. As soon as the poles of the battery are closed, a bell begins to ring. The working of the apparatus is as follows: —

"A sensitive flame is lighted about 10 inches from the metallic ribbon. This burns quietly so long as there is no noise, but a shrill whistle, or any unusual disturbance, will cause it to diminish one half in length, and to spread out wide in the middle, like the wings of a bird. It thus heats the metallic ribbon, which expands unequally, and occasions the contact of the poles of the battery, which rings a bell."

Such a light as this in a banking-house would betray to the watchman the noise of robbery, and the inventor proposes to use it as a species of burglar alarm. As sound can be transmitted in water 4 times as rapidly as in the air, it is also suggested to employ this method on shipboard, to make known the approach of a vessel in time of a fog.

There is probably the germ of curious applications of sensitive flames in Barrett's invention, and it would not be surprising to hear of its use in war, to warn a sentinel of the approach of the enemy, or of its application to a new species of telegraphy.

ELECTRIC BEACONS.

Thomas Stevenson, C.E., Edinburgh, recently conducted an experiment at Granton, with the view of showing the practicability of illuminating beacons and buoys at sea with the electric light produced by means of a battery on shore. A submarine cable, fully half a mile in length, was laid between the east breakwater of Granton Harbor and the chair pier at Trinity. The operator occupied a station near the centre of the breakwater, and the light was shown at the point of the pier in front of an ordinary light-house reflector, producing a most brilliant flash. The flashes were emitted with great rapidity; as many as 500 can be transmitted in a minute, but the machine can be regulated so as to send one every second, or at any other desired interval. The experiment gave entire satisfaction.

8*

PORTABLE ILLUMINATIONS.

Mr. Alvergniat, a French electrician, has made an improvement first suggested to him when using the tubes invented by Giessler, which are cylinders or bulbs of glass filled with rarefied gas that becomes luminous in the dark when a current of electricity is passed through it. The improvement consists in filling a glass cylinder or phial, hermetically sealed, with a substance which becomes phosphorescent by the action of the frictional or static electricity. A tube of this kind may be of some service to those on night duty; for all that is requisite to produce a feeble and ephemeral light is to rub the tube briskly with a silk handkerchief.

WARMING CHURCHES BY GAS.

The following method has been patented in England: A brick chamber is made beneath the floor of the building, and a grating is placed over it to allow of the passage of hot air. Beneath this chamber an air-flue in connection with the flooring, and covered with an iron grating, is introduced. By these means a current of air is made to pass into the building, and this air is brought into contact with a ring gas-burner, which is supplied by an ordinary main by means of a spanner, by which the amount of heat can be regulated. Underneath this ring-burner is placed a small cistern made of fire-clay, filled with water; the heat from the gas-burner acts upon the water, steam arises, and this is passed through pumice stone contained in a cylinder above the cistern; the use of this vapor is to moisten the atmosphere contained in the reservoir. Around this is a circular cylinder made of fire-clay, to contain heat. The whole is covered with a dome of fire-clay. This dome is worked by a lever for the purpose of lighting the ring-burner. By these arrangements, it is said that a pure heat, free from smell or smoke, is obtained, and that with a very small consumption of gas.

GAS FOR LIGHT-HOUSES.

A series of letters and reports sent to the Commissioners of Light-houses and the Board of Trade has resulted in a request being made to Professor Tyndall, by the latter body, that he would report upon the proposal to substitute gas for oil as an illuminating power for light-houses, as illustrated in the light-houses of Howth Baily and Wicklow Head. Various experiments were made at Howth Baily, and Professor Tyndall says that the superiority of the gas over the oil flame is rendered very conspicuous by these experiments. The 28-jet-burner possesses two and one half times, the 48-jet-burner $4\frac{1}{4}$ times, the 68-jet-burner $7\frac{1}{2}$ times, the 88-jet-burner $9\frac{3}{4}$ times, and the 108-jet-burner 13 times the illuminating power of the 4-wick flame. The oil lamp with which the gas flame was compared was the most perfect one employed by the Commissioners of Irish Lights. Further experiments were also made, and it appeared that the whole of the gaslighting apparatus was entirely under the control of the keeper, and that no damage was likely to arise from it. The 28-jet gasburner, when seen from a position some miles off, appeared to be very nearly upon an equality with the oil lamps, but when muffled to represent a fog it had a slight advantage. Of course with the brighter jet-burners a great improvement was apparent, and before the 108-jet-burner the oil lamp grew quite pale. By the adoption of a system of gas-lighting a great saving in cost would be effected; but such a system would not be possible on rock light-houses. Professor Tyndall recommends the encouragement of this system of illumination in Ireland. He was assisted in his investigations by Mr. Valentin, Captain Roberts, and Mr. Wigham. — *Brit. Trade Journal.*

DISPOSITION OF GAS-BURNERS.

Much of the economy and effect of gaslight, says the "Gaslight Journal," depends upon the arrangement of gas-burners in relation to each other, to the surroundings of furniture, height of ceilings, distance, and angles of walls, hangings, etc.

The general practice in this country and in Europe, of disposing burners in chandeliers in the centre of rooms, although pleasing to the eye in its artistic effect, simply as an ornament to the room, is far from being the most philosophical manner to obtain the best effect from the light.

The diffusion of light, in its effects, is materially modified by the laws of reflection and refraction.

Light decreases in intensity in proportion to the square of the distance from the burner or point of illumination. This is a general rule; but in a room with four white walls and a ceiling, the reflection of the light upon itself, as it were, will apparently modify the rule.

Shadows have much to do in the effective and satisfactory lighting of any hall or room. Hence it is that a single light, or a centre-piece, or nucleus of lights as represented by a chandelier, is objectionable, because your shadow will appear in any part of the room opposite to the light, and is more or less inconvenient in proportion as it differs in that respect from daylight, which is so diffused as to avoid this evil except in peculiar conditions.

Now, in view of these suggestions, is it not apparent that the proper and most efficient position for gas-burners is at the different sides, or, better, the different angles of a room? Then the intensity of light will be more uniform in every part of the room, no shadows will be formed, and the reflective action of the walls will be most effective. These *reflections* will show the folly of using bracket-lights at one side only of a room, where shadows fall in every direction it is possible to move from it, and with increased intensity as you go, until the gloom of the opposite side brings you back like a moth, to be blinded by the glare of the immediate proximity of a single luminary. If brackets are to be employed, let there be at least two in a room, and these disposed *vis-a-vis*, or as nearly so as possible.

Reflectors. — The value of reflectors is not appreciated as it should be, and the reason is principally because few people, even those whose business is to make apparatus for artificial light and attend to the introduction of gas-fixtures, etc., are sufficiently acquainted with the laws that govern reflected light, and when so, they fail in the mechanical ability to properly arrange reflectors so as to obtain the proper effect. Reflectors should be made of a material that will not tarnish by the action of the atmosphere or the temperature they may be exposed to. A very slight film of dust, moisture, or smoke on a reflector will almost entirely destroy its value as a reflector. The surface of the reflector should be perfectly smooth, and free from scratches and abrasions. Hence it is apparent that metallic reflectors are not the best in that respect.

Glass reflectors are superior, inasmuch as they do not become tarnished, abraided, scratched, but their action is impaired if the glass is too thick, owing to the absorption of light. The late American invention of a mica reflector is advantageous on that account, because the plates or lamina are very thin. It has also the advantage of not being fragile or liable to fracture.

Reflectors are better placed overhead. A reflector which throws the light in a horizontal direction, unless neutralized by another opposite, will be very disagreeable, owing to the dazzling glare. As a rule, reflectors should be so placed that the reflective rays shall never reach the eye in a straight line. This will avoid the evil effects of glare. As a rule, all the direct rays of a lamp or burner thrown upward may be thrown downward by reflectors, producing a great economy of light, and an effectiveness of illumination very pleasant and satisfactory.

HEATING BUILDINGS BY GAS.

In the United States this art has lately acquired a new impulse, owing to the late discoveries and improvements in the art of manufacturing hydrogen and oxide of carbon gases, at a very trifling cost, compared to the cost of ordinary coal gas. These gases are especially adapted to heating purposes instead of solid fuel and for use in gas engines as a substitute for steam-power, and also for illuminating purposes when carburetted or charged with vapors of hydro-carbons.

The hydrogen and oxide of carbon gases are produced by the American process, under the Gwynne-Harris patent, which consists in decomposing superheated steam, by means of incandescent anthracite coal, in a peculiar manner, and in a simple yet novel apparatus.

Great improvements have also been made in the stoves and other apparatuses for heating and cooking, which overcome most if not all the difficulties heretofore experienced in this department.

The use of gas as fuel has been tried to a considerable extent in France and other countries, but the progress has neither been rapid nor very satisfactory; one reason of this lies, perhaps, in the imperfection of the modes of combustion, although something has been done of late to remedy this; another is the natural hesitation of the directors of gas works to keep pressure of their gasometers all day for a small supply.

Still enough has been done to supply a certain amount of information on the economical part of the question, both as regards gas-cooking apparatus and stoves for churches and other large buildings. The average consumption of the cooking-stoves in use in France, which consume a mixture of gas and air, is found to be as follows: For a large fire, 260 litres per hour; for a moderate fire, 140 litres per hour; for a small fire, 50 litres per hour. When the stove is used, what the French call *pot-au-feu*, it is found that it is sufficient to keep up a large fire for about 20 minutes only, after which the gas may be turned down, and the cooking completed with a very small fire. Taking the average duration of this kind of cooking at 4 hours, and the cost of gas at 30c. per cubic metre, — the present price in Paris, — the consumption amounts to 1,050.20 litres, the expense of which is 31.20c., or little more than 14d. The cleanliness and handiness of gas as fuel, and the great economy arising from its instantaneous lighting and extinction, give it, *in the hands of careful persons*, a great advantage over charcoal, with few of its inconveniences, — one of which is the impossibility of using it for broiling with a special arrangement, as the smallest quantity of fat falling upon heated charcoal fills the house with stifling fumes.

In a coal-using country, however, like England, the use of gas for the heating of apartments, and especially large buildings like churches, is of more importance than its application to cooking; and considerable improvement has been made of late in France in apparatus for the warming of ordinary rooms, to which we shall shortly have to refer more particularly.

The most important results yet produced refer to the heating of churches, which has been essayed on a large scale at Berlin. The method generally adopted is that of placing a horizontal gas-pipe with 3 jets within a stove made of sheet iron, and over the gas-jets a piece of brass wirework, of which the openings are not more than one-twenty-fifth of an inch in diameter. The cathedral at Berlin has a cubical contents of about 13,800 metres, and it is heated by means of 8 of these stoves, each of which has 22 of these brass gratings, 11¼ inches in length by 1½ inches in width, making in all about half an inch square of grating for each cubic metre to be warmed. The consumption of gas in raising the air within the edifice to the required temperature — an operation which takes 3 hours — is 83,400 litres, or 4.82 litres per cubic metre; to maintain the same heat afterwards requires only seven-tenths of a litre of gas per cubic metre.

The parish church of Berlin, whose cubic contents is 13,800

metres, is heated by 4 stoves, each having 15 brass gratings, each rather more than 12 inches long by 1¼ inches wide, or little more than one-fifth of an inch of grating per cubic metre to be warmed. The annual consumption of gas in the cathedral above mentioned is 2.210 cubic metres, costing 20 pounds; this consumption is equal to 552 metres per stove, and 300 litres per four-fifths of an inch square of grating. The consumption in Parisian churches warmed by gas is found to agree very closely with that of the cathedral of Berlin, but other cases give different results.

The church of St. Philippe at Berlin has a contents of 2,780 metres, and is heated by two stoves 1.40m. high, and 1.10m. long, and 65 centimetres in width, each having 7 brass gratings 16 inches by two inches, equal to two-fifths of an inch square per cubic metre of the contents of the church. The annual consumption in this church is 1,485 cubic metres, or at the rate of 410 litres of gas per cubic metre of contents. But this church is only warmed 3 times a week.

The church of St. Catherine at Hamburg is heated by 8 gas stoves, each having 32 brass gratings, 12 inches long by rather more than 1½ inches wide; the cubic contents of the edifice is 33,900 metres. The heating takes 3½ hours, and consumes 220 metres of gas, costing about 27s. 6d., so that 3 litres of gas are required in this church per cubic metre of capacity; the temperature is kept up subsequently by the consumption of three-fourths of a litre per cubic metre and per hour.

In the churches of St. Mary and Nicholas in Berlin, and in Paris also, a kind of large rose burner has been substituted for the brass grating; these are known in France as mushroom burners (*champigons*). The result with these burners in the first of the above-named churches is as follows: The cubical contents of the building is 15,450 metres, and the consumption of gas in 4 hours is 150 cubic metres, costing about 35s., and as it is heated by 10 stoves, each having 3 of these rose burners, the consumption per hour is 1½ cubic metres of gas per burner, and nearly 2½ metres for each metre of the contents of the church. In this case only we have the effect as shown by the thermometer, which is to raise the temperature of the church from one degree below zero to 5° above, or from below 30° to 40° F.

In heating churches and large buildings the economy of gas exhibits itself quite differently as compared with its application to cooking; in the former case, the more continuous the operation the less the relative cost, whereas in the latter the more frequent the interruptions the greater the economy. The objection to gas on account of its vitiation of the atmosphere of a building is one which neither the wire grating nor the mushroom burner has yet obviated.

MIXTURE OF GAS AND AIR.

Professors Silliman and Wurtz conclude that, —

1st. For any quantity of air, less than 5 per cent., mixed with gas, the loss in candle-power due to the addition of each one per cent., is a little over six-tenths of a candle (.611 exactly); above that quantity the ratio of loss falls to one-half a candle power for each additional one per cent. up to about 12 per cent. of air; above which, up to 25 per cent., the loss in illuminating power is as shown by column 12 of the table, nearly four-tenths of a candle for each one per cent. of air added to the gas. In column 11 of Table 1, the ratio of loss in candle power is given in percentages for the several volumes, while in column 10 the destructive effect of air upon the illuminating power is most conspicuously exhibited, 12 per cent. of air destroying over 40 per cent. of the illuminating power. In the diagram this loss of power is represented by the numerals in the right-hand column, which are inverse to those in column 10, and stand with the maximum intensity = 100.

2d. With less than one-fourth of atmospheric air, not quite 15 per cent. of the total illuminating power remains; and with between 30 per cent. and 40 per cent. of air it totally disappears.

In large gas works the liability to contamination by air accidentally introduced by various causes diminishes in proportion to the total make of gas, and an amount of air which, when diffused in a very large volume of gas, becomes insignificant, if confined to 10,000 or 15,000 feet daily product, will become a most serious injury to its illuminating power. This cause of deterioration in gas has been overlooked almost entirely by gas engineers; but in small gas works it deserves special attention, and we have no doubt that the low illuminating power too often obtained in such works is largely due to this cause.

Results of Messrs. Audouin and Berard. — We have already alluded to the results obtained by Messrs. A. and B., which form part of an important memoir published in 1860, under authority of the French Government, " upon the various burners employed in gas-lighting and researches on the best conditions for the combustion of gas." Their table shows " a considerably higher ratio of loss than we have obtained, being rather more than 6 per cent. loss for each one per cent. of air added to the gas, reaching a total loss of 80 per cent. with 15 per cent. of air added; while we obtain 57.53 per cent. loss with 16 per cent; and 93 per cent. loss with 20 per cent. air, while with the latter volume of air added we get 72.90 per cent. loss. These differences may be accounted for by the French trials being made upon a gas of not more than 12 candle-power, our trials being made on a gas averaging nearly 15 candles; also, by the fact that in the French experiments the gas was burned from a batswing burner, ours from a standard Argard.

It appears that the introduction of 6 to 7 per 100 of air suffices to diminish the intensity by one-half, and a mixture of 20 of air with 80 of gas leaves almost no illumination. Unfortunately Messrs. A. and B. do not record the actual illuminating power of their standard gas, which, however, we are led to believe cannot be more than 12 candles of the English and American standard.

For a fuller discussion of this subject the reader is referred to the memoir of Prof. Silliman and Wurtz.

ON THE RELATION BETWEEN THE INTENSITY OF LIGHT PRO-
DUCED FROM THE COMBUSTION OF ILLUMINATING GAS AND
THE VOLUME OF GAS CONSUMED.

In photometric observations made to determine the illuminating power or intensity of street gas, it is the practice of observers
to compute their observations upon the assumed standard of 5 cubic
feet of gas, consumed for one hour; and in the constantly occurring case of a variation from this standard, whether in the volume
of the gas consumed or in the weight of spermaceti burned, the
observed data are computed by the "rule of three," up or down,
to the stated terms. The standard spermaceti candle is assumed
to consume 120 grains of sperm in one hour, a rate which is
rarely found exactly in actual experience.

For example, a given gas, too rich to burn in a standard argand
burner at the rate of $3\frac{1}{2}$ cubic feet to the hour, with an observed
effect of 20 candles' power. This result, previously corrected by
the same rule for the sperm consumed, is then brought to the
standard of 5 cubic feet by the ratio $3.5 : 20 = 5 : 28.57$.

The candle-power of the gas is, therefore, stated as 28.57 candles, and the result has been universally accepted as a true expression of the intensity of the gas in question, or the relative
value of the two consumptions.

In common with other observers, I have long suspected that
this mode of computation was seriously in error, as an expression
of the true intensity of illuminating flames, and that there were
other conditions, besides the volume of gas or weight of sperm
consumed, which must influence and greatly modify the results.
As most of these conditions are considered somewhat at length
in a paper on "*Flame Temperatures*," prepared chiefly from researches conducted by Professor Wurtz and myself, and presented
at the Salem Meeting of the Association, they need not be discussed in this connection.

The results of many trials, made with the purpose of determining the value of these photometric rations, indicate clearly, that the
true ratio of increase in intensity in illuminating flames is, within
certain limits, expressed by the following theorem, namely : —

The intensity of gas flames, that is, *illuminating power, increases*
(within the ordinary limits of consumption) *as the square of the
volume of the gas consumed.*

As the first experimental demonstration of this theorem was
made by Mr. William Farmer, the photometric observer at the
Manhattan Gas Co.'s works in New York, I propose to speak of
it as "Farmer's theorem." I am also indebted to Mr. Farmer,
and to Mr. Sabbaton, the well-known and courteous engineer of
the Manhattan Gas Light Company, for the free use of their experimental data, and the permission to employ them here.

The fundamental importance of this new mode of computation
will at once appear, if, assuming it for the sake of illustration to
be true, we apply it to the case already given above, which then
becomes —

$$3.5^2 : 20 = 5^2 : 40.$$

Showing an increase of 40 per cent. over the old rule of correction.

From experiments with different burners and with gas from rich coals, Prof. Silliman says : —

"A comparison of the results will show that the coincidences with the requirements of the theorem of Farmer are, within the limits assigned, too numerous, and too closely accordant, to be considered as otherwise than pointing clearly to its general truth. A rigorous demonstration cannot be expected, as there are too many variable functions of unknown value involved in the best methods at present known for photometric measurements, to permit more than an approximate proof of its general accuracy. Every photometric observer must recognize its importance, and the necessity in his observations of bringing the consumptions of gas and sperm to the agreed standard.

"To the consumer of gas the evident inference from the data here presented is that where it is important to obtain a maximum of economical effect from the consumption of a given volume of illuminating gas, this result is best obtained by the use of burners of ample flow.

"Where a moderate light of equal diffusion is required over a large space, as in public rooms, it may be expedient to use numerous small jets; but when the maximum intensity obtainable from a given volume of illuminating gas is desired, intensity of burners of large consumption is plainly indicated."— *Abstract from a paper read by Prof. Silliman at the Salem meeting of the Am. Association, Aug.,* 1869.

GAS FROM WOOD.

The following fact may be mentioned in connection with the manufacture of gas from wood. In those countries where this material is abundant, and coal not accessible, wood, aided by the addition of some substance furnishing a rich hydro-carbon, may be made to furnish a very useful illuminating gas, and an economical one, especially when the residue in the retorts and material distilled with the gas can be rendered serviceable. In Coburg, Canada, it is said to have been used advantageously, furnishing a good gas and a valuable residue, namely: —

Two parts pine wood.
One part hard wood.
One part bones.

The residue in the retorts is an excellent charcoal for bleaching purposes, and the other residues are quite serviceable. Where bones cannot be obtained, offal and other coarse animal matter can be used to mix with the wood. This suggestion is worthy of consideration, especially for many small towns peculiarly situated.

9

LITTLE-KNOWN FIBROUS PLANTS.

There has been of late a considerable search after plants producing fibres that could be advantageously used in the arts of paper-making, rope-making, and the manufacture of textile fabrics. Some of these materials have been discovered in North and South America; but a large majority of those claiming the attention of manufacturers are found in Southern Asia, more particularly in India.

Among these stands most prominently a plant of the nettle family, called by the natives "*Tchuma*," the botanical name of which is *Urtica nivea*. In Assam, both a cultivated and a wild variety are found, and in the Malayan peninsula, Panang, and Singapore, another variety grows wild, the fibre of which is unusually strong. This has a Malay name, "*Ramee*," and is in botany known as the *Urtica tenacissima*. This plant is identical with the ramie, now cultivated in the Southern States, brought originally, we believe, from Java.

Mr. Leonard Wray, in a paper read before the Society of Arts, in London, describes the beautiful fibre of the "Rheea" as being worth in England two shillings and four pence per lb., and says, "the fabrics made from it are of so strong and so lustrous a character as to be in universal demand. Pity, indeed, is it that this splendid fibre can be obtained only in such small quantities! No other supplies can be looked for, except from China, nor can we expect much from that country either. Its growth and preparation have been tried by most intelligent Englishmen in India; but they found, first, that the separation of the fibres from the plants was a most difficult and laborious operation; and, secondly, that the yield per acre, per annum, was exceedingly small. Indeed it is said to yield only one to one and a half hundred weight of fibre to the acre, — a fact which forbids any European from entertaining hope of cultivating it at a profit, which is much to be regretted."

Mr. Wray also believes the plants called *Pederia fœtida*, the "*Jettee*," "*Moorva*," and the pine-apple, each and all of them, hold out the promise of amply remunerating any European who will attempt in a judicious manner to utilize the beautiful fibres they contain. Their fibres are fine, silken, and strong. He says, "The *Pederia fœtida* certainly has the most silky and lustrous fibre any one can desire, and its being only in lengths from joint to joint seems the sole objection to it. Still, these joints are often 12 inches apart, while the finest Sea-Island cotton is not more than one inch to an inch and a half in staple. Attention ought, therefore, to be directed to this lustrous fibre-yielding plant.

"The Jettee, again, is jointed, but the joints are sometimes two feet apart, and the fibre proportionably long. It is a most excellent fibre, and will be sure to make its way.

"The pine-apple, with its beautiful fibre, exists in thousands of acres in the Straits of Malacca, and may be had at Singapore in any quantity for the trouble of gathering, yet no one seems to regard it."

Another important fibre-producing plant is the *Bromelia penguin*, from which the surprisingly beautiful Manilla handkerchiefs are made, as well as the celebrated "Pigna" cloth, an Indian fabric commanding always an extreme fancy price. This is a kind of wild pine-apple said to be exceedingly abundant.

The late Mr. Temple, formerly Chief Justice of British Honduras, some years since exhibited a quantity of this fibre to the Society of Arts, calling it silk grass.

Mr. Wray says we may search the world through and not find another plant capable of yielding so rich, so abundant a supply of a fibre which in quality cannot be excelled, and that it is a plant which we may look to, to provide us with a large amount of the very best quality of fibre.

The fibre alluded to can be grown exceedingly cheap, and it is asserted that the manufacture involves no difficulty. The fibre is said to be separated by a machine constructed somewhat on the principle of the threshing machine, the plant being passed at a slow rate along a platform having a yielding surface, through rollers and beaters; and, when this is done with the plant in a green state, it comes out at the other end of the machine very good fibre, which is improved by repeating the operation: A stream of water is used to wash the pulp away as it is expressed from the fibre.

Among cordage fibres there is the nettle and the canna; the latter often growing 14 feet high. The whole stalk and leaf are said to be one mass of fibre; and the root furnishes a species of arrow-root said to be the most nutritious of all the starches.

It is thought that some if not all of these plants can be grown in Europe, and if so they ought to thrive in parts of the United States. It is not a just inference that because a plant is a native of a tropical clime it will not thrive in temperate climates. Though this may be the rule, there are numerous exceptions. Our Commissioner of Agriculture would do the country a service by obtaining and distributing the seeds of these plants in sections most favorable to their growth, if he has not already done so. We are far from believing the vegetable kingdom contributes to the wealth of mankind all, or nearly all, it is capable of doing. It is within the memory of yet young men, that the tomato was considered a useless vegetable; yet to-day there is probably no fruit grown in this country — if we except the apple — more generally used and esteemed. It is quite probable that many plants indigenous to our soil possess fibre which would be of great service, if properly worked. Among those which seem most promising are some of the "*Asclepias*" family, popularly known as "milkweeds," "silkweeds," and so forth. The plants are large, rapid and thrifty growers, and their pods contain a large amount of cotton-like fibre, which, though it might not be sufficiently strong for textile fabrics, would make, we think, excellent paper stock.

THE IXTLE FIBRE.

The following is a letter from Hon. J. McLeod Murphy to the Commissioner of Agriculture, accompanied with 3 skeins of the ixtle fibre, *Bromelia sylvestris*, each produced from a single leaf, of which a single plant might average 20. We extract the substance of this letter from the " Report of Department of Agriculture " for May and June.

" First of all, before I describe the plant and the method of its cultivation, I beg to call your attention to the extraordinary length and strength of the individual fibres, their susceptibility of being divided almost infinitesimally without breaking, their flexibility without kinking, and the readiness with which they receive and hold vegetable or chemical dyes without being impaired. Since my return from Mexico, I have had little or no opportunity of testing this plant practically ; but some samples, such as I send you, were given to an old and experienced maker of fishing-tackle, and he does not hesitate to pronounce the ixtle fibre as superior, in every respect, for the manufacture of trout and other fishing lines, not only on account of the readiness with which it can be spun, its extraordinary strength, but its perfect freedom from kinks when wet. The only secret, if there is one, consists in the preliminary precaution of boiling the fibre (as you have it here) before twisting it. In this one respect it will supersede the use of silk.

" Apart, however, from its use as a thread, I hazard nothing in saying that it forms the best paper stock that can be obtained. I speak now in reference to the imperfect, withered, rejected, and dried leaves, from which the fibre cannot be conveniently extracted by the indifferent mechanical means that the Indians employ. Although I have no samples of paper made from this source just now at hand, yet I can assure the department that several magnificent samples of paper for banking and commercial purposes have been made by manufacturers in the Eastern States, from the dried leaves of the ixtle plant, brought from the neighborhood of Tabasco.

" The samples of fibre I send with this were obtained by the most primitive means, namely, by beating, and at the same time scraping, the leaf of the plant (in a green state) with a dull machete. Then, after the removal of the glutinous vegetable matter, it is combed out and rubbed between the knuckles of the hand until the fibres are separated. The next step is to wash it in tepid water and bleach the skeins on the grass. This is the method pursued by the Indians on the Isthmus of Tehuantepec ; and the average product for the labor of a man is from 4 to 5 pounds per day.

" It is scarcely necessary to tell one so well informed as yourself that this spontaneous product is the *Bromelia sylvestris*, which differs, in some respects, from the *Agave Americana*, the *pulque de maguey*, and *Agave sisalana*, of Campeche ; a difference arising solely from soil and climate influences. The name *ixtle* is given to that species which is characterized by the production of the long fibre; and chiefly because the leaf, being shaped like a sword, has its edges armed with prickles, similar, in fact, to the weapon formed from *itzli*, or obsidian, used by the Aztecs Hence the term. The *pita*, on the other hand, although obtained from a variety of the same plant, is a coarser and shorter fibre, which grows in the *tierras templadas*. The name comes from the word *pittes*, which is given to the plantations of the pulque plant in the uplands of Mexico. But the peculiarity of the ixtle is, that it grows almost exclusively on the southern shore of the Mexican gulf, or in what is known as the 'sota vento,' that is to say, between Alvarado and Tabasco, and extending as far inland as the northern slopes of the dividing ridge which separates the Atlantic from the Pacific. The points generally selected for its cultivation are the edges of a thick forest, from which the small undergrowth is removed by cutting and burning. The roots of the plants are then set out at a distance of 5 or 6 feet apart; and at the end of a year the leaves are cut and 'scraped.' The chief object is to obtain a constant shelter from the rays of the sun, which would otherwise absorb the moisture, and so gum the fibres together as to make them inseparable.

"The average length of the leaf is 6 feet, and the time to cut it is clearly indicated by the upward inclination it makes. In other words, the radical leaves cease to form curved lines with their points downward, but stiffen themselves out at an angle, as if to guard the source of efflorescence. When the ixtle is young its fibres are fine and white, but as it grows in age they become longer and coarser; and in a wild state the thorns are very numerous, but by cultivation they are diminished both in size and number, and in many instances there are none at all. Where any quantity of leaves require to be handled, a pitchfork would be very useful, especially if gathered for paper stock. A few days after cutting, the sun would dry them out, the thorns would drop off, and then they could be easily baled. Independent of the great value which the ixtle has for textile fabrics, and for paper, it possesses many valuable medicinal properties, to which I need not allude. It requires no labor to cultivate it, and no insect is known to feed upon it. It grows everywhere in the primeval forests of the Gulf coasts, and, in my opinion, is far superior to any of the textile fabrics. But as yet no mechanic has succeeded in devising a means of effectually extracting the fibre, and until this is done I presume that its real commercial value will remain unappreciated.

"You will readily discover the superiority of the ixtle over the *jenequin* of Cuba, or the hemp which comes from Sisal and Campeche."

SIGNALLING ON BOARD THE CABLE FLEET.

The London "Gazette" gives the following interesting description of the manner of signalling through the cable on board the Great Eastern:—

9*

" The method of signalling used between the ship and the land is that now universally adopted in working all long submarine lines —the reflecting galvanometer. The principle of this most delicate instrument was discovered a few years since by a German electrician, named Weber. It was then, however, a large machine, and the condensation of all its powers into the smallest and lightest form is due to the scientific research and skill of Sir William Thompson.

" This instrument consists of a small mirror with a magnet on its back. That the two are very small indeed may be judged by the fact that both together weigh less than three-eighths of a grain. This infinitesimally small reflector, which is intensely bright, is suspended by a silk thread, as fine as a hair, in the midst of a small circular coil of insulated copper wires. Directly a current is sent through this circular coil, no matter how slight, it induces another electric current within its circle, which acts in an opposite direction, and this causes the magnet at the back of the mirror to turn to the right or left, and, of course, to turn the little mirror with its reflecting ray of light with it. By a very simple arrangement, this fine ray of light is thrown upon a horizontal graduated scale, about 3 feet long and 3 feet distant from the mirror.

" Thus, when a current is sent through the little circular coil around the mirror, the magnet is acted upon, and turns the mirror with its ray of light, say on the left of the scale in front of it. When the current is reversed, and that is instantly done by pressing a little key in the speaking instrument, the current in the circular coil is reversed, and sent in the opposite direction, and this in turn sends the ray of light from the mirror on to the opposite side of the scale to the right. When the ray of light rests stationary on any part of the scale, it means a dot; when it moves rapidly to the right or left, it means so many dashes, according to the distance it goes. This reflecting galvanometer tells with unerring certainty whether or not the Great Eastern is steady.

" The vessel now at the end of the cable is, with its coils of insulated wire and iron hull, a mere electro-magnet, so to speak. The course of the Great Eastern is east and west, and therefore at right angles with the course of the magnetic current, which is north and south. Thus every time the ship rolls, either to port or starboard, a slight current, but still a current, is induced in her vast coils, and then transmitted through the cable to the shore end at Minou, where it acts upon the reflecting galvanometer, and turns its rays of light a little to the right or left of the centre of the scale, and thus shows in a fraction of a second of time the precise degree and rapidity at which the vessel is rolling."

THE FRENCH ATLANTIC TELEGRAPH.

In the first place, it is interesting as being longer by about 1,500 miles, and laid in deeper water by 500 fathoms, than any direct submarine line yet in existence; then its track lies through a part of the Atlantic which until very recently had been unexplored, and the nature of the bottom comparatively unknown; and, thirdly, we look upon it with interest because it shows that the importance of submarine telegraphic communication is commending itself to other countries besides our own. Hitherto, nearly all the more important submarine lines have been the direct offspring, and have remained in possession of English companies, but the present cable, although manufactured and laid by an English firm, is the result entirely of French enterprise, and to a large extent owes its existence to French capital.

The vital part of the longer section of the cable — or technically the "core" — is a copper conductor of 7 wires twisted together, insulated by 4 concentric coatings of gutta-percha, separated from each other by an equal number of coatings of the material known as "Chetterton's compound," exactly after the pattern of the cores in the last Atlantic cables, the only difference between them being in the weight of the conductor, which in the present case is 400 pounds per mile, instead of 300 pounds. This increase is to compensate for the additional length of the cable. Experiments have shown that the speed of signalling through submarine cables varies *inversely* according to their length, and *directly* as the weight of the conductor; so that, by adding to the weight in due proportion to the increased length, the speed obtained is the same as through a shorter cable.

The core is surrounded with a serving of yarn, called the "wet serving," allowing of the ready access of the water to the core. Until comparatively recently, this serving was saturated with tar, but experience showed that, should a slight defect occur in the gutta-percha, the tar, from the serving being in itself an insulator, would sufficiently stop it up to prevent its being discovered by the electrical tests, until perhaps it was too late to remedy it. The present wet serving, however, containing no insulating fluid, permits of the instant detection of a fault.

Around the serving are twisted spirally 10 homogeneous iron wires galvanized, each of them embedded in 5 strands of Manila hemp. The cable thus completed is of a diameter of about one and a quarter inches, weighing about 86 cwt. to the nautical mile, and capable of bearing a strain of 7 tons.

The core of the shorter section — St. Pierre to Boston — is of the same description as that of the Brest to St. Pierre section; but owing to its much shorter length, the weights of the copper conductor and insulator are only 107 pounds and 150 pounds per mile respectively. This core is also covered with a wet serving, and then surrounded with about a dozen iron wires galvanized, the outside covering consisting of a silicated material, known as "Clark's compound;" the whole forming a cable of about one inch in diameter, weighing about two and three quarter tons to the mile.

The Brest to St. Pierre section was manufactured at the Telegraph Construction Company's Works at Greenwich, and transmitted piece by piece in old hulks to the Great Eastern steamship, lying off Sheerness. This section is of 3 kinds, namely, 1. The heavy shore-ends for protection against ships' anchors, tides, etc., weighing 360 cwt. per mile. 2. The "intermediate," of a size between the shore-end and the deep-sea portion, 127 cwt. per mile. 3. The deep-sea portion already described.

The whole of the above, 2,788 knots in length, with the exception of 15½ miles of shore-end, and 20 miles of intermediate, was taken to the Great Eastern. We calculate that if the various component parts of it were laid end to end, they would make a chain of over 192,000 miles in extent, or nearly 8 times the circumference of the globe. The whole of the work, including the manufacture of the two sections, and the fitting out of the Great Eastern, occupied little more than 8 months.

For the accommodation of the cable on board the Great Eastern, 3 gigantic tanks were constructed, situated in the centre, stern, and fore part of the ship, and known as the main, after, and fore tanks, respectively. Their diameters were as follows: Fore, 51 feet 6 inches diameter, by 20 feet 6 inches deep; main, 75 feet diameter, by 16 feet 6 inches deep; after, 58 feet diameter, by 20 feet 6 inches deep; with a total capacity of 169,760 cubic feet, — being 27,750 feet greater than the capacity of the tanks in 1866. These immense structures were fixed to the sides of the ship, and supported by about 30,000 cubic feet of timber. The weight contained in them was about 5,520 tons, distributed as follows: Fore, 1,270 tons; main, 2,580 tons; aft, 1,670 tons; total, 5,520 tons.

The cable paying-out apparatus, consisting of an elaborate series of brake-wheels and stoppers, with the measuring-machine, and the "dynamometer," a machine constantly recording the strain on the cable, contained all the improvements that science and experience have suggested. The dynamometer especially claims our notice, as being, to our mind, one of the most ingenious and useful contrivances connected with the apparatus. It is placed between the stern of the ship and the paying-out brakes, and consists of a vertical framework of iron, in the centre of which is fitted a grooved wheel, for the cable to pass under as it runs out over the stern of the ship. The wheel is made to slide up and down the frame as the strain on the cable varies, or, in other words, as the cable becomes tighter between the stern and the brakes. At the side of the machine is a scale, with the calculated strains in hundred-weights marked upon it; and a hand fixed to the sliding-wheel traverses this scale, and indicates at any moment the strain on the cable. From the indicated strain, of course, the depth of water may be judged, and the brakes arranged accordingly; but the dynamometer is of most service in cases of hauling back the cable.

The ship was also fitted with a powerful set of picking-up machines and tackle, together with buoys, buoy-ropes, mushroom anchors, and everything requisite for picking up the cable in case of a breakage, as in 1865.

We must not forget to mention that the ship was also fitted

with a complete set of "Wier's Pneumatic Signals," such as we believe are in use on several of the Cunard steamers. The uses to which this excellent apparatus is put are as numerous as they are effectual. The apparatus is rather complicated in its details, but simple enough in the principles on which it works. By pressing down a lever on a series of chambers of compressed air, the air from the latter is forced along a very small leaden pipe, producing instantaneously at the distant end some mechanical effect, — either ringing a bell, or moving a hand, or lifting up a small flap, under which is written the signal meant to be observed. On the Great Eastern there were, 1. An apparatus at both ends of the ship for communicating various messages to both-screw and paddle engines; 2. An apparatus at each of the 3 cable tanks for signalling to screw and paddle, to stop and reverse, in case of a hitch or foul-flake in the tank; 3. An apparatus connected, by means of cams, with the shafts of the screw and paddle engines, registering the revolutions of the same on a clock placed in the engineer's office; and, 4. A communication was placed between the bows and the steering-wheel, to be used in case picking up should become necessary. Connected with some of the apparatus was also a telltale, which by an automatic action would indicate whether the order sent had been obeyed or not.

We have made a rough calculation of the cargo of the ship, including her engines and boilers, when she left Portland, and believe the following to be a very near approximation; it is certainly not *over* the mark: Cable, 5,520 tons; cable-tanks and water, 400 tons; timber-shorings for tanks, 500 tons; paying-out and picking-up machinery, 120 tons; ship's stores, 250 tons; coals, 6,400 tons; engines and boilers, 3,500 tons; total, 16,690 tons. Her draft at starting was about 34 feet aft, and 28 feet forward. This, of course, decreased as the cable was paid out, until, at the end of the voyage, it was only about 25 feet aft, and 23 forward.

The arrangements made for the electrical testing of the cable during submersion were, with one or two slight exceptions, identically the same as in 1866. Their most interesting feature is the keeping up of a constant test on ship and shore for insulation, by a plan devised by Mr. Willoughby Smith in 1865, at the same time allowing of tests for the continuity of the conductor, and free communication between ship and shore to be kept up without in any way interfering with the insulation test. By this means, should a "fault" pass overboard into the sea, it is detected at once, and the paying-out may be stopped before any considerable length of the cable has been allowed to run out. The advantage of this system over the old is apparent from the fact, that formerly it was possible for 3 or 4 miles of cable to run out between the occurrence of the fault and its detection; whereas now, except under very peculiar circumstances, within two or 3 minutes after a "fault" passes overboard, it can be detected, and the signal given to stop the ship.

To give our readers some idea as to how a fault is detected, we may (for this purpose only) compare the cable to a long pipe sealed up at one end, into which water is being forced. As long as the pipe remains perfect, only a certain amount of water can be put into it, according to its capacity, and once filled, there is no flow of water; but if, when the pipe is full, a small hole be made in it, the water will of course rush out at once, indicating the existence of the hole by causing a fresh flow of water into the pipe. Now, the cable is always kept charged with electricity up to its full capacity, — or, in other words, till it can take no more, — and as long as it remains perfect there is practically no current flowing from the battery into it; but immediately on the development of a fault, or communication between the conductor of the cable and the earth, a portion of the charge escaping through the fault causes a fresh supply of electricity to flow from the battery. By having a delicate instrument fixed between the battery and the cable, this increased flow is at once made apparent.

As to the track of the cable, it seems from the soundings taken that the bottom is composed, the greater part of the distance, of the fine mud usually called "ooze," consisting of very minute shells, — so minute that without a microscope the shape is not discernible. This "ooze" constitutes the very best bed for a submarine cable. In fact, judging from the experience of 1866, the cable lies in it as securely and as free from harm as when coiled in the tanks at the manufactory; and if picking up should become necessary, the softness of the "ooze" renders the grappling of the cable comparatively easy.

The position of the present cable has one advantage over that of the English cables, namely, that it has been kept carefully off the Newfoundland Banks, and will therefore not be liable to the breakage by icebergs which have already caused such expense and trouble to the English company. The cable is conducted several miles to the south of the "Great Newfoundland Bank," and then proceeds in a north-westerly direction to the western side of St. Pierre Island, passing along a deep gully between the "Green Bank" and the "St. Pierre Bank." The length of the course selected is about 2,330 knots, and the amount of cable paid out 2,580 knots, — making about 10 per cent. allowance for "slack," or spare cable paid out to cover the inequalities of the bottom, and to allow of picking up, should such become necessary. Without taking notice of the 300 knots from the Brest shore, and the 500 knots from Newfoundland, where the water is shallow, the depth varies from 1,700 to 2,700 fathoms, the deepest part being situated in about 45° north, and longitude 43° west. — *Chambers' Journal.*

THE FRENCH ATLANTIC CABLE.

Various plans of testing submarine cable during paying out have been tried, but all have their disadvantages. None, however, are in any way to be compared to the plan now adopted. This is the invention of Mr. Willoughby Smith, a gentleman of very great experience, the electrician engaged during the paying out of the old Atlantic cables, and who is again in charge of the electrical arrangements on board of the Great Eastern. In the old form of testing, the official at the shore-end had to insulate the cable, when any test was taken, and consequently was unaware of what was going on. In the present plan a constant test can be kept up, with the knowledge of both ship and shore. The cable is attached at the shore-end having high-resistance through a galvanometer to earth; this resistance is so high that, on the ship keeping up a current from a large battery, the resistance is so great that a readable deflection can be obtained. A galvanometer is also inserted in the circuit on board ship. If the current were maintained, the deflection on the two galvanometers would remain constant, and during the paying out the deflections would be constantly watched; if they remained constant, the cable remained in the same electrical condition, but if they altered, they would show at once, both ship and shore, that something was wrong: to ship that by the increased deflection through a fault there was less resistance, and consequently more current flowing in to cause the increased deflection. On the shore the effect would be different, as, there being another method to escape, less current would arrive. By this means we see how the appearance of a fault would be easily detected. The system of speaking or exchanging signals is very simple: by means of a condenser attached to the cable, which is charged with the same potential or opposite potential as the cable, the deflection is slightly altered in one direction or the other, and communication can be exchanged without interfering with the constant test.

THE BLACK SEA CABLE.

It is announced that the cable of the Indo-European Telegraph Co. across the Black Sea, about 200 miles, has been successfully submerged. — *Engineering, July* 16, 1869.

THE INDO-EUROPEAN TELEGRAPH.

The lines from London to Norderney, which constitutes part of the system, are in working order, and from Norderney to Thorn, on the Prusso-Russian frontiers, two wires are being constructed by the Prussian government.

From Thorn to Balta, via Warsaw, the section will consist of 800 miles of line, which will be laid on posts of heavy timber, principally of oak. From Balta the system will be continued via Odessa to Kertch, on through the Crimea to Ecaterneador, and thence to a point which will correspond with the northern end of the Black Sea cable. This section, which will, as far as regards the land part, be constructed of iron posts, will be about 750 miles in length, and will comprise two cables, — one 15 miles long, which will be submerged in the Straits of Kertch, and another, 4 miles long, which will cross the River Dnieper. The continuation of the system proceeds towards Tiflis and thence to Teheran, where it will join existing lines.   In its course it may be added that it will comprise a 3-wire cable of about 100 miles in length, ending at Souchum Kaleh, the conductors of which will be of stranded wire, covered with alternate layers of the mixture now known among scientific men as Chetterton's compound and gutta-percha, and will weigh a little over 270 lbs. per knot.

In order that the means of communication with India may be as complete as possible, it is intended to improve the lines at present constructed from Teheran to India.   These agencies of correspondence proceed from Teheran via Ispahan and Shiraz to Bushire, on the Persian Gulf, and from that point to Kurrachee. The improvements, to which reference has been made, will include the substitution of iron for wooden posts on the lines from Teheran, the submergence of a cable, about 500 miles long, from Bushire to Jask, and the completion of a land-line from Jask to Kurrachee.   The result of these extensions will be, that two cables between Bushire and Jask, and a cable and a land-line from Jask to Kurrachee, will duplicate the facilities of communication through the whole of the Persian Gulf.   The shore-ends of the Black Sea cable, which will probably be laid during the approaching summer, are to be sheathed with heavy galvanized iron wires protected by tarred jute. The section to which Teheran will form the eastern terminus will, it is expected, be completed by the end of next July.   Meanwhile, the project for establishing complete submarine communication between this country and India is being vigorously promoted.   Of the probable results of the competition of the rival systems there are but few data, at present, upon which to erect an opinion.

TELEGRAPH ENTERPRISE.

Another great European telegraph project is on foot.   A company just formed in London has purchased, with concessional rights, the following cables, namely, 1st, Denmark to England, from Sondervig to Newbiggin, actual distance 334 miles; 2d, Denmark to Norway, from Hirtshalts to Arendal, actual distance 60 miles; 3d, Denmark to Russia, from Moen to Bornholm, and Bornholm to Libau, actual distance 304 miles; 4th, Norway to Scotland, from Egersund to Peterhead, actual distance 270 miles; 5th, Sweden to Russia, from Grislehamn to Nystad, actual distance 96 miles.   Of these, the three first are already laid, and have been for some time working; the fourth is shipped on board ready for laying; and the arrangements for the fifth are in course of completion, and both the latter are to be laid at the risk and cost of the old companies.   The new company undertakes the working, and will be entitled to the receipts from the 1st of June.   The cost of purchase was 2,500,000 dollars. The ultimate intention of the company is a connection with North America via the Russian dominions.

THE OCEAN TELEGRAPH.

Expert operators are able to transmit from 15 to 20 words per minute through the Atlantic cable. The velocity with which a current or impulse will pass through the cable has been ascertained to be between 7,000 and 8,000 miles per second; the former being the velocity when the earth forms a part of the circuit, and the latter when it does not.

FRENCH MILITARY TELEGRAPHS.

The following are details of the military electric-telegraphic apparatus used in the experiments in the camp at Chalons, last summer: *Electric Telegraph.*—For military purposes it is desirable that the apparatus should not only be simple in itself, but should be capable of being used in connection with the permanent lines of telegraph already established. Keeping these ends in view, a modification of Morse's recorder, constructed by M. Duguy, from designs furnished by the Bureau des Télégraphie, and known as Le Poste Militaire, was adopted and found to answer well. This apparatus is contained in a box, to the bottom of which it is attached by slides. The manipulator is placed on the right of the small shelf supporting the recorder; on the left are the galvanometer to show the strength of the current, and a *paratonnère* to protect the operator from the shock of unforeseen accumulations of electricity in the wires in stormy weather. The sides and front of the box fold down, so as to permit of the instrument being used without necessitating its removal from its case. The connection between the stations was kept up partly by wires, partly by a cable laid along the ground. *Wires.*—These were of copper, 1.6 mil. in diameter, weighing 22.5 kilog., and costing about 100 francs per kilom. This wire proved an excellent conductor, and, with care, could be used with intervals of 200 and 300m., or even more, between the supports. *Cables.*—Several kinds were tried. In the last experiments the cable was formed of a core of 5 annealed copper wires, bound round with white cotton thread, over which was a coating of gutta-percha, and then a layer of oakum, the whole being bound round twice with cotton tape steeped in vulcanized India-rubber. It weighed 35 kilog., and cost 320 francs per kilom. It was perfectly insulated, and a good conductor. When laid along the ground it suffered little from wheels and the feet of horses passing and repassing over it. But it had serious defects. It was rather too large in its diameter, and very weak, stretching sufficiently to injure the core with a strain of 30 kilog. The wires of the core were so fine as to be frequently cut through in removing the covering for the purpose of splicing. *Supports.*—The wires were supported on light staves called lances, 3m. 80c. in length, 200 of which made a military wagon load. They were sunk 12 inches in the ground, and weighed up with wooden pickets. Where the line made an angle, the lances were strengthened with guy-ropes,

10

known as *haubans*, attached to iron pickets. The lances could be lengthened by attaching two or more, end to end, by means of rings called *anneaux de rallonge*, fitted with clamp-screws. *Insulators.* — With spires of India-rubber made hollow so as to fit over the end of the lances, and surmounted by a small cylinder of the same material. The wires were attached to the insulators by a couple of turns. Iron cramps were also supplied which could be driven into the ground, or into the walls and trees *en route* to support the cable when used in place of wires. The work was very arduous of laying the wire. The average rate obtained on the most favorable ground was two kilom. the hour with suspended wires, and 5 kilom. with cable. In passing villages, etc., double the above time proved requisite. For taking up the line, 5 or 6 men marching in inverse order were sufficient. The rapidity with which this manœuvre was executed equalled and sometimes exceeded that of ordinary route marching. In joining the lengths of cable, the covering was first removed and an elastic India-rubber tube slipped over one length; the wires were then spliced and the India-rubber tube drawn over the joint and secured by tying down the ends firmly with twine. This was found to answer perfectly; but, as the tying process took up some little time, small cylinders were sometimes substituted for the India-rubber tube. These contained two India-rubber discs, having holes in them for the passage of the cable, and hollow screws at each end working against them. The screws were made hollow so as to allow of the passage of the cable through them. The splice was made in the ordinary way, the tube drawn over the joint, and the discs compressed round the cable by the action of the screws. A joint could be thus made in 30 seconds. It was found, however, that the vibration of the cable loosened the screws and allowed water to leak into the joints. — *Van Nostrand's Engineering Mag.*

THE PALLISER GUN.

Some particulars are at hand relative to the practical working of a number of guns converted upon Major Palliser's system. In 1866, 8 cast-iron 24-pounder and 32-pounder smooth-bore guns were converted by Major P. into 56-pounder and 64-pounder rifled guns, with a view of ascertaining whether our large stock of cast-iron guns could be advantageously converted into rifled cannon. Of these 8 experimental guns, one was tested for endurance, by firing continuously, with shot of 64 lbs. weight, until it had completed 2,285 rounds, of which 2,170 were with 8 lbs. weight, 88 were with 14 lbs., two with 12 lbs., one with 10 lbs., and 24 with 16 lbs. and 86 lbs. shot. The power of endurance of the converted guns was thus thoroughly proven. Six of the remaining guns were issued for service to home and foreign stations, in order that the royal artillery might have an opportunity of practising with them. The preliminary reports have now arrived from these stations, and are, on the whole, very satisfactory. The 64-pounder issued to Davenport has fired over 500 rounds; the gun is reported to be perfectly serviceable, and no complaints have been made of any difficulty in working. The Sheerness gun has fired 200 rounds, and the practice is reported as exceedingly accurate. The report from Gibraltar speaks in high terms of the accuracy of the 56-pounder issued to that station. The gun has fired 400 rounds, and is perfectly serviceable. The 56-pounder issued to Malta has fired 250 rounds. At Dover a 64-pounder has fired over 180 rounds with remarkable accuracy. The gun is spoken of as being, for handiness and fitness for rough work and exposure, in every way equal to the old 32-pounder. The 64-pounder on board the "Excellent" has fired over 180 rounds with great accuracy, the working of the gun-carriage, etc., being in every way satisfactory. These reports are of much interest, proving, as they do, that the converted 64-pounder gun is fully equal to the more expensive wrought-iron gun of the same calibre. — *Mechan. Mag.*

PROOF OF GUNS.

Mr. Whitworth says of the late trial of the 9-inch Frazer gun, pronounced so wonderful by the British press, — namely, firing 19 tons of powder and 124½ tons of shot in 1,114 rounds, — that as more than one-half the rounds fired were powder charges, only one-half the most effective charge, and the remainder with three-quarters the charge, while all the shots fired were only two-thirds the best weight for that size of bore, I contend that it was no proper test of endurance, but sheer waste of ammunition.

Mr. Whitworth thus describes his own mode of proof; it consists in preventing the shot from moving when the powder is ignited, the gases generated by the explosion escaping only through the touchhole. About one-sixth of the regular powder-charge fired in this way gives the same strain to the gun as a full charge fired in the ordinary manner. To prevent the movement of the shot, a screw is cut on the periphery of the gun at the muzzle, and on it is fitted a screwed cap having a solid end. The gun is loaded with a cartridge of the ordinary length, but containing one-sixth of the regular charge, and supported by tin disks in the centre of the bore; a flat-fronted shot with tight wads to prevent any escape of gas, and a round steel bar reaching from the shot to the end of the bore, are then introduced, and the cap with the solid end screwed on. The gun is then ready for firing, after which my measuring instrument is introduced into the bore, and any enlargement to the ten-thousandth of an inch may be ascertained.

If there be no enlargement, the powder charges may be gradually increased, until a slight enlargement has been produced. The real strength of each gun is thus positively ascertained, and this strength I would have stamped and recorded on each gun. This would give confidence to the gunners, and would act as a check on those engaged in the manufacture When the ultimate endurance of any gun is thus to be ascertained, the regular powder-charges, or any less quantity deemed desirable, may be used, the enlargements being recorded after each discharge. A 9-pounder bore gun made of my metal but reduced 12 inches in diameter has been so tested, and has had 18 full charges of $1\frac{1}{2}$ lbs. fired from it. The expansion in the bore is now .1903 inches, and that of the outside diameter is .0485 inches. — *Van Nostrand's Eng. Mag.*

VELOCITY OF CANNON BALLS.

At the late ordnance experiments at Fortress Monroe, the initial velocity of cannon balls was tested by a very delicate instrument, "the Schultz Chromoscope." The apparatus, which is operated by electricity, is thus described: two wire targets are placed, one about 20 yards from the gun, and the second about the same distance further on. These are connected by a fine insulated wire with the instrument, which is about 400 yards in the rear of the ordnance. The instrument is adjusted on a plan similar to an electro-balistic machine. When the shot is fired, it cuts the wire in the first target, and then that of the second, — the instant each wire is severed being recorded by the instrument. The interval of time occupied by the ball in passing from one target to the other furnishes the data for obtaining the initial velocity of the shot.

SYSTEM OF MONCRIEFF.

It consists of three parts: 1st. The mechanical principle of the gun-carriages. 2d. The form, internal and external, of the batteries. 3d. The selection of ground for placing the batteries, and the arrangement for working to the greatest effect; or, in other words, the *tactics* of defence for positions where the system is employed. The principle on which the carriage is constructed is the first and most important part of the new system, because on it depends the possibility of applying the other parts. This principle may be shortly stated as that of utilizing the force of the recoil in order to lower the whole gun below the level of the crest of the parapet, so that it can be loaded out of sight and out of exposure, while retaining enough of the force above referred to to bring the gun up again into the firing or fighting position. This principle belongs to all the carriages; but the forms of these carriages, as well as the method in which this principle is applied, vary in each case. For instance, in siege guns, where weight is an element of importance, the recoil is not met by counterpoise. With heavy garrison guns, on the other hand, which when once mounted remain permanent in their positions, there is no objection to weight. In that case, therefore, the force of gravity is used to stop the recoil, because it is a force always the same, easily managed, and not likely to go wrong; and as these carriages are employed for the most powerful guns, it is a great advantage to have the most simple means of working them. It has been already mentioned that the principal difficulty arose from the enormous and hitherto destructive force of the recoil of powerful guns; and here I shall point out the manner in which that difficulty is overcome. That part of the carriage which is called the elevator may be spoken of and treated as a lever; this lever has the gun-carriage axle at the end of the power arm, and the centre of gravity of the counter-weight at the end of the weight-arm, there being between them a moving fulcrum. When the gun is in firing position, the fulcrum on which this lever rests is almost coincident with the centre of gravity of the counter-weight, and when the gun is fired the elevators roll on the platform, and consequently the fulcrum, or point of support, travels away from the end of the weight-arm towards the end of the power-arm; or, in other words, it passes from the counter-weight towards the gun. Notice the important result of this arrangement. When the gun is fired, its axle passes backward on the upper or flat part of a cycloid. It is free to recoil, and no strain is put upon any part of the structure, because the counter-weight commences its motion at a very low velocity. As the recoil goes on, however, the case changes completely, for the moving fulcrum travels towards the gun, making the weight-arm longer and longer every inch it travels. Thus the resistance to the recoil, least at first, goes on in an increasing progression as the gun descends, and at the end of the recoil it is seized by a self-acting pawl or clutch. The recoil takes place without any jar, without any sudden strain, and its force is retained under the control of the detachment to bring up the gun to the firing position at any moment they may choose to release it. The recoil, moreover, however violent at first, does not put injurious horizontal strain on the platform. In my experiments at Edinburgh with a 32-pounder, I found that so slight was the vibration on the platform caused by firing, that the common rails on which the elevators rolled in that experiment, and which were only secured in the slightest manner, did not move from their position, nor even when heavy charges or double charges were used did sand and dust fall off their curved tops. — *Nostrand's Eclectic Engineering.*

GUNPOWDER HAMMER AND PILE-DRIVER.

At a late meeting of the Franklin Institute, there was exhibited a gunpowder hammer, invented and constructed by Mr. Thomas Shaw, of Philadelphia. In describing the apparatus, Mr. Shaw said: —

" A weight or hammer is suspended between vertical guides, and is provided on its under-side with a plunger that fits into the bore of a cylinder held between the same guides beneath the hammer. It is intended that the cylinder should rest upon the object to be pounded, and that the hammer should be held by a pawl, which catches into a rack secured parallel with the guides. The pawl is released from the rack by a cord connected with the same, whereupon the hammer is allowed to fall. A small amount of powder is placed in the cylinder; the hammer, falling, forces its plunger into the cylinder, compressing and heating the air, which explodes the powder, forcing the hammer up again, and forcing the cylinder downward, with an effect fully 8 times as great as from the falling of the weight alone. At the top of the guide-frame is suspended a plunger, which fits into a cylinder in the top of the hammer, thus making an air-chamber to receive the blow of the hammer, in case of an over-charge of powder, that no danger may result to the machine. The model which was exhibited on this occasion had a ram of about 8 pounds' weight, and a fall of 8 feet. The charge employed was half a grain of white gunpowder, made of chlorate of potash, ferrocyanide of potassium, and sugar. With a larger instrument, whose ram weighed 73 pounds, with a fall of 20 feet, the charge was 14 grains of the same powder. A pile placed under this, and driven one quarter inch at a stroke by the fall of the ram, without the use of powder, was driven two inches at each stroke when the powder was used, and after being driven, with a square end, into hard ground, to a depth of 4 feet, showed no splitting or injury to its head."—*Journal of the Franklin Institute.*

AMMONIA POWDER.

The following account of a new explosive material appears in the "Kölnische Zeitung," May 19, which gives the "Militör-Wochen-blatt" as its authority: "It is now some time since the proprietors of the Nora-Gyttorn Powder Mills obtained a patent in Sweden for the discovery of the so-called 'ammonia powder,' a substance which has hitherto been only employed in a few mining-districts, but which otherwise seems wholly unknown. We are, therefore, fully justified in calling attention to the particular properties of this new explosive material. During the short time that it has been employed, it has won the approval, not only of the proprietors of mines, but also of the working miners themselves. Its explosive force may be compared to that of nitro-glycerine, and, consequently, far surpasses that of dynamite. It cannot be exploded by a flame or by sparks, and the explosion is effected by a heavy blow from a hammer. Blast-holes loaded with this powder are exploded by means of a powerful cap, or, better, by means of a cartridge containing common powder, for this forms a more reliable exploder. Miners who have been obliged to give up the use of nitro-glycerine, on account of the danger connected with this powerful explosive agent, have a most satisfactory substitute in the ammonia powder, as the danger of using it is so small that it surpasses in safety every other blasting material. One of the useful and important properties of this new powder is, that it does not require heating in cold weather, whilst nitro-glycerine and dynamite must first of all be warmed, and this has been the cause of many accidents. The price of ammonia powder is the same as that of dynamite." The same paper further adds: "According to information we have received, ammonia powder was discovered by the chemist Norrbin." The German "Building News" contains extracts from a report of the Prussian architect, Steenke, who makes the following remarks upon the safety of ammonia powder: "Experiments were made by fastening a lamp to a pendulum, which was caused to oscillate; gunpowder, gun-cotton, nitro-glycerine, and dynamite all took fire as the flame passed over them, but the ammonia powder did not begin to burn till it had been touched by the flame 20 times. In making experiments upon the force of the blow required to explode it, it was found that, with the apparatus employed, where the fall of a weight from 4 feet to 5 feet would explode gunpowder, nitro-glycerine only required 1½ feet to 2 feet, dynamite 2½ feet to 8 feet fall, whilst a fall of from 12 feet to 15 feet was necessary to cause the explosion of the ammonia powder.

PROCESS FOR THE PRESERVATION OF THE BOTTOM OF IRON SHIPS.

A writer in the Comptes Rendus of July 26, 1869, says:—
"The iron actually employed in maritime construction is nearly always of an inferior quality, and presents a very great heterogeneity. From that cause foci of electric action exist which, provoking the decomposition of water or saline matter that it contains, lead to a prompt deterioration of the shell; the points attacked are then the parts left vacant by clusters of mollusks and weeds which clog the passage of the ship. The problem proposed to us, and which we believe to have solved, is to prevent this oxidation, the first cause of the clusters. In our system the ship is transformed to a kind of a vast pile of buckets; reservoirs in zinc are placed, under the form of tubes or boxes, on the interior sides. These tubes, in perfect communication with the iron of the ship, instead of bolts, rivets, or other instruments, are filled with seawater that is renewed every day. Plates of zinc between windows circulate in the interior of the ship, and hoop the different parts with the tubes or reservoirs. In the course of oxidation, the zinc charges itself with negative fluid, which it transmits by electricity to the iron; the shell becomes then like an immense electrode charged with this fluid. We thought at first that the iron, recovered, so to speak, with an envelope of negative fluid, ought to take, by this means, a certain electric polarity, and thus avoid the action of the electro-negative bodies contained in the air or the ocean; the negative fluid ought to flow out in a continuous manner into the water, and the positive fluid of the liquid to dissipate little by little into the humid air, and thus independently of the particular currents establish themselves in the interior of the boxes between the liquid and the iron bolts which fasten the reservoirs to the ship. Whether the electric communication was imperfect, whether the flow of the positive fluid into the air was insufficient, the carrier-boats of this kind of preparation have presented only a half success; thus the interior has been well

preserved, but the exterior was not slow in presenting traces of oxidation. We then continued the action of the reservoirs by a small plate of zinc, applied to the exterior of the shell, in electric communication with the reservoirs, and with its inferior part plunged into the sea.

"Some experiments made in this condition, for more than a year, have given us a complete success; some boats, plunged since the end of December, 1868, in a pond formed by some old salt-works, and where the water of the ocean is renewed at every tide, have been preserved until to-day, without presenting the least spot of oxidation. Every time that a part of the system was found to be altered, by wear or by accident, some sensible traces of rust appeared, and then disappeared after the preparation was renewed. Many boats placed in the same circumstances, but without preparation, have been perforated successively during this time. Some of these boats were scoured with acid before being submitted to this experiment; the others, immersed immediately after their departure from the work-shop, presented at the time of their putting in water numerous spots of rust, which all disappeared in the first 8 days of their immersion. To avoid the employment of the electrodes of zinc, we plunged one of the extremities of a copper wire, covered with gutta-percha, in the liquid of the reservoirs, and the other in the sea; but in this case, the results have been less satisfactory."—*Comptes Rendus, July* 26, 1869.

MAKING FOUNDATIONS IN MARSHES.

A new process of making foundations for bridges in marshy soils has been recently used on a branch line of the Charentes Railway Company, in France. This line crosses a peat valley to the junction of two small rivers. The thickness of peat was so great that any attempt to reach the solid ground would have been very expensive. In order to obtain cheaply a good support for the bridge two large masses of ballast accurately rammed were made on each bank of the river, and a third one on the peninsula between the two. The slopes of these heaps were pitched with dry stones, for preventing the sand from being washed away by the rains or by the floods in the rivers. Over the ballast a timber platform is laid; this platform carries the girders of the bridge, which has two spans of about 60 feet each. When some sinking down takes place, the girders are easily kept to the proper level by packing the ballast under the timber platform; this packing is made by the plate layers with their ordinary tools. This simple and cheap process has succeeded quite well. The same difficulty was overcome by a different plan on an ordinary road near Algiers. This road crosses a peaty plain nearly one mile broad; the floods and elasticity of the ground prevented the formation of an embankment. The road was to be carried over a viaduct across the valley, but the foundations of this viaduct presented serious difficulties, the thickness of peat or of compressible ground being nearly 80 feet. It was quite possible to reach the solid ground with cast-iron tubes sunk with compressed air, or with any other system; but neither the implements nor the suitable workmen were available in the colony, — and it was a great expense to bring them, and especially the workmen, from France. The use of timber piling was, of course, out of question, as timber is very expensive in Algiers and quickly becomes rotten; but there was a set of boring implements with which the men used to work it. The engineers began boring holes 10 inches diameter down to the solid ground. These holes, lined with thin plate-iron pipes, were afterward filled with concrete up to the very level of the ground. Each of these concrete columns bears a cast-iron column; these columns are properly braced together, and support the girders of the viaduct, which is divided into spans of about 20 feet, and is 20 feet high over the ground. This system has succeeded very well, and is to be extended to another larger valley. — *Van Nostrand's Eclectic Engineering Magazine, Sept.,* 1869.

EXPERIMENTS ON HEAVY ORDNANCE.

The following conclusions, deduced from experiments on heavy ordnance, are given in the Report of the Ordnance Committee, presented to the Senate, February 15, 1869: —

1. That no more heavy guns should be purchased for mounting in the fortifications or use on shipboard until such improvements are made in methods of fabrication as will insure more reliable endurance than has heretofore been exhibited.

2. That the Rodman system of gun-making, while partially successful in smooth bores and small calibres, has so far failed in rifles of large calibre as to show it to be unworthy of further confidence. Recent improvements in defensive works and armor-plating render heavy rifled guns the most efficient means of attack, and no system of fabrication which does not furnish such guns should be adopted or continued. The principle of initial tension, which is the basis of the Rodman system, appears to be of doubtful utility, as applied by General Rodman, especially for rifled guns. This tension, it is admitted, gradually disappears from the gun with age, and in time is entirely lost.

3. That guns cast solid, in the manner practised in the navy under the direction of Rear-Admiral Dahlgren, while exhibiting satisfactory endurance as smooth bores with small charges and hollow projectiles, have not the requisite strength for rifles of large calibre. This mode of casting seems to be defective in principle, as the tensions inaugurated in cooling have a tendency to aid the powder to rupture the gun.

4. That experiments should be at once conducted for the purpose of ascertaining the real cause of the bursting of heavy guns, and of determining upon some method of fabrication that will secure uniform endurance.

5. That every encouragement should be given to inventors,

and a full and fair trial accorded to all devices offered to the government that promise a solution of the ordnance problem.

6. That more efficient means for harbor defence should be adopted. The late war demonstrated that sand was the best material for defensive works, and that forts of masonry, such as we have now mainly to rely upon for the protection of our seaboard cities, are inefficient to prevent the passage of armored, or even wooden, vessels. The destruction of such defences is only a question of time to ordinary guns of heavy calibre. It was also demonstrated that forts alone, of whatever character, cannot resist the entrance to harbors of powerfully armed ships if the preponderance of guns on the assailing fleet is sufficient. In the opinion of the committee, obstructions must be largely relied upon for harbor defence, in connection with properly constructed fortifications.

7. That no officer of the army or navy should be allowed to receive a patent for any article required, or likely to be required, for use in those branches of the public service, or to be in any way interested in the manufacture or procurement of such articles. It should be the duty of Congress to recognize in suitable rewards the services of such officers as might make inventions of especial value to the government.

8. That the Ordnance Department of the army can be entirely abolished with great advantage as to economy, and without detriment to the good of the service. The duties now performed by officers of that corps could be performed by officers detailed from the artillery service, under the direction of a chief stationed at Washington. In this manner the whole expense of the ordnance establishment would be saved, and artillery officers, who have not only scientific training, but practical experience, would have a voice in the selection of the guns and ammunition they are required to use.

The committee are of the opinion that, for the reasons shown, the interests of the public service demand a change in the system of procuring ordnance and ordnance stores, and the manner of conducting experiments with a view to determining the value of the same. The present system has failed to answer the purpose for which it was designed, and the United States is in the position to-day of a nation having a vast coast-line to defend, and a large navy, without a single rifled gun of large calibre, and a corps of ordnance officers who have thus far failed to discover a remedy for the failure of the guns, or to master the rudiments of the science in which they have been trained at the public expense. The importance of an immediate change is shown by the fact that the chief of ordnance of the army asks for appropriations to purchase over 1,900 guns to arm the forts, not of a new and better system to be decided upon after more thorough and careful experiment, but of a kind that experience has shown to be inferior in range and penetration to the guns of foreign powers, and unreliable as to endurance.

It is proposed that 85 of these guns shall be smooth bores of 20-inch calibre, 490 of 15-inch calibre, and 600 of 13-inch calibre.

The experience of all nations goes to prove that the most effect-ive way of developing ordnance power is by rifled guns. To return to smooth bores, throwing huge spherical masses of iron with low velocities, is to disregard all modern progress in the science of gunnery, and to go back to the arms in use two cen-turies ago. Furthermore, the advisability of using guns of such great size is very doubtful; for the slowness with which they are handled and fired makes them less effective than smaller guns delivering a more rapid fire. Two hundred of the guns required it is proposed shall be Rodman 12-inch rifles, notwithstanding all of that class of guns heretofore procured for the army or navy, and subjected to test, have either burst disastrously before the lowest reasonable test has been completed, or have given such indications of failing, after a few rounds, as to be considered unsafe. It is proposed also to purchase 610 10-inch Rodman rifles, although the committee cannot learn that any gun of this class has ever been subjected to test in this country, except the Parrott rifles of that calibre, which are acknowledged failures, having been condemned by both branches of the service.

No progress toward obtaining better guns is likely to be made while the ordnance bureaus are organized as at present; and the committee deem the best way to secure such impartially con-ducted experiments as will determine with certainty what are the best arms, and to insure greater economy and regard for the pub-lic interests in their purchase and adoption, is in the formation of a mixed ordnance commission composed of officers of high char-acter, detailed from both the army and navy, who shall have no interest in patents on devices for arms.

CONCRETE BUILDING.

Tall's system has been used in the construction of a large num-ber of houses in Paris, erected under the directions of the em-peror, who takes great interest in the improvement of the dwell-ings of the working-classes, and has also been applied in other parts of Europe, and to some extent in the United States.

The work can be performed by ordinary laborers, who, after 4 or 5 days' experience, acquire all the requisite expertness. Even boys have been successfully employed in this kind of building. The only skilled workman necessary is a common car-penter, whose duty is to adjust the framework or apparatus to receive the successive courses of material, and place joists, doors, and window-frames properly.

The apparatus is designed to construct 18 inches in height daily over the entire extent in hand. What is done in the even-ing of one day is hard next morning, and quite strong, the best proof of which is, that the wall itself, as it rises in height, sup-ports the necessary scaffolds. A double curb, entirely surround-ing the upper part of the walls, serves to hold the plastic material in place, until it acquires sufficient hardness to support itself.

The material consists of one part of Portland cement to 8 parts of coarse gravel. The cement and gravel are first well mixed together in a dry state, and when this is done it is damped by means of a large watering-pot, and again mixed by a pronged drag, such as is used for dragging dung out of a cart, until the entire heap has been wetted and mixed together. It is then put in iron or zinc pails, and poured into the frame, where it is levelled by men stationed for the purpose. In order to save concrete, large lumps of stones or brickbats are put into the centre of the wall, and covered over and about with concrete. Frost does not affect the concrete after it has once set, which, with good cement, will be in about 5 or 6 hours. Nor do heavy rains appear to injure it in the slightest degree, though they may chance to fall ere the concrete has hardened. The walls can be made straight and even as it is possible for walls to be, and the corners as sharp and neat as if they had been formed of the most carefully dressed stone.

Concrete makes excellent floors, and the walls and floors are quite impervious to vermin of all kinds, and also to wet. Many kinds of building-bricks will absorb water; hence brick houses, when the walls are saturated with water, are cold. This is not the case with houses constructed of concrete, as it is non-absorbent of moisture, and such houses must be, therefore, more healthy.

This novel mode of building houses has excited great interest in the neighborhood of Runnamoat, Ireland, and the proceedings have daily attracted numbers of people from all parts.

While concrete may be used in constructing buildings of every description, it is peculiarly adapted, from its cheapness, for the construction of cottages for laborers, and also for farm buildings. Its cost is not more than half that of brick-work; almost any material can be used along with the cement, and, as we have already shown, the most ordinary class of country laborers are quite competent to carry out the details of the system. With reference to its adaptability for large buildings, we may mention that a warehouse 70 feet long, 50 feet wide, and 60 feet high, 5 stories in all, has been erected on Mr. Tall's system for Mr. H. Goodwin, Great Guildford Street, Southwark, England, and that gentleman testifies in the warmest terms to its satisfactory character, and is making arrangements at the present time for the construction of another similar building. The warehouse already erected has attracted universal admiration from the practical and scientific gentlemen who witnessed its erection.

The chief element of success, when the cement is of good quality, seems to be the thorough mixture of the dry materials, to secure uniform strength.

ENGINEERING UNDER GROUND.

We learn from the "Artisan," London, that a new length of the line of the underground railroad of that city has been completed at a cost of 3,500,000 dollars per mile, the bulk of which has been applied towards compensation for damages. The length of the new line is nearly 3 miles, and has 6 stations, — one at Westminster Bridge; one in the Broadway, at St. James's Park; one at Victoria, where it joins the Chatham and Dover line; one at Chelsea, near Sloane Square; one at South Kensington; and one in the Gloucester Road, West Brompton. Of the whole length of line about one-third is tunnel and the rest open cutting.

No very special engineering difficulties were met with in the construction of the line, except the continued presence of water, as some parts of the works are below low-water mark. The greatest depth below the surface to the rails is not more than 32 feet, the quickest curve is 440 feet radius, and the greatest incline one in 250 feet. Considerable difficulty was experienced during the construction of the line, from water, both from the sewers and from the surface drainage. On one very wet day in the early summer no less than 6 sewers burst at once, and gave the pumps enough to do to keep their contents, with the surface drainage, from flooding all that was then built of the line. To this day, and as long as the line is in use, there must always be permanent pumping-stations for the mere surface drainage, there being no outlet toward the river without raising it to a higher level. This water difficulty, however, is very ingeniously met by Messrs. Fowler and Johnstone, the engineers of the line. The side walls, both of the arched tunnels and open cuttings, are made of extra thickness, and, above all, are connected beneath the ground by an inverted arch of concrete nearly 3 feet thick. This effectually prevents the water rising up through the floor of the line, and equally prevents the surface water from draining off. For this surface drainage, therefore, special provision is made, by means of pipes laid in the centre of the line, which carry the water on to the pumping-stations, where it is raised and sent away into the Thames. Passing under the middle of the Broadway, the line is carried, not in a tunnel, but in a broad, lofty, square chamber, with a flat roof, on massive wrought-iron girders. This is a beautiful piece of work, both in its design and finish, and is of the most unexceptionable character from beginning to end. While passing along the Broadway special precautions were taken to guard against any possible vibration affecting Westminster Abbey. The walls on the Abbey side are here made 7 bricks thick. Behind this comes the Victoria sewer in a tube of iron, and behind all a bed of peat 7 feet thick. The peat checks all vibration, but as the nearest point at which the line passes is more than 90 feet from the Abbey walls, its deadening properties are scarcely required.

After Westminster Bridge the first station is St. James's Park, and leaving this the line continues in an open cutting to Buckingham Row, where it enters a tunnel of about 500 yards in length. Here the water occasioned so much difficulty that engines had to be kept going night and day, pumping at the rate of nearly 4,000 gallons a minute. The tunnel at this point passes but a few feet below the surface of the ground, yet it forms the foundation of the brewery belonging to Elliot, Watney, & Co. above. This building is now carried on a series of girders, but the work had to be done with great care, for the superincumbent weight was immense, and the soil below poor and treacherous.   After finishing this portion of the line a fresh difficulty arose with the King's Scholar's Pond sewer, the largest sewer next to that of the fleet in London.   This had to be entirely diverted, and reconstructed in an iron tube, 11 feet wide by 14 feet high.   So very limited was the space at command that this sewer had to be built over the up and down line in a deeply arched form, in order to make room for the funnels of the locomotives.   This most difficult of all the tasks on the line has been admirably executed by Mr. T. A. Walker, the resident engineer, who has had charge of the works throughout.   A few yards from this point is the station at Victoria, which, like all the others on the line, is open, or rather only closed in with light glass and iron roofs.   From this point the line passes on to Sloane Square, a wide and lofty station, but the architectural effect of which is much marred by the Ranelagh sewer being taken in a huge cylinder of cast iron right across its very centre at the springing of the arches.   Continuing westward, the next station is near the site of the Exhibition building of 1862, and to this a new road will be made by a continuation of the Exhibition Road from Kensington.   The last station is at Gloucester Road, West Brompton, where the junction is effected with the Metropolitan Extension.   The District line then branches to the south, and forms a double junction with the West London, by means of which a communication is gained with most of the southern lines.

EARTHQUAKE-PROOF BUILDINGS.

The recurrence of earthquake shocks in California has led to a discussion of the methods of building houses in such a manner as to be virtually earthquake-proof.   A San Francisco architect, Mr. Saeltzer, has read a paper on this subject before the California Institute of Architecture, in which he contends that flexible materials only should be used in building.   His theory is as follows : —

"By distributing the whole weight of the building on piers of stone, brick, or iron, or on wooden piles, — in fact, isolating the foundation in such a manner that these piers or piles form part of the foundation, — and by connecting them with iron beams screwbolted together, the building is then well anchored at the proper place ; in fact, this style of foundation will form a girding all round the building longitudinally and transversely.

"This mode of construction will insure, first of all, the least contact with the earth ; secondly, concentration of the whole mass of the building on single points only with strong anchorage ; thirdly, more elasticity of the foundation, and consequently more elasticity in the whole mass of the building ; fourthly, a combination of heterogeneous materials in one mass, — an amalgamation, — one of the most important points to be gained ; fifthly, this style of building is the cheapest of all, and in most cases applies to our wants and climate, and to the desired architectural arrangements, and is applicable to any material."

▪ ▪ ▪ "The advantage of the concentration of the whole mass on piers will at once be visible. A pier has more elasticity than a solid wall, and if placed isolated, in the proportion of about 8 times the height to its base, this pier would, by a slight movement of the earth, lose its point of gravity; but by connecting a number of piers horizontally, transversely, and longitudinally, and by resting the weight of the whole building upon them, they become restrained in their natural action till the whole mass of the building begins to move.

"That piers will facilitate the rapidity or velocity of the movement of the whole mass, nobody will deny; inasmuch as they stand isolated, are comparatively weaker than a solid wall, and have solely to depend on themselves, in their own strength and nature, without any assistance from a connecting wall. It is hardly necessary to mention that the piers should, of course, be in proportion to the weight they have to support, and should be placed at proper distances for security."

▪ ▪ ▪ "To many it may seem strange that the towers of San Francisco stood so well during the late earthquakes, with hardly any apparent damage, and that also in European cities the towers have also been less injured; a fact which proves, in a most striking manner, that the flexibility or elasticity of a mass is a necessity for safety. A tower is a pier of high proportion, and forms a high pendulum, and naturally swings with more rapidity than a longer mass, and hence there is less danger. The tower of the Dom of Erfurt, at present a fortified city in Prussia, contains the largest bell in the world except the celebrated bell in Moscow. This bell requires 24 men to set it in motion, and when in motion has always caused an oscillation of the tower varying from 4 to 5 feet from the perpendicular line. For centuries this bell has been used, and the tower remains as perfect as ever. This tower is built of cut stone, with the finest details of Gothic architecture. I merely give this example to show the flexibility even of stone, provided the proportions are right.

"All our hotels stood well, also a large number of stores; in fact all buildings supported on piers or columns. All the bodies of churches also stood well, especially where buttresses were introduced. Each buttress forms a pier, and has, consequently, more elasticity, and always will stand well, provided the proportions are artistically carried out. Very low churches, built more in the proportions of a stable, are unsafe; in fact, all buildings one story high, and of considerable extent, are liable to danger, more so than two or three story buildings, no matter of what materials soever."

WATER-PROOFING WALLS.

One of the most recent of the many uses to which Mr. Frederick Ransome's process of manufacturing artificial stone has been applied, is in protecting the outer walls of buildings, so as to enable them to resist the action of the weather by making them water-proof. Through well-built and substantial walls, moisture will make its way, and the ordinary type of dwelling-house is very pervious to wind-driven rain. We recently noticed what Mr. Ransome is doing in preserving stone, and his system of water-proofing is only an application of the same process.

The external surfaces of the walls to be protected are first washed with a silicate of soda or solution of flint, which is applied again and again, until the bricks are saturated, and the silicate ceases to be absorbed. The strength of the solution is regulated by the character of the bricks upon which it is to be applied, a heavier mixture being used upon porous walls, and a lighter one on those of denser texture. After the silicate has become thoroughly absorbed, and none is visible upon the surface, a solution of chloride of calcium is applied, which, immediately combining with the silicate of soda, forms a perfectly insoluble compound, which completely fills up all the interstices in the brick or stone, without in any way altering its original appearance. By this operation the wall is rendered perfectly water-tight, and, as the pores of the bricks are thoroughly filled for a considerable depth from the surface with the insoluble compound, which is entirely unaffected by atmospheric influences, no subsequent process is necessary.

Already Mr. Ransome has successfully applied this process to a large number of buildings, several of which were previously almost uninhabitable from the constant dampness, and a lengthened experience has proved that it is not only thoroughly effective; but, from the comparative insignificance of its original cost, and the fact that renewals are never required, the system recommends itself for general adoption in preference to all other methods of water-proofing.

THE NEW MODE OF FIRING GUN-COTTON.

An interesting practical exhibition of the newly discovered properties of gun-cotton when fired by concussion, instead of by the direct application of flame or heat, was afforded recently at Woolwich. The huge 36-inch Mallet mortar, weighing 52 tons, which was placed in the marshes in 1857, and designed to fire a shell 2,548 lbs. (empty), has, for some time past, been sinking in its great wooden bed, owing to the gradual decay of the wood. It was thought dangerous to run the risk of its falling upon any visitor by leaving it in this position. But weights of 52 tons cannot be moved for nothing. To erect sheers and the necessary appliances for raising the mortar would have entailed an expenditure estimated at about 50 pounds. Under these circumstances, recourse was had to gun-cotton to destroy the bed, and precipitate the fall of the mortar. Four charges of 4 ozs. each, 4 of 6 ozs., and one of 8 ozs. (total, 48 ozs.), were placed on the wooden bed, and exploded by means of mining fuses charged with detonating composition. The material being rotten was especially unfavorable for the exertion of explosive force, for the force had, so to speak, nothing to act against. But what could be done was done. The huge bed was shattered, and particles flew in all directions. The mortar, although it altered its position, refused, however, to fall, being held, to some extent, by a thick wrought-iron screw-bolt. The next experiment was made upon this bolt. A one-lb. disc of compressed gun-cotton was tied to the belt and exploded. The explosion was then wholly unconfined. Nevertheless the bolt was broken in two places, a result which exceeded the most sanguine anticipations. Still the huge mortar remained in its position. A third operation had, therefore, to be made. This time two one-lb. charges were disposed under the left trunnion, and a one-lb. charge was so placed as to give the mortar a kick behind. The explosion of the charges completed the work. The monster mortar slowly and gracefully bowed forward and fell to the ground. The gun-cotton had thoroughly done its work, at a cost of 14s. 6d. — *Scientific Review*.

PICRATES. THEIR USE AS GUN AND BLASTING POWDERS.

In 1867, Designolle, of Paris, made powder for firearms and for blasting purposes by means of picrates. Both kinds consist of a mixture of picrate and nitrate of potassa; the only difference being that the former contains in addition an admixture of charcoal. Their manufacture, as may be inferred from the accident which recently took place in Paris, appears to be carried on to a considerable extent, and the well-known chemist, Payen, in a report to the *Société d'Encouragement*, ascribes to them several advantages over the ordinary powder. He points out that various kinds of powder may be manufactured by means of them, the relative effects of which may be varied between the limits 1 : 10, namely, that, on one hand, a powder may be made, which will possess 10 times the effect of common gunpowder of equal weight; while, on the other hand, it is just as easy to prepare an explosive of the same projectile force, but of a less bursting tendency compared with ordinary powder. It is said that between these limits all desirable kinds can be made. If so, the long-sought-for problem is solved; that is, an explosive can be prepared in a charge of a certain weight, which will impart a definite velocity to a projectile from a firearm of stated dimensions.

Other advantages of the picric-acid compound are that its projectile force can be increased without enhancing its blasting force, or changing its manner of manufacture; the velocity of combustion may be regulated at will; and its ignition is not attended with the generation of disagreeable gases, as they consist simply of steam.

The manufacture of the powder from picrates proceeds as follows: The various ingredients are powdered in a stamping mill for at least 3 or at most 6 hours, under addition of 6 to 14 per cent. of water, according to their composition.   The mass is now subjected to a pressure of from 600 to 1,000 hundred weight per square inch, according to the velocity of combustion to be imparted to the powder.   The cake obtained is then granulated, polished, and dried in the ordinary manner.   The process remains the same for all kinds.

Gunpowder cannot well bear over 20 per cent. of picrate of potassa, while for cannon powder it should not exceed 15 per cent.   For the latter from 8 to 15 per cent. are taken, according to the desired velocity of combustion.   Designolle prepares also colored fire-work compositions by means of picrates, of which the following are recipes: Gold rain — 50 parts of picrate of ammonia, and 50 parts of picrate of iron; Green fire — 48 parts of picrate of ammonia, and 52 parts of nitrate of baryta; Red fire — 54 parts of picrate of ammonia, and 46 parts of nitrate of strontia. Until recently, the picrate of potassa has been very expensive, but improvements made in its mode of preparation enable the manufacturer to sell it at a price sufficiently low to ensure its application for all practical purposes.

NEW PROPERTY OF GUN-COTTON.

According to the "Chemical News," it is possible to burn gun-cotton in the palm of the hand without the least danger; a delicate balance in the pan on which gun-cotton is exploded does not swing from its poise.   The same quantity of gun-cotton, if it be pressed into a cavity, explodes with a force equal to that of nitro-glycerine, and 10 times greater than that of gunpowder, provided it be ignited by percussion in the same way as nitro-glycerine. This discovery may enable us to employ gun-cotton as a substitute for nitro-glycerine, and as the danger of freezing or of premature explosion is avoided, it may prove to have many advantages over other explosive agents.

Some recent experiments made at the Woolwich Arsenal, near London, encourage the hope that gun-cotton can be successfully used as a most destructive agent.   A palisade was built of oak timbers a foot thick, firmly fixed in the ground, and supported in the rear by strong trusses.   Discs of gun-cotton were placed along the face of the palisade about a foot above the ground, and were fired by a battery in the usual way.   The effect may be described as wonderful.   The palisade was literally blown away amid a deafening report, as if the massive timbers offered no more resistance on one side of the gun-cotton than the atmosphere on the other.   The discs require no fixing; merely laying them on is sufficient.   Solid blocks of iron and stone can be shivered into fragments by firing a disc laid on the top.   In future sieges, if some desperate fellow can but get to the gate or a thin part of the walls, and hang on a few discs of gun-cotton, a breach can be made by firing with a galvanic current from a long distance.

PHOTOGRAPHS WITH A WHITE SURFACE.

Put into a small mortar a teaspoonful of kaolin; add thereto about a quarter of an ounce of sensitive collodio-chloride, and stir well with the pestle until it becomes a smooth paste. Add to this three-fourths of an ounce more of the collodion, and again stir, and pour the whole into a bottle with one or two drops of castor-oil. Shake well, and place it aside until the coarse particles have subsided.

Edge a piece of talc or glass for about a quarter of an inch all round with dilute albumen, afterwards coat with the kaolin collodion, and dry by gentle heat, when the talc or glass, if placed upon a piece of white paper, will have the appearance of alabaster.

If the film splits, it should have a trifle more castor-oil in the collodion; but the best remedy is to choose a more powdery collodion.

If the film is upon glass, the progress of printing may be examined from the back; but if talc be the medium used, it may be turned back in the same manner as when printing upon paper.

Tone, fix, and wash in the same manner as with an ordinary collodio-chloride print upon opal glass, and mount in a frame or case, to protect the picture from being scratched. It must not be varnished.

After 3 years' trial the film has been found not to crack or leave the talc or glass after the picture has been once finished.

Many pretty effects may be produced by putting different colored papers behind vignettes produced in this way, as whatever color is placed behind the picture gives a delicate tinge of that color to the picture.

Talc may be obtained in sheets as large as 10 by 8 inches.

IMPROVED PHOTOGRAPHIC PAPER.

The "British Journal of Photography" publishes the following by W. H. Davis: "My method for preparing the surface — for I believe it will do for many other surfaces than paper — is the following for direct printing: Take from 4 to 6 grains of gelatine, soak it in an ounce of water for an hour, then melt it gently over a fire, hot plate, or water-bath, using a clean earthen pipkin. When fully dissolved, add to it, while yet warm, and stirring it gently during the mixing, from 4 to 6 drachms of a solution of white lac in methylated spirit, if for white or pale surfaces; but orange lac will do if the surface be of a darker color. This is made in the proportion of 6 ounces of spirit to one ounce of lac, and digesting it till fully dissolved. The mixture of the gelatine and gum lac in spirits produces a creamy-looking emulsion, to which is added 4 grains of chloride of sodium, or a like equivalent of chlorides of ammonium or barium, and, when fully dissolved, filter through fine muslin into a clean pipkin, and it is ready for use.

"I generally apply the solution warm with a flat camel's-hair brush, crossing it till it lies evenly. When the paper is dry it is ready for sensitizing, which may be done either by flotation on the ordinary printing-bath, or by brushing on the silver solution. I prefer to use the ammonia-nitrate solution brushed on; but there are specimens by both methods before you. I use 40 grains of silver to the ounce of water. Some of the ammonia-nitrate prints contain also a large proportion of citrate of silver in addition to the usual ammonia-nitrate.

"As you will see, the tones of many of the untoned prints are quite as fine in color as are those toned with gold, and I attribute this entirely to the variations in the salting and in the strength of the size and lac solution, and to the minute variation of the silver bath by the addition of various salts in the course of sensitizing.

THE ALBERTYPE.

A recent number of the London "Photographic News" contains a fine example of this new style of photographic pictures. The process is as follows: A plate of glass is covered with a solution of albumen, gelatine, and bichromate of potash, dried and exposed to light until hardened. It is then again covered with a solution of gelatine and bichromate of potash, and when dry exposed under the negative, and the film is then found to possess qualities analogous to a drawing made with fatty ink upon lithograph stone. All those portions of the film that were acted upon by the light will refuse water and take printing-ink, while those portions which were protected from light by the negative will take water and refuse ink. The ink and water will be absorbed by the film just in accordance with the gradations of light and shade in the negative. To produce a picture, wet the surface of the film, then apply ink, lay on paper, and pass through a press; the operation being substantially the same as lithography. The process is said to be rapid, and excellent pictures of all sizes may be printed in admirable style.

SUMMARY OF IMPROVEMENTS IN THE MECHANIC ARTS, ETC.

Photographing a Tunnel. — We have lately seen a photograph, taken by sunlight, of the interior of the tunnel which penetrates the summit of the Nevada for the distance of 1,659 feet, at an elevation of 7,042 feet above the sea level, the greatest height to which a locomotive has yet attained. The success of this picture is due to the position of this tunnel, through which, like that near Bore, on the Great Western Railway, the sun shines for a few days each year. Taking advantage of this circumstance, and also using mirrors by which light was thrown successively upon various points, this picture was produced with an exposure of 15 minutes, and shows the distant heading with perfect distinctness.

as well as the long intermediate cavern. — *Journal Franklin Institute.*

Photography and Gunnery. — During the late experiments at Fortress Monroe, photographs were taken of the target from an adjacent bomb-proof, so as to record the exact amount of damage effected by each shot.

Fuel in the Form of Powder. — Mr. Crampton's process, described in a few words, consists of an arrangement by which a portion of finely powdered coal is blown into a furnace, where, at first, a small fire has been lighted. This immediately bursts into flame, and by properly adjusting the proportions of air and coal powder, a flame is then regularly kept up, giving out an intense heat, and leaving little or no residue in the shape of clinkers or ash.

Drying of Wood. — For this purpose, the wood is kept for some hours under boiling water, whereby all its soluble parts are withdrawn. It is next left to dry, and then boiled for some time in a solution of borax, which causes the albumen to become soluble, and to escape from the pores. After this proceeding, the wood is placed in stoves heated by steam, and in 3 days has become seasoned. — *Cosmos.*

Conservation of Wood. — M. Morin states that he has in his possession wooden water-wheels which have been in use for more than 1,500 years, for the evacuation of water from a copper mine. These wheels have a diameter of 6 metres; and, on a portion of the wood being analyzed by M. Payen, it was found to be perfectly sound, and to be partly converted into a compound of cellulose and copper, precisely similar to that which is formed in Boucherie's process for the preservation of wood by sulphate of copper.

Tanned Cotton. — This is prepared by treating cotton fabrics in a similar manner to that in which skins and hides are treated for the manufacture of leather. Cotton thereby acquires greater strength, and is more enabled to resist the effects of moisture and disintegrating effects. — *Cosmos.*

Strengthening and Rendering Woven Tissues Impermeable to Water. — M. Neuman, in "Les Mondes," Sept. 16, 1869, gives this method: A sulphuric acid bath is made, containing acid varying in strength from 40° to 66° Beaumé (specific gravities 1384 and 1850,) and kept at a temperature of 57°. The woven tissues, cotton or linen, are rapidly passed through this bath, being only left in contact with the acid for from 10 seconds to two minutes, according to the nature of the tissue, which is immediately after passed through very cold water, and next submitted to a thorough washing process. The effect of the action of the acid is an incipient dissolution, and formation of a varnish-like matter, which, especially after it has been regularly spread over the fabric and incorporated therewith, by hot-pressing and calendering, greatly increase the strength of the fabric, rendering it also impervious to water.

Method of Producing upon Iron a Durable Black, Shining Varnish. — Take oil of turpentine, add to it, drop by drop, and while stirring, strong sulphuric acid, until a syrupy precipitate is quite formed, and no more of it is produced on further addition of a drop of acid. The liquid is now repeatedly washed with water, every time refreshed after a good stirring, until the water does not exhibit any more acid reaction. The precipitate is next brought upon a cloth filter, and, after all the water has run off, the syrupy mass is fit for use. This thickest magma is painted over the iron with a brush; if it happens to be too stiff, it is diluted with oil of turpentine. Immediately afterward this paint is burnt in by a gentle heat, and, after cooling, the black surface is rubbed with a piece of woollen stuff dipped in linseed oil. According to M. Weiskopf, the discoverer, the varnish is not a simple covering of the surface, but it is chemically combined with the metal, and does not wear off or peel off, as other paints and varnishes do.

Cast-iron Tubes are now made for water or gas in England, by turning off one end conically, and boring out the end of the tube to which it is to be united at the same angle, so that the end of one tube may be inserted into the other without the addition of the ordinary cement. The junction is effected very quickly, and the joint is perfectly tight. Pipes 36 inches in diameter have been perfectly joined in this way. Liverpool has about 90 miles of gas-pipe joined in this way, and the leakage is said to be much less than in other cities.

A Cement for Leather is made by mixing 10 parts of sulphide of carbon with one of oil of turpentine, and then adding enough gutta-percha to make a tough, quickly-flowing liquid. One essential prerequisite to a thorough union of the parts consists in freedom of the surfaces to be joined from grease. This may be accomplished by laying on a hot cloth, and applying a hot iron for a time; the cement is then applied to both pieces, the surfaces brought in contact, and pressure applied until the joint is dry.

Seaweed Charcoal. — This material, which is prepared from the fine tangle of the Hebrides, is being extensively used in England, as a substitute for animal charcoal, as a filtering medium for water, for deodorizing sewage, clearing white glass, removing acidity from, and decolorizing, wines, and precipitating and decolorizing vegetable alkaloids. — *Chem. News.*

Cement for Stone. — It is stated that an admirable cement is obtained by mixing infusorial silica, such as constitutes the diatoms, for instance, tripoli, with the following substances: The infusorial silica is mixed in about equal proportions with oxide of lead; about half a part of freshly slaked lime is then added, and the whole is made into a paste, with boiled linseed oil. This is especially recommended for securing iron work in marble and other stone.

Coke. — The importance of obtaining coke, free from sulphur, cannot, especially for iron manufacture, be over-estimated. Numerous experiments have, from time to time, been made, with a view to the use of coal in which some pyrites occur, in the manufacture of a pure coke for the blast furnace. Some experiments have been made in France which are stated to have been remarkably successful. The coke, when at a temperature of 300° Cent., was submitted to a strong current of atmospheric air strongly compressed. This current of air is said to convert the sulphur into sulphuric acid and remove it. The coke is reported to produce iron equal to that which has been made with wood charcoal. — *Quarterly Journal of Science, July.*

In Great Britain, the quantity of coal-dust remaining unemployed is calculated at 28,000,000 tons. Various methods have been attempted to convert it into useful fuel by compressing it into cakes, but the operation is not sufficiently remunerative. In Belgium they employ another plan which seems to answer better. They mix coal-dust with 8 per cent. of tar, and then press into cakes, which are found to make excellent fuel for steam-engines. — *Mech. Mag., July 9.*

An Explosive Dye. — The artificial saffron, invented by Mr. Millonsweg, of Poblitz, has of late been found to be as easily exploded as gunpowder, though possessing 40 per cent. less of projectile force.

Moss Rubber Inking Roller. — The editor of the "Mechanics' Magazine," London, speaks very highly, from his own experience, of the above-mentioned article, which is invented by Mr. Stephen Moulton, of Bradford-on-Avon, and prepared in the following manner: Vulcanized India-rubber is reduced to a powder, then placed in a mould, and subjected to a second vulcanizing heat, which converts it into a mossy substance. This core is now covered with skin of rubber, which is then vulcanized, and the roller is then ready for use.

Lining for Fire-Proofs. — There was exhibited, at the last meeting of the Institute, a new material, which, by its remarkable power of non-conduction, presents especial advantages. This was devised and patented by Mr. W. Alford. It consists of a rough papier maché, made of old wall paper, by moistening and compressing it. Its power of resistance to fire was illustrated by a specimen exhibited on this occasion, which had been exposed, as a lining to an iron-box, with a wooden one in the centre, to the heat of a brightly burning anthracite fire, for the space of an hour. The material was charred, on the outer surface, to the depth of about one-fourth of an inch, while all the rest, and the box, of course, within, was perfectly intact. This substance has been favorably reported upon by many of our safe-builders, and seems to be an admirable invention.

Fire Alarm, by M. Diou. — At the last meeting of the Institute, there was presented by Mr. J. Demorat, for exhibition, an improved fire-detector, manufactured by the American Fire Detector Company, 725 Broadway, New York.

This apparatus consists of two parts, one of which is placed in the location where the presence of fire is to be detected, and the other where the alarm is to be given. These are connected by wire, in the manner of ordinary bells, except that the wire is tightly stretched in its normal condition. The first instrument consists, essentially, of a catch (holding one end of the wire), controlled by a copper-helix, whose expansion will liberate the catch, and thus slack the wire. The other instrument consists of an alarm-bell, operated by clock-work, which goes into action as soon as the wire is slacked. By changing the tension of the copper-spring, the instrument may be set to go off at any temperature, indicated by a dial and pointer attached to the regulating-screw. When exhibited to the meeting, the instrument was started by holding it, for a moment, over a gas-flame, and by the mere warmth of the breath.

Steam Generators. — A novelty was exhibited, at the exhibition of the American Institute, by Thomas Mitchell, of Albany,-N. Y. It is a cylinder of wrought iron with welded joints, into which water is thrown by a feed-pump; the same pump operating through a worm gear to slowly rotate the cylinder in the furnace where it is suspended upon two journals, one at either end of the furnace. The design is to only throw water into the revolving generator, as wanted, to make steam. The steam is generated under very high pressure. The water is injected through a core-pipe in one of the journals which extends longitudinally through the axis of the cylinder, and is perforated at intervals throughout its length. The water is thus subdivided into small jets, which the heat of the cylinder converts into steam instantaneously.

A big Belt. — The New York Belting and Packing Company have lately had on exhibition at their store, New York, an India-rubber belt 4 feet wide, 320 feet long, and weighing no less than 3,600 pounds. It is intended for the main driving-belt of the largest grain elevator in Chicago.

The Joy Hammer. — This hammer is peculiarly adapted for drawing down iron or steel, in which operation a rapid succession of uniform blows is required, with only a gradual alteration in the force of the successive strokes.

It therefore becomes possible to dispense with the complication of separate valves, and thus remove much of the risk of derangement and source of wear.

In this instrument the ram contains openings which are brought by its own motion into communication with passages for the inlet and escape of steam, and thus cause its motion to be automatically reversed. The only valve in the hammer is the throttle-valve governed by a treddle, and by the adjustment of its opening both the rapidity and force of the blows is at the same time regulated. As many as 500 blows in a minute may be readily struck, and from the simplicity and solidity of all parts there is the least possible chance of derangement.

Safety Nitro-Glycerine. — We learn from the "London Mining Journal" that a series of interesting experiments for protecting nitro-glycerine were recently made at the Manorfield House. A small quantity of the material was put into a basin, and hot water was poured upon it, the result being that in two minutes the original oil sunk to the bottom, and (the surplus water being poured off) was run into a small phial ready for use. Into this the fuse (pointed with a percussion cap) was inserted, and fired, and the loud explosion testified to the unimpaired force of the nitro-glycerine thus recovered. It is obvious that by this invention this highly dangerous but very useful compound can be conveyed by rail or ship, and be stored with perfect safety, and that it may be "recovered" in small quantities on the very spot where it is required for use, so as to avoid, in a great measure, the peril to miners or others who have to handle it in their operations.

Painting Zinc. — A difficulty is often experienced in causing oil colors to adhere to sheet zinc.   Boettger recommends the employment of a mordant, so to speak, of the following composition : One part of chloride of copper, one of nitrate of copper, and one of sal-ammoniac, are to be dissolved in 64 parts of water, to which solution is to be added one part of commercial hydrochloric acid. The sheets of zinc are to be brushed over with this liquid, which gives them a deep black color ; in the course of from 12 to 24 hours they become dry, and to their now dirty gray surface a coat of any oil color will firmly adhere.   Some sheets of zinc prepared in this way, and afterwards painted, have been found to entirely withstand all the atmospheric changes of winter and summer.

Very Durable Cement for Iron and Stone. — M. Pollack, of Bautzen, Saxony, states that, for a period of several years, he has used, as a cement to fasten stone to stone, and iron to iron, a paste made of pure oxide of lead, litharge, and glycerine in concentrated state.   This mixture hardens rapidly, is insoluble in acids (unless quite concentrated), and is not affected by heat.   M. Pollack has used it to fasten different portions of a fly-wheel with great success ; while, when placed between stones, and once hardened, it is easier to break the stone than the joint.

"Dingler's Journal" recommends as a lute for covering the corks of vessels containing benzine or any of the light hydrocarbons or essential oils, a paste made of finely-ground litharge and concentrated glycerine.   The mixture is spread over the corks or bungs, and soon hardens.   It is insoluble in the said liquids, is not acted upon by them, and is quite inexpensive, as the commonest kind of glycerine can be used.

A writer in "Comptes Rendus" says that if articles made of copper be immersed in molten sulphur having lamp-black in suspension, they assume the appearance of bronze, and can be polished without losing that aspect.

Treating Textile Fabrics. — M. Pierre Armand Neuman, of St. Denis, Paris, treats textile fabrics with sulphuric acid, for the purpose of rendering them impermeable.   By this process the fibres on the surface of the fabric are partially dissolved, and converted into a glutinous substance, without the fibres in the body of the fabric being destroyed.   The fabric, after being passed through the sulphuric acid, is quickly washed and rinsed in water, to stop the action of the acid, and remove all traces of it, and it is afterwards dried, when the part which has been acted on by the acid, having impregnated and coated the fibres of the fabric, and filled up the interstices between the warp and the weft, will convert it into a parchment-like and impermeable material.

Effect of Steam Heat on Hay. — A correspondent from Rancocas, N. J., favors us with a specimen of hay-wrapping which had been on a steam pipe for 9 years ; the pipe carrying steam at 55 lbs. The specimen is of a chocolate brown and very friable ; but it burns no more readily than well-dried fresh hay, although its appearance would seem to indicate great combustibility. We should have less fear of its ignition than of pine wood similarly carbonized. — *Scientific American.*

The Hydraulic Scraping of the Torquay Water Main. — Mr. R. E. Froude, at the meeting of the British Association, read a paper on the operations which were rendered necessary by the continually decreasing supply of water, which resulted in raising the supply from 320 gallons, in 1864, to 564 gallons per minute in 1867, to 634 gallons in 1868, and to 660 gallons in 1869. The plan adopted was that of passing through the main a piston, armed with a scraper.

Average Duty of Cornish Engines. — An estimate of the average duty of this class of engines, based on observations made upon 18 engines during one month, shows the following results: They have consumed 1,377 tons of coal, and lifted 10.2 million tons of water 10 fathoms high. The average duty of the whole is, therefore, 50,100,000 lbs., lifted one foot high, by the consumption of 112 lbs. of coal.

Aluminium Bells. — It appears that some Belgian manufacturer has just had a bell cast of aluminium, and with good results. It is of course extremely light, so that, though large, it can be easily tolled; its tone is reported to be loud and of excellent pitch. Aluminium is the most sonorous of all metals. — *Engineer.*

A new Alloy, forming a beautiful white metal, very hard and capable of taking a brilliant polish, is obtained by melting together about 70 parts of copper, 20 of nickel, 5½ of zinc, and 4½ of cadmium. It is, therefore, a kind of German silver, in which part of the zinc is replaced by cadmium. This alloy has been recently made in Paris for the manufacture of spoons and forks, which resemble articles of silver.

How Oroide is Made. — Oroide, the beautiful alloy resembling gold, is a French discovery, and consists of pure copper, 100 parts; zinc or (preferably) tin, 17 parts; magnesia, 6 parts; sal-ammoniac one half part; quicklime, one-eighth part; tartar of commerce, 9 parts. The copper is first melted, then the magnesia, sal-ammoniac, lime, and tartar in powder are added little by little, briskly stirring for about half an hour, so as to mix thoroughly; after which zinc is thrown on the surface in small grains, stirring it until entirely fused. The crucible is then covered, and the fusion maintained about 35 minutes, when the dross is skimmed off, and the alloy is ready for use. It can be cast, rolled, drawn, stamped, chased, beaten into a powder or leaves; and none but excellent judges can distinguish it from gold.

S. T. Clements, D.D.S., writes to the "Dental Cosmos" that although wax and resin, shellac, varnish, and liquid silex are recommended for mending plaster models, neither, in his experience, can compare with sandarac varnish. Saturate the broken surfaces thoroughly, and press them well together. Allow it to dry, and the model will stand all the manipulation required.

Safety Envelopes. — It is stated that the thick, tough sap, found in large quantities in the leaves of New Zealand flax, may be converted into a gum for sealing envelopes, which, when dry, unites the surfaces of paper so thoroughly that no process of steaming or soaking will permit them to be separated again. For this reason, it is now being used in large quantities in England, in the preparation of what are called " safely envelopes."

Paper from Shavings and Sawdust. — Dr. Matthiessen, a well-known *savant*, now appears in the character of an inventor and patentee in England of an important improvement. He submits wood when in a state of division, such as shavings, sawdust, or disintegrated wood, to what is known as a rotting process, — that is to say, the wood in a state of division is steeped either in running or stagnant water, and is allowed to undergo a rotting or fermenting process, by which process certain constituents of the wood will be decomposed and removed, and the subsequent treatment of the residual ligneous fibre for the production of pulp or paper will be thereby rendered more economical, and the process of boiling and bleaching is more easily effected.

Ineradicable Writing. — A French technical paper, specially devoted to the art and science of paper manufacture, states that any alterations or falsifications of writings in ordinary ink may be rendered impossible by passing the paper upon which it is intended to write through a solution of one milligram (0.01543 English grain) of gallic acid in as much pure distilled water as will fill to a moderate depth an ordinary soup-plate. After the paper thus prepared has become thoroughly dry, it may be used as ordinary paper for writing, but any attempt made to alter, falsify, or change anything written thereon, will be left perfectly visible, and may thus be readily detected.

How to make Paper Transparent. — Artists, architects, land surveyors, and all who have occasion to make use of tracing-paper in their professional duties, will be glad to know that any paper capable of the transfer of a drawing in ordinary ink, pencil, or water-colors, and that even a stout drawing-paper, can be made as transparent as the thin yellowish paper at present used for tracing purposes. The liquid used is benzine. If the paper be damped with pure and fresh-distilled benzine it at once assumes a transparency, and permits of the tracing being made, and of ink or water-colors being used on its surface without any " running." The paper resumes its opacity as the benzine evaporates, and if the drawing is not then completed, the requisite portion of the paper must be again damped with the benzine. The transparent calico, on which indestructible tracings can be made, was a most valuable invention, and this new discovery of the properties of benzine will prove of further service to many branches of the art profession, in allowing the use of stiff paper where formerly only a slight tissue could be used.

NATURAL PHILOSOPHY.

TYNDALL'S DISCOVERY.

"IT consists," to use his own words, "in subjecting the vapors of volatile liquids to the action of concentrated sunlight, or to the concentrated beam of the electric light;" and some of the results which he records are of such singular, almost inconceivable, beauty, that for this reason alone, and putting aside their important application to many atmospheric phenomena, and probably to art, they have a claim to be noticed in these pages.

He uses the *experimental tube.* It is connected with an air-pump and with a series of tubes used for the purification of the air, and at one end of the tube, which lies horizontally and is closed by plates of glass, is placed an electric lamp, so arranged that the axis of the tube and that of the parallel beam issuing from the lamp are coincident.

The substances whose vapors were passed into the tube, and there exposed to strong light, are known to chemists as nitrite of amyl, iodide of allyl, iodide of isopropyl, hydrobromic acid, hydrochloric acid, hydriodic acid. When these vapors are exposed to the above-described action, clouds of the most beautiful appearance, and at some points vividly iridescent, show themselves in the tube. When the nitrite of amyl vapor is mixed with a little air the cloud is white; but if air is freely admitted, and the nitrite vapor thus attenuated, the cloud varies in color from a milky-blue to a pure, deep blue. "There could scarcely," says the author, "be a more impressive illustration of Newton's mode of regarding the generation of the color of the firmament than that here exhibited; for never, even in the skies of the Alps, have I seen a richer or a purer blue than that attainable by a suitable disposition of the light falling upon the precipitated vapor. May not the aqueous vapor of our atmosphere act in a similar manner?"

The cloud yielded by iodide of allyl was extremely beautiful. The whole column revolved round the axis of the decomposing central beam, and was nipped so as to have an hour-glass appearance, while round the gobular dilatations delicate cloud-filaments twisted themselves in spirals. It also folded itself into convolutions resembling those of shells. When hydrogen is made the vehicle of this vapor, the cloud assumes a pearly lustre, such as Dr. Tyndall has often noticed in certain conditions of the atmosphere in the Alps.

The action of light upon the vapor of iodide of isopropyl occasions in the course of a few minutes some singularly graceful developments. The column of cloud is seen to divide into two parts near the middle of the tube, and in one experiment a globe of cloud formed at the centre with axes projecting right and left. Sudden commotions were observed in the nebulous mass, buds of cloud shooting out and growing into flower-like forms. In one case the cloud-bud grew rapidly into a serpent's head; a mouth was formed, and from the mouth a cord of cloud, resembling a tongue, was rapidly discharged.

The aqueous vapor of hydrobromic acid mixed with air gave rise to the formation of two clouds 5 inches apart, and united by a slender cord of cloud of the same bluish tint as themselves. After undergoing various modifications of form, both clouds presented the appearance of a series of concentric funnels set within one another, the interior ones being seen through the gaseous walls of the outer ones. As many as 6 of these concentric funnels were observed.

The aqueous solution of hydrochloric acid yields a vapor which required an exposure of 15 or 20 minutes to the electric light for the production of a fully developed cloud. It was then divided into several sections, united to each other by a slender axis. "Each of these sections," says Dr. Tyndall, "possessed an exceedingly complex and ornate structure, exhibiting ribs, spears, funnels, leaves, involved scrolls, and tridescent *fleurs-de-lis.* Thus the structure of the cloud from beginning to end was perfectly symmetrical; it was a cloud of revolution, its corresponding points being at equal distances from the axis of the beam."

The aqueous vapor of hydriodic acid yields a nebula which so far resembles those of the two preceding acids that the process commences by the formation of two small clouds united by a cord; but it exhibits more vivid colors (green and crimson) than the other vapors. Of the various substances experimented on, none gave such astonishing results as this. "The development of the cloud," says Dr. Tyndall, "was like that of an organism, from a more or less formless mass at the commencement, to a structure of marvellous complexity;" and this grand simile is fully borne out by his description of the changing phenomena which he observed. After a time the cloud formed into a spectral cone with a circular base, from which filmy drapery seemed to descend. On this base was an exquisite vase, with a vase of similar shape in its interior, and from the edges of the vases fell the faintest clouds. The anterior portion of the cloud assumed in succession the forms of roses, tulips, and sunflowers; it also presented the appearance of a series of beautifully shaped bottles placed (like the funnels in a previous case) one within the other; and once it positively assumed the form of a fish, with eyes, gills, and feelers. "The *twoness* of the animal form," says the observer, "was displayed throughout, and no disc, coil, or speck existed on one side that did not exist on the other." For nearly two hours Dr. Tyndall looked in wonder at the extraordinary vision which his magic skill had evoked.

These experiments are capable of almost any degree of modification and extension. They have already revealed to us a new

12*

world abounding in images of almost inconceivable beauty; but it is very probable that they have more than an æsthetic value. The assistants who watched the phenomena with the professor, and whose minds were probably of a more practical cast, remarked that these reactions " would prove exceedingly valuable to pattern-designers; " and if artistic skill can seize these fleeting phantoms there is no reason why this idea should not be carried out.

The chemical reactions which occur in these experiments are only slightly noticed, and do not admit of a popular explanation; it is, however, in the highest degree probable that future chemists will make this form of experiment a potent auxiliary to the laboratory, while future meteorologists will find in it the true explanation of various atmospheric phenomena which as yet remain in more or less obscurity.

THE BLUE COLOR OF THE SKY, ETC.   BY PROF. TYNDALL.

The idea that the color of the sky is due to the action of finely divided matter, rendering the atmosphere a turbid medium through which we look at the darkness of space, dates as far back as Leonardo da Vinci. Newton conceived the color to be due to exceedingly small water particles acting as thin plates. Goethe's experiments in connection with this subject are well known and exceedingly instructive. One very striking observation of Goethe's referred to what is technically called " chill " by painters, which is due, no doubt, to extremely fine varnish particles interposed between the eye and a dark background. Clausius, in two very able memoirs, endeavored to connect the colors of the sky with suspended water-vesicles, and to show that the important observations of Forbes on condensing steam could also be thus accounted for. Helmholtz has ascribed the blueness of the eyes to the action of suspended particles. In an article written nearly 9 years ago by myself, the colors of the peat smoke of the cabins of Killarney and the colors of the sky were referred to one and the same cause, while a chapter of the " Glaciers of the Alps," published in 1860, is also devoted to this question. Roscoe, in connection with his truly beautiful experiments on the photographic power of sky-light, has also given various instances of the production of color by suspended particles.

In his experiments on fluorescence, Prof. Stokes had continually to separate the light reflected from the motes suspended in his liquids, the action of which he named " false dispersion," from the fluorescent light of the same liquids, which he ascribed to " true dispersion." In fact, it is hardly possible to obtain a liquid without motes, which polarize by reflection the light falling upon them, truly dispersed light being unpolarized. At p. 530, of his celebrated memoir, " On the Change of the Refrangibility of Light," Prof. Stokes adduces some significant facts, and makes some noteworthy remarks, which bear upon our present subject. He notices more particularly a specimen of plate glass which, seen by reflected light, exhibited a blue which was exceedingly like an effect of fluorescence, but which, when properly examined, was found to be an instance of false dispersion.

"It often struck me," he writes, while engaged in these observations, "that when the beam had a continuous appearance, the polarization was more nearly perfect than when it was sparkling, so as to force on the mind the conviction that it arose merely from motes. Indeed, in the former case, the polarization has often appeared perfect, or all but perfect. It is possible that this may, in some measure, have been due to the circumstance, that when a given quantity of light is diminished in a given ratio, the illumination is perceived with more difficulty when the light is diffused uniformly than when it is spread over the same space but collected into specks. Be this as it may, there was at least no tendency observed toward polarization in a plane perpendicular to the plane of reflection, when the suspended particles became finer, and therefore the beam more nearly continuous. Through the courtesy of its owner I have been permitted to see and to experiment with the piece of plate-glass above referred to. Placed in front of the electric-lamp, whether edgeways or transversely, it discharges bluish polarized light laterally, the color being by no means a bad imitation of the color of the sky. Prof. Stokes considers that this deportment may be invoked to decide the question of the direction of the vibrations of polarized light. On this point I would say, if it can be demonstrated that when the particles are small in comparison to the length of a wave of light, the vibrations of a ray reflected by such particles cannot be perpendicular to the vibrations of the incident light; then assuredly the experiments recorded in the foregoing communication decide the question in favor of Fresnel's assumption. As stated above, almost all liquids have motes in them sufficiently numerous to polarize sensibly the light, and very beautiful effects may be obtained by simple artificial devices. When, for example, a cell of distilled water is placed in front of the electric lamp, and a slice of the beam permitted to pass through it, scarcely any polarized light is discharged, and scarcely any color produced with a plate of selenite. But while the beam is passing through it, if a bit of soap be agitated in the water above the beam, the moment the infinitesimal particles reach the beam the liquid sends forth laterally almost perfectly polarized light; and if the selenite be employed, vivid colors flash into existence. A still more brilliant result is obtained with mastic dissolved in a great excess of alcohol. The selenite rings constitute an extremely delicate test as to the quantity of motes in a liquid. Commencing with distilled water, for example, a thickish beam of light is necessary to make the polarization of its motes sensible. A much thinner beam suffices for common water; while with Brücke's precipitated mastic, a beam too thin to produce any sensible effect with most other liquids suffices to bring out vividly the selenite colors.

Note on the Formation and Phenomena of Clouds. — It is well known that when a receiver filled with ordinary undried air is exhausted, a cloudiness, due to the precipitation of the aqueous vapor diffused in the air, is produced by the first few strokes of the pump. It is, as might be expected, possible to produce clouds in this way with the vapors of other liquids than water. In the course of the experiments on the chemical action of light which have been already communicated in abstract to the Royal Society, I had frequent occasion to observe the precipitation of such clouds in the experimental tubes employed; indeed several days at a time have been devoted solely to the generation and examination of clouds formed by the sudden dilatation of the air in the experimental tubes. The clouds were generated in two ways: one mode consisted in opening the passage between the filled experimental tube and the air-pump, and then simply dilating the air by working the pump. In the other, the experimental tube was connected with a vessel of suitable size, the passage between which and the experimental tube could be closed by a stopcock. This vessel was first exhausted; on turning the cock the air rushed from the experimental tube into the vessel, the precipitation of a cloud within the tube being a consequence of the transfer. Instead of a special vessel, the cylinders of the air-pump itself were usually employed for this purpose. It was found possible, by shutting off the residue of air and vapor after each act of precipitation, and again exhausting the cylinders of the pump, to obtain with some substances, and without refilling the experimental tube, 15 or 20 clouds in succession. The clouds thus precipitated differed from each other in luminous energy, some shedding forth a mild white light, others flashing out with sudden and surprising brilliancy. This difference of action is, of course, to be referred to the different reflective energies of the particles of the clouds, which were produced by substances of very different refractive indices. Different clouds, moreover, possess very different degrees of stability; some melt away rapidly, while others linger for minutes in the experimental tube, resting upon its bottom as they dissolve like a heap of snow. The particles of other clouds are trailed through the experimental tube as if they were moving through a viscous medium. Nothing can exceed the splendor of the diffraction phenomena exhibited by some of these clouds; the colors are best seen by looking along the experimental tube from a point above it, the face being turned towards the source of illumination. The differential motions introduced by friction against the interior surface of the tube often cause the colors to arrange themselves in distinct layers. The difference in texture exhibited by different clouds caused me to look a little more closely than I had previously done into the mechanism of cloud-formation. A certain expansion is necessary to bring down the cloud; the moment before precipitation the mass of cooling air and vapor may be regarded as divided into a number of polyhedra, the particles along the bounding surfaces of which move in opposite directions when precipitation actually sets in. Every cloud particle has consumed a polyhedron of vapor in its formation; and it is manifest that the size of the particle must depend, not only on the size of the vapor-polyhedron, but also on the relation of the density of the vapor to that of its liquid. If the vapor were light, and the liquid heavy, other things being equal, the cloud-particle would be smaller than if the vapor were heavy and the liquid light. There would evidently be more shrinkage in the one case than in the other; these considerations were found valid throughout the experiment. The case of toluol may be taken as representative of a great number of others. The specific gravity of this liquid is 0.85, that of water being unity; the specific gravity of its vapor is 3.26, that of aqueous vapor being 0.6. Now, as the size of the cloud-particle is directly proportional to the specific gravity of the vapor, and inversely proportional to the specific gravity of the liquid, an easy calculation proves that, assuming the size of the vapor polyhedra in both cases to be the same, the size of the particle of toluol cloud must be more than 6 times that of the particle of aqueous cloud. It is probably impossible to test this question with numerical accuracy; but the comparative coarseness of the toluol cloud is strikingly manifest to the naked eye. The case is, as I have said, representative. In fact, aqueous vapor is without a parallel in these particulars; it is not only the lightest of all vapors, in the common acceptation of that term, but the lightest of all gases except hydrogen and ammonia. To this circumstance the soft and tender beauty of the clouds of our atmosphere is mainly to be ascribed. The *sphericity* of the cloud-particles may be immediately inferred from their deportment under the luminous beams. The light which they shed when spherical is *continuous;* but clouds may also be precipitated in solid flakes; and then the incessant sparkling of the cloud shows that its particles are *plates,* and not spheres. Some portions of the same cloud may be composed of spherical particles, others of flakes, the difference being at once manifested through the *calmness* of the one portion of the cloud, and the *uneasiness* of the other. The appearance of such flakes reminded me of the plates of mica in the River Rhone at its entrance into the Lake of Geneva, when shone upon by a strong sun. — *American Journal of Science and Arts, Sept.,* 1869.

ZIRCONIA LIGHT.

The news spread in England, through the medium of the scientific newspapers, that a discovery had been made in France, which would have the effect of abolishing the lime light by substituting zirconia for the lime cylinder. The advantages were stated to be that zirconia is not eaten away by the oxyhydrogen flame, and that, when not in use, it does not absorb moisture and crumble to pieces like lime; also, that, in consequence of this stability, the ordinary clock-work of oxyhydrogen lamps to turn the lime cylinder would be unnecessary with zirconia. It was further said, that the zirconia gave more light than lime under the same oxyhydrogen flame. Considerable interest in the new invention was, consequently, raised in this country, among the many who use the lime light, but weeks passsd away without anybody being able to procure the zirconia cylinders in London. One night, however, at a soiree at King's College, the zirconia light was exhibited, burning with great steadiness and brilliancy, in the presence of Professor W. Allen Miller, F.R.S., and many others, but no accurate tests were made, and both then and afterwards the zirconia cylinders were as unprocurable in London as ever. Three weeks since, however, one of the first zirconia lamps procurable for examination, in this country, reached London, and was sent by Mr. R. J. Fowler, the Parisian correspondent of the "British Journal of Photography," to Mr. John Traill Taylor, the editor of that journal, with the request that he and Mr. W. H. Harrison would test its working qualities. The lamp was the property of Messrs. Harvey, Reynolds, & Co., Leeds. Accordingly, some experiments with the lamp were tried at the workshops of Messrs. Darker Brothers, philosophical instrument manufacturers, at Lambeth.

At present, the French company refuses to sell the zirconia cylinders without their lamp be also purchased. According to the "Engineer," this lamp, made for special use with the zirconia, gives a vertical flame, and the piece of zirconia is held in it by a little brass support. The piece of zirconia was excessively small, — about as big as a pea, — and here at once was a source of great loss of light, because the flame was competent to raise to whiteness several times the area presented to its action. On this account alone, the total amount of light was very much less than the same flame gave with a lime cylinder, so as to put competition between the two out of the question, unless the zirconia surface be very greatly increased in size. The experimentalists then cut down a piece of lime till it equalled the zirconia in size, and the lime and zirconia were exposed in turn to the flame, the result being that the zirconia was found to emit a less white and brilliant light than the lime under the same conditions, nor did variations in distance from the nozzle of the jet alter this result. Next, many variations in the pressure of the gases were tried, but the result was not altered. Then, substituting an English "blow-through" jet for the blow-pipe sold by the French company, the same inferiority of the light from the zirconia was perceptible, nor did variations of pressure affect the result. Lastly, a good orthodox oxyhydrogen blow-pipe was tried, wherein the two gases mix thoroughly some little distance behind the nozzle, and again the results were the same. These conclusions do not in any way affect the question of the permanency of zirconia under the fierce heat of the oxyhydrogen flame; but such permanency, if purchased at the expense of inferior light, is too dearly bought, and will condemn the invention. Unless the inventors are acquainted with some peculiarities of zirconia unknown to those who are versed in the use of the lime light, and can, by an unknown method, bring out a light from the zirconia equal to that given by lime, the zirconia light, from an economical point of view, is a failure.

A few other experiments were tried, showing that soft lime and hard lime have to be placed at different distances from the blow-pipe nozzle to get the maximum amount of light from each. Chemical composition even more than hardness varies the amount of whiteness of the light. Magnesia cylinders were found to take a longer time to heat to whiteness and a longer time to cool than either lime or zirconia. Quartz rapidly vitrified under the flame, and asbestos could not resist the intense heat. It requires time, and repeated heatings and coolings, to test the permanency of zirconia under the oxyhydrogen flame to ascertain whether it does away with the necessity for clock-work apparatus. The piece used looked, at the close of the experiments, none the worse for the operations it had undergone, and a native zircon crystal, which, on previous occasions, Messrs. Darker had occasionally ignited under the oxyhydrogen blow-pipe, is now as hard as ever, having shown no tendency to crumble, or soften, like lime, beneath atmospheric influences. The heat had produced in it traces of vitrification, which could be seen only by the aid of a lens.

MAGNESIA BLOCKS FOR THE LIME LIGHT.

They are square prisms of about three-quarters inch base, and five-eighths inch in height, of remarkably even texture, and notable density. Notwithstanding all that has been said in their praise, they do not prove on trial to be by any means equal in powers of resistance (when submitted to the oxyhydrogen flame) to the average quality of lime. With a pressure of about 3 inches of water at the jet, they are rapidly eaten away, and, moreover, split by action of the heat. It is just possible that these specimens have suffered some deterioration in their transit across the ocean, though, considering their method of packing and the properties of the material, this is hardly probable.

Then one undoubted advantage seems to be their security from injury on exposure to the air. In this respect, they have a marked advantage over lime. Except, however, where exceedingly low pressures are employed, their rapid destruction before the jet more than compensates for the other advantage.

THE ACTION OF LIGHT UPON VAPORS.

This was a valuable paper by Professor A. Morren, read in English by Mr. R. B. Hayward, M.A., at the meeting of the British Association, "On the Chemical Reaction of Light, discovered by Professor Tyndall." Professor Morren said that he had repeated Dr. Tyndall's celebrated experiments on the action of light upon vapors in tubes, but that, living in the South of France, he used the rays of the sun, instead of the light from the electric lamp. His tubes, like those of Dr. Tyndall, were of glass, with flat glass ends, and glass stopcocks. After exhausting the air from the tube, he permitted a mixture of absolutely pure dry hydrogen and nitrogen gas to enter, and, on passing a cone of sunlight from a lens through the long axis of the tube, he was surprised to see a cloud forming, because of chemical decomposition set up. At first he thought that the resinous cement fastening the brass ferules to the ends of the glass tube had liberated some volatile hydro-carbon, such as turpentine, and so introduced foreign elements into the experiment. He consequently substituted for the tube a long, narrow measuring glass, with a foot, and a wide circular mouth, ground flat. Over the flat mouth he cemented a flat plate of glass, by means of a mixture of oil, wax, and tallow. A glass stopcock was let into the side of the tube. Still, with the dry hydrogen and nitrogen, he obtained cloudy decomposition under the action of sunlight. This led him to question the method employed to dry the gases, which was by passing them through powdered glass wetted with sulphuric acid. When the chloride of calcium and other methods of drying gases were tried, no clouds were formed by the sunlight, so at last he came to the conclusion that the source of error lay in a trace of sulphurous-acid gas, taken up by the hydrogen and the nitrogen from the sulphuric acid. The latter acid employed by him was absolutely pure, and contained no trace of arsenic from the use of impure sulphur in its manufacture. In the remainder of his paper he explained the exact nature of the chemical reactions which took place in his tube, which reactions he, like Dr. Tyndall, ascribed to a motion of separation set up between the atoms of each molecule, by the short blue and violet waves of the solar spectrum. Dr. J. H. Gladstone, F.R.S., spoke highly of the philosophical character of the paper, and said that such researches promised ere long to explain what action sunlight has upon gases and vapors which are often present as impurities in the atmosphere.

ROCK-SALT PRISMS.

Mr. C. Brooke, F.R.S., said at the meeting of the British Association that, in his attempts to grind and polish rock-salt prisms in planes not parallel to the lines of cleavage of the crystal, he found that the partly ground prisms usually cracked and broke at the thinnest end. He and Mr. Browning, the optician, consequently tried the plan of slowly heating the rock salt buried in sand in a tin vessel, and then permitted the whole to cool very slowly. After this annealing had been performed, it was possible to grind the rock-salt into good prisms.

TWILIGHT, AND THE UNEQUAL EFFECT OF LIGHT IN PHOTOGRAPHY.

1. *Cause of the unequal Visibility of the Colors in the Twilight.* — The visibility of the colors of a picture imply ethereal waves, excited by their vibrations, and which transmit themselves to the retina. But these vibrations of the colors want themselves to be

excited by a light enclosing rays in their keeping. In this respect, the white light can alone render visible the proper color of the whole body, because each one finds there rays capable of exciting its vibrations. From thence if, in a studio receiving the light from above, the red, orange, and yellow of a picture appear obscure and black in the twilight, apparently the faint crepuscular light of the raised part of the heavens does not send rays vibrating in unison with these colors; and if, on the contrary, the violet, blue, and green are bright, it is because some rays in unison with them have penetrated into the studio. Or, indeed, at sunset, the elevated region of the heavens furnish, according to Father Secchi, a shortened atmospheric spectrum, destitute of red, orange, and yellow, and enclosing only green, blue, and violet, doubtless because the atmospheric prism refracts only towards the earth rays of the greatest refrangibility. From thence, as the frangibility of the rays augment with the rapidity of their vibration, the absence of the red, orange, and yellow rays, in the zenith crepuscular spectrum, is due to the insufficient vibratory rapidity of these rays. On the contrary, the green, blue, and violet rays owe their presence in the zenith crepuscular spectrum to their greater refrangibility due to their greater vibratory rapidity.

2. *Cause of the Unequal Photographic Work of the Colors.* — The photographer transfers in black, the red, orange, and yellow of a picture, and in milky-white the blue, indigo, and violet. It is the same with the photographs after nature. Now these infidelities result necessarily from the unequal photographic work of the colors, for the pictures of monochromatic objects, of edifices, statues, in gray, are perfectly faithful. In a monochromatic painting, the luminous vibrations are all in unison, and have the same amplitude under the same bright light. Now the efficient work corresponding to the photographic impression represents, for every part of the picture, an even amount of quick vibratory forces absorbed. From thence the duration of the work will be reciprocal to the sensibility of the photographic retina, and, with equal sensibility, this duration will be reciprocal to the amplitude of the vibrations, or to the intensity of the light; in short, in equal intensity with the light, the duration of the efficient work will be reciprocal to the rapidity of the vibrations, and, in consequence, to the refrangibility of the gray color, for it must be operated by the same number of vibrations for each color, if all have the same vibratory amplitude. Thence, the more rapid vibrations of the more refrangible colors achieve their efficacious work in a less time than the slower vibration of the less refrangible colors; and they cannot impose, with impunity, the same duration to the photographic work of all the colors. For if this duration was regular upon the middle color of the spectrum, or upon the efficacious work of the green, the vibrations of which are more rapid than those of the yellow, orange, and red, these last colors, not having been able to achieve their efficacious work, will be obscured with black in their positive image; on the contrary, the more rapid vibrations of the blue, indigo, and violet, finish their efficacious work before the green, their excessive vibrations will have swept

13

off the image, and carried away its plainness. Thus the slowness of the vibrations of the red, orange, and yellow is the cause of their obscurity, in photography as in the crepuscule light, and the greater rapidity of the vibrations of the blue, indigo, and violet is the cause of their milky or cloudy appearance, as well in photography as in the glimmer of the *crepuscule.* — *Comptes Rendus, July* 26, 1869.

A NEW POLARIZING PRISM.

It is a trough, parallelopipedon in form, of glass filled with sulphuret of carbon, and in which is placed, with a suitable inclination, a very thin plate of spar. All natural luminous rays tend to decompose in the spar into two rays, — the one ordinary, and the other extraordinary; but as the index of this last ray is inferior to that of the sulphuret of carbon, it is totally reflected, and the ordinary ray alone traverses the trough, and is polarized in the plane of incidence. This apparatus replaces successfully the prism of Nicol in all its uses; and as it requires only a very thin plate of spar, it is cheap, and affords a wide field of vision. — *M. Jamin.* — *Comptes Rendus, Feb.* 1, 1869.

COMPLEMENTARY COLORS.

Complementary colors, by reflected and transmitted light, are admirably shown by a simple arrangement, to which attention has been called by Prof. E. C. Pickering, of Boston. A plate of glass is coated with a layer of the violet-colored ink, made from aniline color, now much used, and this fluid is allowed to dry upon it. If we then place this in such a position that light is reflected from its surface to our eyes it will appear of a metallic golden color, as though coated with a gold bronze; but if we look through it at the light, the color will be a very rich purple. There are many other bodies having a similar action, but in none that we know of is it so striking as in this.

Thus, glass flashed with silver has a green color by reflected, and an orange-red by transmitted light. Salts of the sesquioxide of chromium, which are green by reflected, are red by transmitted light; a solution of ordinary litmus is blue by reflected, but red by transmitted light. — *Journal of the Franklin Institute, April,* 1869.

ABSORPTION LINES PRODUCED BY THE PASSAGE OF THE SOLAR LIGHT THROUGH CHLORINE.

Morren has found that by employing a spectroscope of 5 prisms of highly dispersive flint-glass, absorption lines are distinctly visible in the spectrum of light which has traversed a tube filled with chlorine two metres in length. The lines begin to be visible in the part of the spectrum near *b*. They vary in intensity, fineness, and mode of grouping, and exhibit some slight free spaces. They have no regular order, and extend beyond the ray F toward the ray 2,110 of Kirchhoff's scale. In this last portion they are very numerous and almost equidistant. The solar spectrum proper continues visible as far as 2,210, but after that the light is completely absorbed. Chlorine, therefore, absorbs the colored portion of the spectrum, where the chemical rays are most abundant.

SOME PHENOMENA OF DECOMPOSITION PRODUCED BY LIGHT.

M. Morren, in the "Comptes Rendus," of Aug. 9, 1869, in referring to Tyndall's late researches on the vapors of different bodies submitted to light, says: —

"If a body forms and maintains itself in certain undulatory conditions, it is necessary that the oscillations of the atoms which constitute its molecule should be different from those of the medium where the body has been produced. But if the body is transported into another medium, where vibrations synchronous with those of its atoms are produced, the vibrations of these last become more energetic, and the live force, which they accumulate, thus becoming considerable, the atoms are thrown to a distance from each other greater than the radius of their sphere of action. The atomic edifice, previously formed, is demolished; the atoms preserving their special attractions for a new edifice, possible in the conditions of oscillation which surround them, consequently not possessing longer the same synchronous oscillation as those of the medium."

We refer the reader to the "Comptes Rendus," of Aug. 9, 1869, for a more extended exposition by M. Morren; he says, in addition, that the acid-sulphate of quinine placed between two plates of glass, and of a thickness of from 4 to 5 millimetres, affords an admirable screen for cutting off chemical rays, and can replace advantageously the yellow glass of the photographer.

A NEW THERMO-ELECTRIC PILE.

This apparatus is formed of 60 elements; these elements are composed of little bars of galena, or sulphuret of lead (*sulphure natural de plomb*), and some plates of sheet iron; the bars are 40 millimetres in length, and 8 in thickness; the plates of iron 55 millimetres in length to 8 in breadth, and 6mm. in thickness. In these couples the galena is the electro-negative element, the iron the electro-positive. The form of the bars is such, that in placing them side by side they form a crown of 12 couples, the interior of which is formed by the extremities, which are heated. The couples are united in tension by a soldering of tin. They are isolated from one another by some thin plates of mica. In superposing upon each other 5 of these crowns, one forms a battery of 60 couples.   These crowns are isolated, and spaced between by washers of amianthus, the whole is strongly bound, by means of 8 iron pins, between two circles of iron.   The piles constitute then a hollow cylinder, the interior of which it is necessary to heat. The cooling of the junctions, the temperature of which ought to be very low, is effected by simple radiation in the air.   The interior cylinder measures 50 millimetres in diameter to as much in height; the heated surface is, therefore, 78 square centimetres.

The apparatus is heated by gas, by means of a special burner, which is, properly speaking, only an iron cylinder of 56 millimetres in diameter, closed at the top, opened at the base, and pierced by little holes upon its convex surface.   This cylinder is placed in the centre of the pile.   A pipe, pierced with little holes, surrounds this cylinder, and distributes the gas in a uniform manner around it.

The gas, arriving opposite the holes of the burner, meets the air, which is blown out by the draught from the iron pipe which surmounts the apparatus.   Each hole of the burner accordingly forms a blow-pipe, the flame-point of which strikes the opposite side.

Forty couples of galena and iron have an electro-motive force neighboring that of a Bunsen element.   The apparatus that we have described then possesses a force equivalent to one and a half that of a Bunsen element.   Between the two electrodes quite visible sparks are obtained.   The current reddens a platinum thread of 3mm. in diameter at a distance of 35 millimetres; it decomposes water.

This pile working during 6 consecutive hours consumed 785 litres of gas, at a cost of nearly two centimes and a half per hour.

M. Edm. Becquerel, in some observations on the above pile, says: "The results obtained with the preceding pile, the dimensions of which are restrained, which offers some interest in a scientific point of view, and which is of easy use, show that the thermo-electric piles are not yet so economic as one supposes. It is true that the heat produced by the burner can be better utilized by putting a greater number of elements around the chimney; but, in this condition, as happens with the other thermo-electric piles, the portion of the heat which is utilized in the production of the thermo-electric current is only a small fraction of that which is communicated to the elements.   The greater part of the heat is lost by radiation. — *Comptes Rendus*, May 31, 1869.

ACTION OF HEAT UPON THE ELECTROMOTIVE FORCE OF PILES.

Heat exercises a very variable influence upon the electromotive force of piles.

The results of the researches of M. Crova are: —

1. That the electromotive force of the elements of the first kind (the Daniell type) diminishes regularly when the temperature rises.

2. That that of the elements of the second kind (the Grove type) augments with the temperature.

3. That that of the Smée type is independent of the variations of temperature. In order to verify these results, it suffices to oppose pole to pole two elements quite identical, and to place in the circuit a galvanometer, the needle of which points to zero. By heating one of the elements with suitable precautions, the needle will deviate in a permanent manner, in a sense which varies with the nature of the element. — *Comptes Rendus, Feb.* 22, 1869.

DURATION OF ELECTRIC DISCHARGES.

In the last number of "Silliman's Journal" we notice an admirable paper by Prof. O. N. Rood on the above subject. His apparatus, in general arrangement, resembled that used by Wheatstone in his remarkable experiments for determining the velocity of electric conduction, which were, no doubt, the basis of all similar processes for the measurement of extremely small intervals of time which have been since devised. The improvement introduced by Prof. Rood consists chiefly in throwing the image of the spark elongated by the rotating mirror, by means of a lens, on a plate of ground or polished glass, and viewing it with a magnifying lens. There were, besides, various ingenious devices in the details of structure and arrangement, such as have distinguished other investigations of this eminent physicist. As a result of various experiments, Prof. Rood finds, in the first place, that the discharge from a Leyden jar charged by an induction coil is composed of three parts or successive acts, — a white flash, a brownish-yellow gleam, and a fainter and more lasting glow, which, with brass electrodes, is green, and with platina gray in color. The duration of the entire phenomena is from .000017 to .000050 seconds, that is, 17 to 50 millionths of a second; the duration of the white and yellow light together, 6 to 8 millionths; and the duration of the white flash less than 24 hundred millionths of a second.

ARTIFICIAL COLORATION OF THE ELECTRIC SPARK.

Mr. E. Becquerel has shown that the electric spark may be diversely and beautifully colored by being made to pass through saline solutions. If an electrical spark from an inductive apparatus be made to pass into the extremity of a platinum wire suspended over the surface of the solution of a salt, this spark will acquire special coloration according to the chemical composition of the solution traversed. The saline solutions are best concentrated, and the platinum wire positive. The experiment is readily performed in a glass tube.

Salts of strontia will color the spark red; chloride of sodium, yellow; chloride of copper, bluish green, etc.

The light from these sparks, analyzed by the spectroscope, furnishes a method for the determination of the nature of the salts contained in the solution.

MAGNETISM.

M. Trève, in pursuing his researches on magnetism, has conceived the design of submitting cast iron to an electro-magnetic influence.

In the axis of a powerful bobbin, he has placed a mould with sand, which receives the jet of melted iron; then he made an energetic current from 12 couples of Bunsen's pass through it; he placed, at some distance from that, a small cylinder of the same melted iron, withdrawn from all magnetic influence. As soon as the cooling process was complete, he took the moulds, broke the cylinders, and examined the grain of each of them. MM. Douzel, iron-founders, have immediately studied it, and have found no difference in crystallization. Two smaller patterns have been exactly measured by M. Deleuil, which have only shown the trifling difference of 3 milligrammes in their weight. An important fact is, however, revealed by these first attempts. The presence *of a powerful magnetism in the casting*, from its liquid state answered to 1,800 degrees, until the cooling was complete. The cylinder of cast iron, hardly cold, attracted very strongly a large bar of iron. It has remained magnetized since its solidification, magnetizing feebly, it is true, but, in short, characterized by its two poles. It is proved, then, that no incompatibility exists between heat and magnetism, that is to say, that iron can be magnetized at *any temperature*, when the action is constant, as in the experiment written above. M. Faye, in the session of the 16th of August, 1865, had shown a remarkable result, which is not without analogy to that which we have just shown.

After having dissolved in an acid some soft iron, destitute of restraining force, and having deposited it in a thin layer upon the surface of a sheet of copper, the illustrious academician established in this iron, chemically pure (but rough and broken), a restraining faculty so energetic, that it has been able to heat a plate thus prepared to the point of fusion of red copper itself, without making the magnetism disappear that it had first communicated to it. This plate has preserved its magnetism to this day. . . . If now, as these analogous results tend to show, temperature high or low is not incompatible with the existence of magnetism, *when the first cause is persistent*, as in the case of the earth, perpetually submitted to the action of the currents which envelop it from east to west, there would be some reason to accord more of probability to the hypothesis of central magnetism, which explains more completely the variation and the inclination of the magnetic needle, or, indeed, the centre might be magnetic, whatever the temperature, might it not be this perpetual magnetism in rotation from west to east, which determines in the surrounding atmosphere the currents from east to west, which have been established by Ampère? — *Comptes Rendus, Feb. 1, 1869,*

TELEGRAPH LINES AND THE AURORA BOREALIS.

Mr. George B. Prescott, well known as an electrician and author of valuable works on the telegraph, makes the following interesting explanation of a phenomenon noted in the case of a recent auroral display : —

"On the evening of the 15th of April a magnetic storm of unusual force prevailed over the entire northern section of the country, which so seriously affected the operation of the wires that, on some circuits, they could only be worked by taking off the batteries and employing the auroral current instead. The effect of this great disturbance of the earth's magnetism was manifested with particular power upon the wires between New York and Boston, and for several hours the lines upon this route depended entirely upon this abnormal power for their working current. During the prevalence of this storm, however, I operated upon two wires between the above cities by a plan which rendered them as free from the effects of these earth currents as a local circuit.

"Every one has observed that the auroral current comes in waves of ever-changing polarity, corresponding in length and direction with the scintillations of the visible aurora. Sometimes these waves continue but a few seconds, and sometimes for a longer time ; but their constant change of polarity prevents the successful operation of a wire, because at one moment the auroral wave may augment the strength of current on the line, while at the next it entirely neutralizes it. Therefore, it has frequently been found advisable to remove the batteries entirely, and work with the auroral current alone. But the operation of the lines in this manner is very unsatisfactory, owing to the uncertain and fitful character of this force ; and, therefore, any feasible plan by which the wires may be worked under such circumstances is worthy of adoption.

"The plan by which I overcame the difficulties arising from the disturbance of the earth's magnetism was by disconnecting two wires from the earth at Boston, and connecting them together, while I grounded them both at New York, thus forming a loop extending from New York to Boston. As the two wires were both upon the same supports, the auroral wave travelled over each in the same direction, and, by uniting the two wires at one end, the auroral influence upon one wire was made to neutralize that upon the other, and thus the wires were left entirely free.

"Of course it makes no difference how often the polarity of the auroral current changes, or how much the strength of this current may vary, since the direction of the current, and its strength, change as much upon one wire as the other, and therefore the current upon one always exactly equals and neutralizes the other."

INSULATION OF THE ATLANTIC CABLE.

The "Boston Journal of Chemistry" asserts, on the authority of a gentleman intimately connected with the working of the Atlantic Telegraph Cable, that the insulation is growing monthly more perfect, and that the first cable, laid 4 years since, leaks less than the last one. The loss, at the present time, does not reach *half of one per cent.* upon both cables. This is surprising, and very encouraging to the owners of the line. The extreme cold of the deep-sea basin, in which the wires repose, is favorable to the retention of the electrical impulses in the channel provided for them. The time consumed in charging and discharging the conductors is a bar to rapid communication; but this is to be overcome by new methods of insulation. A device has recently been brought forward which promises to fully remove this obstacle, and thus enable submarine cables to perform double the work in the same length of time. The success of deep-sea cables is now fully assured, and we may look for a large increase in the number during the next quarter of a century.

MAGNETISM.

The French Academy of Sciences has received a paper from M. J. Jamin, in which he shows that magnetism may be condensed, just like electricity. Having, for some special purposes, had a large horse-shoe magnet made, consisting of 10 laminæ of perfectly homogeneous steel, each weighing 10 kilogrammes, he suspended it to a hook attached to a strong beam, and, having wound copper wire around each of the legs, which were turned downwards, he put the latter into communication with a battery of 50 of Bunsen's elements, by which means the horse-shoe might be magnetized, either positively or negatively, at pleasure. The varations were indicated by a small horizontal needle, situated in the plane of the poles. There was, further, a series of iron plates, which could be separately applied to each of the laminæ. Before attaching any of the latter, the electric current was driven through the apparatus for a few minutes, and then interrupted, whereby the magnet acquired its first degree of saturation, marked by a certain deviation of the needle. One of the iron plates (usually called "contacts") was then put on, and it supported a weight of 140 kilogrammes. A second trial was now made; and, the current having passed through again for a few seconds, it was found that the horse-shoe would support 300 kilogrammes, instead of 140. The number of contacts being now increased to 5, which together, in the natural state, supported 120 kilogrammes, it was found, after the passage of the current, that they could support the enormous weight of 680 kilogrammes, which they did for the space of a full week. No sooner, however, were the contacts taken off than the horse-shoe returned to its usual permanent strength of 140 kilogrammes. This tends to show that magnetism may be condensed like electricity for a short period.

ELECTRICITY AND THE PULSE.

At the meeting of the American Association at Salem, after explaining the improvements in the diagnosis of aneurisms which the case had suggested, Dr. Upham proceeded, with the aid of the telegraph and magnesium light, to render audible and visible the pulsations of patients in the City Hospital in Boston; Mr. Farmer having charge of the telegraph instruments in the lecture-room, Mr. Stearns at the City Hospital, and Dr. Knight, assisted by the internes of the hospital, taking the medical direction. The Franklin Telegraph Company placed their entire line between Salem and New York at the disposal of the Association, and every pulse-click of the magnet was heard simultaneously at every station on the entire line.

AN IMPROVED BATTERY.

We have recorded so many improvements (as they are all called) in galvanic batteries, that the number and variety become bewildering. The last we meet with is that suggested by Böttger, who proposes to substitute metallic antimony for carbon. An amalgamated zinc plate is immersed in a strong solution of common salt and sulphate of magnesia. The antimony, like the carbon, is placed in a porous pot, but the liquid used is dilute sulphuric acid. A combination of this arrangement is said to give a stronger and more lasting current than a cell of Daniell's battery. — *Mechanics' Magazine.*

APPLICATION OF LEICHTENBERG'S EXPERIMENT TO THE MINERALOGICAL ANALYSIS OF ROCKS.

M. S. Meunier proposes to make use of the well-known experiment of Leichtenberg's electric figures to separate from each other the divers mineralogical constituents of some kinds of rock. We briefly remind our readers that the experiment alluded to consists in charging with electricity a cake of resin or sealing-wax, by means of a previously charged Leyden jar; it is thus possible to charge certain portions of the cake with positive, others with negative, electricity. In order to exhibit this to sight it is usual to blow, by means of a small pair of bellows, on to the cake of the resin, a mixture of very finely powdered red lead and sulphur; the friction, on leaving the nozzle, causes the powders to become electrified, and the sulphur, being negatively electric, is attracted by the curved figures positively electric on the cake, while the red lead follows the opposite course. M. Meunier has tried thus to separate sulphur-bearing trachite into its mineral constituents, and succeeded perfectly in getting the sulphide and fieldspar from each other; he states that he has equally well succeeded with rocks made up of two different silicates. — *Cosmos.*

CHLORIDE OF SILVER PILE.

This pile, inclosed in a rubber-box hermetically closed, can advantageously replace the bulky apparatus called continuous currents, which are ordinarily employed in medical practice. A battery of 42 couples of chloride of silver correspond, in electro-motive force and intensity, to 34 of the sulphate of copper couples of Remack, and to the volume and weight of one only of these last.

It can render great service in inflaming mines, torpedoes, etc. Attached to a bobbin of Ruhmkorff it can serve in the case of inflammations; it can also replace the electrophorus of chemical laboratories. Its use is indicated on the electric telegraph in signalizing an accident, or in notifying of danger. — *Comptes Rendus, May 3*, 1869.

VELOCITY OF ELECTRIC CURRENTS.

At the meeting of the American Association at Salem, Prof. G. W. Hough, director of the Dudley Observatory, read a paper "On the Velocity of the Electric Current over Telegraph Wires."

He stated that the law of apparent velocity was directly proportional to the magnetic force of the current. This was shown to be the fact from a large number of experiments made over lines of different lengths. He also stated that the real velocity of the wave had never been measured, but the velocity observed was due to the difference of mechanical effects produced by the current when the line was opened at alternate ends.

ELECTRIC SPARK FIGURES.

Mr. E. W. Blake, Jr., described a new method of his own discovery, of producing by the electric spark figures similar to those of Leichtenberg. Warming a plate of tin or mica upon which pitch had been allowed to fall up to the softening point of the pitch, the communication of the electric spark produces a star-shaped figure from positive electricity, and circles from negative electricity. Leichtenberg's process prepares the pitch by covering it with some fine powder. No impression is produced upon cold pitch. Resin and sealing-wax give good impressions, but the best come from common pitch or Burgundy pitch. It is essential that the under side of the plate be held to the flame. — *Meeting of the Am. Ass.*

NON-EXISTENCE OF THE ELECTRIC FLUID. BY PROF. VANDER WEYDE, M.D.

In the same manner that the investigations and discoveries of 20 years ago have proved that the so-called caloric fluid has no existence, and that heat is only a state of matter, — a mode of motion of its particles; so the investigations of the present day prove that the so-called electric fluid has no existence, and that even electricity is nothing more than a state of matter, — another mode of motion of its molecules. Without matter there is no electricity, as will be proved by this little glass tube, in which the vacuum is so perfect that no electricity can possibly pass through it, notwithstanding the ends of the two platinum wires melted in the glass, and projecting outside on both ends, and which conduct the electricity interiorly, are only one-quarter of an inch apart. I have here a similar tube filled with common atmospheric air, the ends of the wires are also one-quarter of an inch apart, and may be separated a half or a whole inch, but the electric current will be seen in the form of sparks to pass easily between the wires, and to charge this Leyden jar. I have here also a so-called Geisler tube, in which the ends of the wires are separated to the distance of 20 inches, and through which the electric current could not pass at all while filled with air; but the air in it is rarefied to such a degree as to make it a good conductor of electricity, and you see the current pass not in sparks, as in the second tube filled with common air, but as a glowing fire, resembling the northern light; through this tube, also, we can charge this Leyden jar. Through the first tube, in which, by great precautions, an almost perfect vacuum has been produced, there is not only no current seen to pass, but it is impossible to load this Leyden jar when the tube is interposed between the jar and the machine developing the electricity.

The verification of the passage or non-passage of the electric current by means of this charge in the jar, obtained or not obtained, is important, as otherwise it would be doubted if the electricity passed invisibly through the vacuum.

This striking and novel experiment, demonstrating the impossibility that an electric current can overlap a really empty space, even to the small distance of only one-quarter inch, proves that there are two errors in our present theory of electricity. First, that the transmission of electricity in vacuo, so called, is really a transmission through rarefied air or gas, these being good conductors; common air, we know, is a bad conductor. The vacuum is proved by this new experiment to be an absolute non-conductor. Secondly, this experiment proves that if that which we call electricity was really a fluid distinct from common matter, there is no reason why it should not overlap the small empty space of a quarter of an inch. As we saw, however, that electricity cannot possibly overlap that small space, nor be transmitted where no matter exists, we are forced to the conclusion that the phenomena of electricity are not due to a peculiar fluid, which moves rapidly through conducting media, but that the propagation is effected by peculiar motions of the molecules, which, being rapidly transmitted from molecule to molecule in the conducting body, form that which we call electric currents. In short, that electricity is transmitted like sound, by some kind of waves, undulations, or rotations, only with much greater velocity. In fact, there exists as little necessity to adopt a special electric fluid to explain the electric phenomena, as there exists to adopt a special sonorous fluid to explain the acoustic phenomena. — *Scientific American.*

SUBSTITUTE FOR COPPER IN THE DANIELLS BATTERY.

Few persons, in experimenting upon voltaic combinations, ever consider economy in their construction, and experiments which tend to cheapen their first cost should be made public.

An expensive part of the Daniells battery is the copper plate, the cost of which can be reduced two-thirds, in the following manner : —

Procure sheets of the ordinary sheet tin of commerce, brighten and plunge into a very weak copper plating solution, in connection with a voltaic battery of very low quantity. In 15 to 18 hours a tenacious film of copper will have been deposited upon the tin, and the plate can then be bent in shape suitable for a Daniells battery. — *Telegraph.*

THE "WAVE" TIME OF THE ELECTRIC TELEGRAPH.

The Boston "Traveller" gives the following official figures from the records at Harvard College : "It was proposed to begin with a comparatively short loop, extending from Cambridge to Buffalo and back, and then to extend the loops successively to Chicago, Omaha, Salt Lake, Virginia City, and finally to San Francisco. The plan was put into execution on the nights of February 28th and March 7th, and in both instances the results were extremely successful. It was quite fascinating to stand before two instruments, a few inches apart, and to see and hear a signal made upon one, repeated upon the other in a fraction of a second, after having traversed a distance of over 7,000 miles.

"Below is given a table which shows the time, to hundredths of seconds, occupied by a signal passing from Cambridge to each of the stations and back. The numbers of repeaters in the circuits are also given : —

"TIME OF TRANSMISSION FROM CAMBRIDGE.

	Seconds.	
To Buffalo and return,	0.10	1 repeater.
To Chicago and return,	0.20	3 "
To Omaha and return,	0.33	5 "
To Salt Lake and return,	0.54	9 "
To Virginia City and return,	0.70	11 "
To San Francisco and return,	0.74	13 "

"The actual time of transmission from Cambridge to San Francisco and back does not probably exceed three-tenths of a second; the 'armature times' of the 13 repeaters, in all probability, amount to four or five tenths of a second."

Herr Paalzow has been making experiments from which he concludes that there is no relation between the conductibility for heat and that for electricity. He has experimented on the following substances, and has found that they have the following order in point of conductibility of heat and· electricity : — Heat: Mercury, water, sulphate of copper, sulphuric acid, sulphate of zinc, solution of sea salt. Electricity: Mercury, sulphuric acid, solution of sea-salt, sulphate of zinc, sulphate of copper, water.

THE GALVANIC BATTERY.

Prof. G. W. Hough, in his recent report as Director of the Dudley Observatory at Albany, N. Y., gives the conclusions arrived at, after a series of experiments with galvanic batteries, as follows: 1. In the sulphate of copper battery (Daniells' form), the principal cause of decline in the strength of the electric current is due to the formation of the sulphate of zinc. 2. The quantity of electricity flowing in the external circuit depends on the specific gravity of the sulphate of zinc solution. 3. When the sulphate of zinc solution approaches saturation, polarization takes place in the battery itself, and, although electric motive force remains the same, the internal resistance may be increased more than a hundred times. 4. The sulphate of zinc solution (or any fluid about the zinc) is useful only as a conductor of electricity. 5. The copper, or negative metal, is useful only as a conductor; since it can be replaced by any negative metal, even by zinc itself. 6. The internal resistance of the battery has been separated into two parts, namely, that due to the porous cell and that due to the liquids employed. The specific resistance of the liquids was found to be 13; that for a small clay cell 17, and for a leather cell 7; since the resistance of the leather cell is less than one-half that of a clay cell, we have used it in the construction of batteries, as the quantity of electricity is nearly doubled, without any increase of the surface. For the negative metal, in place of the copper heretofore employed, we have used sheet lead. The investigations have enabled us to compute, with great precision, the length of time a battery will generate its normal quantity of electricity, provided the amount of electricity flowing in the external circuit is known, and the capacity of the vessel holding the sulphate of zinc solution is determined. The specific gravity of the sulphate of zinc solution should not be less than 15°, nor more than 30° Baumé.

SOUNDS OF TELEGRAPH WIRES.

As the cause of the sounds frequently heard to proceed from the wires in the open air, it has been customary to accept the wind, and its producing the soundings by direct vibration, similar to those of the Æolian harp. A different view of it, however, and one which will recommend itself perhaps more generally, is given by a railroad officer in the " Austrian Railway Gazette."

14

He calls observation to the fact that one who gives his close attention to both the wires and sounds will find that the latter make their appearance likewise when there is a total absence of wind, and in a quiet morning in winter, when the wires appear covered with frost to the thickness of a finger, they nevertheless carried on lively vibrations and swinging while the air was totally quiet. The observer had noticed this for 18 years past, and at last was led to the real cause of the phenomenon.

According to him, therefore, the vibrations are due, not to the wind, but the changes of atmospheric temperature, and especially through the action of cold, as lowering of the temperature induces a shortening of the wires, extending over the whole length of the conductor. A considerable amount of friction is produced on the supporting bells, and this gives the explanation for the sounding both in the wires and the poles. This explanation also concurs with the fact that poles bearing but one or a few wires give off far louder sounds than when loaded with many, because in the latter case the vibrations produced must be less uniform and simultaneous.

EXPERIMENTS WITH THE GREAT INDUCTION COIL AT THE ROYAL POLYTECHNIC.

We extract from the " Chemical News " the following abstract of a paper communicated to the Royal Society, by J. P. Gassiot, F.R.S. : —

" The length of the coil from end to end is 9 feet 10 inches, and the diameter 2 feet; the whole is cased in ebonite; it stands on two strong pillars covered with ebonite, the feet of the pillars being of a diameter of 22 inches. The ebonite tubes, etc., are the largest ever constructed by the Silver Town Works.

" The total weight of the great coil is 15 cwt., that of the ebonite alone being 477 lbs.

" The primary wire is made of copper of the highest conductivity, and weighs 145 lbs. ; the diameter of this wire is 0.0925 of an inch, and the length 3,770 yards. The number of revolutions of the primary wire round the core of soft iron is 6,000, its arrangement being 3, 6, and 12 strands.

" The total resistance of the primary is 2.201400 British Association units, and the resistance of the primary conductors are respectively, for three strands, 0.733800 British Association units; six, 0.366945 B.A. units; twelve, 0.1834725 B.A. units.

" The primary core consists of extremely soft straight iron wires 5 feet in length, and each wire is 0.0625 of an inch in diameter. The diameter of the combined wires is 4 inches, and the weight of the core is 123 lbs.

" The secondary wire is 150 miles in length; it is covered with silk throughout, and the average diameter is 0.015 of an inch.

" The total weight of this wire is 606 lbs., and the resistance is 33.560 B.A. units. The length of the secondary coil is 55 inches, and the insulation throughout is calculated to be 95 per cent. beyond that required. The secondary wire is insulated from the primary by means of an ebonite tube of one-half an inch in thickness and 8 feet in length.

" The length of the secondary coil is 54 inches, the diameter is 19 inches, and without the internal ebonite tube containing the primary wire and iron core it is a cylinder 19 inches in diameter and 6 inches thick.

" The condenser, made in the usual manner with sheets of varnished paper and tinfoil, is arranged in 6 parts, each containing 125 superficial feet, or 750 square feet of tinfoil in the whole.

" A large and substantially made contact breaker, detached from the great coil and worked by an independent electro-magnet, was constructed, and worked very well with a comparatively moderate power of 10 or 20 large Bunsen's cells, when, however, the battery was increased to 30 or 40 cells, it became unmanageable.

" A Foucault break, with the platinum amalgam and alcohol above it, was now tried, and answered very much better than the ordinary contact breaker; there was no longer any burning or destruction of the contact points, although the great power of the instrument appeared to cause continued decomposition in the water of the alcohol placed above the platinum amalgam; and every now and then the spirit was violently rejected, probably by explosion of the mixed gases taking place in the amalgam, in which they collected in bubbles; the alcohol took fire constantly and had to be extinguished. A large and very strong glass vessel (in fact, an inverted glass cell belonging to a bichromate battery) was bored through, and the neck fitted into a cap with cement, a thick wire covered with platinum being inserted in the bottom; the platinum amalgam was poured on this, and over it a pint or more of alcohol; the contact wire was also very thick and pointed with a thick stud of platinum, and, being attached to a spring, contact was easily made and broken. Explosions did not occur, flashes of light could be seen between the amalgam and the alcohol, and the height of the column of the latter prevented the forcible ejection of the spirit, which no longer took fire. The break was used for 8 hours in a continuous series of experiments.

" The Bunsen's battery used in the experiments was made with the largest porous cells that could be obtained, and each cell contained about one pint of nitric acid.

" Some experiments were tried with the battery arranged for intensity, and used with the complete condenser of 750 square feet of tinfoil, and 1,500 square feet of paper. At first, 5 cells were used, and these gave a spark 12 inches in length. The number of cells were gradually increased until 50 were in operation, when a spark from 28 to 29 inches in length was obtained.

" In order to ascertain whether any variation in the size of the condenser would affect the length of the spark, a number of experiments were tried; and it was found that when half the condenser was used the spark increased in length up to 20 cells, but not after.

"Experiments were now tried to ascertain whether any increase in the length of the spark could be obtained by arranging the battery and the primary coil for quantity, but no material advantage was obtained by this arrangement; even where 3 groups of cells were connected, a decrease in the length of the spark is observed when compared with the 45 or 50 cells arranged for intensity, the difference being as 20 to 28.

"The spark obtained from the large coil is thick and flame-like in its appearance, and therefore it will be alluded to as the 'flaming spark.'

"When the discharging-point and circular plate are brought within 6 or 7 inches of each other, the flaming nature of the spark becomes still more apparent.

"Two light-yellow flames curving upwards appear to connect the opposite poles. If a blast of air from a powerful bellows is directed against a flaming spark, the flaming portion can be blown away and increased in area, and thin, wiry sparks are now seen darting through it, sometimes in one continuous stream, at another time divided into three or more sparks, all following the direction in which the flame is blown.

"The flaming spark is very hot, and, if passed through asbestos (supported on an insulating pillar), quickly causes the latter to become red-hot.

"When powdered charcoal is shaken from a pepper-box into the flaming spark in a vertical line and in considerable quantities, the greater part of the light is obscured, and the whole form of the flaming spark presents the appearance of a black cloud with a line of brightly ignited particles fringing the bottom parts. If the charcoal is dusted through in small quantities, each particle becomes ignited, like blowing charcoal into a hydrogen flame.

"When the flaming spark is directed on to a glass plate, upon which a little solution of lithium chloride is placed, the latter colors the flame upwards to the height of 3 or 4 inches in the most beautiful manner; and if the point of the discharge is tipped with paper, or sponge moistened with a little solution of sodium chloride, the two colors (the yellow from the salt, and the crimson from the lithium) meet each other, a neutral point being found about half way, and thus illustrating apparently the dual character of electricity, and that + passes to — electrical, and vice versa.

"The flaming spark can be obtained in perfectly dry air.

"While passing through common air, if blown against a sheet of damp litmus paper, the latter is rapidly changed red. In order to ascertain whether the acid product was nitric acid, the flaming spark (9 or 10 inches in length) was passed through a tube connected by a cork and bent tube with a bottle containing distilled water, from which another tube passed to the air-pump. On drawing the air slowly over the spark, and passing the former into the bottle, nitric acid was obtained in large quantities, so much so that it could be detected by the smell and taste as well as by the ordinary tests. The popular notion that nitric acid is always produced during a thunder-storm would therefore appear to be correct. To determine the effect of a cooling surface on the flaming spark, a hole one and one-half inches in diameter was bored through a thick block of Wenham Lake ice, and the spark passed through the air in the tube of ice; no change took place, and the spark was still a flaming one.

"When the spark was received on the ice, it lost its flaming character, and became thin and wiry, spreading out in all directions.

"If the discharging wires were tipped with ice, the spark was always flaming when any thickness of air intervened between them. Even over the ice, if the spark passed a fraction of an inch above the surface, it was always a flaming one, but changed to the thin spark when the point of the discharging wire was thrust into the ice.

"If one of the discharging wires of the great coil is brought to the centre of a large swing looking-glass, and the other wire connected with the amalgam at the back, the sparks are thin and wiry, arborescent, and very bright; the crackling noise of these discharges being quite different from that of the heavy thud or blow delivered by the flaming spark.

"When the discharging wire is brought close to the frame of the looking-glass, or if a sufficient thickness of air intervenes, the spark again becomes flaming; or, as sometimes occurs, if the discharging wire is placed about 5 inches from the frame, the spark is partly flaming and partly wiry, that is, when it impinges on the glass.

"The spectrum is a continuous one with the sodium line.

"When the blast of air is used, and the wiry sparks made apparent, then the nitrogen line appears.

"The flaming spark has been ascribed by some experienced observers to the incandescence of the dust in the air, and especially sodium chloride.

"To ascertain whether the 'flaming spark' could be obtained with a small number of cells, the large Bunsen's battery was reduced to 3 cells, and it was found that no appreciable spark could be produced when the whole primary wire was used with less than 5 cells.

"By reducing the length of the primary wire, and using the 4 divisions separately, with 5 cells, the spark was wiry, and varied from $4\frac{1}{2}$ to $6\frac{1}{2}$ inches; with 10 cells it was wiry, and varied from $8\frac{1}{4}$ to $9\frac{1}{2}$; in the latter the spark was slightly flaming. With 15 cells the spark was slightly flaming, and varied from 10 inches to $11\frac{1}{2}$ inches. With 20 cells a flaming spark, varying from $11\frac{1}{2}$ inches to $12\frac{1}{2}$ inches, was obtained.

"When the two wires from the secondary coil are placed in water, no spark is perceptible, even when the wire was brought very close together, until they touch.

"If the negative wire is passed through a cork, on which a glass tube (a lamp glass) is fixed containing a depth of 5 inches of water, and the positive wire is brought within half an inch of the surface of the water in the tube, it becomes red-hot, and if drawn further away from the surface, the upper part of the

14*

tube is filled with a peculiar glow or light, abounding in Stokes' rays.

"The experiments with the vacuum tube, and especially Gassiot's cascade, are, as might be expected, very beautiful. When a coal-gas vacuum tube of considerable diameter, and conveying the full discharge from the secondary coil, is supported over a powerful electro-magnet axially, the discharge is condensed and heat is produced.

"If placed equatorially, the heat increases greatly, and when the discharge is condensed and impinges upon the sides of the glass tube, it becomes too hot to touch, and if the experiment was continued too long the tube would crack.

"The enormous quantity of electricity of high tension which the coil evolves, when connected with a battery of 40 cells, is shown by the rapidity with which it will charge a Leyden battery.

"Under favorable circumstances, 3 contacts with the mercurial break will charge 40 square feet of glass.

"On one occasion a series of 12 large Leyden jars arranged in cascade were discharged; the noise was great; and each time the spark (which was very condensed and brilliant) struck the metallic disc, the latter emitted a ringing sound, as if it had received a sharp blow from a small hammer.

"The discharges were made from a point to a metallic disc; and when the former was positive the dense spark measured from 18¼ to 18¾ inches, and fell to two and one-half inches when the metallic plate was positive and the point negative.

"Variations of the Leyden-jar experiments were tried by connecting the coil worked by a quantity battery of $25 + 25$ cells with 6 Leyden jars arranged in cascade, and the spark obtained measured 8½ inches.

"The same 6 jars connected with the coil, when the 50 cells were arranged continuously for intensity, gave a spark of 12 inches, of very great density and brilliancy."

ELECTRICITY APPLIED TO REGISTERING VIBRATIONS.

The laws which govern the vibration of cords or wires have been obtained by comparing the sounds they produce with the notes of a syren. Without questioning the accuracy of this method, it will still be desirable to obtain the laws of vibration without regard to the effects which vibrations produce; a *direct* registry cannot fail to be more satisfactory. Now it is clear that however rapid may be the vibrations of a cord, the velocity of the electric force is greater; moreover, it is not impossible to make a succession of electric impulses produce a corresponding succession of *permanent* effects, which can be seen and counted, so that if a vibrating body can be made to open and close an electric current, the electric force may be depended on to register its vibrations. The practical questions are, first, How shall a vibrating body be made to open and close an electric current without having its motion embarrassed? Second, How, in a legible manner, can the number of these rapid impulses be registered? And, third, By what means can the time of vibration be accurately measured? To register the vibration of cords and piano-wires, the following arrangement of apparatus has been made. Through the middle points of the vibrating cord passes a firm cambric needle, the point of which will, when the cord is at rest, be very near, but not in contact with the surface of mercury contained in a cup beneath. A galvanic battery is connected, one pole with this cup, the other with a trough, containing mercury, into which dips the end of a wire bent twice at right angles, and turning freely upon a hinge. To this wire is joined one end of the helix of an electro-magnet, while to the other end of the coil is attached a flexible metallic thread (a ravelling of gilt lace) tied into the eye of the needle, which passes through the vibrating cord. Now, by the vibration of the cord, the needle-point will be brought in contact with the surface of the mercury under it at the end of every double vibration, and a current of electricity darts through the wires, magnetizes the electro-magnet, which pulls the armature to its poles, and brings the registering point in contact with the paper. As the paper is drawn swiftly along by clock-work, while the armature with its sharp and soft lead-pencil point is in motion, the vibrations of the cord are registered upon the paper in a line of distinct black dots, easily counted. To measure time, in the present form of the apparatus, a pendulum is used. The pendulum when drawn to one end of its arc rests against one arm of a lever, while the other arm carries a pair of pluckers which grasps the cord. A pressure of the finger causes this finger to release, at the same instant, the pendulum from one end, and the cord from the other. The wire, whose lower end dips into the trough of mercury, can at any time be brought into the arc of the pendulum, by moving the block to which it is fastened, without breaking the circuit; but when this is done, the ball will strike its upper end, and, knocking it over, lift the lower end from the mercury, and open the circuit. The motion of the armature begins with the beginning of the first vibration of the pendulum, and stops at the end of 1, 3, or any odd number of seconds, and the number of dots left upon the paper shows the number of vibrations of the cord. The vibrations of the wire are made to occur in a vertical plane opening and closing an electric circuit with corresponding rapidity, and a dot is made upon the moving paper at the moment when the lowest point in the vibration is reached. The experiment begins when the wire is above its line of rest; the first dot, therefore, represents one-half of one complete vibration. Should the experiment end when the wire is at the highest point in its motion, the number of dots would show the exact number of complete vibrations made; but since it may end when the wire is at any point of its path, there may be a possible error of less than one-half of a complete vibration in an experiment one second in length. As the time is lengthened, the error is diminished; in a registry of 5 seconds the maximum error would be less than one-tenth of one vibration per second.

The precision with which the laws of vibration may be verified by the use of this instrument is in the highest degree satisfactory. However numerous the repetitions of an experiment may be, the registry varies only by a single dot. Moreover, it makes the law rest upon no comparison of sounds produced by the vibrations, nor upon any other effect of the motion, but upon the vibrations themselves, whose numerical relations are directly shown. Vibrations, sonorous or otherwise, are thus equally the subject of experimental investigation.

Prof. Cooley gives this table of vibrations, which differs from all others relating to music; first, in being the result of a *direct registry*; and, second, in that it shows *all the intervals of the scale*. The piano upon which the registry is based was tuned to the standard pitch of the Boston Music Hall organ.

1st Octave (lowest).		2d Octave.		3d Octave.	
Notes	No. of vibs. per sec.	Notes	No. of vibs. per sec.	Notes	No. of vibs. per sec.
C	30.8	C	61.5	C	123.1
C#	32.7	C#	65.5	C#	130.8
D	34.7	D	69.3	D	138.5
D#	36.7	D#	73.4	D#	146.7
E	38.7	E	77.4	E	154.7
F	41.8	F	83.5	F	166.6
F#	44.2	F#	88.3	F#	176.5
G	46.8	G	93.5	G	187.1
G#	49.4	G#	98.7	G#	197.4
A	52.2	A	104.4	A	208.5
A#	54.4	A#	108.7		
B	57.7	B	115.7		
C	61.5	C	123.1		

The octave above A = 208.5 is the *la* usually referred to in describing the pitch of the orchestra; it is thus produced by 417 *complete vibrations per second.*

In the time of Louis XIV., the pitch of this A was, according to Sauveur, 405 vibrations per second, while by the action of the congress called together by the Society of Arts, at London, in 1860, it was 440. The same note sounded by Handel's tuning-fork (1740) is said to have been made by 416 vibrations per second. It will be thus seen that while the present pitch is nearly one-half of a tone higher than that referred to by Sauveur, and considerably more than that interval lower than that of the London Congress, it agrees with the pitch adopted by Handel, to within a single vibration. — *Prof. Cooley, Journal Franklin Institute.*

CONDUCTING POWERS OF MATERIALS.

According to the experiments of Mr. M. G. Farmer, made some years since, the relative electrical resistance of different metals and fluids at ordinary temperatures is as follows, pure copper being taken as 100 : —

Copper wire,	1.00	Tin wire,	6.80
Silver "	.98	Zinc "	3.70
Gold "	1.13	Brass "	3.88
Iron "	5.63	German silver wire,	11.30
Lead "	10.76	Nickel "	7.70
Mercury "	50.00	Cadmium "	2.61
Pallad'm "	5.50	Aluminum "	1.75
Platinum "	6.78		

His experiments with fluids gave the following results : —

Pure rain water,	40,653,723.00
Water, 12 parts; sulphuric acid, 1 part,	1,305,467.00
Sulphate of copper, 1 pound per gallon,	18,450,000.00
Saturated solution of common salt,	3,173,000.00
" " of sulphate of zinc,	17,330,000.00
Nitric acid, 30 B,	1,606,000.00

The following table gives the specific resistance in ohms (an ohm is an amount of resistance equal to that exerted by one-sixteenth of a mile of common galvanized iron telegraph wire No. 9) of various metals and alloys, at 32° Fah., according to the most recent determination of Dr. Matthiessen : —

NAME OF METALS.	Resistance of wire 1 foot long, weighing 1 grain.	Resistance of wire 1 foot long, 1-1000th inch in diameter.	Approximate per cent. variation in resistance per degree, temperature at 20 degrees.
Silver annealed,	0.2214	9.936	0.377
" hard drawn,	0.2421	9.151	
Copper annealed,	0.2064	9.718	0.388
" hard drawn,	0.2106	9.940	
Gold annealed,	0.5849	12.52	0.365
" hard drawn,	0.5950	12.74	
Aluminum annealed,	0.04822	17.72	
Zinc pressed,	0.5710	32.22	0.365
Platinum annealed,	3.536	55.09	
Iron annealed,	1.2425	59.10	
Nickel annealed,	1.0785	75.78	
Tin pressed,	1.317	80.36	0.365
Lead pressed,	3.236	119.39	0.387
Mercury liquid,	18.746	600.00	0.072
Platinum silver alloy, hard or annealed, used for standard resistance coils,	4.213	148.35	0.031
German silver, hard or annealed, commonly used for resistance coils,	2.652	127.32	0.044
Gold silver alloy, 2 parts gold, 1 part silver, hard or annealed,	2.391	66.10	0.065

The use of this table is as follows : Suppose it is required to find the resistance at 32° Fah. of a conductor of pure hard copper, weighing 400 lbs. per knot. This is equivalent to 460 grains per foot. The resistance of a wire weighing one grain is found by the table to be 0.2106; therefore the resistance of a foot of wire weighing 460 grains will be $\frac{0.2106}{460}$; but the resistance of one knot will be 6,087 times that of one foot; therefore the resistance required will be $\frac{6.087 \times 0.2106}{460} = 2.79$ ohms. If the diameter of the wire be given, instead of its weight per knot, the constant is taken from the second column. Thus the resistance at 32° Fah. of a knot of pure hard-drawn copper wire 0.1 inch in diameter would be $\frac{6.087 \times 9924}{10000} = 6.05$. The resistance of wires is materially altered by annealing them, and a rise in temperature increases the resistance of all metals. Dr. Matthiessen found that for all pure metals the increase of resistance between 32° and 212° Fah. is sensibly the same. The resistance of alloys is much greater than the mean of the metals composing them. They are very useful in the construction of resistance coils.

The highest value which has probably been found for the conducting power of pure copper is 60 times that of pure mercury, according to Sabine. Commercial copper may be considered of good quality when its conducting power is over 50. Different samples of copper vary greatly in their specific conductivity, as may be seen by the following table, which gives the result of careful determinations by Dr. Matthiessen, the conducting power of pure copper at 59.9° Fah. being taken as 100.

Lake Superior, native, not fused,	. . . . . .	98.8 at 59.9°
" " fused (commercial),	. . . . .	92.6 at 59.0°
Burra Burra,	. . . .	88.7 at 57.2°
Best selected,	. . . .	81.3 at 57.5°
Bright copper wire,	. . . .	72.2 at 60.2°
Tough copper,	. . . .	71.0 at 63.1°
Demidoff,	. . . .	59.3 at 54.8°
Rio Tinto,	. . . .	14.2 at 58.6°

Thus Rio Tinto copper possesses no better conducting power than iron. This shows the great importance of testing the conductivity of the wire used in the manufacture of electro-magnets, cables, etc.

VEGETABLE ELECTROMOTORS.

The "Chemical News" contains an article contributed by Edwin Smith, M.A., giving results of researches in a field which, so far as we are aware, has been hitherto untraversed. He says: "It is well known that a voltaic combination may be made of two liquids and a metal, if one of the three acts chemically upon one and only one of the other two; thus, we may employ copper, nitrate of copper, and dilute nitric acid, or platinum, potash, and nitric acid. Connect a platinum crucible with one terminal of a galvanometer, pour in a little solution of caustic potash, place in this the bowl of a tobacco-pipe having the hole stopped up with wax, pour into the bowl a little nitric acid, dip in the acid a small slip of platinum foil, and connect this with the other terminal of the galvanometer; a powerful deflection of the needle indicates the presence of an electric current and shows its direction to be from the alkali to the acid, the platinum serving merely as a conductor. It occurred to me, when performing this experiment, that an electro-motive combination might just as well be made of two vegetable substances, with platinum for conductor, provided only they were of a nature to act chemically upon one another,—an alkaloid and an organic acid, for instance. It also seemed to me not unlikely that, wherever two flavors are habitually conjoined in our cookery and eating, the reason why they mutually improve each other is because a certain amount of electric action is set up between the substances employed to produce them. The *rationale* of the right blending of flavors might be found partly, no doubt, in chemistry, but partly, also, in galvanism.

"Pursuing this idea, I tried pairs of eatables which generally go together, such as pepper and salt, coffee and sugar, almonds and raisins, and the like, and found that a voltaic current more or less strong was excited in every instance which I tested. Bitters and sweets, pungents and salts, or bitters and acids, generally appear to furnish true voltaic couples, doubtless in consequence of the mutual action of some alkaloid salt and an acid or its equivalent. As others may like to repeat or extend the experiments, I will describe shortly my mode of procedure: Cut two pieces of platinum foil about five inches by two and a half inches, and a number of pieces of filter-paper a trifle larger. Well-washed linen is sometimes more convenient than filter-paper. Have a small wooden board near the mercury-cups of the galvanometer, and let a short copper or platinum wire, dipping into one of the cups, rest on the board. The substances to be tried must be brought to a state of solution, the stronger the better, by infusion, decoction, or otherwise. Suppose coffee and sugar are to be operated upon; solutions of both having been prepared, dip into each a slip of filter-paper; place one slip on one of the pieces of platinum foil, and the other on the second piece. Next lay the first slip and its foil on the board, with the metal touching the copper wire before mentioned. Lay the second slip with its platinum upwards, so that the coffee and sugar come into even contact with slight pressure, and immediately connect this upper slip, through a bit of copper wire, insulated from the touch, with the other terminal of the galvanometer. Deflection occurs instantaneously, and may be increased to a considerable vibration by breaking and making circuit at the right swing of the needle. After a few distinct vibrations, it is well to turn over the whole pile of slips just as they are, and connect opposite ends with the galvanometer, so as to reverse the current. This is desirable for the sake of confirming your previous observation, and of correcting any slight disturbing cause arising from the wire and mercury connectors, temperature of the hand, etc. It will be found that coffee and sugar have the same electrical relation to each other as zinc and platinum. Coffee, in fact, is the positive, sugar the negative. I subjoin a table of the results of numerous experiments, conducted in the manner above described : —

ELECTRO-POSITIVE.	ELECTRO-NEGATIVE.
Coffee,	Sugar (loaf).
Tea (black),	"
Cocoa,	"
Nutmeg,	"
Cloves,	"
Cinnamon,	"
Mace,	"
Vanilla,	"
Almonds,	"
Rhubarb (tincture),	"
Starch,	"
Starch caramel,	"
Gum caramel,	"
Cane sugar caramel,	"
Milk sugar,	"
Gum,	"
Almonds,	Raisins.
Horseradish,	Beetroot.
Onion,	"
Horseradish,	Table salt.
Mustard,	"
Pepper (white),	"
Mustard,	Tartaric Acid.
Ginger,	" "
Cayenne pepper,	" "
Pepper (white),	" "
Tea (black),	" "
Tobacco,	" "
Quinine (Howard's),	" "
Gentian root,	" "
Lemon juice,	" "
Horehound,	" "
Lavender water,	" "
Quassia,	" "
Peppermint,	" "
Raw Potato,	Lemon Juice.
Rind of Lemon,	" "
Peruvian Bark,	" "
Camphor (Tincture),	" "
Laudanum,	" "
Arnica (tincture),	Dilute Sulphuric Acid.
Peruvian bark,	" " "
Quinine (Howard's),	" " • "
Iodine (tincture),	Turpentine.
Caustic Potash,	"
Starch,	"
Starch,	Iodine (tincture).
Caustic potash,	Neat's-foot oil.

" It is somewhat difficult to eliminate from these experiments all error arising from difference of temperature, if the galvanometer is tolerably sensitive. Care must be taken to bring the pair of solutions operated upon to the same temperature before testing them; otherwise a thermo-electric current from the hotter to the colder liquid may affect the needle, and mask the true electrical relation between the two, so far as it depends upon their chemical nature.

FRIGORIFIC MIXTURES.

The degree to which the temperature can be reduced by dissolving a salt in water, will, in general, be the greater in the proportion to the dissolved quantity of the salt. Since this quantity depends upon a certain temperature, it will be necessary, in order to obtain the greatest effect, to bring the salt and menstruum together precisely in the proportion in which they yield a saturated solution at the desired low temperature. Any excess of water beyond that needs also to be cooled down, and therefore consumes part of the effect. The fact that this point has generally been left out of view is the cause that the data as to frigorific effect and lowest temperature vary considerably with different observers. The best and safest way is to bring together the ingredients in such conditions that an instantaneous solution must immediately take place, that is, the salt in as fine a state of division as possible, and very slightly in excess of the calculated proportion, after both salt and water have remained for 12 to 18 hours in thin glasses in the same room together, to allow them to equalize their temperature with that of the room. In the following comparative table of averages the results were obtained by adding the water to the salt and stirring with the thermometer. The maximum lowering is attained within a minute at most.

| | Soluble in 100 water. | + Weight 100 water. | Temperature sinks | | |
			from	to	by
Alum, ...	10.0	14	52	49	3° F.
Common Salt, . . .	35.8	36	54	50	4 "
Sulphate Potash, . .	9.9	12	58	53	5 "
Phosphate of Soda, .	9.0	14	51	45	6.5 "
Sulphate Ammonia, .	72.3	75	56	44	12 "
Sulphate Soda, . .	16.8	20	54.5	42	12.5 "
Sulphate Magnesia, .	80.0	85	52.5	38	14 "
Carbonate Soda, . .	30.0	40	51	35	16 "
Nitrate Potassa, . .	15.5	16	56	37.4	18.6 "
Chloride Potassium, .	28.6	30	56	33	23 "
Carb. Ammonia, . .	25.0	30	60	37.5	22.5 "
Acetate Soda, . .	80.0	85	51	24	27 "
Chloride Ammonium,	28.2	30	56	23	33 "
Nitrate Soda, . . .	69.0	75	56	22.5	33.5 "
Hyposulphite Soda, .	98.0	110	51	17.6	33.4 "
Iodide Potassium, .	120.0	140	51.5	11	40.5 "
Chloride Calc'm cryst.,	200.0	250	51.5	9.5	42 "
Nitrate Ammonia, . .	55.0	60	56.6	7	49.6 "
Sulphocyanide Ammonia,	105.0	133	55.7	—1	56.7 "
Sulphocyanide Potash,	130.0	150	51.5	—19	70.0 "

FREEZING MIXTURE.

When citric acid and crystallized carbonate of soda in powder are stirred together, the mass gets into a pasty state, and in a short time becomes quite liquid. If equivalent proportions of the substances are used, the temperature falls from 60° F. to 80° F. The mixture, for a time, is full of air-bubbles, but soon becomes quite a clear, dense, syrupy liquid. The fluid obtained by mixing the powders becomes solid in a day or two, standing in a corked jar. The solid mass has the appearance of set plaster of Paris. The addition of a very little water appears to prevent this settling into a solid mass; but the chalky-looking citrate lies a long time in cold water without being dissolved.

NEW METHOD OF MAKING ICE.

A few days ago a number of gentlemen, by special invitation, witnessed the operations of a new invention which bids fair to be one of great practical value. It is a process of making ice and refrigerating by machinery, in a short space of time, at a comparatively small cost, and to an almost unlimited extent. The working of this machinery was exhibited on board the steamship "William Tabor," lying in the East River, at the foot of Nineteenth Street, and its utility satisfactorily shown to the spectators. This novel invention does two things: it makes ice with the thermometer at 90 degrees in the shade, and preserves meats and fruits for transportation. It accomplishes its purpose upon the chemical principle that if all the heat is extracted out of any object, it becomes intensely cold. The ice is made in this way: A small steam engine, by means of two pumps, subjects carbonic-acid gas to a pressure sufficient to liquidize it. In a liquid state this gas has lost its heat, but recovers it again when converted into gas. Accordingly, a simple apparatus is contrived, by which the acid in a liquid state is made to surround small tubes filled with water. The acid then returns to its gaseous condition, and in doing so takes with it all the caloric out of the water leaving it solid ice. There is no limit to the number of these tubes or apartments of water, and a large quantity of ice can be formed at a time. Yesterday about 20 tubes were filled and frozen to an arctic rigidity.

Upon the same principle air can be rendered cold and dry by being passed through these tubes while carbonic acid is regaining its heat, and then can be pumped into an air-tight chamber. In this chamber, thus filled with dry, frozen air, any meat, fruit, or perishable article can be placed and preserved.

THE BATHOMETER.

This instrument admits of a combination in one sounding of three or more distinct methods of ascertaining and measuring these depths. The discovery of the Messrs. Morse was that of the means of making a buoy which will retain its buoyancy under the enormous pressure of the deep sea. They took a hollow glass sphere between 3 and 4 inches in diameter, the glass only a tenth of an inch thick, and the sphere so light that it floated in water with half its bulk above the surface, and subjecting this fragile body in the cistern of an hydraulic press to a pressure of 7 tons on the square inch, which is the pressure at the depth of about 30,000 feet in the ocean, they found that the sphere was neither crushed nor permeated by the liquid. A tin or wooden tube, 4 inches or more in diameter, and of any required length, is filled with these glass spheres, and ballasted so that it will float upright in the water. An elongated sinker, also, of any required length and weight, is then suspended from the bottom of the tube, and so attached there that it becomes detached when the weight touches, or, if desired, when it is 100 feet, or any required distance, from the bottom, leaving the tube with its spheres to ascend to the surface. As this instrument moves with uniform velocity both in its descent and ascent, the time of its disappearence from the surface indicates the depth to which it has descended. But the inventors do not confine themselves to this mode of determining the depth. They enclose in their tube, and send down and bring back with it their proper bathometer, which is simply a bottle of water with a bag of mercury and water suspended from its neck, the water in the bottle being connected with the mercury in the bag by a glass tube, of very fine bore, passing from the bottom of the bag through an India-rubber stopper in the neck of the bottle into its interior. When this bottle and bag are placed at the bottom of the sea, the pressure of the external water, communicated through the bag and through the mercury in the bag and glass tube to the water in the bottle, compresses that water, and mercury is forced from the bag into the bottle, to supply the void caused by the compression. The amount of the mercury forced into the bottle is the measure of the compression of the water, and the compression of the water is the measure of the height of the compressing column, that is, of the depth of the sea. To facilitate the measuring of the mercury, there is inserted in the bottle, opposite the neck, a graduated tube of even bore, closed at its outer end, so that on inverting the bottle the mercury falls into this metre-tube, and the height of the mercury indicates the depth to which the bottle has descended.

All attempts to measure the deep sea with a line and sinker attached, as in ordinary soundings, have proved failures, and scientific men of the highest reputation, who have devoted much time to the investigation of the problem, have pronounced it impossible ever to send and recover a line with a sinker from the greatest depths of the ocean. Even in moderate depths the measurement by a line is very uncertain and unreliable, in consequence of the effect of currents, and of the drifting of the boat from which the soundings are made. The bathometer of the Messrs. Morse, it is asserted, will descend to, and return from, the greatest depths with certainty, and with a rapidity which hardly admits of a limit. In a recent experiment the instrument rose from the bottom at the rate of 20 feet in a second, or of a mile in less than 4½ minutes. They believe that a sounding in 2,000 fathoms water will ultimately be made easily in less than 15 minutes. The time occupied in a sounding of this depth by those employed by the United States government in sounding between Ireland and Newfoundland, preparatory to laying the Atlantic cable, was ordinarily 6 or 7 hours.

STEWART AND TAIT'S EXPERIMENTS ON THE HEATING OF BODIES BY ROTATION IN VACUO.

Since the theory of a universal, all-permeating, elastic ether, far more subtile than any known gas, even when expanded to the utmost by mechanical means, has been found to account for the phenomena of light and heat more perfectly than any other, the actual demonstration of its existence has been a desideratum. The experiments described in the present article, although to our minds not at all satisfactory, were undertaken to prove the real existence of ether.

The experiments are those of Balfour Stewart, F.R.S., Superintendent of Kew Observatory, London, and P. G. Tait, M.A., of Edinburgh.

These gentlemen, having obtained certain results in air, were encouraged to construct an apparatus wherewith to procure rotation *in vacuo*.

In this apparatus a slowly revolving shaft is carried up through a barometer tube, having at its top the receiver which is to be exhausted. When the exhaustion has taken place, the shaft connected with the multiplying gear revolves in mercury. The train of toothed wheels causes the disc of aluminum to revolve 125 times for each revolution of the shaft. The thermo-electric pile, the most delicate thermometer or test of heat, is connected by two wires carried through two holes in the bed-plate of the receiver with a Thompson's reflecting galvanometer needle. The outside of the thermo-electric pile and its attached cone was wrapped round with wadding and cloth, so as to be entirely unaffected by currents of air.

During these experiments the disc of aluminum was rotated rapidly for half a minute, and a heating effect was, in consequence of the rotation, recorded by the thermo-electric pile.

To obviate the objection that the electric currents which take place in a revolving metallic disc might alter the zero of the galvanometer, the position of the line of light was read before the motion began, and immediately after it ceased, the difference being taken to denote the heating effect produced by rotation.

The thermometric value of the indications given by the galvanometer was found in this way: "The disc was removed from its attachment and laid upon a mercury-bath of known temperature. It was then attached to its spindle again, being in this position exposed to the pile, and having a temperature higher than that of the pile by a known amount. The deflection produced by this exposure being divided by the number of degrees by which the disc was hotter than the pile, gives at once the value in terms of the galvanometric scale of the heating of the disc equal to 1° on Fahrenheit's scale.

The disc of aluminum being blackened with a coating of lampblack, applied by negative photographic varnish, and rock salt inserted in the cone, the following results were obtained: —

No. of set.	No. of observations in each set.	Time at full speed.	Heat indications °Fahrenheit.
I.	3	30	0.85
II.	4	30	0.87
III.	4	30	0.81
IV.	3	30	0.75

To ascertain whether the radiant heat recorded was derived from the rock salt, or from heated air, or from the surface of the disc, the next series of experiments were tried: —

EXPERIMENTS WITH BLACKED ALUMINUM DISC WITHOUT ROCK SALT.

No. of set.	No. of observations in each set.	Time at full speed.	Heat indications °Fahrenheit.
V.	3	30	0.92
VI.	3	30	0.93

With certain modifications of the above experiments it was satisfactorily proved that the effect was not due to heating of the rock salt, or to radiation from heated air; it must therefore be due to the disc of aluminum, which seemed to have rubbed against some matter which remained in the receiver after the air was removed. The question being "Was this ether?" the experimenters further state that: —

1. It may be due to the air which cannot be entirely got rid of.

2. It is possible that visible motion becomes dissipated by an ethereal medium in the same manner, and possibly to nearly the same extent, as molecular motion, or that motion which constitutes heat.

3. Or the effect may be due partly to air and partly to ether.

Not to leave the matter wholly undecided, it was suggested by Professors Maxwell and Graham that there is another effect of air, namely, fluid friction, the coefficient for which they believe to be independent of the tension.

It would appear, however, that the fluid friction of hydrogen is much less than that of atmospheric air, so that were the heating effect due to fluid friction, it ought to be less in a hydrogen vacuum. An experiment proved that the heating effect due to rotation in a hydrogen vacuum was 22.5, while in an air vacuum it was 23.5, and the authors are inclined to consider these numbers

15 *

as sensibly the same, and that the experiment indicates that the effect is not due to fluid friction; at the same time they do not suppose that their experiments have yet conclusively decided the origin of this heating effect, but they hope to elicit the opinions of those interested in the subject, which may serve to direct their future research.

INCREASE OF WEIGHT DURING COMBUSTION.

The "Chemical News" gives a description of an interesting experiment. A small horseshoe magnet is hung up at the beam of a balance sufficiently sensitive to turn with centigrammes; the poles of the magnet are immersed for a moment in the *limatura ferri* of the chemists' shops, and a beard of small particles of iron is caused to adhere to the poles; by means of proper weights placed on the scale-pan at the other end of the beam the equilibrium is restored. This having been done, the finely divided iron is kindled, by approaching to it the flame of a Bunsen gas-burner, and continues to burn. While burning, it will be seen that the arm of the balance on which the magnet is suspended considerably deviates from the horizontal position, thus indicating an increase of weight on the side where the experiment is going on. This experiment succeeds best with a magnet of moderate dimensions; the horseshoe magnet applied in this instance weighed, without its armature, 210 grammes, and can bear a load of 12.5 grammes of iron; when this is altogether converted in magnetic oxide, by combustion, the increase in weight will be about 4.7 grammes.

THE "BLUE CUP" OF THE CANDLE FLAME.

E. W. Hilgard, on "Luminous Flames," in "Silliman's Journal," says: —

"The part performed by the blue cup, namely, that of a self-heating retort with walls impervious to oxygen, in which dry distillation is accomplished; its theoretical import, as the counterpart of the luminous portion, where the same gases are burnt with evolution of light; render the neglect with which it has been treated doubly surprising. That it is totally distinct from the outer veil is rapidly perceived when the eye is protected from being dazzled by means of a screen of the shape and size of the luminous hollow cone. The veil is then seen surrounding the blue cup as well as the higher portions of the flame, and is thus proved to be nothing more than a zone of glowing gas; which, of course, however, cannot be strictly defined from the luminous envelope, the oxidation being a gradually progressive one, from the highly luminous central portion to that brownish, semi-transparent zone of transition, where the carbonic oxide, burning simultaneously with hydrogen, fails to produce its characteristic blue tint because of the excessive temperature existing there."

CONVENIENT METHOD OF ASCERTAINING THE CONSTITUTION OF FLAMES. BY M. L. DUFOUR.

M. L. Dufour recommends the following process for demonstrating, for instance, that the flame of a candle is formed of a hollow cone, luminous on the outside only, and dark in the interior. For this purpose it is necessary to cut the flame; the most preferable method of doing this is by means of a sheet of water or air. The arrangement is as follows: A caoutchouc tube has, at one of its extremities, a gas-jet, such as is used for common gas flames; this jet has an almost semi-circular slit of 0.4 m.m. in depth. The other end of the tube communicates with a reservoir of water placed at a convenient height. Upon a suitable pressure, the water flows out by the slit in the jet, producing a clear-sheet capable of preserving, for a sufficient length of time, an invariable form and size. The slit is placed in such a manner that the sheet presents a horizontal surface; and this will easily cut the flame of a candle showing a perfect section. The hot gases and carbonaceous particles are carried off by the water. On placing the eye above the hollow cone, the luminous wall, etc., can be distinctly seen. Sections may easily be made near the wick or near the point; nothing hinders observation, which may be prolonged at pleasure, and a lens may be used if desired. A flame of gas may be cut and examined in the same manner, but the current of gas must not be strong enough to traverse the sheet of water. If a current of air be caused to come out of the slit by bellows, an invisible sheet of air is formed, which is, also, very convenient for making a section of flame. Close observation is quite possible; for the aerial current prevents the heated gases from reaching the eyes, and a lens may be used; as in the former case, the flame forms a cone, whose luminous walls are extremely thin, and their interior can be plainly seen. A platinum wire may be introduced across the section; and, on being plunged as far as the wick, it will remain unreddened in the dark interior of the cone.

A jet of gas issuing from a circular opening, of from one to two millimetres in diameter, may also be cut very conveniently by the sheet of air. It will be seen to consist of a cone whose walls are brilliant and extremely thin. Upon bringing the sheet of air close to the aperture whence the gas escapes, the flame will be divided at its base and will reappear a little higher. By this means the entire length of the luminous cone, its thin walls, and their interior may be examined.

If a jet of gas produced by a fan-tail burner be cut, the luminous fan will be found to consist of two brilliant blades, between which there is a narrow, obscure space. The blades are at a greater distance apart, and the dark space is wider towards the end of the fan-tails; and, by assuming a suitable position, it is easy to see through the section of flame into the dark space which separates the brilliant walls, and at the end of this will be seen the slit by which the gas escapes.

Instead of throwing the sheet of air perpendicularly to the flame, M. L. Dufour thinks it better to throw it partly on one side, on such a plane as to make a slight angle with the axis of the conical flame, or with the plane of the fan-shaped flame. A lateral section is then produced by the influence of the current, which draws the flame, and inclines it against the sheet of air, by which it is cut. By placing the sheet of air on a more or less inclined plane, and approaching or removing it from the base of the flame, the section is easily made at points more or less distant from that base.

The method described above may, of course, be applied to any kind of flame. M. L. Dufour suggests that it might be of service in the chemical analysis of flames. When a flame is cut by a sheet of water, the water draws off the gases by which it is composed. If the section be made with a sheet of air, it will be easy, by placing suction pipes throughout the length, and ending at fixed points in the interior of the cone, to collect the gases whose composition is desired to be ascertained. — *Chemical News.*

MONCKHOVEN'S NEW ARTIFICIAL LIGHT.

Dr. Desire van Monckhoven recently demonstrated satisfactorily its importance before a meeting of the Vienna Photographic Society, and delivered a lecture upon its mode of application.

One of the most intense lights to be obtained by oxidizing metals or metallic compounds at a high temperature, is that derived from chloride of titanium, or chloro-chromic acid, when exposed to the action of an oxy-hydrogen flame; the light thus produced is of high actinic power, and capable of blackening chloride of silver paper to an appreciable degree in 30 seconds, the formation of titanic acid or chromic acid being brought about at a very high temperature. It is this description of light that has been chosen by Dr. M.

Several kinds of oxy-hydrogen lights have been devised from time to time; the Drummond light, in which the flame acts against a cylinder of unslaked lime, but which requires the constant presence of carbonate of lime, and the surface of the cylinder to be continually changing; the Tessie du Motay light, in which the lime cylinder is replaced by means of a compressed magnesia or zirconia cylinder; and the Carlevaris light, consisting of small parallel pipes of hard charcoal moistened with chloride of magnesium. Of all these lights, that of Drummond is the best, and by substituting for the lime cylinder another composed of titanic acid, magnesia, and carbonate of magnesia, a suitable illuminating power is obtained. A cylinder of this description, measuring 3 centimetres (one inch) broad, and 9 long (3 inches), lasts for 3 hours, and may be produced for the sum of threepence. Instead of hydrogen, ordinary coal gas is employed; and for the supply of oxygen, M. Deville's method of obtaining it by heating a mixture of calcined peroxide of manganese and chlorate of potash is employed.

MR. GRAHAM'S EXPERIMENTS WITH HYDROGEN.

At the February meeting of the Royal Institution in London, Dr. Odling delivered a lecture upon the new discoveries made by Mr. Graham, F.R.S., respecting the properties of hydrogen, tending to prove that hydrogen is a metal having a boiling-point much below the temperature of the air. The lecturer took a tube closed at one end with a single thickness of well-moistened calico, and showed that when the tube, was half filled with water, and its lower end just dipped below the surface of some water in a glass vessel, the water in the tube would not run out, because the wet calico was, practically speaking, air-tight. Air could only enter the tube, by dissolving in the water upon the calico, and then evaporating on the other side, — a very slow operation. Ammonia being a gas much more soluble in water than common air, a jar of it was inverted over the wet calico; it was quickly dissolved in the water, and evaporated on the other side, so as to push down the column of water in the tube. In the same way gases are believed to pass through India-rubber, and colloid septa, by first dissolving in the material of the diaphragm, then passing through it as a condensed volatile liquid, and finally evaporating on the other side.

M. Deville, a French chemist, proved that hydrogen gas would pass through red-hot solid platinum. Mr. Graham took up the discovery of M. Deville, and, by other experiments made, gained fresh information respecting these phenomena. He showed that platinum absorbed a certain quantity of hydrogen before the transmission began, as is the case with India-rubber. Next he tried palladium, and discovered that this metal will absorb or occlude about 1,000 times its own volume of hydrogen gas, the greatest amount taken up in the actual experiments being 980 times the bulk of the palladium. One volume of water will dissolve 800 times its volume of ammonia, the water being then increased in bulk by one-half, — that is to say, that two centimetres of water, after absorbing 800 times their volume of ammonia, will have increased to three cubic centimetres. Palladium does not increase in bulk to anything like the foregoing extent when it absorbs hydrogen; it only enlarges to one-twentieth or one-twenty-first of its former volume, after taking up 900 times its bulk of the gas, in which operation the hydrogen is reduced to one-nineteenth thousand of its former volume.

The enormous mechanical pressure necessary to compress hydrogen to this extent would equal that at the base of a column of mercury three times as high as Mont Blanc, supposing hydrogen, at such a pressure, still to obey the laws of gases, and to possess all the properties of a gas. The weight of hydrogen, thus absorbed, is from eight-tenths to nine-tenths that of the palladium. Mercury can be boiled into an invisible gas, and analogy seems to point out that hydrogen, at all temperatures yet produced by man, is similarly the vapor or gas of a metal, and that, by a sufficiency of pressure or cold, it may be reduced to a liquid metallic state, so as to resemble quicksilver.   Many chemists support this opinion, much evidence on the point having been brought to bear by M. Dumas.

In physical properties the gas acts like a metal, by conducting heat with facility.   Dr. Odling illustrated this by passing a current of electricity through two platinum spirals, till the two coils of wire kept at a white heat.   Over the one spiral he inverted a jar of common air, and over the other a jar of hydrogen, and the latter cooled the wire so rapidly that it ceased to glow.   He said that it was but fair to state that Dr. Tyndal questions whether the cooling effect shown in this experiment is due to the rapid conduction of heat by the hydrogen; still, it is the prevalent opinion, that conduction by heat really causes the cooling, and Professor Magnus, of Berlin, has come to the same conclusion. Mr. Graham's experiments also favor the view that hydrogen is a metal.

Dr. Odling then proved that the condensed hydrogen has a more powerful action upon reducing agents than when in its ordinary state, by showing its bleaching action upon several colored solutions of chemical reagents.   The greatest absorption of hydrogen by palladium takes place at moderately low temperatures, but a high temperature is necessary for the passage of the gas through the solid metal.   He then took a tube of palladium, closed at one end, and connected the other end with the Sprengel air-pump.   A tube of glass was then slipped over the palladium tube, and a stream of hydrogen gas passed between the two, which were then made hot in the middle by the flame of a Bunsen's burner.   The hydrogen gas then passed readily through the solid metal, being, it is supposed, liquefied in the pores of the palladium, and as it evaporated again inside the tube, the Sprengel pump delivered it into a glass vessel inverted over a trough of mercury.   The hydrogen thus collected was then set on fire by the lecturer, to prove that it was hydrogen and nothing else.

Dr. Odling showed that a palladium wire is elongated after being allowed to absorb hydrogen for half an hour; but the remarkable fact is, that when the gas is driven out again by heat the wire contracts, not to its original length, but to less than its original length.   The cause is not known.   As a final illustration of the probable metallic nature of hydrogen, a bar of palladium, charged with the gas, was suspended by a fibre of silk in the field of an electro-magnet, and was seen to be attracted like iron, though not so strongly.   The bar had thus acquired a metallic property, not possessed by palladium in its unalloyed state.

THE METAL HYDROGEN.

At a late meeting of the Royal Society, as we learn from the "Athenæum" of January 16th, Mr. Graham presented a specimen of palladium, charged with some 800 or 900 times its volume of hydrogen, by some process which is not described in the above journal, but which, from his previous researches, we presume consisted in heating it in an atmosphere of compressed gas. This specimen was accompanied by a paper, in which it was explained that the variations of density, of conducting power, etc., produced in the palladium by the absorption of the hydrogen, seemed to indicate that a true alloy had here been formed, and thus to establish the metallic character of the consolidated gas. Various rumors of this circumstance have been circulating in our daily papers, in which the specimen presented by Mr. Graham was exalted into "an ingot of hydrogen," and though, in comparison with this, the actual fact may seem disappointing, yet in its true relations it is sufficiently wonderful, and is certainly a decided step towards the not impossible realization of the veritable "ingot" at some future time. As a mere evidence of the intensity of molecular force, this experiment of Graham reaches into the marvellous and the incomprehensible. If the space occupied by the condensed hydrogen had been entirely void of all other matter, the force required to reduce 800 volumes to one volume would have been 800 atmospheres, or 12,000,000 pounds to the square inch, but with a metal like palladium, as dense as lead, it would be a large allowance to suppose that one-thousandth part of its volume were void space, or consisted of the interstices between its particles. To compress the 800 volumes into this bulk would then demand a force of *twelve million pounds*, or *six thousand tons per square inch*. Yet this inconceivable force is quietly exerted by the atoms of palladium in their attraction for those of the hydrogen. This substance, hydrogen, has other evidence of its metallic character besides these experiments of Graham. We do not allude to its chemical and electrical connections with the metals, but to an action closely related to this absorption by palladium, which, though for some time known, presents a new aspect when viewed in the light of this result. In 1863, Dr. Charles M. Wetherill made a series of investigations on the Ammoniacal Amalgam, which very clearly demonstrated that the peculiar compound known by that name was not an alloy of any such compound as NH^4 with mercury, but was, in truth, a "suds" of mercury, frothed up with minute bubbles of hydrogen and ammonia, but yet holding the gas in such close union as evidenced a decided affinity between the two bodies. We might then justly consider this attraction for and retention of the hydrogen by the mercury as being analogous to the infinitely more energetic action which is shown by palladium, and like it, also, as indicating a tendency in the hydrogen to alloy itself in the manner of a metal with other metallic elements. Remarkable as is this element in its chemical relations, it is equally notable in another respect, about which a few words may be appropriate (in connection with the late astronomical discoveries of which we have recently spoken), under the head of The Cosmical Relations of Hydrogen. — When Miller and Huggins attacked, with the spectroscope, the problem of the constitution of the nebulæ, which had successfully defied the most diligent telescopic research, and had demonstrated that many of these were of gaseous consistency, hydrogen was one of the substances first recognized in the wonderful nebula of Orion and in several others.   Now, this nebula of Orion was believed by Lord Ross to have been completely resolved by his telescope into separate points of light, and we should thus be led to conclude that it is, in fact, a vast system — a universe of suns or luminous centres, none of them solid, however, but all, on the contrary, vast spheres of glowing gas, that gas being chiefly hydrogen, mixed with nitrogen.   When, in May, 1866, a star in the constellation of the Northern Crown suddenly burst forth with unprecedented splendor, and when examined with the spectroscope showed a spectrum such as had never before been encountered, consisting of such a one as our sun or an ordinary star gives, but with 4 bright lines, due to a gaseous source of light, superposed, it was found that two of these lines (and those the most brilliant) were such as come from light emitted by intensely heated hydrogen.   The natural conclusion from this was, that some half extinguished star or sun had been encountered by one of these nebulous masses of hydrogen, or else by some vast globe or planetary cloud of the same gas, which had lost its heat and ceased to be luminous.   This true "planet" or "wandering sphere" of hydrogen, coming within range of the star's attraction, was drawn down to it, and, by the arrest of motion and compression consequent upon its encounter, was itself heated to incandescence, and heated also the surface of the dead sun to a temporary but intense brightness.   Here, then, was presented the spectacle of a world on fire, in which the agent of destruction, or reconstruction, whichever it might be, was one of these celestial masses of hydrogen gas.   It is curious to reflect, in this relation, that, making due allowance for the probable distance of this star and the velocity of light, this sphere had been at rest for some 10 or 12 years after its fiery ordeal, at the time when we witnessed the event as in actual progress.   When, about a year since, Graham subjected pieces of meteoric iron to the same treatment which had, in the case of ordinary iron, eliminated the carbonic oxide which it had absorbed while undergoing fusion in the smelting-furnace, it was hydrogen gas in large quantity which was evolved; thus proving that in the furnace in which these "falling stars" were fused and cast into shape, this same widely distributed element was again predominant.   Lastly, in these spectroscopic observations and discoveries in connection with the sun, which we described in our last number, it seems to be very clearly shown that hydrogen gas is again the main constituent of that which Lockyer proposes to call the solar "chromosphere," which surrounds the entire mass of our luminary for a depth of some 5,000 miles, and forms those flames or protuberances, a single tongue of which, as in the last eclipse, may contain some 7,000,000,000,000 cubic miles, or 27 times the earth's volume of this gas.   We have reason, therefore, to wish that our knowledge of these solar appendages may not become too intimate, and that none of them may, by an excursion to this distance, furnish to other planets, at our expense, a second display of the phenomena exhibited in τ Coronæ Borealis.

IS HYDROGEN GAS A METAL ?

It has been long suspected that hydrogen would ultimately prove to be a metal. Our readers will also recollect the announcement that during some recent experiments a substance had been discovered, supposed to be the metallic base of hydrogen. Still more recent experiments by Thomas Graham, F.R.S., Master of the British Mint, throw additional light upon this most important subject.

It has often been maintained on chemical grounds that hydrogen gas is the vapor of a highly volatile metal. The idea forces itself upon the mind, that palladium with its occluded hydrogen is simply an alloy of this volatile metal, in which the volatility of the one element is restrained by its union with the other, and which owes its metallic aspect equally to both constituents. How far such a view is borne out by the properties of the compound substance in question, will appear by the following examination of the properties of what, assuming its metallic character, would fairly be named hydrogenium.

The density of palladium, when charged with 800 or 900 times its volume of hydrogen gas, is perceptibly lowered, but the change cannot be measured accurately by the ordinary method of immersion in water, owing to a continuous evolution of minute hydrogen bubbles, which appear to be determined by contact with the liquid. However, the linear dimensions of the charged palladium are altered so considerably, that the difference admits of easy measurement, and furnishes the required density by calculation. Palladium, in the form of wire, is readily charged with hydrogen, by evolving that gas upon the surface of the metal in a galvanometer containing dilute sulphuric acid, as usual. The length of the wire, before and after a charge, is found by stretching it on both occasions by the same moderate weight, such as will not produce permanent distention over the surface of a flat, graduated measure. The measure was graduated to hundredths of an inch, and by means of a vernier, the divisions could be read to thousandths. The distance between two fine cross lines marked upon the surface of the wire near each of its extremities was observed.

The wire had been drawn from welded palladium, and was hard and elastic. The diameter of the wire was 0.462 millimetres; its specific gravity was 15.38, as determined with care. The wire was twisted into a loop at each end, and the mark made near each loop. The loops were varnished so as to limit absorption of gas by the wire to the measured length between the two marks. To straighten the wire, the loop was fixed, and the other connected with a string passing over a pulley and loaded with 1.5 kilogrammes, a weight sufficient to straighten the wire without occasioning any undue strain. The wire was charged with hydrogen by making it the negative electrode of a small Bunsen's battery, consisting of two cells, each of half a litre in capacity. The positive electrode was a thick, plantinum wire, placed side

16

by side with the palladium wire, and extending the whole length of the latter, within a tall jar filled with dilute sulphuric acid. The palladium wire had, in consequence, hydrogen carried to its surface for a period of one and a half hours. A longer exposure was found not to add sensibly to the charge of hydrogen acquired by the wire. The wire was again measured and the increase in length noted. Finally, the wire, being dried with a cloth, was divided at the marks, and the charged portion heated in a long narrow glass tube kept vacuous by a Sprengel aspirator. The whole occluded hydrogen was thus collected and measured; its volume is reduced by calculation to Bar. 760 m.m., and Therm. 0° C.

The original length of the palladium wire exposed was 609.144 m.m. (23.982 inches) and its weight 1.6832 grm. The wire received a charge of hydrogen amounting to 936 times its volume, measuring 128 c.c., and therefore weighing 0.01147 grm. When the gas was ultimately expelled, the loss as ascertained by direct weighing was 0.01164 grm. The charged wire measured 618.923 m.m., showing an increase in length of 9.779 m.m. (0-.385 inch.) The increase in linear dimensions is from 100 to 101-.605; and in cubic capacity, assuming the expansion to be equal in all directions, from 100 to 104.908. Supposing the two metals united without any change of volume, the alloy may therefore be said to be composed of—

		By volume.	
Palladium	. . . .	100	or 95.32
Hydrogenium	. . . .	4.908	or 4.68
		104.908	100

The expansion which the palladium undergoes appears enormous if viewed as a change of bulk in the metal only, due to any conceivable physical force, amounting as it does to 16 times the dilatation of palladium when heated from 0° to 100° C. The density of the charged wire is reduced by calculation from 12.3 to 11.79. Again, as 100 is to 4.91, so the volume of the palladium, 0.1358 c.c., is to the volume of the hydrogenium 0.006714 c.c. Finally, dividing the weight of the hydrogenium, 0.01147 grm., by its volume in the alloy, 0.006714 c.c., we find

Density of hydrogenium, ... 1.708

The density of hydrogenium, then, appears to approach that of magnesium, 1.743, by this first experiment.

Further, the expulsion of hydrogen from the wire, however caused, is attended with an extraordinary contraction of the latter. On expelling the hydrogen by a moderate heat, the wire not only receded to its original length, but fell as much below that zero as it had previously ridden above it. The palladium wire first measuring 609.144 m.m., and which increased 9.77 m.m., was ultimately reduced to 590.444 m.m., and contracted 9.7 m.m. The wire is permanently shortened. The density of the palladium did not increase, but fell slightly at the same time, namely, from 12.38 to 12.12; proving that this contraction of the wire is in length only. The result is the converse of extension by wire-drawing. The retraction of the wire is possibly due to an effect of wire-drawing, in leaving the particles of metal in a state of unequal tension, a tension which is excessive in the direction of the length of the wire. The metallic particles would seem to become mobile, and to right themselves in proportion as the hydrogen escapes; and the wire contracts in length, expanding, as appears by its final density, in other directions at the same time.

A wire so charged with hydrogen, if rubbed with the powder of magnesia (to make the flame luminous), burns like a waxed thread when ignited in the flame of a lamp.

Numerous other experiments were also performed, with remarkable unanimity of result; the specific density of hydrogenium being found by calculation from several successive experiments to be, respectively, 1.708, 1.898, 1.977, 1.917, 1.927, 1.930, 2.055, the variations resulting from different volumes being used in the alloy, the highest densities being obtained when small quantities were used.

In these experiments the hydrogen was expelled by exposing the palladium placed within a glass tube to a moderate heat short of redness, and exhausting by means of a Sprengel tube; but the gas was also withdrawn in another way, namely, by making the wire the positive electrode, and thereby evolving oxygen upon its surface. In such circumstances, a slight film of oxide of palladium is formed on the wire, but it appears not to interfere with the extraction and oxidation of the hydrogen. The wire measured: —

			Difference.
Before charge,	. . . . . .	443.25 m.m.	
With hydrogen,	. . . . . .	449.90 "	6.65 m.m.
After discharge,	. . . . . .	437.31 "	5.94 "

The retraction of the wire, therefore, does not require the concurrence of a high temperature. This experiment further proved that a large charge of hydrogen may be removed in a complete manner, by exposure to the positive pole — for 4 hours in this case; for the wire in its ultimate state gave no hydrogen on being heated *in vacuo*.

Experiments were also made to determine the conducting power of the palladium and hydrogenium wire, and its magnetic properties, the details of which may be hereafter referred to. The record of these experiments, as communicated to the Royal Society, January 14, by Mr. Graham, forms one of the most important contributions to science that has been recently made, and will immediately arrest the attention of the entire scientific world.

DETERMINATIONS OF FREE OXYGEN.

At a meeting of the Manchester Literary and Philosophical Society, Mr. Peter Hart described his method of making rapid determinations of free oxygen. The apparatus required consists, in addition to an ordinary pneumatic trough, of two tubes, each one-half inch in diameter and 16 inches long, closed at one end. One of the tubes is graduated into fiftieths of a cubic inch, and the other is coated internally with phosphorus. This is effected by dropping into the tube a few pieces of phosphorus; it is then to be closed by a sound cork, and the phosphorus (melted by immersing the tube in hot water) may be spread in a thin coating over the interior by turning it round as it cools. On cooling, the cork is to be withdrawn, the tube filled with water, and a piece of India-rubber tube tied securely over the mouth. This completes the apparatus. The *modus operandi* is as follows: Both tubes are filled with water, and allowed to remain in the trough, a portion of the air to be examined is passed into the measuring tube, which is now allowed to remain for 5 minutes in the trough to allow it to attain the same temperature as the water. It is lifted until the water is at the same level within and without, and may then be closed by the finger, and withdrawn from the trough. The volume is easily noted. This done, it is connected by the India-rubber joint with the phosphorus tube, into which the air is allowed to flow. The whole may now be placed for half an hour in the trough, when the gas may be poured back into the measuring tube, the level once more taken, and the volume read off in the same way as before. The loss is oxygen. No claim is made for strict scientific accuracy in connection with this apparatus; its sole merit consists in its offering an easy and rapid means of approximately determining the free oxygen in an atmosphere. In the working of sulphuric acid chambers it has been found extremely valuable, and possibly may be found so for other technical inquiries. — *Mechanics' Magazine.*

DEFLECTION OF BEAMS.

Professor W. A. Norton, of Yale College, at the meeting of the American Association, at Salem, communicated the principal results of a series of experiments which he had made to test the theoretical laws of the deflection of beams exposed to a transverse strain. In the experiments the beam rested on the supports at the ends, and was loaded in the middle. The accepted formula gives the following laws: (1) The deflection is proportional to the pressure; (2) inversely to the breadth; (3) and to the cube of the depth; (4) directly proportional to the cube of the length. The results of the experiments (fully explained by diagrams and tables) show that the deflection is approximately proportional to the pressure, but, strictly speaking, increases according to a less rapid law, the neutral axis of the cross section of the stick shifting its position and its distance from the centre of gravity of the cross section augmenting. As to the second law, the deviations are not greater than may be attributed to differences in the moduli of elasticity of different sticks, and the greater shifting of the neutral axis of the sticks most strained. The third law cannot be regarded as even approximately true, except in case of sticks whose length bears a high proportion to their depth. The fourth law fails as well as the third. Professor Norton has made with the same apparatus a series of experiments on the degree of set or residual deflection communicated to sticks by varied strains and under varied circumstances, and obtained interesting and curious if not important results. But these he did not enter upon at this time.

ELEMENTS OF MATTER.

Prof. Charles A. Seely, at the meeting of the American Association, at Salem, in his paper on the Classification of the Elements of Matter, after alluding to some points in the philosophy of classification in general, remarked that the revised atomic notation and the doctrine of atomicity are the foundation of what is termed " modern chemistry." They are the starting-point of the most reasonable explanations of facts. They test the genuineness of the old grouping of the elements, and they lead us to altogether new systems of grouping. Atomicity divides the elements into two grand divisions, perissads (whose atoms combine singly with an odd number of other atoms), and astiads (whose atoms combine with an even number of other atoms). The author supposed himself the first to observe that if the classes be placed side by side, the members being arranged in the order of their atomic numbers, and at the same time so that those of corresponding atomic numbers be brought into juxtaposition, then the elements of corresponding atomic numbers will be found to be remarkably allied in physical properties; in other words, the astiad is paired with the perissad of corresponding atomic number. It will also be observed that each member of a natural group will be found opposite a member of a related natural group. It thus appears that the physical properties of the elements are closely related to and possibly dependent upon the atomic weight and the atomicity; the relation is so close that the atomic weight and atomicity may be taken as the sole data for a subdivision of the two grand classes. For the best realization of this thought the author acknowledged indebtedness to Prof. Charles S. Peirce, of Cambridge, and exhibited a diagram of classification prepared by him. In this chart the elements are represented at heights corresponding to their atomic numbers, and the natural series appear in vertical columns; in other words, the ordinates of the points fixing the position of the elements represent the atomic weights, and the abscissas of the members of a series are equal. The chart plainly exhibits the fact of the pairing between individuals and between well-recog-

16 *

nized groups, and at the same time indicates new symmetries and new groupings. Prof. Seely believes that no diagram of classification of the elements has ever been devised which is so simple and so comprehensive. The paper continues by pointing out the importance and the consequences of the fact of the pairing of the elements. It is a new confirmation of the doctrine of atomicity and of the truth of the atomic numbers. It indicates the probability that very few more elements are to be discovered, and assists in bringing chemical phenomena into the domain of mathematics and ordinary physics.

HEAT.

M. Le Roux has made some experiments with the vapor of sodium, and examined its capability or incapability of passing through rock salt. Two crucibles of rock salt were prepared, a thin plate of the same substance placed between them, and in one of the cavities sodium was placed. Notwithstanding a bright red heat maintained for several hours, the piece which was not in direct contact with the sodium vapor remained completely unaltered, even where it had been in contact with the plate already completely penetrated. Chloride of sodium is not attacked by the vapor of sodium, but soda corrodes it energetically. A very small quantity of soda suffices to hermetically seal two surfaces of rock salt, sodium preserving its lustre for several months in a crucible of this kind. Potassium vapor does not attack its chloride, but it covers the chloride with a bright blue substance, in which, possibly, chemists recognize the suboxide of potassium.

Mr. W. P. Dexter has described a new gas-lamp for heating crucibles, etc. The ordinary Bunsen burner is known to act upon the surface of platinum vessels brought into contact with the inner line of the flame; the metal loses its polish, becoming superficially porous and spongy, and requires the use of the burnisher to bring it back to its original state. This alteration of the surface is attended with a change of weight, and Mr. Dexter has consequently devised the following arrangement: He removes the air-tube of a common Bunsen lamp, and puts in its place a somewhat longer one of glass or iron, of about 12 millimetres internal diameter. The gas-jet has a single circular aperture, and should be in proper proportion to the diameter of the tube, which may be held in any of the ordinary clamped supports. The tube being raised sufficiently above the jet to allow free entrance of air, and a full stream of gas let on, a " roaring " flame is produced, of which the interior blue cone is pointed, sharply defined, and extends only about half an inch from the top of the tube. A polished platinum surface is not acted upon by this flame, provided it be not brought into contact with the interior cone. In the Bunsen burner, as usually made, the supply of air depends upon the diameter of the tube, the holes at its base being more than sufficient to supply the draught. With the wider tube, it is necessary to limit the admission of air by depressing the tube upon the lamp, when the force of the gas is diminished. Otherwise the proportion becomes such that an explosive mixture is formed. For this reason it is more convenient to use an arrangement in which the excess of air can be regulated by an exterior tube sliding obliquely downward over the air-apertures. The gas-jet should be on a level with the top of these apertures, which must be much larger than those of the ordinary Bunsen burner.

Mr. Brown, of the War Office Chemical Department, has discovered a remarkable property connected with the ignition and explosion of gun-cotton. He has found that the explosive force of gun-cotton may, like that of nitro-glycerine, be developed by the exposure of the substance to the sudden concussion produced by a detonation; and that, if exploded by that agency, the suddenness and consequent violence of its action greatly exceed that of its explosion by means of a highly heated body or flame. It follows, that gun-cotton, even when freely exposed to air, may be made to explode with destructive violence, apparently not inferior to that of nitro-glycerine, simply by employing for its explosion a fuse to which is attached a small detonating charge. Some remarkable results have been already obtained with this new mode of exploding gun-cotton. Large blocks of granite, and other very hard rock, and iron plates of some thickness, have been shattered by exploding small charges of gun-cotton which simply rested upon their upper surfaces. Further, long charges or trains of gun-cotton, simply placed upon the ground against stockades of great strength, and wholly unconfined, have been exploded by means of detonating fuses placed in the centre or at one end of the train, and produced uniformly destructive effects throughout their entire length, the results corresponding to those produced by 8 or 10 times the amount of gunpowder when applied under the most favorable conditions. Mining and quarrying operations, with gun-cotton applied in the new manner, have furnished results quite equal to those obtained with nitro-glycerine, and have proved conclusively that if gun-cotton is exploded by detonation, it is unnecessary to confine the charge in the blast-hole by the process of hard-tamping, as the explosion of the entire charge takes place too suddenly for its effects to be appreciably diminished by the line of escape presented by the blast-hole. Thus the most dangerous of all operations connected with mining may be dispensed with when gun-cotton fired by the new system is employed. — *Quarterly Journal of Science, April,* 1869.

FACTS IN NATURAL PHILOSOPHY.

Radiation of Heat from the Moon. — The Earl of Rosse is making a series of experiments, by means of a thermo-pile of 4 elements and a 3-foot telescope, to determine, if possible, what proportion of the moon's heat consists of—1. That coming from the interior of the moon, which will not vary with the phase; 2. That which falls from the sun on the moon's surface, and is at once reflected regularly and irregularly; 3. That which falling from the sun on the moon's surface is absorbed, raises the temperature of the moon's surface, and is afterwards radiated as heat of low refrangibility. The chief result arrived at up to the present moment is, that (the radiating power of the moon being taken as equal to lampblack, and the earth's atmosphere supposed not to affect the result) a deviation of 90° for full moon appears to indicate an elevation of temperature = 500° F. The relative amount of solar and lunar radiation was found = 89819 : 1.

Heat Reflected from the Moon's Surface. — The moon's surface emits as much heat as a cube filled with boiling water, covered with lampblack, having a surface of 6.5 square centimetres, and placed at a distance of 85 metres from the thermo-electric measuring apparatus employed by the author in his experiments. — *M. Baille, in Comptes Rendus of Nov. 2,* 1869.

Maximum Point of the Density of Water. — A great many data exist in different text-books as to the precise temperature at which water arrives at the highest density, varying from 38.624° F. to 39.344° F. (3.68° C. to 4.08° C.), the latter being the number indicated by H. Kapp. A new series of researches made by Rossetti has led to very nearly the same result, the numbers being 4.07° C., or 39.326° F., and this temperature should now, as before, be considered the standard for graduation of measures:

Oils on Water. — Dr. Carter Moffat has succeeded in fixing on paper the beautiful figures which are produced when oils, etc., are allowed to fall, drop by drop, on a surface of pure water, and which Professor Tomlinson has shown to be characteristic of each oil. The method is very simple, and is, briefly, to obtain a pattern on water, note the time, lay on the paper, glazed side downwards, for an instant, take out, draw through a plate of ink, remove, and wash with water. The process is capable of great extension, and will be valuable to paper-stainers and others.

The Temperature of Sea-Water at Great Depths. — Several carefully conducted soundings, made near the Faroe Islands, have revealed the fact that while the surface-water has an almost invariable temperature of 52°, the heat at great depths varies exceedingly. At a depth of 500 fathoms the temperature was 32°, — a fact which is explained by the supposition of a cold Arctic stream flowing from the north-east, and apparently coming between the fork of the Gulf Stream. Another interesting fact established by these inquiries is, that even at a temperature in the ocean almost that of our freezing-point, there are an abundance and variety of animal forms which could not have been predicated. — *Med. Times and Gazette.*

The Tides. — Mr. William Ferrel, of Cambridge, at the meeting of the American Association at Salem, gave some results of a discussion of Tide Operations at the Boston Dry Dock, and also at Brest, in France. The most important new term introduced by Mr. Ferrel depends upon friction, and the important modifications consequent upon it were very satisfactorily explained.

Professor Peirce complimented the author very highly upon his results, stating that we may now for the first time feel that we have a theory of the tides.

Transmission of Gases through Colloid Substances. — In a recent lecture at the Royal Institution, Dr. Odling said, in regard to the transmission of gases through India-rubber, etc., that the "gas appears to be condensed at the nearest surface, and to pass through the pores of the material as a volatile liquid, which evaporates on the other side. He took a long glass tube, with its upper end closed with a single thickness of calico. When the tube was half filled with colored liquid, and its lower end placed in a dish of water, the water in the tube ran out, because of the rapid passage of air through the holes in the calico. But when the calico was wetted with water, the column of liquid was sustained in the tube, as air could enter then only by dissolving in the water and evaporating on the other side, — a very slow process. Ammonia, being very soluble in water, passed through quicker; which the lecturer proved by inverting a jar of ammonia over the wet calico, thus causing the liquid in the tube to descend more rapidly. Liquid ammonia dropped upon the wet calico was also seen to act more vigorously than the gas which had to dissolve in the water before it began to pass."

A New Pyrometer. — M. A. Lamy, in the "Comptes Rendus," of Aug. 2, 1869, describes the advantages of this instrument at length. It is based upon the principle that certain compounds, gaseous or volatile, are decomposed in a partial and progressive manner in the same measure that the temperature is elevated, and that the tension of the elements of the mixture, or tension of dissociation, increases with the temperature, and remains constant at a fixed temperature. This law has been extended to the case of solid substance formed by the union of two bodies, one of which is fixed, the other volatile, like carbonate of lime. The pyrometer is formed of a porcelain tube, varnished upon its two faces; closed at one end and put in communication by the other with a tube of glass in two branches containing mercury, or connected with any other manometric system. The porcelain tube contains a certain quantity of Iceland spar, or simply marble powder. The marble powder is heated to redness, and the tube is filled with dry and pure carbonic-acid gas. When such a tube cools down to the ordinary temperature, the carbonic-acid gas is entirely reabsorbed by the lime, and the manometer shows a vacuum. It is then a true barometer when it is not used to indicate high temperatures.

Coloration of Glass under Influence of Sunlight. — M. Bontemps, who is the managing director of the celebrated glass works at Choisy le Roi, states, after referring to the observations on this subject made by the immortal Faraday, in 1824, and MM. Gaffield and Pelouze, in 1863 and 1867, that his observations lead to the following results: Within 3 months after having been exposed to sunlight, the best and whitest glass made at St. Gobain is turned very distinctly yellow; extra white glass (of a peculiar mode of manufacture) has become even more yellow, and gradually assumes a color known as *pelure d'oignon*; glass containing

5 per cent. of litharge was also affected, but far less perceptibly; crystal glass, made with carbonate of potassa (the other varieties referred to contain carbonate of soda), litharge, and silica, was not at all affected; English plate glass, made by the British Plate Glass Company, and exhibiting a distinctly azure-blue tinge, remained, also, unaffected. The author attributes this coloration, which begins with yellow and gradually turns to violet, passing through red *pelure d'oignon*, to the oxidizing effect of the sun's rays upon the protoxides of iron and manganese contained in glass. — *Comptes Rendus*, Nov. 22, 1869.

Luminous Effects of Light. — In the "Comptes Rendus," of Nov. 15, there is a paper entitled, "Researches on the Luminous Effects due to the Action of Light upon different Bodies." This is the fifth instalment of a lengthy memoir by M. Becquerel. The author's experiments lead to the following conclusions: The most refrangible rays, and principally those beyond the violet, are the most active; the different parts of the solar spectrum differ in their activity; the least refrangible rays from the blue, and past the ultra-red, act especially as extinguishers of phosphorescences.

Phosphorescence of the Sea. — The phenomenon is due to electricity, and the infusoria only acts as sharp points do in well-known electrical experiments. — *M. Duchemin, Comptes Rendus*, Nov. 2, 1869.

Constitution and Motion of Glaciers. — In the "Comptes Rendus," of Nov. 2, 1869, MM. Grad and Dupré have a paper on this subject.

The chief results of the labors of these authors are the following: The crystals of ice of the glaciers are arranged in a regular manner, and the constituent molecules of that ice are placed as in frozen water. The velocity of motion of a glacier increases from the bottom to the top, while the maximum of motion coincides with the greatest slope.

Reflection of Heat. — Professor Gustav Magnus, at the meeting of the British Association, read a paper, in which he made known a curious discovery of his own, that fluor spar has the property of reflecting, very largely, the dark, invisible rays emitted by hot rock salt. Dr. Balfour Stewart then called attention to the fact that there is much evidence tending to prove that the heat rays from rock salt are of very great wave length, belonging almost to one of the extremities of the spectrum.

Mechanical Equivalent of Heat. — Mr. P. H. Van der Weyde, of New York, read a paper, at the meeting of the American Association, Aug., 1869, on "The Determination of the Mechanical Equivalent of Heat by Means of the Modern Ice and Cooling Machines." In converting heat into motion there is a great loss, the result being but one-seventh or one-fourteenth part what would be expected. But in converting motion into heat we get very nearly a full equivalent. In the production of artificial cold by abstracting heat we get the same result. The expenditure of one horse-power reduces the temperature of water one degree Fahrenheit in one minute. In the English process of cooling, using ammonia as the agent, 10 horse-power working 10 hours has the cooling power of one ton of ice, and one ton of coal, or a week's supply, has the virtue of 14 tons of ice. The professor finds an excellent evaporation in condensed gas from petroleum wells or stills. This gas can be condensed into fluid by very little pressure, and boils at a temperature of 30° Fahrenheit.

Curious Production of Cold. — Dr. Phipson has recently discovered that an intense degree of cold is produced by dissolving sulphocyanate of ammonium in water. Many salts, more especially salts of ammonia, lower the temperature of water while dissolving; but, according to Dr. Phipson, no compound produces this effect in so marvellous a manner as sulphocyanate of ammonium. In one experiment 35 grammes of this salt dissolved rapidly in 35 cubic centimetres of water at 23° Cent., caused the thermometer to descend in a few seconds to 10° Cent. The moisture of the atmosphere instantly condensed itself on the outside of the glass in thin plates of ice. — *Scientific Review.*

As a general rule, according to experiments by M. Schultz, it has been found that the point of solidification of fluids is lowered by substances dissolved therein, and that gases dissolved in fluids exercise the same effects. Pure acetic acid fuses at 16°; this is lowered to 15.2° when a current of carbonic acid is transmitted through this acid. It is well known that hydrochloric acid gas and ammonia gas lower the freezing temperature of water in which they are dissolved; so do carbonic acid and sulphurous acid gas; and it has been ascertained by M. Schultz that nitrogen, oxygen, and hydrogen gases exert the same effect when dissolved in water. Numerous experiments were made by him with the view of ascertaining the effect of an increase of pressure brought to bear upon the absorption of various gases by water, and the lowering of the freezing-point of that liquid in consequence thereof. By the phenomenon of regelation is understood that property exhibited by ice of freezing together to a solid mass, when pieces of that substance are pressed together at the temperature of 0°. After quoting the opinions of Messrs. Faraday, Forbes, Thomson, and Helmholtz, on this subject, the author says: "When we take it for granted that regelation is the formation of ice from water anew, we must bear in mind that only pure water, or water, at least, not saturated with air, is suitable for this purpose."

Photography — Self-prints from Nature. — At a meeting of the Mass. Inst. of Technology, Mr. Thomas Gaffield exhibited illustrations of what he calls "Photographic Self-prints from Nature." While on a visit to the country, having with him his pressure frames and sensitive paper, it occurred to him that the colored autumn leaves might produce varied effects, just as the colored glasses did on the sensitive paper exposed beneath them. He exhibited various groups of colored leaves taken in this way; the red leaves generally cut off a very large amount of the actinic rays, while the other colors passed a considerable amount; the thickness of the leaves, their dryness from age, and the hardness of the veins and ribs, are elements which determine the amount of chemical effect upon the paper. From wreaths of leaves he went to ferns, arranged in various artistic forms, and as mottoes. By a singular coincidence, the first motto thus printed was, "God is love," and he was thus able to make Nature herself proclaim in letters of light, by the voice of the humble ferns, and in the language of flowers, the essential principle of Christianity. The work is done as follows : Having procured your design, place it under the glass of your pressure frame ; if a motto, it must be written backwards. Place your ferns, with mucilage, upon the glass within the lines of your design ; put your sensitive paper on the glass, press the back board down, and expose to the sunlight until you get a dark impression. Have this print washed, toned, fixed, and mounted by some photographic friend, if you have not a workroom for the purpose at home. The time of exposure varies with the seasons, the hour of the day, and the state of the sunlight. In five or ten minutes, in a bright summer day, he has obtained a good impression. This dark background print, No. 1, is used as a negative to produce No. 2, or a print with a white background, and in which all the lights and shades of No. 1 are reversed ; from No. 2, used as a negative, No. 1 can be reproduced, although the lines are not quite so sharp, nor the effect so good, as in the print taken directly from the ferns. By the aid of a camera any of these interesting pictures may be reproduced of any required size. Many of these were exhibited. From leaves and ferns, he successfully experimented with delicate algæ from the shore, the bright feathers of birds, and brilliant wings of insects ; making thus the sun portray, with its powerful pencil, some of the most beautiful objects of the land, and sea, and air. These designs were of singular delicacy and beauty. What he had thus been able to accomplish in the midst of a busy life, he believed was sufficient to show that very important results might be expected from the further development of this process, especially in the illustration of the works of nature, by the most ethereal and at the same time most powerful agency of sunlight.

Photographs of Nobert's Bands. — In "Silliman's Journal" we have a paper by Dr. Woodward, who has so distinguished himself by his micro-photographic results, describing his success in photographing a new plate by Nobert, containing 19 bands with a one-sixteenth objective, by Powel & Leland. No lens, previously, had been able to resolve the lines on these bands beyond the 15th.

Photographing without a Lens. — The method adopted by Mr. James Thomson, of Glasgow, to photograph the bodily organs of fossil corals : Each of these fossil corals is nearly as large as a hen's egg, and Mr. Thomson, it will be remembered, cut a thin slice out of the centre of each coral, and then ground down and polished the stone slice till it became thin and translucent enough to be used as a negative from which to take photographic prints on paper. When he exhibited these valuable photographs at the British Association at Norwich, last year, Mr. W. H. Harrison recommended him to have them copied in future by the permanent carbon process. Mr. Thomson, in consequence, went to Newcastle-on-Tyne, saw Mr. Joseph W. Swan, the patentee of the chief carbon process, and made arrangements for a large supply of permanent photographs from the stone negatives. Some of these carbon prints were exhibited at Exeter, and met with much approval. Mr. Thomson says that he and Mr. Swan are now trying experiments upon a new process, which they hope will result in the production of blocks from the coral sections which can be used in the common printing press, to print from in printing ink. — *Journal of Franklin Inst., Nov.*, 1869.

17

CHEMISTRY.

HYDROGENIUM.

SOME years since, Deville and Troost discovered that hydrogen passed somewhat readily through platinum at a high temperature, and later Graham discovered the property of palladium even at low temperatures of taking up and retaining within itself a large proportion of hydrogen.

It has often been maintained, on chemical grounds, that hydrogen gas is the vapor of a highly volatile metal. Graham, in two papers read before the Royal Society,[*] details a series of experiments made by him, from which he concludes that "palladium, with its occluded hydrogen, is simply an alloy of this volatile metal, in which the volatility of the one element is restrained by its union with the other, and which owes its metallic aspect equally to both constituents." Assuming that hydrogen does really thus exist in a metallic state, he calls the metal hydrogenium.

The palladium was employed in the form of wire, and was charged with hydrogen by making it the negative electrode of a small Bunsen battery; the positive electrode consisted of a platinum wire extending by the side of the palladium wire in a jar of acidulated water. In this way the palladium wire occluded an amount of hydrogen equal to 800 or 900 times its own volume.

Density. — The density of palladium when charged with 800 or 900 times its volume of hydrogen is perceptibly lowered. The density of the alloy cannot be measured in water in the usual manner, as the mere immersion in water determines the escape of hydrogen. It was therefore estimated, assuming that the two metals united without condensation, by measuring the wire under an equal tension, before and after charging it with hydrogen.

The hydrogen was then exhausted by a Sprengel aspirator and the volume measured.

It was found, on exhausting the hydrogen, that the palladium wire had decreased in length by an amount nearly equal to its increase over its original length. Supposing the increase of volume due to the hydrogenium to be represented by the sum of the elongation and the retraction, the density of hydrogenium calculated from a number of experiments would be in the neighborhood of .85.

[*] Printed in full in the "Chem. News," Vol. xix., p. 52, and Vol. xx., p. 16.

The property of occluding hydrogen belongs also to the alloys of palladium when the second metal does not form more than one-half the alloy. In this case the expansion is about twice as great as in the case of pure palladium, and on expelling the hydrogen the alloy returns to its original dimensions without further retraction. The density of hydrogenium, calculated from a series of experiments with alloys of palladium, gave results between 0.711 and 0.755, the mean of which would be 0.733.

Tenacity. — The tenacity of the alloy of palladium and hydrogenium is less than that of palladium. If the tenacity of the latter be represented by 100, that of the alloy will be represented by 81.29.

Conductivity. — The electric conductivity of copper being represented by 100, that of palladium would be represented by 8.10, and that of the alloy by 5.99.

The conductivity, although diminished, still remains considerable, which would show the metallic character of hydrogenium.

Magnetism. — Palladium is feebly but truly magnetic; the alloy is magnetic to a greater degree, which fact indicates the metallic character of the other component of the alloy.

Chemical Characters. — The chemical properties of hydrogenium also distinguish it from ordinary hydrogen: e. g., the palladium alloy precipitates mercury and calomel from a solution of mercuric chloride without disengagement of hydrogen; that is, hydrogenium decomposes mercuric chloride while hydrogen does not.

The conclusions arrived at are, that hydrogenium is a white solid of metallic aspect, of a density between 7 and 8, and capable of forming with an equivalent proportion of palladium a definite alloy.

CELL-STRUCTURE OF METALS.

A paper, by W. Vivian, recently read before the Liverpool Polytechnic Society, presented some interesting points in regard to the microscopic structure of metals. Mr. Vivian classes metals under two heads, namely, those the structure of which is angular or crystalline, and those in which it is cellular or porous. The cellular structure is most highly developed in those metals which we have found to be the best conductors of heat and electricity; and its perfection is in proportion to the capacity for such conduction. "The 'fibre,' or 'silky lustre,' exhibited in the fracture of good iron," says Mr. V., "is only the effect of the light reflected from the inner surfaces of myriads of minute cells exposed by the fracture. The form of these, in their normal state, is spherical, or nearly so, but becomes changed in the process of rolling. The mechanical properties of tenacity, ductility, etc., must greatly depend on the perfection of the cell system; a crystalline, malleable iron does not show prisms in its fracture, but simply a number of faces or planes crossing the cells at right angles, cutting them off short. The process of rolling iron into plates or sheets does not obliterate these cells, but merely modifies them, as they widen out under the pressure; the thin partitions become laminated, and on the regularity of this lamination the quality of the plate very much depends. The cell system of copper is more perfect than that of iron, a result of the pouring of the copper into moulds, but the cells are afterwards altered by the pressure in rolling, etc., but never destroyed. If it were possible to make a section one-millionth part of an inch in thickness these cells would be seen." — *Druggists' Circular.*

BEHAVIOR OF METALS IN THE ELECTRIC CURRENT.

If an electric current from a couple of cells of a Bunsen battery, the positive pole of which consists of a silver plate, is made to pass through water acidulated with sulphuric acid, the silver becomes covered with a black coating of amorphous peroxide of silver. The formation of this oxide is due to ozone; for, on substituting a platinum plate for the one of silver, the smell of ozone may be at once recognized. The same phenomenon takes place if, instead of acidulated water, a solution of sulphate of sodium be used. No peroxide is formed in a solution of nitrate of potassium, but a flocculent, light-brown precipitate of oxide of silver forms in the liquid. In a solution of ferrocyanide of potassium the silver becomes covered with a white film of ferrocyanide of silver (amorphous), and in a solution of bichromate of potassium with a reddish-black film of crystallized chromate of silver. When a plate of palladium is used as the positive electrode in water acidulated with sulphuric acid, it becomes covered with an almost black film of peroxide. Upon lead a coating of brown peroxide, and upon thallium one of black oxide, is deposited. Osmium, in its ordinary porous condition, is freely converted into osmic acid. If, as an electrolyte, a dilute solution of hydrate of sodium is employed, the solution assumes a deep-yellow color, while at the same time metal is deposited on the negative electrode. The same is the case with ruthenium. Osm-iridium, in its natural state, readily dissolves in the alkaline electrolyte. — *Wöhler, Götting. Nach.*

PURE IRON.

Matthiesen prepares pure iron by the following method: Pure dried ferrous sulphate and pure dried sulphate of sodium are mixed in nearly equal proportions, and introduced gradually into a red-hot platinum crucible. The mass is kept in fusion until the evolution of sulphurous-acid gas ceases, then allowed to cool and extracted with water. If the heat be properly regulated, the whole of the iron is left as a very fine crystalline oxide. This oxide is thoroughly washed by decantation, to remove every trace of the sulphate of sodium, and, after being dried, is reduced by hydrogen in a platinum crucible; the spongy iron thus obtained is then pressed into solid buttons, and melted in lime crucibles with the oxyhydrogen blow-pipe. If proper precautions are taken in purifying the ferrous sulphate and the sulphate of sodium, almost absolutely pure iron is obtained; careful analysis fails to detect phosphorus or silicon, while the amount of sulphur varies from 0.00025 to 0.0007 per cent. — *Chem. News, Aug.*, 1869.

APPLICATION OF CHLORINE GAS TO THE TOUGHENING AND REFINING OF GOLD.

A method of effecting the toughening and refining of gold has been devised by F. B. Miller, F.C.S., of the Sydney Branch of the Royal Mint, which appears to be superior to those now in use, and to answer all the requirements of the case in a single operation. A French clay crucible is saturated with borax by immersing it in a strong and hot solution of the salt and then drying. The gold is melted in this crucible with a little borax, and a stream of chlorine gas is allowed to pass through it by means of a clay tube. In a few hours the whole of the silver is converted into chloride, which floats on the gold. The borax prevents the absorption of the chloride by the crucible, and also its volatilization, except in very minute quantities. As soon as the gold has become solid, the still liquid chloride of silver is poured off, and the gold is now found to have a fineness of say 993 in 1,000. The apparent loss of gold is very little greater than is found in ordinary gold melting, — being 2.9 parts in 10,000, whereas in the ordinary process it is two. A small sample of the gold is removed from time to time during the operation, by means of a piece of tobacco-pipe used as a pipette. This is rapidly assayed approximately, and thus the progress of the operation is judged of. The fused chloride of silver, obtained as a slab by this operation, is reduced by placing it between two plates of wrought iron in a bath of dilute sulphuric acid. The spongy silver thus obtained contains gold, which is separated by nitric acid; the silver is then thrown down as chloride and again reduced. — *Chem. Soc., reported in Chem. News.*

REDUCTION OF OXIDES BY HYDROGEN.

M. W. Müller, as a result of a series of experiments made to determine the temperature at which various oxides are reduced by hydrogen, finds that oxide of iron, prepared by cautiously heating metallic iron in the air, is reduced at 285° C.; that oxide of iron prepared from the nitrate is reduced at 286°; when rather moist hydrogen was employed on oxide of iron prepared from ferrous oxalate, the reduction took place at 278°. Precipitated oxide of copper, previously heated to 300°, was reduced at 135°; strongly ignited oxide of copper at 142°; oxide of cobalt at about 132°; oxide of tin at about 174°; oxide of lead at from 310° to 315°; peroxide of mercury at 230°; oxide of silver at between

17*

73° and 78°; oxide of zinc was not reduced at a temperature at which glass fused.

Experiments were also made on the chlorides and sulphides of certain metals. Chloride of gold does not appear to be acted upon below 200°, but at a higher temperature an explosion took place; the action on chloride of platinum was strong at 85°, violent at 165°; the chlorides of silver and lead require a red heat for reduction. Sulphide of gold is reduced at 200°, and sulphide of platinum at the ordinary temperature; sulphuretted hydrogen is formed in both cases. — *Pogg. Ann.*

PROPERTY OF TEROXIDE OF THALLIUM.

The teroxide of thallium may be obtained as a dark-brown powder by digesting with heat freshly precipitated chloride of thallium in a solution of hypochlorite of sodium containing an excess of alkali. If a mixture of the dry teroxide and flowers of sulphur is submitted to a moderate friction, it ignites with explosion. When, however, to the teroxide is added one-eighth its weight of the product vulgarly known as *golden sulphur*, it is observed that the ignition requires less rubbing and takes place without explosion. This mixture possesses the property of being set on fire by the faintest electric spark, surpassing, in this respect, the well-known mixture of equal parts of chlorate of potassium and black sulphide of antimony. — *Dingl. Polyt. Journ.*

MARGUERITTE'S METHOD OF REFINING SUGAR.

It is well known that the present method of manufacturing sugar, notwithstanding the improvements it has received of late years, does not allow the extraction of the whole of the sugar contained in the beet-root, and that the residue contains about 50 per cent. of its weight of the substance to be obtained. The combinations of barium and calcium with sugar, observed by M. Peligot, and the discovery of osmose and dialysis by Messrs. Graham and Dutrochet, have given rise to many attempts to extract from molasses the sugar which it contains in a non-crystallizable form.

The method employed by M. Margueritte is to mix the molasses with alcohol of 85° acidulated with 5 per cent. of sulphuric acid. The precipitate which forms, and which consists mainly of the sulphates of potassium, sodium, and calcium, is removed by filtration, and to the liquor is added an amount of alcohol of 95° equal to that originally employed. A supersaturated solution of sugar is thus obtained, from which the sugar slowly deposits. To hasten this operation a quantity of sugar is added to the solution, and this addition determines the immediate separation of the greater portion of the sugar dissolved. M. Margueritte claims to obtain 35 to 38 kilos. of sugar from 100 kilos. of molasses, and to increase the total amount of the yield from 24 to 26 per cent.— *Comptes Rendus.*

A NEW COMPOUND OF LIME AND SUGAR.

Messrs. Boivin and Loiseau have formed a new combination of lime and sugar, which, moreover, contains carbonic acid. It is prepared as follows: To 200 kilos. of syrup, containing 60 per cent. of crystallizable sugar, are added 120 kilos. of caustic lime as a thick milk of lime; carbonic acid is then passed through the mixture until a precipitate makes its appearance, when 20 litres of tepid lime-water are added and the passing of carbonic acid is stopped. The precipitate contains 43 per cent. of sugar, 40 of lime, and 17 of carbonic acid. — *Bull. Soc. Chim.*

FLUOSILICIC ACID FOR SUGAR REFINING.

M. Marix has taken in France a patent for the application of fluosilicic acid for the purifying of beet-root and other saccharine juices. The saccharine fluids are first diluted with a sufficient quantity of water to take away the viscosity of these fluids, sufficient fluosilicic acid is then added to precipitate all the potassium salts present, and next powdered chalk is added to saturate any excess of the acid. The fluid is then filtered in order to obtain a clear liquid, and this afterwards treated in the usual manner. — *Bull. Soc. Chim.*

MANUFACTURE OF SUGAR.

The "Journal des Fabricants de Sucre" states that experiments are now in progress in some French colonies to try on a large scale the plan of MM. Rousseau and Bonnaterre, of converting the saccharine juice of the cane or the beet-root into a peculiar saccharate of lime, and of transporting that salt, instead of the raw sugar, for the purposes of refining. It is said that this compound is as hard as sand, and can be transported without the risk of damage and injury to which sugar is subject: it can, moreover, be kept for any length of time. — *Chem. News.*

IMPROVED METHOD OF MANUFACTURING GLUCOSE FROM STARCH.

M. Maubré finds that, by the usual mode of proceeding, a portion of the starch is always left in the state of dextrine; he therefore operates under pressure and at a higher temperature. For this purpose he employs a strong cylinder-shaped iron vessel internally lined with lead; this boiler is charged with 28 kilos. of sulphuric acid at 60° B., and 2,800 litres of water, and the liquid is brought to the boiling-point by means of high-pressure steam. When boiling, there is gradually run in a mixture of 1,180 kilos. of starch, and 2,500 litres of water acidulated with 28 kilos. of sulphuric acid. When the whole of this quantity has been introduced into the boiler, the boiler is closed, and the temperature raised to 160° C. by means of steam; after 4 hours the action is complete. The mixture is run off into tubs, and the acid saturated with finely powdered limestone. After separation of the sulphate of calcium, the fluid is evaporated to 20° B., clarified with animal charcoal, and evaporated in vacuum-pans. An excellent and beautiful glucose is thus obtained. — *Mon. Scientif.*

NOTES ON THE MANUFACTURE OF SOAP.

It is a well-known fact that by an indirect method a potash soap may be converted into a soda soap; this is done by adding to a boiling solution of a potash soap a very concentrated solution of common salt; and it is generally taken for granted that if enough of the latter has been added, the potash is replaced, at least chiefly, by soda, and chloride of potassium is formed. Dr. Oudemans has made experiments to ascertain how much of the potash is replaced by soda, and finds that by the process, as executed in a large scale and yielding excellent produce, only a little more than half, to wit, 53.7 per cent. of potash is replaced by soda, while 46.3 per cent. of potash are left along with the other alkali combined with fatty acids in the curd soap. — *Journ. f. Prak. Chem. v. Erdmann*, I., 1869.

UTILIZATION OF CHROME-ALUM.

The manufacture of aniline green and violet and of valerianic acid gives abundant residues of chrome-alum. M. F. Jean proposes to utilize the chrome-alum by pulverizing and mixing the alum with 3 equivalents of carbon, and then decomposing at a red heat in a retort of refractory earthenware. The reaction occurring may be thus expressed: $KO, SO_3, Cr_2O_3 3SO_3 + 3C = 3SO_2 + KO, SO_3 + Cr_2O_3 + 3CO$. The sulphurous acid is passed into water or into a solution of carbonate of sodium, and the residue boiled with water, to dissolve out the sulphate of potassium, which may afterwards be obtained by crystallization. The sesquioxide of chromium is then drained and calcined in order to get rid of all the water, and although it is too dull for use in printing, it may be used for the manufacture of bichromate of potassium. — *Chem. News.*

PURIFICATION OF BISULPHIDE OF CARBON.

M. Millon purifies the bisulphide of carbon by first washing it several times with distilled water, as in the purification of ether, and then transferring it to a retort of large capacity containing quick-lime. After 24 hours' contact the bisulphide is distilled off from the lime, and received in a flask partially filled with copper turnings, which have been previously roasted to remove all traces of fatty matter and afterwards reduced by hydrogen. The lime remaining in the retort is strongly colored. All the disagreeable odor of the ordinary bisulphide of carbon is removed by this treatment and an ethereal odor only is perceived. — *Chem. News, Jan.*, 1869.

SOLUBILITY OF SULPHUR IN COAL-TAR OILS.

Coal-tar oils at a low temperature dissolve but a small proportion of sulphur; but at a higher temperature this proportion is considerably increased. Thus coal-tar oil of 0.885 sp. gr. and distilling between 146° and 200° C. dissolves

at	15°,	2.3 per cent. sulphur.		
"	40°,	5.6	"	"
"	65°,	10.6	"	"
"	100°,	25.0	"	"
"	110°,	30.3	"	"
"	130°,	43.2	"	"

As the temperature decreases the sulphur is precipitated in the crystalline state, and as the difference in solubility is so great the larger portion of the sulphur dissolved at a high temperature is recovered on cooling the solution. This property of the heavier coal-tar oils is made use of at the Paris gas-works to extract, from the materials which have been used in purifying gas according to Laming's process, the sulphur therein contained. M. Pelouze reports very favorably on this plan, as greatly superior to, and less dangerous than, the use of sulphide of carbon for that purpose. — *Comptes Rendus, May*, 1869.

HÆMATOXYLINE IN PHOTOGRAPHY.

Dr. Tabensky states that since MM. Erdmann and Hesse had discovered that hæmatoxyline reduces solution of silver and becomes colored red by the action of direct sunlight, he has made some experiments in order to discover whether the alcoholic extract of logwood might not be very serviceable in photography. For this purpose he prepared hæmatoxyline in the pure state according to Erdmann's method, taking care to recrystallize the substance repeatedly from an alcoholic solution. Next two glass plates, properly prepared, were exposed in a photographic apparatus to light, and afterwards one of these plates was treated as usual with pyrogallic acid, the other with a solution of hæmatoxyline. The success of the latter operation left nothing to be desired, and further experiments leave little doubt that hæmatoxyline may be advantageously applied in photography. The quantities best suited for the solution are as follows: Hæmatoxyline, 0.5 grams; distilled water, 80 grams; 22 grams of acetic acid of 33° strength; and a small quantity of glycerine. — *Zeitsch. für Ch.*

EXTRACTION OF OXYGEN FROM THE AIR.

MM. Laire and Montmagnon propose to take advantage of the well-known property of wood charcoal, alkaline solutions, and blood, of absorbing a larger portion of oxygen from the surrounding air than of nitrogen. It is proved, by experiment, that 100 measures of wood charcoal, freshly burned, absorb 985 of oxygen, and only about 705 of nitrogen. The blood of animals and solutions of phosphate and carbonate of sodium absorb rapidly, according to the amount of surface exposed to the air, about 12 per cent. of oxygen, and only two per cent. of nitrogen. The proposed method of utilizing these facts in this : — Pump out the oxygen and nitrogen from the substances used to absorb it by means of an air-pump; pass the mixture through fresh absorbing media; re-extract, and repeat the operations as often as required. In this way an oxygen is obtained very free from nitrogen, and at an extremely cheap rate. — *British Journal of Photography.*

ENAMELS.

The fine enamels of trade are generally prepared by fusing, at high temperatures, silica, oxide of tin, and oxide of lead, and spreading the mixture over the surface of a sheet of copper, of gold, or of platinum.

The objections to these enamels are, in the first place, their high cost, and, secondly, the impossibility of giving them a perfectly flat surface.

Mr. E. Duchemin has advantageously replaced them by the following economical and efficient compound : Arsenic, 30 parts by weight; saltpetre, 30; silica (fine sand), 90; litharge, 250. This is spread on plates of glass of the required shape and size, care being taken, however, that the kind of glass employed be not inferior in point of fusibility to the enamel.

Enamelled glass prepared from the above substances may be drawn or written on as readily as if it were paper, and in less time than one minute the writing may be rendered indelible by simply heating the plate in a small open furnace or muffle.

First-class photographs, either negatives or positives, may be taken on such enamels without collodion, by using bitumen, or citrate of iron, or perchloride of iron and tartaric acid, or bichromate, or any other salt.

A good solution for this purpose is, water, 100 parts by weight; gum, 4 parts; honey, one part; pulverized bichromate of potassium, 3 parts. Filter the liquid, spread it over the enamel, and let it rest, after which : —

1. Expose it to the camera.
2. Develop the image by brushing over it the following powder: Oxide of cobalt, 10 parts by weight; black oxide of iron, 90 parts; red lead, 100 parts; sand, 30 parts.

3. Decompose the bichromate by immersion in a bath formed of, water, 100 parts by weight; hydrochloric acid, 5 parts.

4. Wash it in clean water and dry it.

5. Vitrify the proof on a clean piece of cast iron, the surface of which has been previously chalked. One minute will suffice for indelibly fixing and glazing the photograph, which must be carefully and slowly allowed to cool.

Photographs on enamel of any size, taken in this manner, are perfectly unalterable. under all atmospheric conditions, and may consequently and aptly be called "everlasting photographs."— *Scientific American.*

PRESERVATION OF WINES.

The process for improving and preserving wines, originally proposed by Pasteur in his "*Études sur le Vin,*" by simply heating it to a temperature of 55° to 75° C. (131° to 167° F.), previous to bottling, or after partial decomposition had set in, has lately been reported upon by a commission of the French Navy Department — a series of experiments and trials on an extensive scale having been made for the purpose of determining its value. The report states that Pasteur's process will preserve French wines permanently, or for an indefinite length of time, from acidity and change of taste or clearness; that a temperature of from 55° to 60° C. (131° to 140° F.) is the one desirable to apply to the wines; and that this heating should be performed in vessels of tin or tinned copper. — *Dingler's Journal, from Armengaud's Génie.*

ANALYSIS OF LAGER BEER.

Prof. C. F. Chandler, of the School of Mines of Columbia College, has recently concluded a series of chemical tests with lager beer, undertaken in order to ascertain the extent of its intoxicating properties, and the hygienic character which it has been represented to possess. His report is eminently successful in proving that the nourishing qualities which have been ignorantly assigned to lager beer are only fictitious, and also that it is entirely objectionable as a drink. It is composed chiefly of water, with a certain amount of alcohol, — enough to cause intoxication when copiously imbibed. During the brewing of the beer — which, if properly done, occupies 8 months, the brewing commencing in cold weather — great care has to be taken to prevent its becoming mouldy, which it sometimes does by the slightest variation in temperature. It is necessary to cool the brewing-vault in summer and warm it in winter, in order to keep it at the requisite temperature, averaging from 41 to 45 degrees Fahrenheit. Frequently, however, the weather continues to act on the beer after it has been barrelled and sold to retail dealers, rendering it flat and bitter, in which condition it is very often sold as a drink. Prof. Chandler's analyses embraced 5 samples of different breweries, which, when examined, developed trifling and unimportant differences in their quality. The following is the tabulated result: —

No.	Specific Gravity.	Water.	Alcohol by volume.	Extractive matter of the Malt and Hops.
1	1.008	90.75	6.25	3.00
2	1.006	89.98	4.99	5.03
3	1.008	91.59	5.39	3.02
4	1.018	89.61	4.99	5.40
5	1.005	87.16	7.74	5.10
Average	1.013	89.82	5.86	4.32

It was found that all the specimens contained small quantities of grape sugar; of lupuline, the bitter principle of the hops; of acetic acid (merely a trace), produced by oxidization of some of the alcohol; and of carbonic-acid gas generated during the fermentation. A most thorough examination failed to reveal any indications of the presence of picric acid, picrotoxin (the peculiar principle of cocculus Indicus), alum, copperas, or any other adulteration whatever. — *Druggists' Circular*

NEW ALKALOID IN FERMENTED LIQUORS.

According to M. Ozer, every time that solutions of sugar ferment under the influence of yeast, beside alcohol, a new alkaloid is produced, to which he attributes the formula $C_{26} H_{20} N_4$. The chlorhydrate of this base crystallizes in hygroscopic tables, which become brown on exposure to the air. It appears that all fermented liquors contain the new alkaloid, or at least one of its compounds. The existence of this new alkaloid may explain certain effects of fermented liquors which cannot be attributed to alcohol alone. — *Cosmos*.

TURACINE.

The turaco, or plantain-eater, of the Cape of Good Hope is celebrated for its beautiful plumage. A portion of the wings is of a fine red color. This red coloring matter has been investigated by Prof. Church, who finds it to contain nearly 6 per cent. of copper, which cannot be distinguished by the ordinary tests, nor removed from the coloring matter without destroying it. The coloring matter is, in fact, a natural organic compound, of which copper is one of the essential constituents. Traces of this metal had previously been found in animals; for example, in oysters, to the cost of those who partook of them; but in these cases the presence of the copper was merely accidental; thus, oysters that lived near the mouths of streams which came down from copper mines assimilated a portion of the copper salt without apparently its doing them either good or harm. But, in the turaco, the existence of the red coloring matter which belongs to their normal plumage is dependent upon copper, which, obtained in minute quantities with the food, is stored up in this strange manner in the system of the bird. Thus, in the very same feather, partly red and partly black, copper was found in abundance in the red parts, but none, or only the merest trace, in the black. This red coloring matter is soluble in water; and a pair of birds, kept in captivity, lost their fine red color in the course of a few days, in consequence of washing in the water which was left them to drink; except as to the loss of their beauty, however, it does not appear that the birds were the worse for it. — *Address of President Stokes before the British Association,* 1869.

ALIZARINE.

M. Martin, taking advantage of Shützenberger's investigation of madder, has invented a process for transforming orange-madder, purpurine, pseudo-purpurine, and tantho-purpurine, into alizarine. The several coloring matters are first dissolved in concentrated sulphuric acid; powdered zinc is then added, and heat applied. When the reaction is completed, the mass is diluted with water, and an abundant precipitate falls, which is the required dye. This, after washing with water, is ready for use. — *Chem. News.*

ARTIFICIAL ALIZARINE.

Messrs. Græbe and Liebermann, of Berlin, have discovered a process for converting anthracene (paranaphthaline), a constituent of gas-tar, into alizarine, the principal coloring matter of the madder-plant. This conversion is accomplished by three successive operations : —

First : the anthracene ($C_{14} H_8$) is transformed into oxanthracene, or anthraquinone ($C_{14} H_{10}$) by heating one part of anthracene with two parts of bichromate of potassium in the presence of sulphuric acid or of crystallized acetic acid, or by the action of a mixture of nitric and acetic acids.

Second : the anthraquinone is heated with two equivalents of bromine, and the product formed heated with alcoholic potash. There results the compound $C_{14} H_6 Br_4$, and from this, by the oxidizing action of nitric acid and bichromate of potassium, is obtained the brominated compound $C_{14} H_6 Br_2 O_2$, which is purified by recrystallization. In this process chlorine can be used instead of bromine.

Third : the brominated compound thus formed is heated with a very concentrated solution of potash to from 180° to 260° C., until the blue color which the mass assumes no longer increases in intensity. The mass is then treated with an acid which precipitates the alizarine. — *Bull. Soc. Ch., June,* 1869.

MM. Græbe and Liebermann have recently stated that they

can dispense with the use of acetic acid and bromine, and will shortly be able to bring into the trade a superior article manufactured by a method different from that already described by them. — *Mo. Sci.*

NEW DYE FROM MADDER.

Prof. Rochleder, of Prague, has found that, when madder is treated with dilute mineral acids, it yields, beside alizarine and purpurine, a small quantity of a third tinctorial substance, which in alkaline solution has a great similarity to chrysophanic acid in alkaline solution; acids precipitate it from this solution in the amorphous, flocculent state, the precipitate being of a pale yellow color. This substance is soluble in alcohol and acetic acid, from which solutions it is obtained by evaporation in orange-yellow colored crystals. Its aqueous solution, mixed with acetic acid and brought to the boiling point, imparts to silk and wool a beautiful and durable golden-yellow color. — *Cosmos.*

A NEW COLORING MATTER.

The discovery of fuchsine and other colors derived from aniline first caused the existence of very rich sources of coloring matters to be predicted in mineral oils and hydrocarbons in general. Therefore, since that period, chemists have devoted themselves to laborious researches in the same direction, in order to find new products for use in dyeing. The method which M. Clavel has adopted was suggested by the study of the circumstances, which have since been explained, regarding the formation of fuchsine. It is now known that commercial aniline is a mixture of aniline and toluidine; and M. Hofmann has proved that it is a mixture of these two bases which produces the brilliant color. Guided by an examination of these facts, M. Clavel has not sought in naphthylamine for a coloring matter by itself, but for one likely to produce the color, by a mixture with another base like naphthylamine, from which it has been derived, or with any other isomeric substance. The new coloring matter, then, is obtained by the direct oxidation of a product isomeric with naphthylamine and mixing the products of higher distillation with the naphthylamine.

The mode of operation is as follows: The naphthaline is first treated with nitric acid of 1.33°, and the resulting nitronaphthaline is washed, and reduced either by iron and acetic acid, or by zinc and hydrochloric acid, or by other appropriate reagents. The distillation is then proceeded with. There comes over at first naphthylamine, and then at a higher temperature a second body discovered by M. Clavel.

This second product is treated at 120° with 50 per cent. of very dry nitrate of mercury, and subsequently left in contact with its own bulk of naphthylamine for about a quarter of an hour; the mixture is then treated with boiling water containing a vegetable acid, by which the coloring matter is dissolved. After filtration the solution is treated in the ordinary manner with a salt and the coloring matter is precipitated; the solution of this substance in alcohol gives a red color, finer and more solid than the colors hitherto extracted from naphthaline and naphthylamine. No analysis has yet been given of this body. It distils at 300°; its vapors form in condensing a deposit which rapidly becomes brown on exposure to the air; in a state of purity it is solid below 15°, becoming liquid at a higher temperature. — *Mon. Sci.*

ANILINE GRAY.

M. Bloch publishes the following receipt: One kilo. of aniline at 190° and 5 kilos. of arsenic acid at 75° are heated in a caldron over an open fire, care being taken to maintain the heat at the boiling-point till the substance thickens and rises, when the operation is terminated. The substance obtained presents a black appearance; it is thick and insoluble in water. In order to purify the product it is boiled with the aid of steam in a mixture of about 20 litres of water and one kilo. of chlorhydric acid, for half an hour, collected on a filter, washed first with water and then with a dilute solution of carbonate of sodium. Finally the collected matter is dried, and gives a fine black powder. For dyeing, a solution of this product is made in alcohol to which 10 per cent. of sulphuric acid is added. With this liquor, when filtered, magnificent grays of all shades can be dyed.

A NEW METHOD OF DYEING A FAST GRAY.

It is stated by M. Barreswil that protonitrate of mercury is successfully used as a mordant; the dye employed is a solution of sulphide of potassium, one kilo. of the salt being employed to 18 kilos. of woven tissue or yarn. The gray color thus produced is essentially due to the formation of sulphide of mercury on and in the tissues, and, according to M. Barreswil, the color is fast, that is, it is not destroyed by washing with soap or alkalies, and resists acids, but it is destroyed by chlorine. — *Bull. d. l. Soc. d'Encour., June,* 1869.

SOLUBILITY OF INDIGO.

Koechlin has discovered that indigo is soluble in alkaloid salts, and particularly in the acetates and chlorides of aniline, morphine, etc.

Stockvis announces the solubility of indigo in chloroform, stating that this solvent takes up the color largely and readily. — *Bull. Soc. Chim.*

CHROME GREEN.

Oxide of chromium prepared in the dry way varies in the shade of color, but never possesses such brilliancy or freshness that it may be used in printing paper or textile fabrics. It is possible, however, in the wet way, to produce a green oxide of chromium not devoid of beauty. MM. Casthela and Leune prepare what they style *imperial* green, by slowly precipitating salts of chromium by treating them with hydrated metallic oxides, carbonates, or sulphides; the action proceeds gradually, and the color of the hydrated oxide precipitated is a deep emerald green. Practically the reagents employed are gelatinous alumina and the oxides, carbonates, and sulphides of zinc and iron. The color of the green precipitate may be modified by the use of reagents forming with the acid of the salt of chromium insoluble salts. — *Mon. Sci.*

BLEACHING WOOD-PULP.

The difficulties encountered in the bleaching of wood-pulp are, (1) that chloride of lime, however little in excess, has a tendency to produce a yellow tint; (2) that strong acids turn the paste red under the action of the sun, or after some time without sunlight in the presence of moisture; (3) that the slightest trace of iron is sufficient to blacken the paste in a short time.

M. Orioli obviates these objectionable results by the use of oxalic acid, the energetic action of which on vegetable coloring matters is well known. For 100 kilos. of wood-pulp he employs 800 kilos. of oxalic acid, which serves the double purpose of bleaching the coloring matters already oxidized, and of neutralizing the alkaline principles favorable to oxidation; two kilos. of sulphate of alumina, perfectly free from iron, are also added. This sulphate of alumina does not bleach of itself, but forms with the coloring matter of the wood a nearly colorless lake, which, remaining in the pulp, enables the brilliancy of the product to be heightened. — *Chem. News, Jan.*, 1869.

BLEACHING PAPER-PULP.

M. Gauny proposes to bleach paper-pulp by means of bichromate of potassium. For 100 kilos. of pulp (supposed to be dry) he uses 50 kilos. of bichromate and 150 kilos. of hydrochloric acid, mixed with a sufficient quantity of water to make the pulp float. After 12 hours' standing the chloride of chromium is washed out by means of clean water, and the pulp treated with a small quantity of bleaching powder to make it thoroughly white. The chloride of chromium is precipitated with excess of lime, and this mixture calcined in a reverberatory furnace, where it is converted into chromate of calcium.

NEW METHOD OF BLEACHING FEATHERS.

This process is a new one, and by it even black feathers of ostriches and other birds may be bleached. The feathers are allowed to stand for 3 or 4 hours in a lukewarm dilute solution of bichromate of potassium, to which a small quantity of nitric acid has been added. After the expiration of this time the feathers are found to have assumed a greenish hue, owing to the sesqui-oxide of chromium deposited upon them; in order to remove this, use is made of a dilute aqueous solution of sulphurous acid, which leaves the feathers perfectly white. The solutions should all be dilute, and particular care exercised in the employment of the nitric acid. — *Duflot in Dingl. Pol. Journ.*

BLEACHING PALM OIL BY CHROMIC ACID.

The following is a detailed account of the process used by M. Engelhardt, of Leipzig, for bleaching palm oil by means of chromic acid: A convenient quantity of palm oil is placed in a caldron and heated to about 62° C., and allowed to repose during a whole night; the next day it is poured into a perfectly clean vessel, and cooled down to 40° or 37° C. While this operation is being performed, a certain quantity of water is heated to ebullition; for 1,000 parts by weight of palm oil, 45 of water; in this quantity 15 parts of bichromate of potassium are dissolved. As soon as the solution has cooled a little, 60 parts of hydrochloric acid are added, and it is then mixed with the palm oil, which is vigorously agitated during the mixing. Five minutes suffice for the oil to be colored a dull green. By continuing the stirring, the oxide of chromium becomes completely separated, the oil becomes clearer and clearer, and finally quite limpid; when this point is arrived at, it is washed with hot water; the product is perfectly white. If the palm oil has not been thoroughly bleached by the treatment, the process is repeated with 23 parts of bichromate of potassium, and one of hydrochloric acid. This method is capable of rapid execution, and gives very good results. — *Druggists' Circular.*

ALBUMEN.

It frequently happens that among the dried albumen met with in commerce a variety occurs which is soluble in water, but not coagulated by heat. Dr. Monnier, of Lyons, has found that when white of eggs is slowly evaporated by exposure to the heat of the sun, or rapidly evaporated in a water-bath after exposure for a considerable time to sunlight, a modification of albumen is obtained, which is not coagulated by heat. From a dilute aqueous solution, this variety is not precipitated by acetic, formic, or tartaric acid, but on the addition of a few drops of either of these acids it passes into the coagulable modification. It was found that 5 milligrams of crystallized acetic acid in 0.5 c.c. of water were sufficient to cause the conversion of 20 grams of this dry albumen dissolved in 10 c.c. of water. When ammonia was added in sufficient quantity to exactly neutralize the acid, the albumen passed back into the modification not coagulated by heat. — *Deutsche Ind. Zeitung.*

18 *

MANUFACTURE OF CHLORINE.

When air is passed through a mixture of MnO and CaO, suspended in water, there is formed *manganite of calcium*, a compound of MnO_2 and CaO. This compound, perpetually regenerated, is used in the manufacture of chlorine as follows: The residual liquor, after a charge of MnO_2 has been acted upon by chlorhydric acid, is treated with twice the quantity of lime necessary to decompose the chloride of manganese; and through the resulting precipitate suspended in the liquor air is passed, forming the manganite, which is used again to generate chlorine. — *W. Whelden before the Brit. Ass.*, 1869.

FILTRATION.

The operation of filtration being one of constant necessity, and occupying so much time in any analytical operation, attempts have often been made to improve the common method with a view of shortening the time required. Various devices have been proposed to utilize the principle of the syphon; and in 1865 Piccard proposed to filter under pressure by fitting the funnel into a flask in which the air was rarefied. This rarefaction was effected by connecting the flask with a tube through which a thin stream of water flowed, sucking down with it a continuous stream of air-bubbles. No one, has, however, devised a simple and inexpensive apparatus suitable for general use until recently. Bunsen ("Ann. der Ch. u. Ph.," vol. XLVIII., p. 269) has published a paper "On the Washing of Precipitates,"[*] of which the following is an abstract: —

"A precipitate is washed either by filtration or decantation, or by a combination of these two methods. In either case the time required is so long, and the quantity of wash-water needed is so great, that some simplification of this continually recurring operation is in the highest degree desirable. The following method, which depends, not upon the removal of the impurity by simple attenuation, but upon its displacement by forcing the wash-water through the precipitate, appears to me to combine all the requisite conditions, and therefore to satisfy the need.

"The rapidity with which a liquid filters depends, other things being equal, upon the difference which exists between the pressure on its upper and lower surfaces. Supposing the filter to consist of a solid substance, the pores of which suffer no alteration by pressure or by any other influence, then the volume of liquid filtered in a given time is nearly proportional to the difference in pressure, as was experimentally shown, using pure water and a filter of artificial pumice-stone. With a difference of pressure amounting to 0.179 metre the time required for a given quantity of water to run through was 91.7″, while under

[*] Reprinted in Silliman's Journal, May, 1869.

a pressure of 0.472 metre the same quantity ran through in 33.0″. In the ordinary process of filtration the difference in pressure amounts to scarcely more than 0.005 metre. The advantage gained, therefore, is easily perceived when we can succeed by some simple, practicable, and easily attainable method in multiplying this difference in pressure one or two hundred times, or, say, to an entire atmosphere, without running any risk of breaking the filter. The solution of this problem is very easy; a glass funnel is chosen possessing an angle of as near 60° as possible, the walls of which must be perfectly free from inequalities of every description, and into it is placed a second funnel made of extremely thin platinum-foil, the sides of which possess exactly the same inclination as those of the glass funnel. An ordinary paper filter is then introduced into this compound funnel in the usual manner; when carefully moistened and so adjusted that no air-bubbles are visible between it and the glass, this filter, when filled with a liquid, will support the pressure of an extra atmosphere without breaking. In order that the additional pressure of an atmosphere may be produced the filtered liquid is received in a strong glass flask instead of in a beaker. This flask is closed by a doubly perforated caoutchouc cork, through one of the holes of which the neck of the glass funnel is passed; through the other is fitted a narrow glass tube connected with the apparatus designed to produce the requisite difference in pressure.

"It is impossible to employ any of the air-pumps at present in use for this purpose, since the filtrate not unfrequently contains chlorine, sulphurous acid, hydric sulphide, and other substances which would act injuriously upon the metallic portions of these instruments. A *water* air-pump is, therefore, employed, constructed on the principle of Sprengel's mercury-pump, by connecting the flask which receives the filtrate with a vertical pipe through which a stream of water continually flows. This stream of water sucks down with it the air from the flask in a continuous series of bubbles. With a fall of from 30 to 40 feet, the rarefaction can be carried to within 8 or 12 millimetres of a perfect vacuum; but even with a fall of 10 feet only, a great advantage is gained.

"Bunsen gives a number of examples to show the efficiency of this new method, from which it appears that the time necessary to filter and dry a quantity of sesquioxide of chromium, hitherto requiring about 7 hours, is reduced to 18 minutes; and the total length of time needed to filter the sesquioxide of chromium, wash and dry the precipitate, and evaporate the filtrate, is reduced from 14 or 15 hours to about 32 minutes.

"Other advantages gained by this method are that the precipitate is obtained so dry as that it can be immediately ignited, or, if necessary, it can be readily removed from the filter without loss, and without being mixed with particles of the paper. Moreover, if the filtrate is to be used for further investigation, there is a much smaller bulk to be evaporated than if the precipitate had been washed in the old way."

AN IMPROVED QUALITATIVE FILTER.

A mode of folding filters for qualitative analysis superior to the one in common use is suggested by C. E. Avery. In place of folding the filter doubled upon itself down the middle in the usual way, he turns down on each side of the paper a fold equal to one-quarter of the semicircle, and then folds the sectors of 45° thus formed back upon themselves. The filter is then opened without disturbing the folded portion, and placed in the funnel. In this form the triple side of the plain filter is broken up, and the folded portions keep open passages instead of hindering filtration. A gain of some 50 per cent. is obtained in the rapidity of filtration. — *Amer. Jour. Phar.*, *XL.*, *p.* 200.

THE PHENOMENA OF SUPERSATURATION AND BOILING.

Oersted noticed in 1806 that dilute acids might be cautiously added to solutions of the alkaloid carbonates without producing any action, but that on the introduction of a solid body, such as a platinum wire, a glass rod, or the finger, brisk effervescence ensued. He inferred that gas in solution is never given off, except in contact with a solid, and he adduced the influence of solids in promoting crystallization in support of his view. Analogous experiments were made by Schönbein in 1837, who suggested that the solids acted by carrying down air. Further illustrations were supplied, in 1839, by Liebig, who concurred in attributing the effects to the influence of the air introduced. Tomlinson refers all such phenomena, together with that of the sudden deposition of crystals from a supersaturated solution, to the action of *nuclei*, and defines a *nucleus* as "a body which has a stronger adhesion for a gas, salt, or vapor in solution than for the liquid which holds it in solution." The action of solids in these cases he ascribes to the greasy film which after exposure to the air they are sure to acquire; for it is found that a platinum or a glass rod, which, by means of chemical agents, is made perfectly clean, is powerless to bring about such changes. He considers the sudden crystallization of a supersaturated solution of a salt by mere exposure to the air as due to particles of dust falling upon the liquid.

The effect of dropping a crystal of the salt into the solution is due to its having acquired the condition of a nucleus from exposure to the air. If a crystal of sulphate of sodium be suspended in the neck of the flask in which the supersaturated solution is being prepared, it ceases to be a nucleus, and when the solution is cold the crystal may be lowered into it without determining the separation of the salt. Tomlinson uses the term *catharism* to express the condition of a body which is made chemically clean, and which does not act as a nucleus. Considering a boiling liquid as a supersaturated solution of its own vapor, he refers to the same theory the phenomena of boiling. If any solid body be introduced into a boiling liquid, bubbles of vapor collect on the solid and are given off from it. This action does not take place if the body introduced has previously been made chemically clean, nor will the body introduced continue to promote the action indefinitely if the liquid is of such a nature as to render it clean after a time.

"It has been recommended to use sharp-pointed or roughened bodies, under the impression that steam is given off with greater facility from the points or the teeth. This is a mistake. Make these rough or sharp-pointed bodies clean, and they cease to act. Sharp, angular fragments of glass, washed in sulphuric acid and rinsed, no longer act as nuclei. A rat's-tail file passed through the flame of a spirit lamp also becomes denucleized. A body such as a file is apt to collect between its teeth the greasy kind of matter that acts so well as a nucleus; and this has led to an idea in favor of rough bodies. The air is not a nucleus. When Dr. Bostock, in his experiments, found his thermometer cease to act, and by taking it out of the liquid and waving it in the air it liberated vapor when restored to the liquid, the thermometer had caught from the air some unclean particles of dust, which acted for a moment as nuclei, until, by the action of the ether, they became denucleized."

Looking, then, at the matter from a practical stand-point, what is wanted in conducting the processes of boiling and distillation is a body which will act permanently as a nucleus. Such bodies are charcoal, coke, pumice-stone, meerschaum, and a few others, which act by virtue of the powerful force of capillarity. The same force which, according to Saussure, enables one volume of box-wood charcoal to absorb 90 volumes of ammoniacal gas, 85 of hydrochloric acid gas, 65 of sulphurous acid gas, and so on, enables these porous bodies to absorb vapor from boiling liquids, and, under the continued action of the heat, to give it out in never-ceasing jets, thus relieving the vessel of all tendency to bumping, making the boiling soft, gentle, and regular, and increasing the quantity of the distillate. Charcoal made from cocoa-nut shell answers best for this purpose. Thus, methylated spirit of wine, boiling at 171° F., was distilled in a glass retort. The amount of distillate collected in a given time was weighed, and bore to the amount collected in the same time after the addition of a few fragments of cocoa-nut shell charcoal, the ratio of 100 : 133. Even a short bundle of capillary glass tubes, united like a fagot by a thread in the middle, is an active nucleus in liberating vapor. Such a bundle, weighing only 10 grains, put into a retort from which methylated spirit was being distilled, raised the amount of distillate in the ratio of 100 : 110. — *Tomlinson, Lecture before Chem. Soc.*

ACTION OF BOILING LIQUIDS UPON GLASS AND PORCELAIN VESSELS.

Dr. A. Emmerling publishes ("Ann. Ch. u. Ph.," June, 1869) the results of a series of extended and carefully conducted experiments on this subject, the general result of which may be summed up as follows: —

(1.) The action of boiling liquids upon glass vessels is, within certain limits, proportional to the time of boiling. The action upon new vessels is somewhat greater for the first few hours than afterwards.

(2.) The action is proportional to the extent of surface in contact with the boiling liquid.

(3.) The action is independent of the quantity of liquid evaporated in a given time.

(4.) The action decreases rapidly with the temperature.

(5.) Alkalies, even in very dilute solutions, attack the glass strongly.

(6.) Dilute acids (with the exception of sulphuric acid) attack the glass less than pure water.

(7.) Solutions of salts whose acids form insoluble calcium salts attack the glass more violently, those whose acids form soluble calcium salts less violently, than pure water.

(8.) The amount of action depends on the composition of the glass, soda glass being attacked more than Bohemian glass.

(9.) The component parts of the glass are dissolved in about the proportions in which they exist in the glass.

(10.) Vessels of Berlin porcelain were sensibly attacked by alkalies only.

DECREASE OF TEMPERATURE CAUSED BY THE SOLUTION OF SALTS IN WATER.

The decrease of temperature caused by the solution of a given salt in water is greater the larger the quantity of the salt dissolved in a given time. Since, however, the amount of the salt which can be dissolved by water of a given temperature is a fixed quantity, it follows that the maximum decrease of temperature will be produced by employing a quantity of salt sufficient to form a saturated solution. As the decrease of temperature will be greater the more rapid the solution, the salt employed should be in as fine a state of division as possible; moreover, the relative decrease of temperature is greater, the lower the temperature of the water, and of the salt before mixing; therefore, the greatest effect will be obtained by cooling each separately before making the solution. In no case is it possible to obtain a temperature lower than the freezing-point of the saturated solution, although that point can in some cases be very closely approached. A number of experiments made upon various salts, were conducted in the following manner: — The finely powdered salt and the requisite quantities of water were, previous to the making of the experiments, each put in separate beakers made of very thin glass, and placed for from 12 to 18 hours in a room wherein the temperature could be kept as nearly as possible constant; in consequence of this, the beakers and contents attained the same temperature throughout. The mixing was effected by pouring the water on to the salt, and stirring up with a very delicate and highly sensitive thermometer; the maximum decrease of temperature took place within a minute after the mixing of the salt and water. Of a considerable number of salts experimented upon, the sulphocyanide of potassium caused the greatest decrease of temperature. When 150 parts of the salt were mixed with 100 parts of water, the temperature fell from 10.8° C. to — 23.7° C., that is, through 34.5°.

When 133 parts of sulphocyanide of ammonium were mixed with 100 parts of water, the temperature fell from 13.2° to —18°, or through 31.2°.

When 60 parts of nitrate of ammonium were mixed with 100 parts of water, the temperature fell from 13.6° to —13.6°, that is, through 26.2°. — *Rudorff. Deut. Ch. Ges., Berlin*, 1869.

Freezing Mixture. — If citric acid and crystallized carbonate of sodium in powder be stirred together, the temperature falls from + 60° F. to — 80° F. — *Chem. News.*

PURIFYING WATER.

The inhabitants of the towns and villages along the River Maas are dependent upon its waters for domestic and drinking purposes. The water is turbid, does not become clear on standing, and produces, in those not accustomed to its use, a diarrhœa, sometimes accompanied by dangerous symptoms. Analysis fails to reveal the cause of this property. Dr. Gunning, of Amsterdam, has found that perchloride of iron added to this water . (and the same applies to far more foul waters experimented upon) renders it wholesome and even agreeable to use.

To one litre of the water is added 0.032 gram of the dry salt dissolved in pure water, and the liquid, after stirring, is allowed to stand for 36 hours. On a large scale, a small quantity of carbonate of sodium is subsequently added to neutralize any free chlorhydric acid. Comparative experiments have proved that the application of this process is far superior to filtration, even through animal charcoal. The result obtained with the Maas water having been so eminently successful, the committee has applied this method to the purifying of water, otherwise undrinkable, such as is met with in the smaller canals, brooks, and wells containing surface water; thus treated such waters become available for use.

The precipitate formed by the addition of perchloride of iron and carbonate of sodium contains a large quantity of organic matter. Analysis shows that the only addition to the inorganic constituents of the water is one part of chloride of sodium to 40,000 parts of water. — *From the Report of the Netherlands Committee. — Chem. News.*

SEWAGE.

The sewage water from Paris taken at the bridge near Asnieres contains one kilo. of solid matter to the cubic metre; of this amount 37 grams are nitrogenous matter. This water is treated with sulphate of aluminum, whereby all the phosphoric acid, two-thirds of the nitrogenous matter, and rather more than one-half the potassium salts present are completely precipitated, and perfectly clear, inodorous water is left, which may be run off into the rivers without injury to the purity of the water of the same. — *Chem. News.*

At Rheims experiments have been tried on a large scale to determine the value and applicability of various processes for treating the sewage of that city. The processes tried have been: (1) treatment with sulphate of iron and lime; (2) treatment with lignite and lime; (3) treatment with fine coal and a small quantity of sulphate of iron and lime. The first two processes yield a manure, the third a fuel. The use of lignite is said to prove completely successful. — *Les Mondes.*

ACTION OF WATER ON LEAD.

Dr. Frankland has made the observation that water which acted on lead lost this power after passing through a filter of animal charcoal. This he discovered to be owing to the fact that a minute quantity of phosphate of calcium from the charcoal passed into the water.

On comparing two natural waters, that of the River Kent, which acts violently on lead, and that of the River Vyrnwy, which, though very soft, has no action on lead, he found that the latter water contained an appreciable amount of phosphate of calcium, while none could be detected in the Kent water.

Solubility of Carbonate of Calcium in Water saturated with Carbonic Acid. — Cossa finds that 1,000 parts of water saturated with carbonic acid at the atmospheric pressure dissolve, of Carrara marble, at from 7.5° to 9.5°, 1.181 parts; of Luneburg chalk, at from 20° to 22°, 0.835 parts; of precipitated carbonate of calcium, at 18°, 0.950 parts; of Oölithic limestone, at 15°, 1.252 parts; of dolomite, at 15°, 0.573 parts. — *Jour. f. Prak. Ch.*

SPECTRUM ANALYSIS.

It is stated, in regard to the delicacy of the method of spectrum analysis, that it is possible to detect 1-180,000,000th part of a grain of sodium, 1-6,000,000th part of a grain of lithium, and 1-1,000,000th part of a grain of strontium.

The most important application which has yet been made of spectrum analysis to manufacturing purposes is its use in the making of steel by the Bessemer process. In this operation it is all important that the blowing of air through the molten mass should cease the instant the proper amount of carbon has been burned out. The precise moment at which to interrupt the blast is determined by examination of the flame issuing from the converter. As soon as the carbon lines disappear from the spectrum the blast is shut off. — *Roscoe, Lectures on Spect. Anal.*

Gaseous Spectra. — Frankland and Lockyer find, that under certain conditions of temperature and pressure the spectrum of hydrogen is reduced to one line in the green corresponding to F in the solar spectrum; that the spectrum of nitrogen is similarly reducible to one bright line in the green, with traces of other more refrangible faint lines; that from a mixture of hydrogen and nitrogen a combination of these spectra is obtained, the relative brilliancy of the two lines varying with the amount of each gas present in the mixture; that, by reducing the temperature, all spectroscopic evidence of the nitrogen vanishes, and by increasing it many new nitrogen lines make their appearance, the hydrogen line always remaining visible. These observations render unnecessary the assumption made by Huggins, that the visibility of a single nitrogen line in the spectra of the nebulæ indicates a form of matter more elementary than nitrogen, and which our analysis has not yet enabled us to detect. We can gather that the temperature of the nebulæ is less than that of our sun and that their tenuity is excessive. It is also a question whether the continuous spectrum observed in some cases may not be due to gaseous condensation. — *Chem. News.*

JARGONIUM.

The existence of absorption bands in the spectra, obtained from light transmitted through certain specimens of zircons, was first observed by Prof. Church, in 1866. Recently Mr. H. C. Sorby, acting independently, observed the same phenomena, and has inferred therefrom the existence of a new element, to which he gives the name of jargonium. He has also succeeded in separating chemically the oxide of jargonium from that of zirconium, altogether not in a state of purity.

NEW ACID FROM SULPHUR.

A solution of sulphurous acid in contact with zinc becomes of a yellow color, and acquires the property of powerfully decolorizing indigo and litmus, which Schönbein laid to the conversion of the oxygen in combination into ozone. The same effect is produced by the action of zinc on a solution of bisulphite of sodium. As the color of the indigo and litmus returns on exposure to the air, it is evident that the phenomenon is due to a reduction. M. Shützenberger shows this is due to the formation of a compound made up of a double atom of sulphurous acid, wherein one atom of oxygen is replaced by one atom of hydrogen; this free and anhydrous acid would be represented by the formula $S_2 O_3 H$. M. Shützenberger proposes to call this compound hydrosulphurous acid. He prepared the *hydrosulphite* of sodium by heating a solution of bisulphite of sodium with zinc out of access of the air, cooling the mixture to avoid a rise of temperature, and decanting the liquid into three times its bulk of alcohol. This mixture is hermetically sealed in a flask, until there has fallen a crystalline deposit, consisting mainly of the double sulphite of zinc and sodium. The clear alcoholic solution is then decanted into another flask, which it should fill, and sealed up. There forms in the flask a mass of colorless, needle-like crystals, which, dried in a vacuum, effloresce to a white powder of the composition, S_2O_3H,NaO.

This sodium compound is more stable than the acid itself, which may be obtained in solution by adding dilute sulphuric or oxalic acid to the crystals.

If a solution of bisulphite of sodium be placed in a porous vessel, this vessel put into one containing water acidulated with sulphuric acid, and the negative pole of a battery be inserted into the bisulphite, while the positive pole is in the acidulated water, oxygen is disengaged from the positive pole, while no gas escapes from the negative pole. At the same time the bisulphite solution acquires the decolorizing property, owing to the formation of the hydrosulphite of sodium. — *Comptes Rendus, July* 19, 1869.

RESEARCHES ON RESINS.

M. Sacc had published the results of his researches, which extend to copal, amber, dammar, colophony, lac (or shellac), elemi, sandarac, mastic, and carnauba wax (a resin). The author has studied the greater or less degree of readiness wherewith resins are reduced to powder, the action thereupon of boiling water, of alcohol of 86 per cent. strength, of ether, of ordinary acetic acid, of a hot solution of caustic soda of 1.074 specific gravity, of sulphide of carbon, of oil of turpentine, of boiled linseed oil, of benzine, of naphtha, of sulphuric acid of 1.83 specific gravity, of nitric acid of 1.329 specific gravity, and of caustic ammonia. All the resins were treated in powder; and the solvents, three times as large a bulk as that of the resins, have acted for at least 24 hours, at temperatures varying between 15° and 22°. The results arrived at are briefly as follows: All resins submitted to experiments fuse quietly when heated, excepting amber, shellac, elemi, sandarac, and mastic, which swell up, and increase in bulk. Only the carnauba wax melts in boiling water; colophony becomes pasty therein, while dammar, shellac, elemi, and mastic agglutinate. Copal, amber, and sandarac do not change. Alcohol does not dissolve amber nor dammar; it agglutinates copal, partly dissolves elemi and carnauba wax, while colophony, shellac, sandarac, and mastic are readily soluble therein. Ether does not dissolve amber and shellac, makes copals swell, and partly but slowly dissolves carnauba wax; dammar, colophony, elemi, sandarac, and mastic are readily dissolved therein. Acetic acid does not dissolve amber and shellac; causes copal to swell; acts somewhat upon carnauba wax, and does not act at all upon any other of the resins above named. Caustic soda solution readily dissolves shellac, with difficulty colophony, and has no action upon the rest. In sulphide of carbon, amber and shellac are insoluble; copal swells therein; elemi, sandarac, mastic, and carnauba wax are with difficulty dissolved, while dammar and colophony are readily soluble. Oil of turpentine has no action upon amber or shellac; causes copal to swell; dissolves readily dammar, colophony, elemi, sandarac, carnauba, and very readily mastic. Sulphuric acid does not dissolve carnauba wax; all other resins are dissolved and colored brown, excepting dammar, which becomes bright red. Nitric acid does not act upon the resins, but colors carnauba wax straw-yellow, elemi a dirty-yellow, and mastic and sandarac bright brown. Ammonia does not dissolve certain of these resins, but causes copal, sandarac, and mastic first to swell, afterward dissolving them; colophony is easily soluble therein. — *Sci. Am.*

A SUBSTANCE HOMOLOGOUS WITH BORNEO CAMPHOR.

The substance known in perfumery and in pharmacy as patchouli camphor is, according to recent researches of M. Gal, a substance homologous with Borneo camphor, which is represented by $C_{20}H_{28}O_2$. The average results of several elementary analyses of patchouli camphor gave for 100 parts: C, 80.1; H, 12.6; the formula just quoted requires C, 80.3; H, 12.5; the vapor density of this substance taken at 324° is 8.00; patchouli camphor is solid, fuses between 54° and 55°, and boils at 296°; its specific gravity is 1.051, at a temperature of 4.5° C. The camphor is insoluble in water, readily soluble in alcohol and ether; it crystallizes in hexagonal prisms. While Borneo camphor is a right-handed rotatory-substance, the patchouli camphor is left-handed. When patchouli camphor is distilled with chloride of zinc, at between 248° and 252° C., it yields a carbide of hydrogen, $C_{20}H_{26}$. The essence of patchouli is isomeric with the camphor, which is, it appears, simply formed by a molecular change. — *Druggists' Circular.*

FORMATION OF UREA.

Basarow has discovered that anhydrous carbonate of ammonium is converted into *urea* by heating in a sealed tube to 130° C. (266° F.) The carbonate he obtained by the action of carbonic acid gas on ammonia gas dissolved in absolute alcohol. He offers the following equation to express the reaction : —

$$(C_2O_2) H_2NO, H_4NO - 2 HO = C_2O_2 H_2 N \begin{Bmatrix} \\ H_2 \end{Bmatrix} N.$$

Even when commercial carbonate of ammonium is subjected to a temperature of 130° — 140° C., a considerable quantity of urea is formed. — *Zeitschr. für Ch. IV.*, 204.

DIRECT OXIDATION OF HYDROCARBONS.

Berthelot has made the extremely interesting discovery that various hydrocarbons may be oxidated immediately, and without loss of carbon, with the production of neutral bodies, such as aldehydes and their congeners. He operated with crystallized chromic acid, dissolved in a small quantity of water. Pure *ethylene* (freed from vapor of ether by repeated washings with concentrated sulphuric acid) is attacked slowly at 120° C. (248° F.) with formation of aldehyde

$$C_4 H_4 + O_2 = C_4 H_4 O_2.$$

In the cold, or even at 100° C., after many hours, no appreciable reaction was found. The aldehyde was separated by distillation and crystallized aldehyde-ammonia prepared from it.

Pure *propylene* was oxidated much more readily and almost at the ordinary temperature, in a few hours a great quantity of *acetone* being formed : —

$$C_6 H_6 + O_2 = C_6 H_6 O_2.$$

This acetone is easily isolated by simple distillation. Some acetic acid appears, being a secondary product from the acetone. *Amylene* is attacked violently, at the ordinary temperature, with formation of complex products, derived, however, doubtless as secondary products of oxidation of an acetone, $C_{10}H_{10}O_2$, which may be obtained by moderating the reaction. *Acetylene* is oxidated in the cold, with heat, and production of formic and carbonic acids.

Crystallized *camphene* is changed easily into *camphor* by pure CrO_3, on heating gently : —

$$C_{20}H_{16} + O_2 = C_{20}H_{16}O_2 ;$$

the reaction being easier than that with platinum-black, long since discovered by Berthelot.

The name *camphene* is given by Berthelot and some other French chemists to the solid hydrocarbon, isomeric with oil of turpentine itself, which is separated by alkalies from the crystalline compound that turpentine forms with muriatic acid.

In conclusion, he remarks that the oxidating action of pure CrO_3 is not exactly equivalent to that of mixed bichromate of potassium and sulphuric acid ; in the latter the presence of the sulphuric acid, as well as the heat evolved in the formation of the chromic and potassic sulphates, modifying the action. — *Amer. Gas Light Journal.*

ACTION OF THE ELECTRIC SPARK ON MARSH GAS.

The production of *acetylene* by this process was announced by Berthelot eight years ago ; he now says all organic gases and vapors (of course which contain both C and H) yield acetylene under the same influence. Indeed, this is a characteristic and sensitive reaction, permitting him to detect the presence in hydrogen gas of compound vapors of feeble tensions at ordinary temperatures.

A current of sparks through marsh gas augments its volume rapidly, with deposition of carbon. One hundred volumes became in two minutes 127, in 10 minutes 154; but still for complete action hours are necessary, the maximum final volume being 181. On the old view that free C and H are formed, the volume should have been doubled. Nevertheless, in 1860, Burr and Hoffman obtained results similar to the above, which they inferred to be due to impossibility of complete decomposition, not knowing of the formation of acetylene. Berthelot's results show the surprising fact that but one-eighth of the original marsh gas can really be converted directly into its elements. After some hours, when no further carbon is deposited, the residual gas contained 13 or 14 volumes of acetylene, showing that half the marsh gas has undergone the following reaction: $2C_2H_4 = C_4H_2 + 3H_2$. But on removing the acetylene now by absorption, it is found that a new state of equilibrium is established, and the amount rapidly increases again, the final amount of acetylene producible (39 volumes), proving a transformation, by the above reaction, of *four-fifths* of the marsh gas (as the condensation, from marsh gas into acetylene, is to one-half; the latter containing its own volume of hydrogen). Hence a far easier mode of preparing acetylene than heretofore known. Common coal gas may be passed slowly through a tube permeated by a current of sparks, and then through an absorbent of acetylene.

The 39 volumes of condensible matter above is not wholly represented, however, by acetylene. The latter, as Berthelot has proved, is gradually condensed by heat into hydrocarbons of heavier molecules, and the heat of the spark converts it partially into benzole (which is *triacetylene* $C_{12}H_6 = C_4H_2, C_4H_2, C_4H_2$) and still heavier hydrocarbons, some of which are even tar-like and precipitate with the carbon. The action of the spark thus assimilates itself to that of simple heat, the first transient action of which, on marsh gas, according to previous researches of Berthelot, is to produce acetylene, which is then gradually condensed by prolonged action. — *Am. Gas Light Journal.*

RELATIVE PROPORTION OF ALKALIES FOUND IN THE ASH OF DIVERS PLANTS.

The same plants grown near the sea, and at remote distances therefrom, alter their saline constituents, so that, while growing near the sea, soda prevails, as a rule, over potash, the reverse being the case while the same plant vegetates at a distance more or less remote from the sea; of this fact some instances are given in this paper. The relation of the soda to the potash of the ash of *Crambe maritima*, when grown near the sea, was as 960 to 1,000; when grown at Paris, as 89 to 1,000. The relation of soda to potash in the ash of black mustard seed grown near the sea was as 200 to 1,000, while when grown in Paris it was as 96 to 1,000. — *Bulletin Mensuel.*

APOMORPHIA.

Dr. Matthiessen found that, by the action of hydrochloric acid on morphia, a new base was produced, which, as to composition, differed from the former merely by the removal of one equivalent of water. But the physiological action of the new base was utterly different from that of the original one. While morphia is a powerful narcotic, the use of which is apt to be followed by subsequent depression, the new base was found to be free from narcotic properties, but to be a powerful emetic, the action of which was unattended by injurious after-effects. It seems likely to become a valuable remedial agent. — *Druggists' Circular.*

EVOLUTION OF AMMONIA GAS FROM MUSHROOMS.

M. El. Borscow says that, many years ago, the late Professor Sachs observed that when a glass rod, moistened with dilute hydrochloric acid (specific gravity 1.12), was brought near vigorously and healthily growing mushrooms, there appears a white vapor, evidently due to the formation of chloride of ammonium. This fact has been confirmed by Dr. G. Lehmann, while the late Alexander von Humboldt stated that mushrooms constantly give off not only ammonia, but also hydrogen. The author of this paper has thoroughly investigated this subject, taking due care to eliminate all sources of error from his experiments by every precaution modern science can suggest and successfully apply. Several engravings would be absolutely necessary for the proper understanding of these researches; but we briefly notice the following results: (1) different kinds and species of mushrooms give off, while growing vigorously, weighable quantities of ammonia; (2) this evolution of ammonia is not confined to full-grown mushrooms only, but belongs to young individuals, and even to some varieties of mushroom spawn; (3) this evolution of ammonia is a proper function of the living organism of these cryptogamic vegetables, and is very little, if at all, influenced by exterior causes; (4) there is no direct relation between the quantity of ammonia and that of carbonic acid given off during a given period of time. The quantity of ammonia given off during a certain length of time bears no direct relation to the weight of the substance from which it is given off. — *Druggists' Circular.*

INCLOSED CRYSTALS IN DIAMONDS.

Sorby argues that the supposed cavities in diamonds, described by Brewster, are in reality inclosed crystals, and the conclusion arrived at from the consideration of the whole structure of the diamond is not opposed to its having been formed at a high temperature.

The crystals inclosed in diamonds are frequently seen to be

surrounded by a series of fine, radiating cracks, which are the result of the contraction suffered by the diamond in solidifying over the inclosed crystal, and this explanation is verified by observing crystals formed in fused globules of borax glass cooled slowly, where the same phenomenon is seen. — *Chem. News.*

MOLYBDENUM AND CHROMIUM.

These metals can, according to Loughlin, be easily prepared as follows: A mixture of one part of pure molybdic acid and one and a half parts of cyanide of potassium is placed in a porcelain crucible and the lid luted on; this is placed in a large crucible and the interstices packed with animal charcoal. The entire apparatus is then exposed to a strong white heat for 12 hours; when cold the inner crucible is found lined with a white, silver-like metal, not acted upon by hydrochloric acid, but readily dissolved by nitric acid, and having a specific gravity of 8.56. By substituting oxide of chromium for molybdic acid, metallic chromium is obtained. — *Engineer.*

MINERAL CAOUTCHOUC.

Recent communications from Adelaide, South Australia, have made known the discovery in the southern portion of the colony of a remarkable carboniferous substance, which hitherto has only been found in small quantity in the coal strata of Derbyshire (England). It is a mineral caoutchouc, so called from its general appearance and elasticity. In Australia it is found on the surface of the sandy soil, through which it would appear to exude from beneath, as, burnt off occasionally by the bush fires, it is again found after the winter season, occurring in quantity and of varying thickness. Analysis proves it to yield 82 per cent. or more of a pure hydrocarbon oil; its value for the manufacture of gas there will be great, and it is also believed to be applicable to the making of certain dyes. The discovery is also important from its indication of the existence of oils or other carboniferous deposits. This material, known in mineralogy as elaterite, is also found in a coal-pit at Montrelais, near Nantes, France, at Neufchâtel, and on the island of Zante. According to the analysis of the late Professor Johnston, of Durham University, it is a hydrocarbon, containing from 83.7 to 85.5 per cent. of carbon, and from 12.5 to 13.28 per cent. of hydrogen. The variety found in Derbyshire (near Castleton) has a specific gravity varying between 0.9053 and 1.233; the substance is highly inflammable, its color blackish brown, its lustre resinous. — *Chem. News.*

SUMMARY OF CHEMICAL NOVELTIES.

Decomposition of Alkaline Chlorides. — According to Messrs. Kuentz and Jossinet, the decomposition of alkaline chlorides may be readily and economically effected by forcing through them when in the state of fusion a jet of steam; chlorhydric acid is formed together with caustic alkali, or, if a stream of carbonic acid be introduced with the steam, the carbonated alkali remains. — *Mon. Sci. No.* 165.

Extraction of Zinc from its Ores in the Wet Way. — Owing to the scarcity of fuel, and to the fact that the main bulk of the zinc ores now obtained in Silesia contain only from 7 to 10 per cent. of metal, experiments have been tried with a view of devising a process for extracting the metal in the wet way. Ammonia-water, chloride of ammonium, and hydrochloric acid were tried, but did not answer the purpose. Chloride of calcium was then tried, and found to answer well, even when the percentage of metal was as low as 4; a nearly concentrated solution of chloride of calcium and a boiling heat are required, and the process is less expensive than the ordinary method of extraction by the dry way, and the material obtained is readily reduced by the common method of zinc smelting. The ore operated upon is an impure carbonate of zinc. — *Journ. f. Prak. Ch.*

Welding Copper. — The great obstacle hitherto experienced in welding copper is that the oxide formed is not fusible. Rust has found that the use of microcosmic salt gives a fusible slag. This salt being expensive, he has substituted a mixture of one part phosphate of soda and two parts borax, and finds that it answers the purpose very well, although the slag formed is not so fusible as that formed by the microcosmic salt. — *Dingl. Pol. Journ.*

Welding Compound. — An improved compound for welding has been recently introduced in Belgium. It consists of iron filings 1,000 parts, borax 500 parts, resinous oil 50 parts, and sal-ammoniac 75 parts. The materials are mixed, heated, and powdered; the surfaces to be welded are dusted over with the composition and then brought to a cherry-red heat, at which the powder melts, when the portions to be united are taken from the fire and joined. Another composition for the same object consists of 15 parts of borax, two parts of sal-ammoniac, and two parts of cyanide of potassium. These constituents are dissolved in water, and the water itself afterwards evaporated at a low temperature. — *Druggists' Circular.*

Blackening Zinc. — Zinc may be given a fine black color by cleaning with dilute sulphuric acid and sand, and then immersing for an instant in a solution of 4 parts of sulphate of nickel and ammonium in 40 parts of water acidulated with one part sulphuric acid. After washing and drying, there remains a black coating, which adheres firmly, and takes a bronze color under the burnisher. Brass may be stained black with a liquid containing two pts. arsenious acid, 4 pts. hydrochloric acid, one pt. sulphuric acid and 80 pts. water. — *Ch. News.*

Tinning by the Moist Way. — It is a well-known fact that, when it is desirable to cover metals, especially brass or copper, with a strongly adhering coating of tin, this is usually effected by boiling the articles to be thus coated with an aqueous fluid, to which is added cream of tartar, crystallized protochloride of tin, and some lumps of pure metallic tin. The author states that, instead of this mixture, he uses, with very good success, a solution of one part of protochloride of tin in 10 parts of water, to which he next adds a solution of two parts of caustic soda in 20 parts of water; the mixture becomes turbid, but this does not affect the tinning operation, which is effected by heating the objects to be tinned in this fluid, care being taken, at the same time, to place in the liquid a piece of perforated block-tin plate, and to stir up the fluid during the tinning with a rod of zinc. — *Dr. Hillier, in the Moniteur Scientifique.*

Silvering Cast Iron. — M. Böttger recommends the use of a bath prepared in the following manner: 15 grams of nitrate of silver are dissolved in 250 grams of water, and 30 grams of cyanide of potassium are added; when the solution is complete, the liquid is poured into 750 grams of water wherein 15 grams of common salt have been previously dissolved. The cast iron intended to be silvered by this solution should, after having been well cleaned, be placed for a few minutes in a bath of nitric acid of 1.2 sp. gr., just previous to being placed in the silvering fluid. — *Druggists' Circ.*

Adulteration of Sulphuric Acid. — (*Rev. Hebd. de Chim.*) — It appears that some Continental makers of this acid are in the habit of adding to ordinary chamber acid a sufficient quantity of some cheap acid sulphate, so as to bring the sulphuric acid, as far as hydrometrical tests are concerned, up to the desired degree of density. M. Fleischer, having cause to complain about the bad quality of indigo-carmine prepared with a certain sample of sulphuric acid, was induced to evaporate some of the acid, and on doing so discovered the formation of crystals of sulphate of soda. This kind of adulteration, however readily detected, might cause in many dye and madder and garancine works very serious loss and great inconvenience, and is a gross fraud; the inducement is the saving of the cost of evaporation and apparatus connected therewith. — *Ch. News.*

Metallic Uranium. — Dr. Bolton has succeeded in preparing uranium by reducing the double fluoride of uranium and potassium by means of sodium. The double salt is prepared from the oxyfluoride by exposure to sunlight in the presence of an organic acid. It falls down as a beautiful green powder. This powder is mixed with proper equivalents of sodium and anhydrous chloride of potassium, and is fused in a porcelain crucible inclosed in a Hessian crucible lined with charcoal. The heat required at first is moderate, but, as soon as the reduction is accomplished, must be rapidly raised to prevent oxidation and loss of the metal. This method is analogous to the preparation of aluminum from cryolite, and appears to have been perfectly successful in the hands of Dr. Bolton. — *Jour. of App. Chem.*

Tungstate of Barium is said to form an excellent white paint, which has as good a tone and depth as white lead, and is not blackened by exposure to atmospheric influences.

Luting. — Prof. Hirzel, of Leipsic, recommends as a lute for covering the corks of vessels containing volatile substances (as benzine, light petroleum, etc.) a mixture of finely ground litharge and concentrated glycerine. Common glycerine, if concentrated, will answer the purpose.

Preparation of Nitrogen. — A new and elegant method of preparing this gas has been devised by Levy, an Italian chemist. It consists in heating bichromate of ammonium in a retort. The salt is transformed into green sesquioxide of chromium, and disengages vapor of water and nitrogen. — *Cosmos.*

Sulphurous Acid for Dissolving Bones. — It is well known that hydrochloric acid is used for the purposes of dissolving the earthy salts of bones, in order to obtain the gelatine in such a state as to render that substance readily soluble in boiling water. The use, however, of hydrochloric acid is rendered rather inconvenient for this purpose on account of the formation of chloride of calcium, which interferes with the drying of the gelatine. M. Coignet, at Paris, has found that sulphurous acid answers the purpose of hydrochloric acid in this instance perfectly well. The bones are placed in cold water, and through the water a current of sulphurous acid gas is forced so long as is required to completely soften the bones, which are afterwards washed in fresh water wherein some sulphurous acid gas has been previously dissolved. — *Druggists' Circular.*

Liquefied Hydrochloric Acid Gas. — In a paper read before the Royal Society, Mr. Gore gives the following summary : Out of 86 solids, liquefied hydrochloric acid gas only dissolved 12, and some of those only in a minute degree ; of 5 non-metallic substances it dissolved one, namely, iodine ; of 15 metals it dissolved only one, namely, aluminum ; of 22 oxides it dissolved 5, namely, titanic acid, arsenious acid, arsenic acid, teroxide of antimony, and oxide of zinc ; of 9 carbonates it dissolved none ; of 8 sulphides it dissolved one, namely, tersulphide of antimony ; of 7 chlorides it dissolved two, namely, pentachloride of phosphorus and protochloride of tin ; and of 7 organic bodies it dissolved two. The results show also that liquid hydrochloric acid in the anhydrous state manifests much less chemical action upon solid bodies than the same acid mixed with water, as under ordinary circumstances. — *Abstract of Proceedings of the Royal Society.*

Cyanogen in Coal Gas produced by Ammonia. — Romilly (*Erdmann's Journal für Chemie,* vol. 103) has shown that cyanogen is formed if illuminating gas is passed through weak water of ammonia, and then the lighted burner is turned upon the surface of a solution of a caustic alkali (potash, soda, or lime). After a few minutes the presence of a cyanide can be shown in the alkaline fluid by the iron test ; and if the alkaline solution used was strong potash lye, holding in suspension some fine metallic iron, there will be produced both ferro and ferri cyanide of potassium. This happens only when the flame is bright from incandescent carbon ; that of a Bunsen burner (blue or colorless) is without effect when directed on alkali after passing through ammonia, the carbon being not free, but already oxidized.

Black Phosphorus. — M. Blondlot states that the production of black phosphorus depends on two things, — the state of purity to which phosphorus is brought by distillation, and the temperature to which it is afterwards submitted.

Phosphorus which has been exposed to the sun is carefully distilled and collected in a flask, which is slowly cooled in a water-bath. The product forms a transparent white mass at ordinary temperatures, but if cooled down to 5° or 6° C., it suddenly turns to a beautiful black color. It can be redistilled or fused; it is colorless while liquid, but becomes black on again cooling to near zero. M. Blondlot regards black as the proper color of phosphorus. — *Comptes Rendus.*

White Phosphorus. — M. Baudrimont shows that white phosphorus is neither a hydrate nor an allotropic state of ordinary phosphorus, nor does it result from devitrification of transparent phosphorus; but that it is ordinary phosphorus irregularly corroded on the surface by the action of the air dissolved in the water, — a slow combustion, which is accelerated by the action of light, and which ceases as soon as the water holds no more oxygen in solution. — *Comptes Rendus.*

Oreide. — Composition — copper 79.7 parts, zinc 83.05 parts, nickel 6.09 parts, iron 0.28 parts, tin 0.09 parts.

The last-two ingredients are purely accidental. This alloy resembles gold.

Silver Ware may be kept bright and clean by coating the (warmed) articles with a solution of collodion diluted with alcohol.

Austrian Non-Explosive Blasting Powder consists of 30 per cent. of nitrate of potassium, 40 per cent. of nitrate of sodium, 12 per cent. of sulphur, 8 per cent. of charcoal, 4 per cent. of pit-coal, and 6 per cent. of tartrate of potassium and sodium. This powder is explosive only when it has been rammed tight.

Glycerine in Crystals. — M. Werner, by passing a few bubbles of chlorine gas through the glycerine of commerce, obtained small octahedral crystals, which are very hard, and without the sweet taste of glycerine even when melted. — *Chem. News.*

Platinum in Scotland. — Small quantities of platinum have been in Scotland associated with the gold existing there in the quartz. The metal is found in small scales resembling silver, but not magnetic, as is much of the crude platinum found in South America. — *Mining Journal.*

Topaz. — In a very difficultly accessible cave in the mountain of Galenstock, which separates the canton of Berne from that of Urich, a very rich deposit of topaz has been recently found, valued at more than 100,000 francs.

Salt Deposit near Berlin. — It appears that there has been discovered near Berlin, at Sperenberg, a rock-salt deposit, which in some localities has a depth of 669 feet, and from borings made it seems in every respect to be a highly valuable mineral deposit.

A new Crystalline Form of Silica. — De Rath has found, in a volcanic porphyry from Cerro San Cristobal, Mexico, a mineral he calls *tridymite*, which is pure silica, of the density of what has heretofore been regarded as "amorphous" silica, 2.3; the den-

sity of ordinary quartz being 2.6.   Tridymite, like quartz itself,
is hexagonal, but occurs in very beautiful macles.   It is uniax-
ial. — *Bull. Soc. Ch., June,* 1869.

Beauxite. — Between Taraon and Antibes in the south of
France there exists a valuable and extensive bed of beauxite
(hydrate of alumina), which has been used for the manufacture
of sulphate of aluminum.   This material has been applied, at the
suggestion of M. Audouin, for the manufacture of crucibles and
fire-bricks, and it was found that the best English, French, and
German fire-brick could be melted in crucibles made of beauxite
and heated by mineral oils and a blast. — *Cosmos.*

Formation of Nitre in Egypt. — A. Houzeau. — At Tantah,
a town of the Delta of the Nile, the houses are built simply
out of the river mud, after mixing it with straw and drying the
mass in the sun.   They have little stability, for this reason, and
frequently tumble to pieces; whenever this happens the natives
at once proceed to erect another building of precisely the same
character on the same spot.   Hence it comes that most buildings
are placed on a species of hills, some of which are of considerable
age, and that the ground retains both liquid and solid secretions
of numerous former generations.   The author examined some of
these earth-hills, both of old and later creation, especially for the
purpose of establishing the particular form in which *nitrogen* is
contained in them.   The quantity of the latter appears to be the
same in earths of different periods; that of older generations .670
per cent., of later .690 per cent.   This was divided in : —

	New Ground.	Old Ground.
Nitrogen as nitric acid	.044	.246
" " ammonia	.032	.300
" " organic compounds	.620	.124

proving the gradual passage of organic nitrogen into ammonia
and nitric acid. — *Comptes Rendus,* lxviii., p. 821.

Testing Antimony for Arsenic. — During the last year, on the occasion of the inspection of the apothecaries' shops in Prussia, a
quantity of tartar emetic was found to contain arsenic; in consequence thereof a vigorous investigation was set on foot by the
minister for medical affairs and police.   The method adopted for
testing for arsenic is as follows: Two grams of the suspected
tartar emetic are reduced to a fine powder and dissolved in 4
grams of pure chlorhydric acid.   A quantity of pure chlorhydric
acid, at least 30 grams, saturated with sulphuretted hydrogen, is
then added, the vessel corked tightly, shaken, and set aside.
The slightest trace of arsenic gives rise to a yellow coloration,
and very soon after to a perfectly perceptible pure yellow precipitate. — *Jahrb. f. Pharm.*

Arsenic in the Soda of Commerce. — Fresenius (*Zeitschrift*) calls
attention to the fact that the carbonate of sodium as met with in
commerce contains arseniate or arsenite of sodium.   A sample
purporting to be chemically pure, heated with cyanide of potassium in a stream of carbonic acid, gave distinct traces of a
mirror of arsenic.   Five grams of the same salt gave, when dis-

solved and acidulated with chlorhydric acid, a distinct yellow precipitate with sulphuretted hydrogen.

The arsenic is undoubtedly derived from the sulphuric acid used in converting the common salt into sulphate of sodium, as the pyrites used in the manufacture of sulphuric acid often contain arsenic in notable quantities and are rarely entirely free from it.

Test for Prussian Blue. — Nickles found that Prussian blue might be distinguished from the blue of indigo or aniline by means of fluoride of potassium, which bleaches the former and is without effect on the other two. — *Journ. Frank. Inst.*

Test for Hydrocyanic Acid. — Schönbein moistens filtering paper with fresh tincture of guiacum, containing 3 or 4 parts of resin, and, after drying, moistens the paper with a solution containing one quarter of one per cent. of sulphate of copper. This paper is instantly rendered blue in the atmosphere of a 20-litre vessel containing one drop of dilute hydrocyanic acid of one per cent. — *Schw. Wochenscrf. f. Pharm.*

Binoxide of Hydrogen as Test for Prussic Acid in Blood, which was proposed by Schönbein and again by Buchner, requires great care in its application, according to Dr. Huizinga, inasmuch as any acid reaction of blood, produced by the usual mineral or organic acids, causes the same brown color. At the same time it must be noted that the spectroscopic reactions for the color produced by prussic acid or cyanides are quite distinct, and so are the chemical tests for them. — *Fresenius, Zeitsch. f. Analy. Chemie.*

Reagent for Alkaloids. — M. Marme proposes the use of the double iodide of cadmium and potassium as a reagent for alkaloids. This compound precipitates the following alkaloids from very dilute solutions mixed with sulphuric acid: Nicotine, conicine, piperine, morphia, codeia, thebaine, narcotine, narceine, quinine, quinidine, cinchonine, strychnine, brucine, veratrine, berberine, atropine, aconitine, and some others. The precipitates are white and flocculent, but for the most part become crystalline. Quinine and strychnine, diluted with 10,000 parts of water, are entirely precipitated. These precipitates are insoluble in ether, soluble in alcohol, slightly soluble in water, and soluble in an excess of the double iodide.

This reagent does not precipitate glycosides. — *Chem. News.*

On the Estimation of the Iodine of Commerce by Volumetric Analysis. — M. Bobierre dissolves a weighed quantity of the iodine, the true value of which has to be estimated, in a concentrated solution of iodide of potassium; the solution is diluted to 100 c.c., and is dropped into an alkaline solution of arsenious acid of known strength. Instead of using starch-water as a means of recognizing the end of the reaction, the author adds a few cubic centimetres of benzol to the solution of arsenious acid, and ceases to add more of the solution of iodine as soon as the former solution becomes rose-colored. The arsenical solution is made by weighing off 49.95 grms. of arsenious acid, and 14.5 grms. of crystallized carbonate of sodium, and dissolving these in one litre of water, representing 12.688 grms. of iodine to the litre; 10 c.c. of this solution are taken for each assay, and 4 c.c. of benzol are added. — *J. de Pharmacie.*

Detection of Alcohol. — M. Lieben adds to the liquid suspected to contain alcohol a small quantity of iodine and a few drops of caustic potash or soda. On heating, but not boiling, the mixture the presence of alcohol is denoted by a very characteristic yellowish precipitate of iodoform. It is possible in this way to detect one-two-thousandth part of alcohol dissolved in water. — *Mon. Sci.*

Testing Glycerine for Sugar and Dextrine. — To 5 drops of the glycerine to be tested add 100 to 120 drops of water, 3 to 4 centigrams of ammonium-molybdate, one drop pure nitric acid (25 per cent.), and boil for about a minute and a half. If any sugar or dextrine be present, the mixture assumes a deep blue color. — *Polyt. Notizbl.* 143, 1868.

Detection of Phosphorus. — According to Dr. Schönn, of Stettin, when inorganic combinations of phosphorus and phosphates are ignited (after being previously well dried) with small quantities of pure magnesium (best is powder), phosphide of magnesium is formed, and the fused mass, on being moistened with water, will disengage phosphuretted hydrogen gas, which, in many cases, will be found to be the spontaneously inflammable variety of this compound. Phosphorus may thus be detected in organic substances, which, however, should be previously calcined. — *Zeitcsh. f. Anal. Ch.*

Test for Nitrates and Chlorates. — To one c.c. of pure concentrated sulphuric acid is added one-half c.c. of a solution of sulphate of aniline, prepared by adding 10 drops of the aniline of commerce to 50 c.c. of dilute sulphuric acid (1 to 6). If a glass rod be dipped in the substance to be tested, and then into the mixture, the presence of nitric acid, or of a nitrate, causes red streaks to appear in the path of the rod, or if the quantity of nitric acid be considerable, a tint varying from carmine to a deep red will pervade the mixture. The presence of a chlorate is indicated by a blue coloration. — *Chem. News.*

Chlorate of Potassium as a Blow-pipe Test. — In the "Neues Jahrbuch für Pharmacie" M. Landauer enumerates several instances in which chlorate of potassium may be made very useful before the blow-pipe in the search for certain metals. This salt, giving up at higher temperatures some of its oxygen to certain metals, becomes itself colored by the oxides of those metals. From *iron* and its compounds it receives a flesh color; from *lead* a pale brown; from *copper* a shade of light or dark blue, in some cases so deep even as to be nearly black. Manganese imparts to the alkaline salt a purple of variable intensity, and nickel (sesquioxide = $Ni_2 O_3$) turns it to black. The reaction is best performed in a tube closed at one end, 5 or 6 inches long by one-fifth to a quarter of an inch in diameter, into which is introduced a mixture of equal parts of the substance under examination, and of chlorate of potassium, previously rubbed fine with a few drops of alcohol and then carefully dried. The tube is heated gradually, at first over the lamp, and finally by means of the blow-pipe.

Determination of Silver. — The method of Gay Lussac for the determination of silver by titration as chloride is subject to a slight error, on account of the solubility of the chloride of silver in the liquid from which it is precipitated. Stas proposes to determine the silver as bromide, and thus avoid this error. — *Compt. Rend.*

New Test for Wool. — Wagner dissolves a decigramme of the material to be analyzed by boiling it in 10 to 15 c. c. of a strong solution of potash, dilutes to 100 c. c., and then tests this solution with nitro-prusside of potassium. The presence of the smallest quantity of wool causes a violet coloration of the liquid — *Mon. Sci. d. Quesn.*

Action of Heat on Tartaric Acid. — Dr. Sace has observed that, when tartaric acid is heated in a glass retort, acetic acid distils over; there is left in the retort a carbonaceous mass, while carbonic acid escapes.

Oxidation of Acetic Acid into Oxalic Acid. — When one part of acetate of sodium, one part hydrate of sodium, and two parts of permanganate of potassium are dissolved in a little water, the solution concentrated by boiling, finally evaporated to dryness, and the residue heated until it ceases to give with water a green colored solution, oxalic acid is found to exist in the saline mass.

Action of Cyanogen on Hydrochloric Acid. — When a current of gaseous cyanogen is passed into hydrochloric acid as concentrated as possible, no coloration is observed, but after twelve hours crystals of oxamide make their appearance, and the supernatant liquid contains oxalate of ammonium. With hydriodic acid the result is the same; oxamide is likewise formed, but iodine is displaced, and the liquid is found to contain hydrocyanic acid and iodide of ammonium. — *Engineer.*

Horse-chestnut leaves, according to Rochleder, contain a tannin which is found also in the tormentilla root; in the former it is converted into aescigenin, $C_{24} H_{20} O_4$, in the latter into kinovic acid. — *Chem. Centralb.*

Discovery of a New Base. — M. Wurtz has succeeded in obtaining a new base by making chlorhydrate of glycol act upon toluidine at a temperature of from 200° to 220° C. This substance exhibits a beautifully green fluorescence, has a bitter taste, and is precipitated by iodine in solution of iodide of potassium. It contains two atoms of hydrogen less than toluidine, while for two other hydrogen atoms are substituted a vinyl and an hydroxethylen group. The chloroplatinate of the base is a crystalline substance readily decomposed by heat. — *Bull. Soc. Ch.*, *Nov.* 4, 1869.

Determination of Silver. — The method of Gay Lussac for the determination of silver by titration as chloride is subject to a slight error, on account of the solubility of the chloride of silver in the liquid from which it is precipitated. Stas proposes to determine the silver as bromide, and thus avoid this error. — *Compt. Rend.*

New Test for Wool. — Wagner dissolves a decigramme of the material to be analyzed by boiling it in 10 to 15 c. c. of a strong solution of potash, dilutes to 100 c. c., and then tests this solution with nitro-prusside of potassium. The presence of the smallest quantity of wool causes a violet coloration of the liquid — *Mon. d. Quesn.*

Action of Heat on Tartaric Acid. — Dr. Sace has observed that, when tartaric acid is heated in a glass retort, acetic acid distils over; there is left in the retort a carbonaceous mass, while carbonic acid escapes.

Oxidation of Acetic Acid into Oxalic Acid. — When one part of acetate of sodium, one part hydrate of sodium, and two parts of permanganate of potassium are dissolved in a little water, the solution concentrated by boiling, finally evaporated to dryness, and the residue heated until it ceases to give with water a green colored solution, oxalic acid is found to exist in the saline mass.

Action of Cyanogen on Hydrochloric Acid. — When a current of gaseous cyanogen is passed into hydrochloric acid as concentrated as possible, no coloration is observed; but after twelve hours crystals of oxamide make their appearance, and the supernatant liquid contains oxalic ⋯ ⋯ acid the result is the same; ⋯ ⋯ iodine is displaced, and the ⋯ ⋯ anic acid and iodide of amm ⋯ ⋯

Horse-chestnut leaves, acc ⋯ ⋯ which is found also in the ⋯ ⋯ converted into aescigenin, C_{x} ⋯ ⋯ acid. — *Chem. Centralb.*

Discovery of a New Base. — M. W ⋯ ⋯ ing a new base by making chlor ⋯ ⋯ dine at a temperature of from ⋯ ⋯ its a beautifully green fluor ⋯ ⋯ itated by iodine in solution of ⋯ ⋯ atoms of hydrogen ⋯ ⋯ ⋯ ⋯ ⋯ ⋯ atom ⋯ ⋯ ⋯ ⋯ ⋯ — *Bull.* ⋯

GEOLOGY.

IT has already been shown, in a paper in the "Proceedings of the Boston Society of Natural History" for 1866, that there are good reasons for supposing that there is an essential difference in the nature of the two series of phenomena of elevation, continents and mountain chains; that they are entirely different in character, and are not connected by a series of forms. An effort has been made, in the paper referred to, to account for this dissimilarity by supposing that mountains are the product of the contraction in an outer crust in some way separated from the internal mass, if that mass be solid or floating on it, if we accept the old and now questionable theory of a molten interior. Pursuing the same line of reasoning, it can be shown that the causes of the continental surfaces and the sea basins are due to the wrinkling of all that portion of the earth which is called, even by those who do not acknowledge the implication of internal fluidity, its crust. A diminution of the earth's radius to the amount of four and a half metres in 2,500 years, according to Mayer, has resulted from loss of heat. It has long been seen that the contraction must be accompanied by a wrinkling of the crust, which, not losing heat, or not losing it as rapidly as the internal mass, must adapt itself to the diminished nucleus; but as yet nothing has been done to determine the forces which cause certain parts of the crust to bend up and others to bend down as this wrinkling goes on. The idea has been generally prevalent among naturalists and geologists that the position of these up and down curves of the crust of the earth is not permanent, but that the continental curves may become flattened out or even replaced by the depressions of the seas. This supposition is necessarily made by all those who, following the distinguished leader of our science, Sir Charles Lyell, call in such changes to account for alterations of climate and the destruction of organic life. The following reasons militate against this view:—

1st. When the contraction of the central mass has once thrown the crust into ridges and furrows, that is, formed continents and sea basins, all further contraction will necessarily tend to develop these ridges and furrows; nor can we legitimately suppose that these ridges and depressions have ever changed places, unless we can show some cause competent to overcome the very great resistance which they must oppose to such changes.

2d. The accumulation of sedimentary matter on the ocean floors causes the isogeothermal lines steadily to rise. The laying down of one hundred thousand feet of strata would bring a temperature of about 1,700° into the lowest part of the beds which were formed in water having the ordinary temperature of the sea. This must cause a great lateral strain in the lower part of the section beneath the sea floor where strata are being accumulated, and as there is no such lateral strain in the upper part of the section the result will be, necessarily, to cause the crust beneath such an area of deposition to tend to bend downwards. The result in this case is comparable to what occurs when two metals having different coefficients of expansion are soldered together and then subjected to the action of heat. The compound bar tends to arch in the direction of the metal which expands the most. In the section of the crust beneath the sea, the lower part, which expands the most, is also on the outside of the curve. Even if the whole crust section beneath the areas of deposition expanded equally, the tendency of the strain produced would still be to cause the actual curve of the sea floor to be deepened whenever the crust came to contract further in order to readjust itself to the diminished nucleus.

The frequent submergence of parts of the continents after they had been lifted above the sea does not conflict with this theory; the alteration of the pivot point of the movement would go far to account for these changes.*

The truth of these conclusions does not depend upon the internal condition of the earth in any way, except that the mass is supposed to be intensely heated. It may be either fluid or essentially solid without affecting these conclusions. — *Abstract of View set forth in Lectures at Harvard University in 1864 and 1869, by N. S. Shaler.*

GEOLOGY.

The question, How far the variation of the eccentricity of the earth's orbit may have brought about the great changes of climate indicated by geological phenomena, has been often discussed, more especially as regards the cause and date of glacial epochs. During the past three millions of years there have been three periods when the eccentricity attained a high value. The first of these began about 2,630,000 years ago, and terminated about 2,460,000 years ago. The second began about 980,000 years ago, and terminated about 720,000 years ago. The third began about 240,000 years ago, and terminated about 80,000 years ago. The third period, Mr. Croll considers, was the date of the glacial epoch; the second was that of the upper miocene period; while the third corresponded to the glacial epoch of the middle eocene period. Few geologists believe that during the two latter periods our country passed through conditions of glaciation as severe as it has done during the post-pliocene period. Mr. Croll, however, argues that subaerial denudation, by destroying the whole of

---

* See abstract of paper on the changes of level of seashores, p. —.

the land surfaces, has effectually removed all direct proof, although the indirect evidence is very much in favor of their occurrence. From calculations based upon the amount of sediment brought down by the Ganges, Mississippi, and other rivers, it would follow that from the close of the miocene and eocene glacial periods to the present day, supposing the rate of deposition to be constant, 120 feet and 410 feet respectively have been removed and carried down to the sea in the form of sediment. The cosmical theory of climate also requires that if glacial conditions obtained at these periods, warm and equable climates must have prevailed immediately before and after them; and the author maintains this is just what has happened. In the Turin miocene, conglomerates, considered glacial by Sir Charles Lyell, are overlain and underlain conformably by strata indicating a subtropical condition of climate. The same phenomena are also observed in Switzerland in rocks of the middle eocene period, where we find " flysch" closely associated with nummulitic strata, which contain genera characteristic of a warm climate. The cretaceous and permian periods afford similar evidence, and in the post-pliocene glacial period we have undoubted evidence of a warmer climate during part of its duration, as evidenced by the occurrence of animals and shells existing in latitudes where they could not otherwise have lived in consequence of the cold. — *Chronicles of Science, Jan.*, 1869.

THE SOURCE OF VOLCANIC ACTION.

The limitation of volcanic activity to the seashores was long since noticed, and has been much commented upon. A careful study of the relation of former seats of igneous activity to the ancient seashores will convince the student that volcanoes always cease to be active when the ocean abandons their bases. It is evident, therefore, that we must seek the origin of volcanic action in some process or other which is going on in the crust of the earth beneath the sea floor, which does not take place beneath the dry land.

There is but one cause competent to produce such effects which is peculiar to the sea, and that is the accumulation of strata going on upon its floor. The beds first laid down contained, it may be, large quantities of organic matter in the shape of animal and plant remains, and a great deal of water was imprisoned in their structure. After a time the accumulation of superincumbent beds causes the heat of the beds first laid down to become very great. A thickness of sedimentary beds much less than what we have good reason to suppose may have been laid down on the greater part of the ocean floors, would be sufficient to bring the heat of materials lying at the level of the original sea bottom to a temperature high enough to decompose the water and vaporize the carbon which they contained. As this heat increased, the tension of these materials seeking to take on the gaseous form would become greater and greater. If at any point the pressure was suddenly removed the water would be decomposed and the carbon vaporized. If, as we have reason to suppose, the sea floors constantly bend downwards by virtue of the forces brought into action by the deposition of strata, there would naturally be a tendency to fracture along the shore line. Such fissures penetrating to the bed of these pent-up gases would give them relief. The reconstruction of the oxygen of the water, taking place at a distance from the point of decomposition, with the gaseous carbon, would generate heat enough to melt the walls of the channel, and this molten matter would be pushed out by the escaping gases.

All, or nearly all, volcanic eruptions begin with a rush of gases. After an interval, which may be supposed to correspond to the time required for the molten rock to accumulate and clog the channel, comes an outbreak of lava, succeeded, if the eruption continues, by another rush of gases, followed, it may be, by another escape of molten matter. The character of the gases poured out during an eruption corresponds very well with what would be required by this theory. — *Abstract of a View presented in a Course of Lectures at Harvard College, by Prof. N. S. Shaler.*

THE FROZEN WELL AT BRANDON, VERMONT.

Descriptions of this well have been published in the "Annual Sci. Disc.," 1860, p. 316; ibid., 1856, p. 190. In the "Hours at Home" for Feb., 1870, there is an article upon this well. The scientific observations will be of interest. We condense the following from a paper presented to the American Academy of Arts and Sciences, by Prof. F. H. Storer, in behalf of Prof. John M. Ordway and himself, and contained in vol. v. (Records from May, 1860, to May, 1862) of the proceedings of that body.

"On visiting the locality in the early part of the summer of 1860, we ascertained the existence of a variable but well-marked current of cold air continually flowing upwards out of the mouth of the well. Bits of any light material dropped in were buoyed up and forcibly blown out. The mature pappus of the dandelion, which was then in full puff all around, afforded an abundance of very sensitive current indicators.

"At the opening of the well the thermometer indicated 43.5° F., the temperature of the external air being 78°. Five feet below the mouth, the thermometer *stood* at 43°, and 12 feet down, at 40°. Water drawn up from the bottom, without stopping to cool the bucket, was at 34°. Water drawn up at other times contained lumps of ice detached from the coating of ice lining the well to the height of some 5 feet above the surface of the water.

"We had hardly begun to make close observations, before it occurred to us that we were dealing with a case of compressed air, which might be accumulated by some natural subterranean *Trompe* (Wassertrommel), or "Catalan blower," and which, expanding as it approached the surface of the earth, or escaped into this artificial outlet, would absorb and render latent a large amount of heat, and could thus effect the gradual refrigeration and actual freezing of a considerable body of wet gravel.

" Considering that the drift heap in which the well is situated rests on limestone, and is not far distant from the junction of the limestone with the mica slate, or gneiss, we may easily conceive of the occurrence of such caverns, fissures, natural conduits, and subterranean watercourses as might complete an arrangement on the principle of the water-tromper, one of the oldest contrivances for securing a blast to be used in iron furnaces, — and thus afford a constant and ever-renewed supply of condensed air. And, as the experiments of Dr. Gorrie show that but a moderate degree of condensation is necessary to enable air to become freezing cold by its return to the normal bulk, we may be warranted in saying that such a cause, though of moderate power and having various impediments to overcome, would be sufficient to produce all the effects observed in the case under consideration . . . The actual freezing must proceed with greater rapidity at that time of the year when the accumulated heat of the soil is allowed the freest radiation, together with the least chance of increase. In fact, it is said to be a matter of yearly observation, that the well " begins to feel the cold weather," and to freeze over in autumn, long before there are any heavy frosts above, and; indeed, while the ground is still open for tillage. This would seem to indicate a cause operating with almost uniform force.

" But not intending to lay too much stress on the water-tromper hypothesis, which, of course, is not entirely free from drawbacks, and may or may not be the true explanation of the singular phenomenon under discussion, we wish more particularly to bring forward to the notice of the academy the fact of the continual rush of cold air out of the well at Brandon, — a current probably having some connection with the freezing below. And we may be allowed to remark that in the case of this particular well, at least, any theory which fails to assign a sufficient cause for the continued efflux leaves out of account a matter hardly less wonderful than the perennial congelation itself."

Profs. Storer and Ordway put on record the temperature of sources of water open near this limited drift bed.

" 1. In a spring sunk to about the depth of 10 feet from the surface, — a stone's throw north-west of the frozen well, at the side of the lane leading out of the main road, — the water at top stood at 54° F., and that at the bottom at 50°.

" 2. A similar spring about 12 ft. deep, 3 or 4 rods west of No. 1, showed a temperature of 50° in water drawn from the bottom.

" 3. In a shallow spring at some distance south-west of the frozen well, in lower ground, and apparently near the limit of the drift, the water stood at 48° F. A deep well in the mica slate formation, about half a mile west, stood at 45° F."

This well is of great interest at the present time, acting as it does upon the principle of Bunsen's filterer, now attracting attention among chemists. A description of this filterer will be found in this volume (see Index).

CHANGES OF LEVEL OF SEASHORES.

Numerous observations have been made upon the changes of level of shore lines now in progress on the borders of the different continents, but as yet little effort has been made to determine the nature of the movements involved in these changes.

Inasmuch as we have no other means of readily perceiving the changes of level of the earth's crust except such as may be afforded by the consequent alterations in the position of the line of contact of sea and land, our observations are limited to the shore lines. But unless we form some idea of the way in which the continents and sea floors are affected during these movements, we cannot fully understand the phenomena. It needs no argument to show that it is exceedingly unlikely that these movements are mere accidents of the shore. It is evident that they must be a part of an extensive movement, which is only rendered evident at a few points by changes in the position of the sea. The only way in which any considerable portion of the earth's crust can change its level is by a sinking of the ocean furrow and a lifting of the adjoining continental folds. As the earth must be essentially incompressible to any pressure which any part of the outer surface could suddenly apply to it, we can only conceive of subsidence over an extensive area by supposing a proportionate elevation at another point. This idea is thoroughly borne out by all we know of the geological history of the earth's crust; for we have as the main feature of that history the continued elevation of continents attended by the continual depression of the ocean troughs. That the continents have been continually elevated is sufficiently proved by the fact that they are still in existence, although large portions of them have been from the earliest time subjected to the erosion of atmospheric agents. Over a large portion of the basin of the Mississippi the erosion is as rapid as a foot a thousand years; yet this region has been above the level of the sea for millions of years. The evidence of the continued subsidence of ocean floors is also easily seen. Now a movement wherein the lands go up and the seas down is comparable to that of a lever, or bar, about a fulcrum point. The whole section from the centre of the sea to the centre of the continent is not like a rigid bar, in which case the centre of either land or water area would have to describe a great curve in order to have any considerable motion near the shores. The sea floors probably sink and the land areas rise at something like the same rate over the greater part of their surfaces. Still, for convenience' sake, we may regard the section of the earth's crust for a little distance on either side of the shore line as moving as a rigid mass as the uplift of the continents and the sinking of the sea bottom goes on.

It is evident that much will depend upon the position of the fulcrum point of the movement in relation to the shore line; if this point should be exactly at the coast, then the movement of uplift and subsidence could go on without any change on the shore line; as this point departs from the shore the extent of the alteration in the position of that line would increase. The way in which the sea would move would, however, depend entirely upon the question, whether the fulcrum point was to the seaward or landward of the shore. Where this point lay to the seaward, then the rotative movement would cause the land to gain on the sea; if, however, the pivot point be beneath the dry land, then the same movement would cause the sea to advance upon the land. The rapidity of the advance or retreat of the sea would depend, other things being equal, upon the remoteness of the pivot point from the shore line.

Since we cannot suppose that the line connecting the different fulcrum points can often coincide exactly with the outline of any shore, it is evident that at different positions this line may correspond precisely with the course of the shore, or may pass to the seaward or landward of that shore, so that we may have the three different conditions of an unchanging, an advancing, or a retreating sea all brought about by variations in the position of the fulcrum points of the moving crust of the earth. — *Abstract of Paper by Prof. N. S. Shaler, in the Proceedings of the Boston Soci. of Nat. Hist.*

PLASTICITY OF PEBBLES AND ROCKS.

Professor W. P. Blake, at the meeting of the American Association at Salem, read an interesting paper on the peculiar elongated structure of the pebbles of the conglomerate at Purgatory, near Newport, which Professor Hitchcock had maintained had been elongated, compressed, and distorted by tension and pressure after being rendered plastic by an elevation of temperature.

Professor Rogers, at the Newport meeting of the Association, had contended that the peculiar forms of these pebbles were due entirely to wave action on the oblong fragments of the original metamorphic rocks. Some difference of opinion had existed among geologists upon these points, but he (Prof. Blake) presented some fresh evidence from a conglomerate in Arizona Territory. This conglomerate consisted of a paste of micaceous schist filled with pebbles of varying size, and elongated and compressed similar to those of the Newport conglomerate. They presented even more conclusive evidence of having been drawn out and compressed by tension and enormous pressure than even the Newport pebbles. Eminent geologists had alleged that deep-seated rocks often became plastic, and that those not much exposed to air were softer than those on the surface. Prof. Blake then adduced arguments and facts tending to substantiate this theory. The distortion of hard rocks was found on a large scale in the flanks of the Sierra Nevada, of California. After dilating on some details bearing on these points, and referring to various hypotheses which had been adduced thereon, Prof. Blake said that the consideration of the phenomena led him to conclude that enormous and long-continued pressure and tension, probably at a moderate elevation of temperature (but not necessarily so), had been sufficient to produce the molecular movement of these hard and apparently unyielding materials. Mechanical force alone appeared to have been the agent, and M. Tresca had shown that under enormous pressure solids could be made to flow in the same manner as liquids, or that in their movements they followed the same law. The remainder of the paper pointed out certain facts and illustrations tending to strengthen these views. By the careful study of these phenomena of plasticity new views were opened of the structure of great rock masses; of the phenomena of plication, lamination, and of the origin of some structural peculiarities of mineral veins and their enclosing walls. In view of all the facts, Prof. Blake thought that geologists should admit that very great changes had been produced in the structure of rock masses by simple mechanical pressure, unaided by any great elevation of temperature, or by extraordinary chemical agencies.

Mr. J. B. Perry exhibited some pebbles obtained at Purgatory, in which one pebble appeared driven into another, showing the effects of this kind of compression.

Mr. T. Sterry Hunt made a few remarks bearing on these points.

HINTS ON THE STRATOGRAPHY OF THE PALÆOZOIC ROCKS OF VERMONT.

Prof. J. B. Perry, at the meeting of the American Association, read a long and elaborate paper on the above subject, throwing much light on many geological phenomena connected therewith.

Prof. Agassiz said that Prof. Perry had stuck to a difficult subject with unusual perseverance, and had, he thought, solved it to the satisfaction of all those who should afterwards critically go over the ground. He said that Prof. Perry's object was to establish the precise stratification of the rocks in question and their relation to each other, in order to prevent future mistakes of palæontologists in mixing up fossils of different periods. He thought American geologists were under an obligation to him for what he had done.

FLORA AND FAUNA OF THE MIOCENE TERTIARY BEDS OF OREGON AND IDAHO.

Prof. J. S. Newberry exhibited, at the meeting of the American Association, a beautiful series of fossil plants collected by Rev. Mr. Condon, of Dallas City, Oregon.

These plants, the professor said, were from the fresh-water deposits which cover so large a surface of the Great Basin in Nevada, Idaho, and Oregon, and were of special interest both from their geological position and botanical character. They were contained in the sediments deposited by a series of great fresh-water lakes which once existed in the area lying between the Rocky Mountains and Sierra Nevada.

In the report of his explorations in California and Oregon Prof. Newberry had described these lacustine deposits, and had shown how the lakes at the bottom of which they accumulated had disappeared by the cutting down of their outlets, the gorges through which the Columbia, Klamath, and Pitt Rivers now flow.

The Klamath Lakes, etc., were miniature representatives of these ancient lakes, which were apparently quite as extensive as our present great lakes.

The fossil plants contained in the collection made by Rev. Mr. Condon were most beautifully preserved, and consisted of a great number of species, most of which were new; but a number were identical with species found in the miocene tertiary of the Upper Missouri.

There are also some species which had been found in the miocene beds of Fraser's River and Greenland.

The present collection will add much to our knowledge of the flora of the miocene period on this continent.

The animal remains found in the same series of tertiaries with the plants consist of fresh-water shells and fishes, with a few mammalian bones.

The shells are numerous species of *Meladia*, *Planorbis*, *Cerbicula*, and *Unio*, — all, so far as known, new to science.

The fishes were *Cyponodonts* allied to *Mylophawdon*, etc., — the fishes now inhabiting the western rivers.

Among the mammalian bones contained in this collection were some that plainly belonged to the horse.

The beds containing the animal remains were perhaps more recent than the plant beds, but still tertiary.

THE COAL-FIELDS OF THE NORTH PACIFIC COAST.

The Pacific Railroad being now nearly ready for traffic, it becomes of importance to inquire what are the fuel supplies — on the Pacific coast — to be relied upon to supply the fleets of steamers and the branch railways which will soon strike off from the main line into almost every valley, and to every little mountain town. No doubt coal might be brought round Cape Horn, as hitherto much of it has been, or across the plains with the railway; but both of these means of supply must necessarily be limited, on account of the expense. It behoves us, therefore, to inquire somewhat narrowly what are the extent and nature of the native coal-fields on the North Pacific coast. I must preface what I have to say by telling you that what notes I may have to lay before you are the result of occasional observations in the course of my wandering in the greater portion of certain regions — explored and unexplored — between California and Alaska during portions of the years 1863, 1864, 1865, and 1866. Though I shall have occasion, now and then, to refer to general geological questions, yet, for the main part, what I shall have to say will almost entirely be looked at from a coal-supply point of view, and then as much with the eye of a physical geographer as that of a pure geologist.

Extending from the borders of California to Alaska are three coal-fields, belonging respectively to the tertiary, secondary, and palæozoic ages; the latter being situated, as far as yet known, only in the Queen Charlotte Islands, off the northern coast of British Columbia, the exact age being as yet undetermined, though the coal is anthracitic, and, in all probability, palæozoic. The other two coal-fields are situated, as regards each other, from south to north, in the order of their age. The tertiary extends from California northwards, through Oregon and Washington Territory, impinging the southern end of British Columbia and Vancouver Island, and extending, with some interruptions, right across the Rocky Mountains,—the miocene coals of Missouri being apparently only a continuation of these same beds. The secondary beds, on the other hand, on the North Pacific are confined to the island of Vancouver, though, in all probability, they are also a continuation of the cretaceous strata of Missouri. The tertiary lignites of the North Pacific are throughout of miocene age, and are associated with beds of sandstone, shale, etc. It burns freely, but leaves behind much slag and ash. It has been wrought at various places on the coast. 1. Mount Diablo, California. Here 59,257 tons were mined last year, from January to August, the coal selling for 8 dollars per ton in San Francisco. At Benicia it was also mined, but has been discontinued. Its analysis is, carbon, 50; volatile bituminous matter, 46; ash, 4. 2. Coose Bay, Oregon. Its analysis shows 46.44 per cent. of carbon, 50.27 of volatile matter, and 3.19 of ash. Its percentage of coke is 49.73; but this is dark, friable, and of little value. It produces abundant gas, of low illuminating power. It is used to some extent in San Francisco, 7,759 tons having been imported from January to August, 1868. 3. Clallam Bay, Washington Territory. Several attempts have been made here to get good coal, but have failed to a great extent, owing to the want of a harbor. Analysis, carbon, 46.40; volatile matter, 50.97; ash, 2.63. 4. Bellingham Bay. Here the lignite has been mined for some years with success, though it is of no better quality than the others. From January to August, 1865, 5,680 tons were imported into San Francisco. Analysis, carbon, 47.63; bitumen, 50.22; ash, 2.15. Coal crops out at various other localities, — Fraser River, Burrard Inlet, islands of the Haro Archipelago, Sanetch Peninsula, the northern (Vancouver) shores of De Fucas Strait, etc., — but has not been worked; and I am of opinion that all these outcrops are of tertiary age, the secondary formation not appearing south of the Chemainos River. There are newer (pleistocene, or perhaps recent) lignites in the cliffs of Useless Bay, Whidby's Island, associated with remains of the mastodon, a tradition of the existence of which animal still lingers among the Indian tribes. This lignite is in small quantity, and quite worthless for fuel. The whole coast of Vancouver on the east coast, north of Chemainos, is bounded by a belt of carboniferous strata, composed of sandstone, shale, and coarse gravel-stone conglomerates, interstratified with which are beds of coal of a much superior character to any hitherto described. These beds, from the contained fossils, appear to be cretaceous. Everywhere the strata named form a characteristic accompaniment of the coal (especially this coarse conglomerate), and nearly everywhere it is underlaid by one or more seams of coal cropping out at some point of the circuit named, though it may reasonably be supposed yet to be found on the opposite shores of British Columbia. Outcrops are seen on some of the coast-lying islands, etc.; but it is only at Nanaimo where it is wrought to any extent, this being the only mine in Vancouver Island (or in the British North Pacific territories) exporting coal. Here is a village of 500 inhabitants, and some 50 miners. Last year, the company exported 43,778 tons, and declared a dividend of 15 per cent. The coal is bright, tolerably hard, and not unlike some of the best qualities of English coal. It is used all over the coast for steaming and domestic purposes. It brings 11 dollars per ton in Victoria, and 13 in San Francisco. An analysis gives carbon, 66.93; hydrogen, 5.32; nitrogen, 1.02; sulphur, 2.20; oxygen, 8.70; ash, 15.83. The fossil remains were then described. North of Nanaimo, on Brown's River, immense seams of coal have been discovered by myself and party; on Salmon River, the Indians report coal; at Sukwash, near Fort Rupert, coal appears; and at Koskeemo Sound, on the western shore, are extensive undeveloped fields of what will ultimately, no doubt, prove the best coal in Vancouver Island, both from its quality and easy shipment. The latter, on analysis, gave carbon, 66.15; hydrogen, 4.70; nitrogen, 1.25; sulphur, 0.80; oxygen, 13.59; ash, 13.60. Other coal-fields will no doubt be discovered as exploration proceeds; but the country is so covered with dense forests and undergrowth as to render exploration very difficult. The anthracite is found on the Queen Charlotte Islands, off the north coast of British Columbia. The beds are much broken up by faults, felspathic trap dykes, and other disturbing influences, so that to work it will always be expensive and troublesome. Still, the value of the discovery is of the highest importance to the coast. The coal is associated with conglomerates, a fine hard slate, out of which the Hydah Indians carve the pipes and other ornaments so common in the European museums, and metamorphosed sandstones. On first sight, I was inclined to believe it only debituminized cretaceous coal; but, from the fossils recently discovered, I am induced to change that opinion, and to believe it of palæozoic age. An analysis gave, carbon, 71.20; moisture, 5.10; volatile combustible matter, 7.27; ash, 6.43. The only good or extensive coal-fields in the North Pacific are, therefore, within the English colonies of Vancouver Island and British Columbia; and in the possession of these coal-fields, these States, at present so depressed, have a mine of wealth, which, if judiciously managed, will ultimately render them the seat of busy industry. — *Abstract of a Paper read by Robert Brown, Esq., F.R.G.S., before the Edinburgh Geological Society.*

COAL IN THE ROCKY MOUNTAINS.

The Union Pacific Railway is not likely, as was at first anticipated, to suffer any inconvenience from the absence of steam fuel. A coal-field, almost unlimited in extent, showing outcroppings for 300 miles on the road, has been "struck" in Wyoming Territory, in the heart of the Rocky Mountains. The locomotives are now fed almost entirely by coal, worked by the company itself, or by contractors, who furnish it at a low price. All the coal for 15 miles in the "alternate sections" on either side of the line is owned by the company. There are 6 mines in working order; there are others in progress. The principal mine, at Carbon station, yielded 4,000 tons to the railway company in the first three weeks in April. One of the drifts is already 540 feet in length; and there is an excellent shaft, with the usual gear, pumps, etc., worked by steam-power. The thickest part of the seam so far opened is 9 feet high. Hitherto, neither fire nor choke-damp has troubled the miners; but there is a certain amount of water in the deepest part. The miners are at present earning from 7 to 12 dollars per day. The coal is of good quality. There is neither bitumen nor sulphur in it. It contains, by analysis, nearly 60 per cent. of carbon, 12 per cent. of water, and 26 per cent. of inflammable gases. It is to bear a new name, — one which is, perhaps, tolerably appropriate. It is to be called "anthra-lignite;" and as coal has been sold lately in Omaha, on the Missouri, at the rate of 21 dollars a ton, whilst the company will probably sell it at half that price, it will be seen that the discovery is one of the greatest importance to the whole central portion of the continent. Iron ores have been found near it; and a good collection of coal fossils has been collected at the Carbon Station. A coal seam has also been recently discovered at Elko, on the Central Pacific Railway, which is the continuation of the Union Pacific line already referred to.

CHINESE GEOLOGY AND MINERALOGY.

Professor A. S. Bickmore, of Madison University, read a paper to the Association at Salem, relating his observations during a journey of some 2,000 miles in the interior of China.

It fortunately happened that the rivers, at the time, were low, as their beds in China constitute the only access in most cases to geological outcrops, there being no railroad and similar excavations there as here. Professor B. found first a basis of granite, overlaid with grits and shales, with no fossils, as yet found. Then ancient limestones, with fossils thought to be Devonian, then limestones equivalent to the carboniferous. (A hill of limestone was visited, which was *interstratified with coal*, and burnt directly to lime by the Chinese. Fossils brought from coal rocks at Pekin are regarded by Dr. Newberry as probably Triassic.) Next over the limestone, a red sandstone.

Coal and iron are the most important minerals observed. China, being mostly bare of forests, is dependent on coal for fuel: but this is very dear, on account of imperfect mining, and the best coal yet lies undisturbed, as, for lack of pumping machinery, they can mine but little below water level. Professor B. thinks the coal inferior, however, to ours. The Chinese burned coal in the time of Marco Polo, A.D., 1290, before it was used in Europe.

There is an important mine at Mun-ti-kau, 35 miles south-west of the capital, which he visited. An inclined shaft has been sunk to a very great depth below the surface of the earth, following the drift of the coal, by which the coal is brought up on sleds, by man-power, one man for each sled, the capacity of which is one bushel and a half. No machinery of any kind is in use. No artificial means of ventilation are employed. By reason of the fact that the Chinese do not go below the water line, fire-damp is almost unknown.

In the north of China coal is ground to dust and mixed with clay, that it may burn more slowly.

The quantity of coal in China is immense and the supply inexhaustible.

Petroleum also was found 160 years ago in the province of Shensi. Du Halde, in his work on China, compiled from the diaries of Jesuit priests, as long ago as 1725, says: "Its mountains distil a *bituminous liquor*, which they call 'oil of stone,' and use for lamps." A kind of petroleum is also found in the Island of Formosa.

The iron yield of China is large, but the best ore comes from the beds of Sungan, in the southern part of the province of Shensi. From this the Chinese razors and other cutlery are manufactured.

Gold is found in nearly all the Chinese rivers in the mountainous districts, and the Yangste is called the "Golden Sanded River." Professor Bickmore thinks Shensi to be the most promising gold field in the empire. It is difficult, however, to determine where gold and silver exist in China, for the law is harshly repressive of all discoveries of their deposit.

There is lead near Tungchan, in Shantung, but exorbitant demands for permission to work it have effectually prohibited its development.

Silver and copper are found in many parts of China, the former being employed mostly in the payment of taxes to the government, and the latter in the manufacture of coin, bells, idols, and articles in bronze.

There are in China extensive deposits of cinnabar, from which the Chinese manufacture mercury, under the name of "water silver," but since the development of the cinnabar mines of California, the cities on the sea-coast of China are supplied with quicksilver chiefly from that source.

Tin has not yet been found *in situ* in China, but the great numbers of bronze idols make it very probable that the tin used was not all imported from Malacca. If tin shall be found in

China then we may expect that it will be found the chief source of the considerable quantities of that metal used in manufacturing the bronze implements that have been found in such numbers, during late years, in the lakes of Switzerland.

"In review, we see that China is well supplied with coal and iron, — the two minerals especially necessary for her future development, — that these minerals are widely distributed over almost her whole area, and that she has thus the requisite materials for manufacturing her own cotton, without being dependent on the looms of England. Again, China possesses her share of the precious metals, and yet nearly all her ample material resources remain to be developed, though she has been the most civilized nation in all the East, and the most populous empire the world has ever seen."

MINING.

Coal in the Colorado district is a matter of great importance. According to the "Denver News," Gen. Pierce stated to the Board of Trade that besides the bed of 31 inches, discovered near Fort Dupton, on the Platte, there were also two beds on the Cache-la-Poudre. One of these beds was 4 feet thick, and the other about 18 inches. The "Salina Herald" says that in digging a well on the east side of the Smoky Hill River, less than two miles from town, a bed of good bituminous coal, 18 inches thick and about 20 feet below the surface, was cut through.

The copper mines of Africa have of late years been attracting considerable attention. The copper lodes in the Insizwa Mountain, about 12 miles from the southern boundary of Natal, are remarkable. Some comparatively small workings have been carried on about 80 miles from Fort St. John. The deposit here is described as about 18 feet thick by 2½ feet in depth. From this description it is evidently not a *vein*, but a *bed*. This is clearly in a state of decomposition, since it is said the ore is replaced by a yellow ochreous deposit (*gissan* of miners) containing nodules of very pure carbonate of copper or malachite, varying in size from a pea to masses of 10 or 15 pounds' weight. Some miners from D'Urban penetrated deeper into the mountains, and found a similar deposit. Portions of considerable masses have been found to contain as much as 56 per cent. of metal, the average, however, being from 30 to 40 per cent. Silver was found to the extent of 5.30 ounces to the ton of copper, and a trace of gold was discovered.

Chromium is stated to have been discovered in large quantities in Maryland and Pennsylvania. Chromate of iron, of fine quality, has also been found in Victoria. We understand samples of this mineral and antimonial ores of good quality have been shipped to this country with a view to determining their real commercial value. In a cave in the mountain of Galenstock, which, it is well known, separates the cantons of Berne and Urich, a valuable deposit of topaz has been recently found. — *Quarterly Journal of Science*, *April*, 1869.

21*

DECREASE IN THE PRODUCTION OF GOLD.

Blake, in his late "Report on the Precious Metals," has the following remarks on the probable future decline in the production of gold, which are worthy of notice; as also those on placer and vein mining, and the probable rise in value of gold to be quoted hereafter: —

"The statistics of the production of gold in California, Australia, and other countries show very clearly the familiar fact that in all newly discovered gold regions a maximum production is soon attained, and is succeeded by a gradual but certain decrease, owing to the exhaustion of the placer deposits. Thus, in California, the maximum product was attained in the year 1853, when the shipments were about 55,000,000 dollars, and the production was doubtless from 60,000,000 dollars to 65,000,000 dollars in value. It is now much less than half of that amount. In Australia, in the same year (1853), the reported shipments from Victoria amounted to 3,150,020 troy ounces, and the production was nearly 60,000,000 dollars in value.* In 1867, the shipments were only 1,433,687 ounces, much less than half as much as in 1853. The apparently nearly uniform production of California for the past ten years, judging from the shipments of treasure from the port of San Francisco, is the result of the opening of other gold and silver producing regions in Nevada, Idaho, Oregon, and Arizona, which, so far as their production depends upon placers, are in their turn liable to rapid exhaustion. In British America, and in Idaho and Montana, the production of gold is now rapidly diminishing. Russia is the only country in which a nearly uniform production has been maintained through a series of years. This may perhaps be explained by the fact that the mines have not been free to all, and consequently comparatively few persons have been engaged in developing them. The climate, also, is unfavorable to rapid and continuous working, and the method of washing placer gravel by machinery in use there is necessarily slow, and gives limited results, which cannot compare with those obtained by the gigantic system of sluicing practised in California and Australia. There has also been in Russia a constant extension eastward of the gold region by new discoveries, extending even to the Pacific coast, and there is, doubtless, an immense area of virgin ground from which the gold supply of Russia may be for a long time maintained at the present figures, or, possibly, greatly increased, especially if all restrictions upon mining are removed, and the country is thrown open to the skilled miners of other regions. This Siberian gold-field, with the great mountain region south of it, extending into China and India, is the only extended region now known in regard to which there is any uncertainty in respect to its probable future yield of gold.

"The existence of very ancient workings in the Altai is significant, and leads us to question whether this great interior region has not already yielded up its most accessible treasures." — *American Journal of Science and Arts*, May, 1869.

---

* Calculated at 19 dollars per ounce.

THE NODULAR PHOSPHATES OF SOUTH CAROLINA.

The belt of nodular phosphates appears to extend, more or less interrupted, from the Wando and Cooper Rivers, some 15 to 30 miles above Charleston, in a south-south-westerly direction, parallel to the coast line, as far as St. Helena Sound and Bluffton, near Port Royal. As yet the precise area is unknown; no accurate survey having been made, although this want is daily felt by the community. It would be erroneous to suppose that there is a well-defined stratum of any such extent as this area above mentioned. On the contrary, the bed appears only in patches, some of which, however, are many miles in diameter. On the Wando and Cooper Rivers the nodules are found in comparatively small beds, generally but a few inches in thickness; still, limited deposits, one to three feet thick, have been deposited in some localities of this neighborhood. On the peninsula between the Cooper and Ashley Rivers the deposit assumes the form of a well-defined stratum, in many places attaining a thickness of 18 to 24 inches, and underlying hundreds of acres, at an average depth of about 3 feet from the surface. The nodules vary in size from that of a walnut to masses weighing 200 pounds and over; they lie compactly together with but little marl between them. This marl is composed of 30 to 60 per cent. carbonate of lime, a few per cent. phosphates of iron, lime, and alumina, the balance being chiefly sand and peroxide of iron. At other points on the peninsula the nodules rarely exceed a few pounds in weight, and are sparsely distributed. The favorable localities lie east of Goose Creek, near the Cooper River. The Ashley beds were the first discovered, are the best known, largest in extent, and most mined. This deposit extends, at an accessible depth, over, perhaps, 1,000 acres, on both sides of the river, and running back from it for several miles in some places. The beds are quite accessible, not only on account of the depth of Ashley River and their proximity to Charleston, but because of their lying close to the surface (generally within two feet), in a light soil, which separates easily from the nodules on handling or washing. The nodules are of a yellowish-gray color, of less specific gravity than those elsewhere found, their surface but slightly irregular, and their composition tolerably uniform. The best beds lie on the river 10 to 20 miles from Charleston; further up stream the nodules are found in a sandy soil, and become permeated with sand to the amount of 30 per cent. and over, when the phosphates do not reach 50 per cent. On some plantations the bed of phosphatic nodules is over two feet in thickness; and the amount of marketable material produced from mining an acre may exceed 1,200 tons. On the Stono and Edisto Rivers there have been found but few rich deposits, the stratum exhibiting continuity in but occasional spots. As a rule, the nodules lie deeper on these rivers than on the Ashley. Heavy deposits have been discovered on the flats in the neighborhood of St. Helena Sound, covering vast surfaces at little depth from the surface, occasionally forming a compact floor, or huge boulder, like masses on the bottom of the creeks which intersect that neighborhood.   Finally, on the Ashepoo River, at one locality in this neighborhood, the stratum has the appearance of an immense pavement, extending over hundreds of acres, at a depth of 3 to 6 feet.   It is with difficulty that the large masses (often several hundred weight each) can be pried apart, so closely are they wedged together, having a smooth, glazed upper surface, but irregular beneath.   The masses, moreover, are often penetrated to considerable depth, sometimes perforated by round holes, which extend generally in a perpendicular direction.   These cavities have a diameter of one-half to one inch. The phosphatic masses forming this floor are 9 to 12 inches in thickness, and overlie a bed of nodular phosphates of smaller size, which extends down to the depth of 12 to 15 inches below the continuous stratum.   The whole deposit is embedded in a tenacious clay, underneath which occurs a yellow-red marl.   This marl is rich in shells and the bones of marine and land animals. It is composed, when air dry, of nearly 70 per cent. of sand, 18 per cent. carbonate of lime, and 5 to 7 per cent. phosphate of lime, alumina, and iron.

The phosphatic nodules and masses generally give on friction of their fresh surfaces a peculiar naphthous odor.   This property is, as a rule, the more decided the denser the nodules, and is in direct proportion to the amount of organic matter contained in them.   The impressions of numerous fossil shells of the eocene period occur throughout the various phosphatic masses.   The specimens analyzed contained from 25 to 30 per cent. phosphoric acid and 35 to 40 per cent. lime.

Concerning the origin of this extensive formation, Prof. Shepard, of Amherst College, Mass., says: —

"Several explanations suggest themselves.   Perhaps the best supposition is, that the great Carolina eocene bed of shell marl on which it rests, formerly, and for a long period, protruded many feet above the present sea level, giving rise to a luxuriant soil (analogous to that now existing over portions of some of the guano islands), and which was then depressed beneath the sea, where it underwent the changes that have resulted in the present formation.   For the superabundance of phosphate of lime, we would point to the deposition of bird guano, as it is now going on upon the Mosquito coast of the Carribbean Sea." — *American Journal of Science.*

THE ROCKY MOUNTAIN ALPINE REGION.

Professor C. C. Perry, at the meeting of the American Association at Salem, read a paper on the above subject.   He said that the Rocky Mountain Alpine Region was of special interest, on account of its extensiveness as compared with anything which they had in the east.   Hitherto it had been mostly inaccessible; but now that railways were making it accessible, further exploration would reveal its flora, and thus it could be compared with the

Alpine flora of Europe. The woody belt of coniferous trees began at an average elevation of 6,000 feet. Its densest growth was at between 7,000 and 9,000 feet elevation, and its termination was at an average height of 11,300 feet. The growth was most dense and varied where there was the greatest and most regular amount of aqueous precipitation. At still higher elevations the actual limit of tree growth was determined by conditions of temperature which satisfactorily explained the peculiar features of vegetation there met with. This belt of trees terminated with singular abruptness. The probable explanation was that this timber line marked the extreme point of minimum winter temperature below which no phenogamous vegetation could exist. After alluding to the meteorological conditions of the region, the paper went on to point out the peculiar dwarfed tree-growth scattered occasionally above the timber line. It was on the most open exposures above that the Alpine flora was most diversified and attractive, presenting from June to September a succession of colors most attractive to the eye of the naturalist. Out of 142 species 56 were exclusively confined to these Alpine exposures. The usual characteristics of Alpine plants were a dwarfed habit of growth, late period of flowering, and early seeding, the forms being exclusively perennial. Of the 34 natural orders in the Alpine flora 31 belong to phenogamous plants, the remaining three were of the higher order of cryptogams. Of the latter, ferns were represented by a single species not exclusively Alpine (*Cryptogramia acrostichoides*). Mosses were more numerously represented, but were still comparatively rare. Lichens were most abundant, and afforded the greatest number of species. The superficial extent of these bare Alpine exposures in Colorado Territory had been roughly estimated at from 1,200 to 1,500 square miles. After a brief allusion to the fauna of the region, the paper stated that when accessible it would doubtless afford a favorite resort for summer pasturage, and eventually yield choice dairy products, equalling those of the Swiss Alps, and produce delicate fibrous tissues rivalling those of the looms of Cashmere. As a summer resort it was unexcelled in the purity of its atmosphere, the clearness of its streams, and its picturesque and extended views. The paper concluded with some topographical details and with a list of Alpine plants.

ON SURFACE CHANGES IN MAINE.

Professor N. T. True, at the meeting of the American Association at Salem, read a paper " On Surface Changes in Maine, indicating the length of time since the close of the Quaternary Period."

The paper began by stating that the almost infinity of time since the earth was spoken into existence was now generally accepted not only by geologists, but by non-scientific men. This had led some writers to give loose reins to their imagination, and to attribute an immense period of time since the close of the last great geological changes on the surface of the earth without duly examining the condition of things within their reach which by their accumulating evidence might lead to different results. The paper then specified the various geological, surface, and other changes that were now going on in New England, and from observations within the range of human experience and record attempted to show how materially a few thousand years might alter the character of a country. From these data the paper inferred that there was no necessity for throwing back the history of the present geological era to a period much if any before the time when man was in the infancy of his race, — not very long before the historic period. Geology had suffered too much from loose conclusions, and the present state of science demanded the most rigid investigation of facts. In conclusion, it was pretty evident that if the present epoch had claims to a very high antiquity, the evidence had not yet been seen in New England, and especially in the State of Maine, and that the present results might more logically be traced back to a period from 5,000 to 10,000 years ago than 50,000.

This paper resulted in a somewhat animated discussion, in which Prof. Agassiz and other gentlemen took part.

BEST ROUTE TO THE NORTH POLE.

At the meeting of the British Association, Captain R. N. Hamilton's paper "On the Best Route to the North Pole" was read, in his absence, by Mr. C. R. Markham, F.R.G.S., one of the secretaries. The conclusions he arrived at were, first, that by sea Smith's Sound offers equal, if not superior, chances for a ship reaching a higher latitude than has yet been attained to that offered by the route by Spitzbergen; secondly, that the prospects of successful sledge travelling are by far superior in Smith's Sound to Spitzbergen; thirdly, the great advantage it possesses in the event of any disaster happening to the expedition.

VEINS CONTAINING ORGANIC REMAINS.

One of the papers read before the British Association was a "Report of the Committee for the purpose of investigating the Veins containing Organic Remains which occur in the Mountain Limestone of the Mendips, and Elsewhere," by C. Moore, F.G.S. This gentleman has for a long time made the organic remains frequently found in mineral veins his particular study. In his report he referred to the various theories extant as to the origin of veins. They could not have been formed by sublimation, or the fossils would not be found in them. Mr. Moore was equally against the doctrine of segregation. Referring to Mr. Wallace's theory that many of the veins had been filled up by superficial action since the glacial period, he pointed to the age of the fossils as decidedly against it. Mr. Moore's idea was that open fissures communicated with submarine floors and dwindled down below. The mollusca, etc., of these seas were deposited in the fissures. Three or four things were necessary to the formation of mineral veins, — open crevices, the presence of certain minerals in the water of the seas, and electrical action. The Mendip hills are intersected with veins, and on their tops some of these are worked. One of them extends for 270 feet downwards, and contains abundant lias fossils, although no liassic rocks are nearer than several miles away. This proves how great must have been the denuding force. Mr. Moore has also discovered both land and fresh-water shells in these veins, as well as entomostraca, as well as seeds of old carboniferous plants. In the mines of North Wales he had found molluscan and fish remains, the latter belonging to no fewer than 10 genera. Intermixed with the contents of some of the mineral veins, the author had found innumerable teeth of fishes, *conodonts*, nearly all of which were so small that they required optical power to see them. In the lead veins he had met with great quantities of foraminifera, all of secondary age. These veins also developed the existence of a fresh-water fauna, of coal-measure age, having no fewer than 9 genera, and 127 species.

Mr. H. Brady said three well-known genera of foraminifera had been mentioned by Mr. Moore, all of which still existed. One of the most abundant of the foraminifera, *Involutina*, was remarkable for its variety of form. Mr. Brady's remarks on the rest of these minute shells were of a purely technical character.

CHANGES IN THE DISTRIBUTION OF THE LARGE AMERICAN MAMMALS, THE SUBSTANCE OF SEVERAL COMMUNICATIONS MADE TO THE BOSTON SOCIETY OF NATURAL HISTORY. BY N. S. SHALER.

In the course of some excavations made at Big Bone Lick, in Kentucky, in the summer of 1869, some interesting information was obtained concerning the former range of several of our large quadrupeds. The peculiarly uniform growth of the beds which are constantly forming in this swamp, which is due to the deposits from the mineral springs, and to the regular accumulation of sediment from overflows of the stream which passes through it, enables us to measure, with tolerable accuracy, the relative age of the several strata.

The most important fact is, that the buffalo did not begin to come to these springs until a very recent day. It is impossible to suppose that more than 500 years have elapsed since they began to range into this part of the Mississippi valley. The stratum in which their remains were found is the uppermost of the bone beds, and is but two feet in thickness at the three points where it was cut through; beneath it was found the fragment of an arrow-head of flint. The evidence of the recent appearance of the buffalo afforded by the swamp at Big Bone Lick is corroborated by that from a number of other sources. It seems fully certain that the buffalo was not in the Mississippi valley at the time of the *mound builders*. That people have preserved in their pottery work, or in the remains found around their sacrificial and lunal fires, the images, or the bones, of all the other large animals which were found there at the time of the coming of civilized man. Nearly every mammal with which they could possibly have come in contact is represented. Even the manitre, which they could have known only by report, is very often figured by them upon their pipes and other utensils. It is hardly possible that the buffalo could have failed to be represented, if they had ever come in contact with it.

The common deer (*Cervus Virginianus*) seems, also, to have frequented these springs for only a few hundred years before the coming of man. It probably came some time before the buffalo, though its remains, also, are never found at such depths as would warrant one in supposing that it had been more than twice as long as the buffalo in the Ohio valley.

Beneath the levels where the remains of the Virginia deer and the buffalo abound were found numerous fragments of the horns of the caribou (*Tarandas rargifer*). This animal has not been found south of the State of Maine or the great lakes since the discovery of this country. The position of these remains indicates that it appeared in the Ohio valley immediately after the disappearance of the *Elephas fumegerens*, or mammoth. It seems, indeed, not improbable that they may have coexisted for a short time. The existence of a boreal species of mammal in this region at the time of the disappearance of the elephants makes it seem very probable that the climate, during the elephant period in this region, was much colder than is generally supposed, and that the change of temperature which accompanied, if it did not produce, the extinction of the fauna in which these animals belonged was more likely from cold to warm than from warm to cold. The fact that the representative of our American mammoth in Northern Europe and Asia was an animal as well fitted to withstand excessive cold as the polar bear, shows how unsafe it is to infer for animals of former ages the climatic restrictions which affect their living relatives.

THE TREND OF THE ROCKY MOUNTAINS.

Professor W. H. Dall read a paper at the meeting of the American Association, at Salem, "On the Trend of the Rocky Mountain Range, north latitude 60°, and its Influence on Faunal Distribution."

The paper stated that the Rocky Mountain range, between latitudes 60° and 64°, bends trending with the eastern coast; so that, instead of there being, as represented on the old maps, a straight line of mountains up to the Arctic Sea, there is an elevated plateau, only broken occasionally by a very few ranges of hills. This bend of the mountains prevented the characteristic birds of the west coast from coming north, while the eastern birds came clear to Behring's Sea, north of it, over the plateau. He also stated that the elevation of the bottom of Behring's Straits, 180 feet, would make dry land between Asia and America, but that a deep ocean valley extended south-west from Plover Bay, just west of the Straits, along the Kamschatka coast.

REPTILIAN REMAINS. BY PROFESSOR COPE.

The fossil which Professor Cope exhibited was the almost perfect cranium of a mosasauroid reptile, the *Clidastes propython*. He explained various peculiarities of its structure, as the movable articulation of certain of the mandibular pieces on each other, the suspension of the os-quadratum at the extremity of a cylinder composed of the opistholic, etc., and other peculiarities. He also explained, from specimens, the characters of a large new plesiosauroid, from Kansas, discovered by William E. Webb, of Topeka, which possessed deeply biconcave vertebræ, and anchylosed neural arches, with the zygapophyses directed after the manner usual among vertebrates. The former was thus shown to belong to the true sauropterygia, and not to the streptosauria, of which *Elas mosaurus* was the type. Several distal caudals were anchylosed, without chevron bones, and of depressed form, while proximal caudals had anchylosed diapophyses and distinct chevron bones. The form was regarded as new, and called *Polycotylusa latipinnis*, from the great relative stoutness of the paddle. He also gave an account of the discovery, by Dr. Samuel Lockwood, of Keyport, of a fragment of a large dinosaur, in the clay which underlies immediately the clay marls below the lower green-sand bed in Monmouth County, N. J. The piece was the extremities of the tibia and fibula, with astragalo-calcaneum anchylosed to the former; in length, about 16 inches; distal width, 14. The confluence of the first series of tarsal bones with each other, and with the tibia, he regarded as a most interesting peculiarity, and one only met with elsewhere in the reptile compsognathus, and in birds. He therefore referred the animal to the order symphypoda, near to compsognathus wagm. The extremity of the fibula was free from, and received into, a cavity of the astragalo-calcaneum, and demonstrated what the speaker had already asserted, that the fibula of iguanodon and hadrosaurus had been inverted by their describers. The medullary cavity was filled with open cancellous tissue. The species, which was one-half larger than the type specimen of *Hadrosaurus foulkii*, he named *Ornithotarsus immanis.* — *Proc. Am. Phil. Soc.*, xi., 117.

PAPERS READ AT THE MEETING OF THE AMERICAN ASSOCIATION.

Prof. O. C. Marsh read a paper upon the "Discovery of the Remains of the Horse among the Ancient Ruins of Central America."

22

The discovery of fossil human remains, accompanying the remains of the fossil horse, seems to establish the fact that the horse existed and was utilized by the aborigines of the section previous to the arrival of the Spaniards and the European horse.   A number of fossil remains from that section were exhibited by Mr. McNeal.

Prof. Squires, by request, spoke in a very interesting manner upon the Migrations of Indian Tribes.   He finds three centres of civilization, so called, upon this continent, and regards it as generally of local growth, and due, except in the case of Mexico, almost entirely to local influences.

Mr. N. T. True gave a paper upon "Physical Geography among the Aborigines of North America."   It is a peculiarity of the Indians that they treat of generic names.   Thus, an Indian has a name for his own father, but no word for fathers in general. They apply the same principle in geography, giving different names, for example, to different parts of the same river, and no one name to the whole.   In answer to a question, Mr. True said that Naumkeag, the Indian name of Salem, means "fish-drying place."

Mr. W. H. Dall gave a very interesting and exhaustive paper, accompanied by a map, on the "Distribution of the Aborigines of Alaska and Adjacent Territories."

Vertebrate Remains in Nebraska. — The locality described by Prof. Marsh was the Antelope Station on the Pacific Railroad, in south-western Nebraska.   While engaged in sinking a well at that place in June, 1868, a layer of bones was found by the workmen at a depth of 68 feet below the surface, which were at first pronounced to be human, but during a trip to the Rocky Mountains Prof. Marsh examined the locality and the bones, and found that the latter were the remains of tertiary animals, some of which were of great interest.   The well was subsequently sunk about 10 feet deeper, and the bones obtained were secured by the professor.   An examination proved that among them there were four kinds of fossil horses, one of which he described in November last as *Equus parvulus.*   Although it was a full-grown animal, it was not more than 2½ feet high.   It was by far the smallest horse ever discovered.   Of the other kinds of fossil horses one was of hipparion type, or the three-toed horse.   Including the above the number of fossil horses discovered in this country was 17, although the horse was supposed to be a native only of the Old World, and was first introduced here by the Spaniards.   Of the other remains there were two carnivorous animals, one about the size of a lynx, and the other considerably larger than a lion, — twice as large as any extinct carnivora yet discovered in this country.   Among the ruminants found in this locality was one with a double metatarsal bone, a peculiar type, only seen in the living aquatic musk deer and in the extinct anaplotherium.   There were also the remains of an animal like the hog, a large rhinoceros, and two kinds of turtles.   These, together forming 15 species of animals, and representing 11 genera, were all found in a space 10 feet in diameter and 6 or 8 feet in depth.   It is supposed that the locality was once the shore of a great lake, and that the animals were mired when they went down to the water to drink.

At the close of Prof. Marsh's address, Prof. Agassiz made a few interesting remarks on the possibility of determining genuine affinities from fragmentary fossil remains, after which he read a paper on the "Homologies of the Palæchinidæ," partially prepared by his son, Alexander E. R. Agassiz.

Mosasauroid Reptiles. — Professor O. C. Marsh read a paper on "Some new Mosasauroid Reptiles from the Green-sand of New Jersey." The striking difference between the reptilian fauna of the cretaceous period of Europe and the same period in America was, that in the former there were great numbers of remains of ichthyosauri and plesiosauri, while hardly a tooth or vertebra of the mosasauroids was to be found. In America, the two former kinds of reptiles appeared to be almost entirely wanting. One or two specimens found here had been alleged to be ichthyosauri, or plesiosauri; but further examination threw strong doubts on the matter. To replace these forms, however, the mosasauroids were found in abundance. The affinities of the mosasauroids were chiefly with the serpents rather than with other reptiles, although they had certain other affinities with swarming reptiles. Professor Marsh produced some fossil remains of different specimens of mosasauroids, showing the peculiar formation of the skull. These reptiles appeared to have no hind limbs, although Cuvier thought he had detected them. The specimens found in this country, however, afforded no evidence of this. He called attention to two new forms of the family, — the *Macrosaurus platyspondulus* and the *Mosasaurus copeanus*, — in which the articulation of the lower jaw was one of the most interesting features. The larger specimens of these animals showed that they must have been the monarchs of the seas of those periods, and in appearance and size not unlike the popular notion of the sea-serpent, being sometimes 75 feet long.

Professor Agassiz said that the examination of the mosasauroid remains reveals much that was new to descriptive palæontology. He was not quite satisfied that the remains showed real serpent-like affinities. The resemblances of the mosasauroids to serpents, he thought, were rather of the synthetic type than of affinity. The articulation of the lower jaw, he thought, in no way corresponded to that of serpents.

Extinct Cetacea. — Professor Cope's observations embraced a description of the characters of a very large representative of the dugong of the modern East Indian seas, which was found in a bed, either miocene or eocene, in New Jersey. It was double the size of the existing dugong, and was interesting as adding to the series of Asiatic and African forms characteristic of American miocenes. Another type was regarded as remotely allied to squalodon; but it was indentulous, and furnished with a broad, shallow alveolus, either that left after shedding a tooth, or that adapted to a broad, obtuse tooth. It constituted a remarkable new genus, which was called *Anopolonassa forcipata*. It was found in postpliocene beds, near Savannah. He also exhibited teeth of two gigantic species of chinchillas which had been discovered in the small West India island of Anguilla, which has an area of but about thirty square miles. The specimens were taken from caves, and were thought to indicate postpliocene age. With them was discovered an implement of human manufacture, — a chisel made from the lips of the shell strombusgigas. The contemporaneity of the fossils and human implements was supposed, but not ascertained. Its interest and connection with human migrations was mentioned; also the supposition of Pomel, that the submergence of the West India Islands took place since the postpliocene period.

PAPERS READ BEFORE THE BRITISH ASSOCIATION AT EXETER.

Report of the Committee on Ice as an Agent of Geological Change. — This was a report by Mr. H. Bauerman, in which the grooving power of ice was traced, as well as its power to transport blocks to a distance, where they accumulated as mordines. He thought there was no proper means known of measuring the erosive power of glaciers, and mentioned several plans which might ultimately furnish that information, although he thought it would require national scientific co-operation.

Professor Phillips said, in reply to the latter idea, he thought a difficulty would arise in interesting nations in such a subject as cold. At the same time, unless something of the sort were done, we should know little of the glacial period. Mr. Vivian thought that the superficial action of ice had not been sufficiently taken into consideration. Devon must have been under ice during the glacial period, and he should like to see some evidences of it. Mr. Pengelly explained how certain beds had been bent on themselves, giving the idea of their having been acted upon by superficial action, along the line of least resistance. He mentioned an instance where the beds were bent against the centre of gravity. The Rev. Osmond Fisher thought the latter was in favor of ice action, instead of being opposed to it. Mr. Godwin Austen thought the report fell short of what he had expected. With regard to Mr. Vivian's theory, it had been taken into consideration by the Swiss geologists. Both Agassiz and Dr. Buckland thought that Devonshire had never been under ice, and, although that idea was perhaps premature, he could not adduce a single valley in the county whose origin could be ascribed to ice action. Without doubt Devon was under the influence of great cold, although not sufficient to support continual masses of ice. In the Chagford valley ice may once have moved. The neighborhood of Bovey also may have received a good deal of its superficial *débris* from ice.

Mr. George Maw, F.G.S., next read a short paper on "Insect Remains and Shells from the Lower Bagshot Leaf-Bed of Studland Bay, Dorsetshire." The author mentioned several species of insects he had met with in the above bed, as well as the shells, which have not been found before, and which are of fresh-water origin. The plant remains most notable were those of the genus *Porano*, still living in sub-tropical latitudes.

The Rev. Mr. Brodie, who is an authority on the subject of fossil insects, made a few remarks on the various insects mentioned by Mr. Maw, and expressed his belief that if the beds were better worked they would yield more species. Mr. Etheridge, of the Geological Survey, said Mr. Maw's discovery was very important, as fresh-water, or indeed shells of any sort, had never been met with before in this bed. Mr. Godwin Austen made a few remarks describing the general character of the strata, stating much of them was deposited in a large lake, during the nummulitic period. Mr. Pengelly congratulated Mr. Maw in finding what he wanted. With reference to the Bovey Tracey lignite series, they lay on a green sand bottom. Fifty species of fossil plants had been found in the lignites, and they were of the same forms as those occurring in the miocene lignites on the continent, and occupying the same horizon. The fossil plants of Bovey Tracey had been found in the Hempstead beds of the Isle of Wight. The Rev. O. Fisher mentioned that some years ago, at Furzey Brook pits, he had found an oyster in the leaf-beds of Mr. Maw. It had all the appearance of being an estuarine shell. He thought the strata were estuarine rather than of a lake character. Mr. Maw, in reply, said that, although there was a variation in the fauna of the eocene and miocene, there was not any in their flora. Mr. Godwin Austen expressed his opinion that the Bovey Tracey beds were upper eocene, and not miocene.

The president (Prof. Harkness) said Mr. Thomson had obtained some of the finest labrynthodont remains ever found in Great Britain. Sir Philip Egerton corroborated this, and said, from an examination of the sections, he had no doubt Dr. Young was right in separating the remains into a new genus, that of *Pteroplax*. He was happy also to coincide with Mr. Thomson as regards the character of the fossil fishes. Mr. Brodie referred to the number of these reptilian remains which the coal measures had recently given. Mr. Miall mentioned that the structure of the teeth in the reptiles might alter according to the age of the animals. Mr. Thomson replied that the differences in the specimens he produced could not be brought under such an explanation.

On the Discovery of Fossil Plants in the Cambrian Rocks near St. David's. — This was a communication by Dr. Hicks. The strata in which the fossil plants had been found were the Upper Longmynds. Their ripple-marked character showed they had been deposited in shallow water. Last year, Prof. Torrell reported his having found land plants in the Cambrian strata; and this encouraged Dr. Hicks to seek for them. He had been successful; and Prof. Harkness said that there was a difference in the nature of the supposed plant remains. He mentioned the various theories afloat as to the nature of these plants, and said they might be fucoidal. Some of Dr. Hicks' specimens were, he thought, the tracks of marine worms. Dr. Hicks had sent fossils which were found 1,500 feet below the horizon where they have hitherto been

met with in the British islands.   They were, therefore, the earliest
types of life which had hitherto been found in this country.   Prof.
Phillips thought that many of the so-called fossil plants in strata
of this age might be referred to annelids.   He thought the finding
of the trilobites and other remains 1,500 feet below the stage they
had been found in before ought to teach geologists a valuable les-
son.   The learned professor went into an elaborate review of the
order of life, succession, and of the natural history classification
of the early geological epochs.   He thought it the duty of the
Association to encourage and support such able workers as Dr.
Hicks.   Prof. Etheridge said that the plants exhibited were quite
of a different character to those shown by Prof. Torrell last year.
He thought they were nothing beyond furrow or tracks of annelids and crustacea.   The number of generic species of trilobites,
etc., showed that life was enjoyed in great abundance during these
early epochs.

*On the Occurrence of a Large Deposit of Terra-Cotta Clay at Wat-
combe, by Prof. Etheridge, Torquay.* — The author described the
discovery, some years ago, in boring, of a deposit of clay resting
on the new red sandstone.   This clay was mineralogically similar
to that formerly used by the Etruscans.   Prof. Etheridge exhibited several beautiful vases which had been made from this clay.
He mentioned that at Copenhagen they were copying the works
of Thorwalsden and others; but the clay at Watcombe was of a
very superior kind.   The communication was illustrated by diagrams, which showed that this clay had been deposited by a river
in a large lake.   There were indications of the Romans, or early
Britons, having been acquainted with the bed, and of their having
worked it.   There was no other combe in the neighborhood which
possessed a similar deposit.   The southern end of the lake, along
whose bottom the clay had been formed, extended far out to sea,
marine action having cut it off.   The clay contained above 60 per
cent. of silicia, and 20 per cent. of alumina, two very important
elements.   There was also 7 per cent. of peroxide of iron.
The alkalies, soda and potash, were present in great quantities.
In fact, the mineral constituents generally were better than anything known to the Romans, and just those most necessary for the
purposes to which this fine clay was to be put.   Prof. Etheridge
pointed out that the Assyrians, Greeks, Etruscans, and Romans
had all left their traces in terra-cotta clay.   He had no doubt
that a good many Roman *Amphora* had been manufactured out of
this identical deposit.   Its thickness, in some parts, was above 80
feet.   He thought the valley had formerly been covered to its
very summit by this clay.   Mr. Pengelly said that clay of the
same character, but not quite so fine, was found further up the
valley.   One bed, 12 feet thick, was underlaid by a layer of pebbles, in which the remains of man were abundant.   He agreed
with Mr. Etheridge that it was a subaerial deposit.   Under the
layer of stones was a still finer clay.   Mr. G. Maw said he had
examined the clay some years ago, to ascertain the heat it would
stand.   One peculiarity about it was its extremely fine subdivision.   It was almost impalpably subdivided.

The next paper was read by Mr. Pengelly, in the absence of the author, Mr. N. Whitley, on "The Distribution of Shattered Chalk Flints and Flakes in Devon and Cornwall." He had traced these flints over very large areas, to a height of 300 feet above the sea-level. He also mentioned the various localities in the two counties where these flakes, or knives, were most abundant. The author did not concur in the idea that these flakes had been left by man, but suggested that they had a geological, and not an archæological, origin. He thought they might subsequently have been used and adapted afterwards by man. Mr. Pengelly said he thought Mr. Whitley sometimes used the word "flake" for an implement. Mr. Wyatt took exception to Mr. Whitley's conclusions. He had examined many of the flints, and could not concur in the deductions, geological or archæological, which had been drawn. He had no doubt that many of the flints were of human workmanship. The Rev. Mr. Winwood said there was a difference between chips and flakes. He thought that the district mentioned by Mr. Whitley bore undoubted traces of human workmanship. The Rev. O. Fisher said they never got a chip or flake in a natural manner.

The Gulf Stream. — Mr. A. G. Findlay read a paper on "The supposed Influence of the Gulf Stream on the climate of North-west Europe." He submitted that the actual bulk of water which passes through the Florida Channel is from 294 to 330 cubic miles per day, and it receives no accession from the tropics. Fully one-half of this passes eastward and southward from the banks of Newfoundland, and the northern half, cooled down and neutralized by the Arctic current, has, according to this theory, to cover this area to raise its temperature. The known bulk of the stream will only give 6 inches per diem over this area. And he would ask, how is it possible that such a minute film could have any influence, and this, too, at from one to two years after it has left the Gulf of Florida as the true Gulf Stream? He would not advert to the further progress of this warmer water, which might be traced to and beyond Spitzbergen, and its effects throughout the North Polar Basin; and these effects, he contended, were totally and absolutely incompatible with the now well-known particulars of the Gulf Stream proper. He could not go into the isothermal lines which show most markedly the higher temperature in the winter, and much less so in the summer. The equable temperature of the waters causes this change, — the relation of the warm and cold water. It had been propounded by Mr. Crott that the modern method of determining the amount of heat would account for all the phenomena popularly attributed to the Gulf Stream. But he (Mr. Findlay) would deferentially demur to his calculations. He (Mr. Crott) took no account of the time it takes for the water to circulate. He doubled, as he (Mr. Findlay) thought, the volume of the stream, and he took no account of the interferences it encountered. However valuable his suggestions might be, they must be applied in a different way. How, then, can the phenomena of our warm winter climate be accounted for? The reason seemed to him to be simple and obvious. The great belt of south-west winds, called the anti-trade, or passage winds, passes over the North Atlantic throughout its breadth, and drives slowly the whole surface of the water to the northward of an easterly course, or towards the shore of North-west Europe. From the particular configuration of the land, this north-west drift is allowed to pass into the polar area. This south-west wind infuses into high latitudes the temperature and moisture of much lower parallels, and by its greater rate of travelling passes over the warmer water to the southward, and this brings to Exeter in one day the warmth of the centre of France. By its variation from westward or eastward of a southerly direction, we find all the variations or moisture which are induced by this wind passing over land or sea. The excellent observations made in the expedition from the Royal Society, under Dr. Carpenter and Dr. Wyvell Thompson, would, he had no doubt, throw great light on this obscure north-east current, which should not be called the Gulf Stream, but possess a specific term. Mr. Trelawney Saunders remarked that the greatest centres of heat were not at the equator, but were to be found in either tropic.

On Certain Phenomena in the Drift near Norwich. — In this communication, Mr. J. B. Taylor said that, although there was the finest series of the drift beds in Norfolk to be found in Great Britain, still in the upper boulder clay certain anomalies occur which frequently puzzle the geologist. The paper was an attempt to explain these by referring them to the agency of icebergs. Sometimes there were found beds of upper boulder clay lying at lower levels than the middle drift beds. In fact, such phenomena occurred through icebergs having ploughed up the sands and deposited beds of clay in the furrows. This accounted for the out-of-the-way character of what had been termed "third, or valley boulder clay." The sand beds on each side these linear extensions of clay were frequently dragged out of their place and contorted. The chalk also was disturbed, and the flint bands thrown into almost perpendicular positions in the neighborhood of such phenomena. Mr. Taylor also mentioned the exceeding narrow track of these abnormal beds of clay, and concluded by showing that their occurrence only the more fully bore out the glacial hypothesis.

Prof. Harkness said Mr. Taylor distinguished himself by working on the clay and drift beds of Norfolk, and that his paper was very valuable and interesting. He then traced the general relationship of the lower and upper boulder clays, and of the middle drift beds. The first and last, he said, always showed strong evidences of ice action and arctic climature, the middle drift sands being marked by having numbers of non-arctic shells and flint pebbles. Prof. Harkness reviewed the various localities where this was the case, both in England, Ireland, and Scotland.

Mr. S. Pattison, F.G.S., said similar phenomena to those mentioned by Mr. Taylor could be seen in the neighborhood of Whitby. He had no doubt they were due to iceberg groovings.

The Water-bearing Strata in the Neighborhood of Norwich. — This was another paper by Mr. Taylor. It dealt with the origin of sand-pipes in chalk, showing them to be natural drains, and advocating their origin from a chemical point of view. These sand-pipes were most abundant in the disturbed chalk, and less so in the solid strata. The latter allowed the water to get away by means of joints and flint bands. The age of some of the sand-pipes could be told by the material filling them, and by the un-changed contour of the country. In the excavations attending the sewage works at Norwich, much trouble was given by their having to work through strata thoroughly saturated with water. The same sort of strata standing above the water-level gave no trouble whatever. The deduction was drawn that if so much trouble ensued whilst working only twenty feet below the water-level, the excavation of the proposed channel tunnel, under so much more pressure, must necessarily be attended with great diffi-culties. Mr. Taylor gave an interesting statement of the manner in which the wells were drained by the pumping in the neighbor-hood of Norwich, and showed they were affected according to the different nature of the strata in which they were sunk.

Mr. Godwin Austen mentioned several localities in Devonshire where sand-pipes occurred in the sandstone rocks, and thought that the chemical theory could not hold in cases like these, al-though they might do so in chalk districts.

Sir Willoughby Jones expressed his gratification at the papers which had been read, and, as a Norfolk man, said he could thor-oughly bear out the correctness of Mr. Taylor's views. It was a very common thing for holes to be suddenly formed by the caving in of gravel and sand into the sand-pipes.

Mr. Taylor, in reply to Prof. Harkness, said that the upper and lower boulder clays in Norfolk were very distinct. The former were derived principally from the wreck of the lias beds, and the latter from the lower chalk and oolite. One was of a dark-blue color, and the other of an ochreous white.

The next paper was by a French geologist, G. A. Lebour, on the "Denudation of Western Brittany," read by Captain Galton. There was also another communication by the same author, "Notes on some Granites of Lower Brittany." The section closed after a paper on "Some New Forms of *Graptolites*," by Dr. H. A. Nichol-son. This paper was read by the President, who stated there could be no doubt that the fossil *graptolites* were related to the recent sertularia.

The Extinction of the Mammoth. — A very interesting paper on this subject was read by Mr. H. H. Howorth. The various his-torical notices in old authors of the mammoth remains in Siberia and elsewhere were well condensed. The usual idea was, that the mammoth was a sort of huge mole, which rarely came to the surface. This was the way their vast remains were accounted for. Mr. Howorth did not think the extinction of the mammoth ought to be ascribed to the men of the early stone age. Prof. Phillips and Prof. Boyd Dawkins made some remarks on the above paper, the former dwelling at some length upon the more popular geological notions of the former conditions of northern geography, and the latter observing that Mr. Howorth had misunderstood him. He had never said that the extinction of the mammoth in

Siberia was owing to his being hunted down; but he had stated
that in England and Western Europe generally there was no
doubt that the mammoth had become extinct by the hand of man.
Mr. Howorth briefly replied, stating that he still differed from Mr.
Dawkins as to the extinction of the animals mentioned. He
thought that different races of man had become extinct along with
the animals.

*On the Occurrence of the Mineral Scheelite (Tungstate of Lime) at
Val Toppa Gold Mine, near Domodossola, Piedmont; by C. Le
Neve Foster, B.A., D.Sc., E.G.S.*—In this paper the author
stated that *Scheelite*, or tungstate of lime, is now occurring at the
Val Toppa gold mine.   It is associated with quartz, iron pyrites,
zinc blende, calcspar, brown spar, and native gold; whilst wol-
fram, tinstone, molybdenite, fluor-spar, apatite, topaz, and tourmaline, which usually accompany *Scheelite*, are entirely absent.
The *Scheelite* is called "marmor rosso" by the Piedmontese
miners, and is looked upon as a good indication for gold.   Professor Warrington Smyth said this rare mineral might be found
in the neighborhood of Tavistock, in Devonshire.

Mr. Charles Moore, F.G.S., then made a communication relative to a specimen of *Teleosaurus* from the Upper Lias.   He said
he had discovered shells (*Leptœna*) in the Middle Lias, which
had been thought peculiar to the palæozoic rocks.   Above
these was a bed rich in nodules, and these nodules when broken
open were seen to be full of the bones and other remains of *Tele-
osauri*.

*On the Denudation of the Shropshire and Staffordshire Coal-
Fields.* — In the absence of the author, this paper was read by
Professor Warrington Smyth.   The paper read treated on the
mineral character of some of the coal seams in the field in question, and showed how many of the seams were cut off by denudation.   The fauna and flora belonging to these coal seams were
mentioned.   The Staffordshire and Shropshire coal-fields were
only portions of one original tract.   He thought that a sea or
strait had existed over the area of the coal measures which had
denuded them.   Mr. Smyth said he was himself attracted to the
subject from knowing the neighborhood.   The subject was interesting as dealing with the great national question of the practical extension of our coal-fields.   The great question was as to
whether certain seams were capable of being worked at a certain
depth.   Mr. Lionel Brough said that in the neighborhood of
Wolverhampton and Cannock Chase there were great disloca-
tions.   He did not agree with the author that a strait had ever
existed over the area mentioned.   With regard to the continuity
of the South Staffordshire coal-field in Shropshire, it was interrupted by faults.   He thought that if they sunk deeper in Shropshire they might come on the Staffordshire coal seams, although
perhaps under various other appearances.

*On a Specimen of Obsidian from Java, with a Microscopical Ex-
amination; by W. C. Roberts, F.C.S., F.G.S.* — Microscopists have
lately urged the necessity and importance of examining rock
sections with the microscope.   Little, however, appears to have

been done in the accurate identification of the constituent minerals of the rock mass. The present paper was a statement of
the result of the examination of a substance that, from the indefinite character of its composition, partakes of the nature of a rock
rather than that of a mineral. It consists of a specimen of obsidian from Java, originally in the cabinet of Bernard Woodward,
Esq., but the label does not give the exact locality. It appears
to differ much from that, also from Java, now in the British Museum. The specific gravity of the specimen now produced is
2.35; in thin sections it is perfectly transparent. The lecturer gave
a complete analysis of its composition, which he said may be
easily cut into thin sections, and by the aid of a low power, say
200 diameters, at least three distinct minerals (beautifully crystallized) may be distinguished, diagrams of which were produced
with the specimen. These, with the optical properties, were admirably described, some doubt being expressed as to the nature of
the second mineral; but the third was undoubtedly composed of
magnetic iron.

Mr. Thomson then read a paper "On Teeth and Dermal
Structure associated with *Ctenacanthus* as well as on new forms
of *Pteroplax* and other carboniferous *Labryinthodonts* and of
Megalichtys." Sir Philip Egerton, who is a great authority on
fossil fishes, took the chair, for the purpose of being able to com-
ment on the subjects mentioned in the paper, which were of a
purely technical character. Sir Philip Egerton mentioned several instances where genera had been founded on different characters of the same fish. The main object of the communication
was to show that several so-called genera of fossil teeth were in
reality small spines. Mr. Thomson had proved, from actual demonstration, that three or four genera of fossil fish could be
resolved into the same genus.

A short communication was made by Mr. W. Carruthers "On
Reptilian Eggs from Secondary Strata." Some of the eggs were
Chelonian, or turtle, in their character. Many of them had all the
appearance of fruit. They had a peculiarly glossy appearance,
and were very thin. Mr. Carruthers went into some detail on the
origin of small shakeneides found in coal shale, and explained
how they had been formed by gas or air.

M. de Tchipatchef gave a short *viva voce* account of the Palæontology of Asia Minor. To this he has devoted twenty years of
his life. Mr. Godwin Austen said M. de Tchipatchef was well
known as the most enterprising Asian traveller, and all geologists had derived great profit from his labors.

"Occurrence of *Stylonarus* in the Cornstone of Hereford."
This was a new species of crustacean. Mr. Woodward also read
a few notes "On the discovery of a large Myriapod, of the genus
Euphoberia, in the coal measures of Kilmaurs." This fossil is a
centipede nearly two inches long. Their occurrence in the British coal measures is very rare, although Dr Dawson had found
them in the strata of South Loggins, Nova Scotia. The legs, etc.,
of the fossil could be plainly seen with a low optical power. Mr.
Godwin Austen said nothing was more interesting than the nu-

merous forms of life which the researches of geologists were continually discovering in the coal measures.

SUMMARY OF GEOLOGICAL FACTS.

Petroleum in the Netherlands' East Indies. — *Dr. Baumhauer.* — The author gives a complete description of a large number of sources of petroleum discovered in different islands of the Indian Archipelago, dependencies of the Netherlands. From observations and experiments made, there exists at 250 metres' depth an almost inexhaustible reservoir of this fluid.

Smoke-colored Quartz. — A letter from the French minister, resident at Berne, contains full particulars concerning the discovery and the exploration of quartz of rare beauty, accidentally discovered in the Tiefengletscher of the valley of Urseren, Canton Uri, Switzerland. — *Annales des Mines*, Nov. 3.

Mineral Resources of Algeria. — This paper is an excellent monograph. — *Annales des Mines, Nov. 3.*

Copper Mines of Lake Superior — *Tin in the State of Maine, U. S.* — In the shape of a letter, written by the author to M. Elie de Beaumont, Mr. Jackson, of Boston, states that, in June last, there was found in the Phœnix copper mine, near Lake Superior, a mass of native copper measuring $65 \times 32 \times 4$ feet, weighing 1,000 tons, and valued at 400,000 dollars. In some parts, this mass has, instead of its average 4 feet, 7 feet in thickness. As to the site where the tin ore has been discovered, the author states that he received a sample, sent to him from Winslow, and that on analysis he found the ore to yield, in its crude state, 46 per cent. of pure tin, and, after washing, about 75.5 per cent. There exist some 40 mineral veins containing the ore, and these veins are workable.

Highest Peaks of the Caucasus. — There is a capital map of the Caucasus in "Petermann's Mittheilungen," II., 1869. The accompanying notes give the following as the elevations of the four most important peaks of the proper or Great Caucasus: —

Elbrug, ...	18,572 English feet.	17,426 Paris feet.
Koschan-tau, ...	17,123 "	16,066 "
Dych-tau, ...	16,928 "	15,883 "
Kasbek, ...	16,546 "	15,525 "

The Ararat is almost equally high with the Dych-tau, namely, 16,916 English feet, or 15,872 Paris feet.

Geodetic Measurement in Europe. — There is a good prospect that, at an early day, the measurement of an arc of meridian, undertaken by the Russian government, will be extended into the Turkish dominions, and, possibly, into the island of Crete. If the project is carried out, an arc of 35° 35' will have been measured, extending from 35° 5' to 70° 40' N. lat., the utmost possible in Europe. A measurement of the 52d parallel, between Valentia, on the Irish coast, and Orsk, on the Kirgisen Steppe, has lately been completed. — *Petermann*, II., 1869.

Lithographic Researches. — Geologists will be much interested in the reported discovery of Dr. Jenzsch, of Gotha. This *savant*, it is said, has devoted himself for some years to what he calls microscopic lithographic researches, and now announces that in various kinds of crystalline and volcanic rocks he has discovered minute animal forms in prodigious numbers, and in a fossil condition. Some of the creatures he describes as having been petrified in the midst of their "life functions." Among them, he finds *Infusoria* and *Rotiferæ*, intermingled with *Algæ*, and he infers their formation in a large expanse of stagnant water.

The Colorado Expedition. — The expedition under the command of Col. Powell, the Colorado explorer, has returned to Chicago, having successfully travelled through the entire Grand Cañon, from Green River to the point where the Colorado debouches into the open plain, in the territory of Arizona.

From the point where Colonel Powell's last letter was written, the expedition descended the river about 400 miles, between walls almost vertical, ranging from 500 to 1,500 feet high, the exterior of the cañon being from 2,500 to 4,000 feet above the bed of the river. More than 200 waterfalls and cascades, emptying themselves over the walls of the cañon into the main river, were seen in this distance, with almost every variety of natural scenery. The geological formation of the cañon consists principally of limestone and sandstone; granite is only found at three places, and in a limited amount. No discoveries of precious metals were made, and there were no indications of gold or silver found in the bed of the river.

One section of the cañon was found to consist of a very fine, beautifully polished marble, which at present is entirely inaccessible. The country traversed was barren beyond description, and is pronounced by Colonel Powell as not susceptible of cultivation, even by irrigation.

Effect of Irrigation. — The Suez Canal appears likely to produce a radical change in the climate of the surrounding country. From a series of meteorological observations made during two years at three different stations on the isthmus, we are led to infer the interesting fact that introduction of the waters of the Mediterranean into the lakes has caused an atmospheric moisture in places heretofore noted for their dryness, to such an extent that fogs, equal in intensity to those of some European cities, now occur. This appears to support an important conclusion of Colonel Foster, in his recently published work, with regard to the effect that irrigation would have on our western deserts.

Durangite. — The mineral is of a bright orange-red, the crystals having a rhombic aspect; streak, cream-yellow; lustre, vitreous; cleavage, distinct in two directions; crystallizations, monoclinic; hardness, 5; specific gravity, 3.95 — 4.03. The small quantity which could be used for the test did not allow a full and complete quantitative determination. Direct duplicate estimations, however, were obtained of every constituent, except fluorine. This last element was found to exist in such considerable quantity, that the fluohydric acid evolved in attacking the mineral

23

by sulphuric acid, etched the glass with great readiness and dis
tinctness. The following results were obtained by analysis.   No.
1 in the wet way, by sulphuric acid :—

Arsenic acid, . . .	55.10;	Quantity of Oxygen	19.16
Alumina, ...	20.60;	" "	9.63
Ferric oxide, . . .	4.78;	" "	1.44
Managanous oxide, .	1.30;	" "	0.38
Soda, ...	11.66;	" "	3.01
Lithia, ...	0.81;	" "	0.42
Fluorine, ...		undetermined.	

84.33

Analysis No. 2, made in the dry way, by fusion with carbonate
of soda, dissolved in water, acidulated with chlorhydric acid,
gave : arsenic acid, 53.22; alumina, 20.09; ferric oxide, 5.06;
managanous oxide, 1.28.   The low amount of arsenic acid by
this determination, it was thought, might be due to the fact that
the soda fusion was made over a gas-blast lamp, with the possibility that a portion of the arsenic acid might have been reduced
to arsenious acid, and volatilized; or possibly to other accidental
causes.   The small quantity of mineral would not allow of a repe-
tition of this analysis.

An analysis, No. 3, was made, qualitative quantitative, in
which only the alkalies were estimated.   The results of this was :
soda, 11.86; lithia, 0.70; — agreeing very closely with No. 1.
The alkalies examined with the spectroscope showed only the
lines of sodium and lithium.

The composition and oxygen ratio (nearly 1 : 3 : 5), says the
professor, " suggest an *analogy* between the new mineral and
amblygonite, a fluo-phosphate of alumina, lithia, and soda," but
he thinks the results given are sufficient to demonstrate it to be a
new mineral, and, as he thinks, the only observed native fluo-
arseniate.

Geology of Venezuela. — Since the publications of Baron Von
Humboldt, nothing has been contributed to the geology of the
south-eastern portion of Venezuela.   In his grouping of the mountain systems of South America, he groups the entire mountain
series of all Guayana into one system, and calls it the Parimi system.   Its rocks are all gneiss or granite, and crystalline, according
to his description.

Our examination of a large portion of the northern mountains
shows the presence of other rocks, such as schists of various kinds,
talcose rock, limestone, and itacolumite.   A section across the
trend of the Imitaca range, at right angles, exhibits for the first
miles only crystalline rocks.   At San Maria, the culminating
point of this range, it falls off suddenly on the southward full 900
feet, to the plains of Cumé.   Hornblende schists, with interstratified veins of quartz, and bands of syenite and granite, with talcose, chloritic and silicious schists, then obtain for two days' journey, until we reach the valley of the Yuruari River, where we
find limestone, itacolumite, and greater frequency of talcose

rock. After crossing the Yuruari, we first enter the gold fields of the country.

Gold veins occur in brecciated and other slates, which are but little changed from the sedimentary and fossiliferous condition. These slates appear to be changed in places into talcose rock, and then auriferous veins are more abundant. The more silicious portions are changed into porphyroid rock, and dioritic rock is frequent.

The best-known portion of this gold field is the valleys of Mocupio and Iguana. The whole country south of the Imitaca may be called auriferous, for gold is found in all the streams, and on the savanna. In the Mocupio gold is found, —

1st. In the beds of streams, in sands and gravel.

2d. In placer deposits, under cover of earth, clays and gravels.

3d. In red earth, within a few feet of the surface. This is often very rich. A nugget weighing 15 pounds was found in it.

4th. In conglomerate of recent formation,

The geographical area which is auriferous is very great, reaching through the English, Dutch, and French Guianas, and through all of Venezuelian Guyana.

It should be called the "Parima Gold Field."

Difference of Level between the Red Sea and the Mediterranean. — M. Poirée, Inspector General, discusses this question in the "Comptes Rendus" of Aug. 2, 1869. He says: —

"It results from the comparison of the level of 1799 with that of 1856, adopted by the international commission, that the Red Sea is 0.86^m higher than the Mediterranean."

The borings for rock salt near Wylen, Switzerland, have given very favorable results. Near the Rhine, a bed of 80 feet in thickness has been found at a depth of 420 feet below the surface, and another, 50 feet thick, not far off. The salt is hard, pure, and of excellent quality.

Sea Depths. — Soundings for submarine cables show that the Baltic, between Sweden and Germany, is 125 feet deep; the Adriatic, between Venice and Trieste, 130; the English Channel, 300; the Irish Sea, in the south-western part, 2,000; the Mediterranean, east of Gibraltar, 3,100; off the coast of Spain, 6,200; by the Cape of Good Hope, 15,500.

BIOLOGY;

OR, PHYSIOLOGY, ZOÖLOGY, AND BOTANY.

DERIVATIVE HYPOTHESIS OF LIFE AND SPECIES. BY PROF. OWEN.

IN his recently published work on the "Anatomy of Vertebrates," Prof. Owen devotes a chapter to his hypothesis of the origin of species, as contrasted with the theory of Darwin. This chapter is reprinted in the "American Journal of Science" for January, 1869; and from this the following extracts are made: —

"Prof. Owen, like Lamarck and Darwin, rejects the principle of direct or miraculous creation, and recognizes a 'natural law, or secondary cause,' as operative in the production of species 'in orderly succession and progression.' To Cuvier's objection, that, if the existing species are modifications, by slow degrees, of extinct ones, the intermediate forms ought to be found, he replies, that many missing links in the palæontological series have been found since 1830. He gives several examples of these modifications, and dwells specially on *hipparion*, and the other forms between the fossil *palæotherium* and the present genus *equus*.

"Cuvier maintained that the revolutions of the surface of the globe had been numerous and sudden. Owen writes, 'Continued observations of geologists, while establishing the fact of successive changes, have filled up the seeming chasms between such supposed "revolutions," as the discoveries of palæontologists have supplied the links between the species held to have perished by the cataclysms. Each successive parcel of geological truth has tended to dissipate the belief in the unusually sudden and violent nature of the changes recognizable in the earth's surface.'"

Lamarck laid great stress upon the influence of surrounding circumstances in modifying the habits and structure of living beings. In this connection, Owen observes, taking the coral animals as illustrations, the hypothesis "of appetency subsides from the impotency of a coral polyp to exercise volition. The weak point of Lamarck's creative machinery is its limited applicability, namely, to creatures high enough in the scale to be able to want to do something; for the determined laws of the reflex function, in the physiology of the nervous system, and the necessity of the superadded cerebral mass for true sensation, rigorously fix the limits of volitional faculties." So, being "unable to accept the volitional hypothesis, or that of impulse from within (Lamarck), or the selective force exerted by outward circumstances (Darwin), I deem an innate tendency to deviate from parental type, operating through periods of adequate duration, to be the most probable nature, or way of operation, of the secondary law, whereby species have been derived one from the other. . . . According to my derivative hypothesis, a change takes place first in the structure of the animal; and this, when sufficiently advanced, may lead to modifications of habits. As species rise in the scale, the concomitant change of structure can, and does, lead to change of habits. But species owe as little to the accidental concurrence of environing circumstances as Cosmos depends on a fortuitous concourse of atoms. A purposive route of development and change, of correlation and interdependence, manifesting intelligent will, is as determinable in the succession of races as in the development and organization of the individual. Generations do not vary accidentally, in any and every direction, but in preordained, definite, and correlated courses."

" 'Derivation' holds that every species changes, in time, by virtue of inherent tendencies thereto. 'Natural Selection' holds that no such change can take place without the influence of altered circumstances educing or selecting such change.

" 'Derivation' sees among the effects of the innate tendency to change, irrespective of altered surrounding circumstances, a manifestation of creative power in the variety and beauty of the results; and, in the ultimate forthcoming of a being susceptible of appreciating such beauty, evidence of the preordaining of such relation of power to the appreciation. 'Natural Selection' acknowledges that if ornament or beauty, in itself, should be a purpose in creation, it would be absolutely fatal to it as a hypothesis.

" 'Natural Selection' sees grandeur in the view of life, with its several powers, having been originally breathed by the Creator into a few forms, or into one. 'Derivation' sees therein a narrow invocation of a special miracle, and an unworthy limitation of creative power, the grandeur of which is manifested daily, hourly, in calling into life many forms, by conversion of physical and chemical into vital modes of force, under as many diversified conditions of the requisite elements to be so combined.

" 'Natural Selection' leaves the subsequent origin and succession of species to the fortuitous concurrence of outward conditions. 'Derivation' recognizes a purpose in the defined and preordained course, due to innate capacity or power of change, by which homogeneously created protozoa have risen to the higher forms of plants and animals."

" As to epigenesis, or evolution, the 'evolutionists' of the last century 'contended that the new being pre-existed in a complete state of formation, needing only to be vivified by impregnation in order to commence the series of expansions, or disencasings, culminating in the independent individual. The 'epigenesists' held that both the germ and its subsequent organs were built up of juxtaposed molecules, according to the operation of a developmental force, or 'nisus formativus.' Haller maintained the prin-

22 *

ciple of 'evolution;' Buffon that of 'epigenesis;' Hunter would now be classed with the 'epigenesists.' . . . 'Pre-existence of germs' and 'evolution' are logically inseparable from the idea of the origin of species by primary miraculously created individuals. Cuvier, therefore, maintained both, as firmly as did Haller."

To meet the question of "whence the first organic matter?" the nomogenist (epigenesist) "is reduced to enumerate the existing elements into which the simplest living jelly (*protogenes* of Haeckel) or sarcode (*Amœba*) is resolvable, and to contrast the degree of probability of such elements combining, under unknown conditions, as the first step in the resolution of other forces into vital force, with the degree of probability remaining, after the observations above recorded, of the interposition of a miraculous power associating these elements into living germs, or forms with powers of propagating their kind to all time, as the sole condition of their ubiquitous manifestation, in the absence of any secondary law thereto ordained.

"It seems to me more consistent with the present phase of dynamical science and the observed gradations of living things, to suppose that sarcode, or the 'protogenal' jelly-speck, should be formable through concurrence of conditions favoring such combination of their elements and involving a change of force productive of their contractions and extensions, molecular attractions and repulsions — and that sarcode has so become, from the period when its irrelative repetitions resulted in the vast indefinite masses of 'eozoon,' exemplifying the earliest process of 'formification' or organic crystallization — than that all existing sarcodes or 'protogenes' are the result of genetic descent from a germ or cell due to a primary act of miraculous interposition."

Dismissing the old doctrines as absurd, he believes in what has been called "spontaneous generation," or the incessant new development of living beings out of non-living material. He sides with Pouchet and Child against Pasteur. He does not believe in "panspermism," or the doctrine that all the forms of life produced in decaying organic matter come from germs dispersed through the air. He prefers believing that, when the requisite material and conditions are present, other forces are resolved into vital force; and sees "the grandeur of creative power," not in the exceptional miracle of one or few original forms of life, but in the "daily and hourly calling into life many forms by conversion of chemical and physical into vital modes of force." The "Cause which has endowed his world with power convertible into magnetic, electric, thermotic, and other forms or modes of force, has also added the conditions of conversion into the vital mode."

He draws a comparison between life and magnetism, and between all the actions of living beings, from the attraction of the amœba by a bit of meat, to the highest phenomenon of consciousness in man; of which his conclusion is that from the magnet which chooses between steel and zinc, to the philosopher who chooses between good and evil, the difference is one of degree, not of kind, and that there is no need to assume a special miracle to account for mental phenomena.

DISTRIBUTION OF COPPER IN THE ANIMAL KINGDOM.

The presence of traces of copper in the blood of the lower animals has been for years an undisputed fact among chemists. In the blood of the higher animals, however, with few exceptions, no copper has been detected until lately. Wackenroder, for instance, discovered this metal in the blood of the duck, but not in that of the ox, the sheep, or the chicken. Its presence in the blood and in the muscles of man has been asserted as often as it has been denied, and now, as there is no doubt that it sometimes occurs in the bile, and bile stones, and the liver of man, its existence in these organs is still considered to be merely accidental, the more so as it is well known they retain poisonous substances more than other organs. In 1865, Mr. Ulex, in Hamburg, was led to search for copper in various animals, with results which gave rise to the supposition of a general distribution of copper in the animal kingdom. As the tests for copper are very easy and simple, as well as exceedingly sensitive, if properly applied, the respective investigations were extended by Ulex to animals of various zoölogical classes. The reagents employed were tested for copper in every case, and rejected if containing any. The quantity ranged from 0.01 to 0.10 per cent. Among the mammalia, it was found in the stomach and intestines of the European and Canadian lynx, and in those of some species of the leopard, jackal, and repeatedly in the flesh of horses and cattle. It was met with in Liebig's meat extract, which contains the soluble portions of beef in a concentrated form. Moreover, it was discovered in the breast of a " crick duck," in the yellow and white of an egg, more so in the latter than in the yolk; among amphibians, in the geometrical tortoise, the viper, and frog. Among fishes, it was met with in the eel and torsk, and among animals of the lower classes in the following species: In *Crangon vulgaris*, the South American bird-catching spider, *Scolopendra Italica*, in the Spanish fly, the earth-worm and the ascaris, in the edible vine-snail, in sea stars, in the thick-hided echinanthus, and in the bath sponge. It is thus seen that copper was detected in every case where it had been searched for; this having been the case with accidentally chosen animals of various zoölogical classes, it may rightly be concluded that the metal copper, like iron, is of a general distribution in the animal kingdom. From this it follows that copper must also be present in plants, in the ground, and in the sea. Indeed, copper was detected in plants by Meissner and John more than 50 years ago, and later it was ascertained by Sarzeau to be present in more than 500 vegetable species. In the earth, copper has been repeatedly detected, and so in the water of the ocean. If copper is found in the vegetable fibre, it follows that it must also be present in its industrial products. In order to ascertain this, Ulex selected a material that is daily employed by chemists, and, on account of its purity, highly esteemed by them, namely, Swedish filtering paper. Upon analysis it was found that 10 grains of it yielded 6.03 grains or 6.3 per cent. of ashes, from which a piece of copper half the size of a pin's head could easily be obtained. Charcoal also yields a cupreous ash, and as both paper and charcoal are made use of in the analyses spoken of, it might be suggested that the copper of these substances got into the analyzed materials, where, of course, they would have been found. Yet this reaction has its limits. If it is possible to detect copper in 10 grains of paper, and in 100 grains of charcoal, it is not possible to find it in 0.25 grains of paper, or 0.1 grain of charcoal, which are the quantities used in each analysis. Besides, copper has been discovered in animal tissues without the use of either paper or charcoal. The above-mentioned facts are certainly not without importance to physiology, judicial medicine, and pharmacy, but it is to be hoped, that, in following them up, more light will be thrown upon this interesting topic. — *Scientific American: translation from Aus der Natur.*

UNHEALTHFULNESS OF IRON STOVES.

Considerable discussion having arisen as to the permeability of cast iron to gases, and to their morbific effect in ill-ventilated rooms (see " Annual of Scientific Discovery " for 1869, p. 126), the conclusions of Gen. Morin, as given in a report to the French Academy, will be read with interest.

The experiments extended over a year, and were performed at the " Conservatoire des Arts et Metiers," in Paris, being terminated in February, 1869.

His conclusions are as follows : —

1. In addition to the immediate and grave inconveniences arising from the facility with which stoves of the ordinary metals attain a red heat, cast-iron stoves, at a dull red heat, cause the development of a determinate but very variable amount of carbonic oxide, a very poisonous gas.

2. A similar development takes place, but in a less degree, in sheet-iron stoves raised to a red heat.

3. In rooms thus heated, the carbonic acid naturally contained in the air, and that derived from respiration, may be decomposed, and produce carbonic oxide.

4. The carbonic oxide may arise from several different and sometimes concurrent causes, as, the permeability of the iron to this gas, which passes from within outward; the direct action of the oxygen of the air upon the carbon of the iron heated to redness; the decomposition of the carbonic acid in the air by its contact with the heated metal, and the influence of organic dust naturally contained in the air.

5. The effects observed in a room lighted by four windows, and two doors, one of which is frequently opened, would be made manifest and grave in ordinary rooms, without ventilation, in consequence of the presence and decomposition of various kinds of organic dust therein present.

6. Consequently, stoves and heating apparatus in cast or sheet iron, without interior linings of fire-bricks, or other refractory

substances which will prevent their becoming red-hot, are dangerous to the health.

MM. St. Claire Deville and Troost have shown that the air in contact with the external surface of a cast-iron stove may become charged with a proportion of carbonic oxide equal to .0007 to .0013 of its volume. Experiments on rabbits show that carbonic oxide has the property of expelling a part of the oxygen contained in the blood; and that the small amount of .0004 will cause the expulsion of .45 of the oxygen of the blood. Though sheet-iron stoves are less dangerous on this account, they are not so harmless as Dr. Carret supposes, as they are open to the grave objections of the sudden elevation of temperature of their external surface, and of then decomposing the carbonic acid of the air. It has long been admitted as a fact in science, that iron at a red heat decomposes carbonic acid, takes a portion of its oxygen, and transforms it into carbonic oxide. The experiments showed that the amount of carbonic oxide formed was notably less in a moist than in a dry air; this justifies the common use of vessels filled with water on stoves and furnaces.—*Comptes Rendus*, *May 3*, 1869.

BURIAL OF THE DEAD.

The public health in large cities is very apt to be endangered by prevailing practices in regard to the disposition of the dead; and one of the most dangerous, because almost universal and disregarded, is the long time which is permitted to elapse between death and burial. This time is made longer than formerly, from the necessity of placing cemeteries at considerable distances from cities, by the facilities offered by railroads for bringing back the dead to their native places, and by the increasing dread of premature interments. It becomes, therefore, important to protect the living from cadaveric emanations, especially in times of epidemic disease, by various disinfectants and antiseptics, and hermetically sealed receptacles for the dead. In this way many days, sometimes weeks, intervene between the death and the burial.

The danger of burying the dead in the midst of dense populations has been shown by the sad experience of most of the large cities of Europe. The grave, unless the ground be too limited, is much better than the tomb; in the former the earth absorbs and neutralizes the products of decomposition, while the emanations from the tomb, by their imprisonment, acquire frequently a dangerous intensity; this is especially true of the old and absurd custom of placing the dead under churches frequented by the living. Antiseptics, therefore, and all contrivances for retarding decomposition, should, unless in a few exceptional cases, be discouraged; on the contrary, the return of dust to dust, of organic matters to their elements, by the natural agencies of the soil, should be hastened by committing the body to the earth, of such extent and depth as readily to absorb and neutralize all liquid or gaseous products. To avoid all possibility of contamination, the cemeteries should be as far as possible removed from human habita-

tions, and so situated that the natural drainage of the soil should
not convey any deleterious matters into the water used or earth
occupied by man or animals.

RESPIRATION vs. THE TEMPERATURE OF THE BLOOD.

One of the results of Dr. Lombard's experiments, with a thermo-electric apparatus capable of indicating a difference of
temperature of one two-thousandth of a degree centigrade
(described in the "Annual of Scientific Discovery" for 1869, p.
285), is, that, although the air taken into the lungs and thence
into the blood be cold and dry, it does not lower the temperature of the blood sufficiently to be appreciable by this delicate thermometer, as compared with the temperature when
the respired air is hot. In the "Quarterly Journal of Science" for April, 1869, we find the following: "We must all
have noticed the feeling of heat in the lungs on a cold, frosty
day,—a sensation which is not experienced in warmer weather,
and which is the very reverse of what we should expect from
the greater coldness of the inspired air. M. Brown Séquard suggests that the explanation may be this,—the lower the temperature
of the inhaled oxygen the greater will be the amount absorbed,
according to a well-known law of physics, and hence possibly,
there being a larger absorption of oxygen, there may be increased
oxidation, and increased heat accordingly. The tension of the
vessels affected by cold air may have some connection with the
sensation in the lungs.

ASCENT OF HIGH MOUNTAINS.

According to carefully made experiments of Mr. Lortet in the
valley of Chamounix, up to a height of about 3,900 metres the
respiration is but little troubled, if the precautions are taken of
walking with the head low to diminish the orifice of the air-passages, of keeping the mouth shut and breathing through the nose,
and of sucking some small substance, as a nut or stone, to
increase the salivary secretion. Above this height, the respiration
becomes hurried, even to 36 a minute, and difficult; it seems as if
the pectoral muscles became stiff and the ribs were encased; the
amount of air which passes through is much less than in the valley, and the amount of oxygen for purification of the blood
very small.

The pulse increases from 64 to 160, according to altitude, and
is febrile and weak, the arteries feeling almost empty. The
rapid circulation of the blood in the lungs adds to the insufficient
oxygenation arising from rarefaction of the air; the veins become
swollen, and all experience a heaviness in the head and sleepi-
ness, due to imperfect aeration of the blood. The weakness of
the pulse is accompanied by a general refrigeration of the body.
Between 1,050 and 4,810 metres, the heat of the body may
descend 6 to 8° C. during the muscular efforts of ascension, a

very great reduction for a mammal; during the periods of rest, the heat reassumes quickly the normal standard; during the process of digestion, the cooling does not occur; hence the custom of eating frequently during the ascent. — *Comptes Rendus, Sept.* 20, 1869.

A NEW METHOD OF EFFECTING ARTIFICIAL RESPIRATION. BY BENJAMIN HOWARD, M. D.

"The patient is laid on the ground upon his back, his arms fully extended backward and outward, a firm roll of clothing being placed beneath the false ribs, so as to throw their anterior margin prominently forward.

"The tongue being held forward by an assistant, the operator, facing the patient, kneels astride his abdomen, and places both hands so that the balls of the thumbs rest upon the anterior margins of the false ribs, the four fingers falling naturally into four of the lower corresponding intercostal spaces on each side. The elbows of the operator being then planted against his sides, he has but to throw himself forward, using his knees as a pivot, and the entire weight of his trunk is brought to bear upon the patient's false ribs. If, at the same time, the fingers of the operator grasp and squeeze the false ribs toward each other, these combined actions crowd the false ribs upward and inward, producing the greatest possible motion of the diaphragm, and displacement of the contents of the pulmonary air-cells. The operator then suddenly lets go, and returns to the erect position upon his knees, when both the inrush of air and the natural elasticity of the ribs at this part cause instant return to their normal position. This, repeated with proper rhythm and frequency, constitutes the entire process.

"This direct method possesses, in my opinion, the following advantages over and above the *indirect methods*, both of Silvester and of Marshall Hall: —

"1st. It is more simple.

"2d. The degree of compression is felt, and can be regulated by the operator.

"3d. All the available anatomical means for displacement of air in the cavity of the chest are completely used.

"4th. While the necessary motions are in progress, the tongue may be steadily held out, the limbs and entire body be dried and rubbed without interfering with the operator.

"5th. No time is lost in superfluous motions.

"6th. It is less fatiguing to the operator.

"7th. It is more quickly taught to a bystander." — *Medical Record.*

VACCINATION.

Dr. Henry Blanc, at the 1869 meeting of the British Association, read a paper on "Human Vaccine Lymph and Heifer Lymph Compared."

In treating the subject, he dealt with two questions: 1st. Can disease be transmitted with humanized lymph? 2d. Is humanized lymph of long standing a prophylactic against small-pox? In answer to the first question, he did not believe that every possible disease could be transmitted by lymph. To suppose that cholera and some other forms of disease were produced by vaccination was not only irrational, but simply absurd; but, at the same time, he was compelled to admit that the transmission of disease was not only possible, but must be received as an acknowledged fact. Dr. Blanc gave instances to show that two forms of disease, particularly a kind of skin disease and syphilis, have been unmistakably transmitted by vaccination. ·

With regard to the second question, as to the efficacy of humanized lymph, Dr. Blanc answered it in the negative, as he found the humanized lymph of long standing lost much of its anti-variolic power, and stated that, far from being alone in this opinion, he was supported by all the best authorities on vaccination. M. Simon, after a careful study of the progressive successes of vaccination in the Prussian army, found that the vaccinations of 1836, when tested by subsequent susceptibility to cow-pox, were not so successful as those of 1813. There was no longer the same immunity as was formerly given, and the cases of fatal result from vaccination had also largely increased. Dr. Blanc quoted copiously from returns of various public institutions to show that the number of cases of post-vaccinal small-pox had steadily increased since the use of humanized lymph became general. On the other hand, on examination of the cases of people who had taken cow-pox from milking cows, it was found that they still enjoyed perfect immunity from small-pox, as was shown by Dr. Blanc in a variety of statistical extracts. The remedy he proposed was simply to return to the system of Jenner. Vaccination direct from the heifer, or animal, was no new or untried system, and had been established in many large cities of Europe. The advantages of the system were a removal of the danger of infection from other disease, as the bovine race was not subject to such diseases as might be transmitted to man; that the spontaneous cow-pox was not likely to lose its essential qualities; and it was easy always to have on hand a good supply of vaccine matter by these means. No fatal results had been recorded as arising from the use of the animal lymph; and the conclusion of Dr. Blanc is, that to render compulsory vaccination efficacious, and to complete the great work of Jenner, they must return to the system of taking the lymph from the animal, and so restore the glory and usefulness and prestige of Jenner's great remedy.

PHOTOGRAPHIC REPRESENTATIONS OF THE PULSE.

Dr. Ozanam, of Paris, has invented an ingenious apparatus for rendering the variable beatings of the pulse visible. It consists of a camera lucida, about 10 inches wide, in which a piece of mechanism, moving at a uniform rate, pushes a glass plate, prepared with collodion, in front of a very narrow aperture exposed to the light. In this aperture is a glass tube, in which a column of mercury may rise or fall, as in a thermometer. By attaching to the wrist a rubber tube, filled with mercury, in connection with the tube of the apparatus, the beating of the pulse is received on this artificial artery, and the pulsations are transmitted to the recording apparatus. As the column in the tube acts as a screen, light can penetrate the aperture only where the column is deficient; consequently, the prepared plate becomes black under the influence of light everywhere except at such places as the column intercepts it. As the column rises and falls with each pulsation of the heart, these black lines on the prepared plate, pushed regularly forward, will be longer or shorter alternately, and will be successively photographed as being lines perpendicular to a common base, the heart being thus made to register photographically its own pulsations.

Dr. E. J. Marey, of Paris, had discovered, by his "sphygmograph" (see "Annual of Scientific Discovery" for 1866–67, p. 307), that the pulse was double in some diseased conditions. This Dr. Ozanam shows to be not the exception, but the general rule, and that, when we place a finger on an artery, we receive two, and sometimes three, blows. The natural pulse is double, bounding at once to the top of the scale, and then falling, by two or three motions, to the lower level. The first bound is apparently due to the vigorous contraction of the left ventricle, the second and lesser to the contraction of the right ventricle, and the third (the least apparent) to the contraction of the left auricle, or the elasticity of the arteries. These photographic representations can be so magnified as to make them visible across a large amphitheatre. This apparatus may be modified to register the variations of respiration, the irregular action of coughing, and similar physiological and pathological phenomena.

NEW ANÆSTHETICS.

From time to time, new anæsthetics are discovered. First, ether, then chloroform and nitrous oxide; now Dr. Leebach, of Germany, has discovered another, to which he has given the name of chloralhydrat. It is highly spoken of by the medical men abroad, and said to be superior to chloroform in producing a more complete state of unconsciousness, while it neither induces feebleness nor leaves any bad effects behind. He has held rabbits from 12 to 14 hours under the influence of chloralhydrat, during a part of which time he kept them suspended over the back of a chair; and as soon as they awakened, they displayed their usual activity, and fed with unimpaired appetite. It has been successfully applied as a sedative in the treatment of the insane. Chloralhydrat resembles chloroform in appearance, but it is not so heavy; and, being much less volatile than that body, it has a feebler odor. On the tongue, it has a sharp, but not an acrid taste; and, though it reminds one of chloroform, it gives the sensation neither of warmth nor sweet-

24

ness, like the latter. It is absorbed, and not inhaled, and in this respect differs from other anæsthetics. When liquid ammonia is added to a solution of this body, chloroform is precipitated.

Chloral. — At the 1869 meeting of the British Association, Dr. Richardson said that chloral had been introduced by Liebig, in 1832; and it occurred to his assistant at the Academy in Berlin, who suggested that, as chloral had its chloroform set free by the action of an alkali, the introduction of it into contact with the alkali contained in the blood might suggest a means of using it for the purpose of obtaining insensibility in animals, without some of the disadvantages of taking chloroform into the stomach. Dr. Richardson gave a detailed statement of the nature of chloral, a specimen of which had been sent him by Mr. Hanburg, who had received it from Liebig; and he also described some experiments made with chloral. In pigeons, he had found chloral produce sleep and insensibility, lasting from 4 to 5 hours, by the use of from one and a half to two grains of chloral, and that above that quantity would kill. This had been applied both by injection and in the stomach. He had found, as a result of his experiments, that perfect insensibility could not be produced unless the dose was increased to a dangerous extent. Dr. Richardson gave detailed accounts of experiments with chloral upon pigeons, rabbits, and frogs, in 23 separate cases, and also carried on some with pigeons in the room. Dr. Richardson was not of opinion that chloral could be used instead of any of the present anæsthetic agents. It produced vomiting, and reduced the temperature of the body. It had some of the disadvantages of opium, and was no better, in many other respects, than that article. Still, they should be grateful to Liebig, as there might be considerable collateral benefit in suggesting a means for searching for advantages which might be obtained by the decomposition of medicines in the body.

[It has since been found of considerable advantage as a sedative in many diseases.] — *Ed.*

ACTION OF POISONS.

Poison of the Copperhead Snake. — Experiments on the poison of the cobra-de-capello, made by Dr. Halford, are given in the "Annual of Scientific Discovery" for 1868, p. 255; in the volume for 1869, on the rattlesnake poison, p. 306; and more recent observations on the effects of the bite of the American copperhead have been made by Dr. Joseph Jones, of New York. Dogs were subjected to its bite, sometimes with, and sometimes without, fatal results; the blood was examined carefully under the microscope, and in the fatal cases post-mortem examinations were made. "Thousands of small acicular crystals were mingled with the altered blood-corpuscles; and, as the bloody serum and effused blood dried, the blood-corpuscles seemed to be transformed into crystalline masses, shooting out into crystals of hæmatin in all directions. The blood-vessels of the brain were filled with gelatinous coagulable blood, which presented altered blood-corpuscles and acicular crystals." He concludes that the special toxic effect of this poison is due to its destruction of the red blood-corpuscles.

The Cobra-de-Capello. — M. Vulpian, of Paris, in experiments with the poison of this serpent, the activity of which was doubtless considerably diminished by its transmission from India, found that it appeared to act on the central nervous system, gradually suppressing its functions, and producing a remarkable state of somnolence, acting on the muscles and nerves like curare and many other poisonous substances. He did not notice the increase of white corpuscles observed by Dr. Halford, but found that the buccal mucous membrane will absorb the poison, producing the same symptoms as when received from a wound. This is an interesting fact, as it might render dangerous the attempt to extract the poison from a wound by suction. If this poison resembles curare in its action, there is nothing improbable in the native statements that certain herbs are antidotes to its effects, or that vegetable principles should exist having opposite physiological effects, and therefore capable of neutralizing its action.

Woorali. — It has hitherto been imagined that the action of *curare*, when applied to a wound, is to cause death without any visible struggle, and without pain. Dr. Claude Bernard has shown this notion to be utterly erroneous. He states that the paralysis creeps gradually on from limb to limb, depriving the animal of motion, and yet without in the slightest degree affecting its intellectual faculties or power of volition, which remain unimpaired to the last moment. This he considers one of the greatest tortures to which an intelligent being can be subjected. Death is caused by the paralysis of the respiratory organs, which cease to provide the blood with the quantity of oxygen it requires. This being the case, a poisoned animal may be restored to life by the mechanical injection of air into the lungs. This important fact Dr. Bernard proved by actual experiment, finding that, in the course of a few hours, the poison was eliminated. — *Comptes Rendus.*

The Poison Akazga. — This is used as an ordeal on the west coast of Africa, and found by French chemists to resemble nux vomica in its physiological effects. Specimens have been received in Edinburgh by Dr. Fraser, in bundles of long, slender, crooked stems; he comes to the conclusion that it is new to the West African flora, and thinks it may be a new species of strychnos. He has separated from it a new crystalline alkaloid, which he calls *Akazga*, closely resembling strychnia, but differing from it in being precipitated by alkaline bicarbonates. A suspected wizard is made to drink an infusion of the bark, and then to walk over small sticks of the plant; if guilty, he stumbles, and tries to step over the sticks as if they were logs, finally falling in convulsions, when he is beaten to death by clubs; if innocent, the kidneys act freely, and the poison is supposed to be thus eliminated. Some twigs of different structure were found in the bundles received by him, not yielding the alkaloid; and those who escape may, perhaps, have taken, by accident or design, an infusion of the spuri-

ous akazga.   This much resembles, if it is not the same as, the
Boundou poison, used by the natives of the Gaboon for a similar
purpose, the effects of which are described in "Annual of Scientific Discovery" for 1869, p. 256.

ARTIFICIAL PRODUCTION OF MONSTROSITIES.

The researches of M. Dareste on this subject are referred to, in
the "Annual of Scientific Discovery" for 1869, p. 308; further
results obtained are given in "Comptes Rendus" for July and
August, 1869.   He here states that embryos developed at relatively low temperatures *always* present organic anomalies, characterized, also, by arrest of development of different kinds.   Sometimes, the cicatricula is transformed into a blastoderm, without producing an embryo; this remarkable anomaly confirms the recently
expressed opinion of Milne Edwards on the nature of the cicatricula,
which he regards as a living being independent of the embryo, and
as representing the asexual generations in the cycle of alternate
generations.   Spinal fissure is one of the most frequent anomalies,
and is evidently the result of an arrest of development of the
primitive groove.   In the very remarkable case of arrest of development of the primitive groove, the embryo appears reduced simply to the cephalic region, the rest of the body being more or less
completely wanting.   In these anomalies, the embryo itself is
primitively affected; others result from arrested development of
the amnios, as before observed.   Cyclopism is the result, he states,
of the juxtaposition, at a certain period of embryonic life, of the
two orbits, or rather their rudiments, at the anterior end of the
body.   If the orbits are not separated by the ulterior development
of the anterior cerebral vesicle, they remain in juxtaposition, and
the eyes are united at the moment of their appearance.   Arrest of
development of the head is often accompanied with arrested car-
diac development; the formation of the heart resulting from the
union of two blastemas at first separate; arrest of development
maintains the separation, and thus two distinct hearts are produced.   When the head continues to grow, while the cephalic
hood is arrested, the former is reversed backward, and forms a
hernial protuberance in the upper part of the umbilical opening,
behind the heart.   The slowness of development of the blood
globules and vascular area is an obstacle to the formation of the
blood, and tends to produce a dropsical condition, a frequent cause
of anencephaly.

Embryos, thus rendered anomalous by the action of relatively
low temperatures, — 30° to 34° C., — perish very early, at about
the time of the turning of the embryo upon the yolk, and before
the appearance of the allantois; but if, before this period, the eggs
be submitted to the normal temperature of incubation, — 40° C.,
— development may be considerably increased before death, with
results very interesting to the embryologist.   A very remarkable
fact resulting from these experiments is, that embryos submitted
to identical physical conditions present great diversity in their

development, — showing that germs, as well as adult beings, are not identical, either anatomically or physiologically. The one thing certain is, that arrest of development produces anomaly. There are other anomalies in the forms of the blastoderm and vascular area which may be produced with certainty; so that development may be modified by two kinds of causes, direct and disturbing. This consideration will tend to throw light upon the much discussed and still obscure question of the influence of surrounding media on the development of living beings, which may be effected either by the production of a determined modification, or simply by a tendency to variation whose results depend on original differences in the germs.

Temperatures, also, a little above, as well as below, that of normal incubation, determine the same anomalies in the forming embryo, all by arrest of development. The partial application of an impermeable coating, the vertical position of the egg, and any considerable change in the ordinary process of incubation, produce a condition of variation characterized by arrest of development.

HUMAN LONGEVITY.

At the 1869 meeting of the British Association, Sir Duncan Gibb read a paper on " An obstacle to European Longevity beyond 70 years." He had previously drawn attention to the position of the leaf-shaped cartilage at the back of the tongue, known as the epiglottis, in 5,000 healthy people of all ages, and in 11 per cent. it was found to be drooping or pendent, in place of being vertical. He discovered the fact, that, in all persons above 70, its position was vertical, without a single exception, — a circumstance of the highest importance bearing upon the attainment of old age among Europeans. In a number of instances, where the age varied from 70 to 95, in all was this cartilage vertical. Many of these he cited as examples, such as the well-known statesmen, Lord Palmerston, Lord Lyndhurst, Lord Campbell, and Lord Brougham. He also gave some among old ladies, still alive, at ages from 75 to 92, whose epiglottis was vertical. But the most remarkable was that of a gentleman, still alive, 102 years of age, in whom it occupied the same position. He summed up his views in the following conclusions: First, as a rule, persons with a pendent epiglottis do not attain a longevity beyond 70; a few may overstep it, but such examples are exceptional. Second, with pendency of the epiglottis, life verges to a close at or about 70, and the limit of old age is reached. Third, a vertical epiglottis, on the other hand, affords the best chance of reaching the extreme limit of longevity. Lastly, pendency of the epiglottis is an obstacle to longevity of 11 per cent. of all ages amongst Europeans.

He stated that a considerable portion of the Jewish race possesses a physiognomy to which he gave the name of sanguineooleaginous expression, characterized by varying degrees of flushed face, sleepy aspect, greasy look, guttural or husky voice, and fulness of body. With this expression is usually associated pen-

24*

dency of the epiglottis.   As a rule, longevity is rare among such persons, for they are liable to those diseases of a congestive character which influence the heart, brain, and liver.   The cause of all this is eating food, especially flesh, cooked in oil, which tends to the destructive processes in the system, and induces premature old age, although the individual may appear to be the personification of comparatively good health.   The extensive use of oil in the south of Europe has the same effect in giving rise to congestive diseases and diminished longevity.   Pendency of the epiglottis, associated with the sanguineo-oleaginous expression, is of serious import.   The persistent use of oil, therefore, as an article of diet, is pernicious, unless in persons of spare habit of body, delicate constitution, and liability to disease wherein its employment would prove useful.

HAY FEVER.

Helmholz says, in "Virchow's Archiv," that since 1847 he has been attacked every year, at some time between May 20th and the end of June, with a catarrh of the upper air-passages.   These attacks increase rapidly in severity; violent sneezing comes on, with secretion of a thin, very irritating fluid; in a few hours there is a painful inflammation of the nose, both externally and internally; then fever, violent headache, and great prostration.   This train of symptoms is sure to follow if he is exposed to the sun and heat, and is equally certain to disappear in a short time if he withdraws himself from such exposure.   At the approach of cold weather these catarrhs cease.   He has otherwise very little tendency to catarrhs or colds.

For five years past, at the season indicated, and only then, he has regularly succeeded in finding vibrios in his nasal secretions. They are only discernible with the immersion lens of a very good Hartnak's.   The single joints, commonly isolated, are characterized by containing 4 granules in a row; each two granules being more closely connected, pairwise, and the combined length equalling 0.004 mm.   The joints are also found united in rows, or in series of branches.   As they are seen only in the secretion which is expelled by a violent sneeze, and not in that which trickles gradually forth, he concludes that they are probably situated in the adjoining cavities and recesses of the nose.

On reading Binz's account of the poisonous effect of quinine upon infusoria, he determined to try it in his own case.   He took a saturated neutral solution of quiniæ sulph. in water = 1 : 740. This excites a moderate sensation of burning in the nasal mucous membrane.   Lying upon his back, he dropped 4 centim. of the solution, by a pencil, into each nostril; moving his head meanwhile in all directions, to bring the fluid thoroughly into contact with the parts, until he felt it reach the œsophagus.   Relief was immediate.   He was able, for some hours, freely to expose himself to the heat of the sun.   Three applications a day sufficed to keep him free from the catarrh, under circumstances the most unfavorable.   The vibriones, also, were no longer to be found.

The experiment was made in 1867, and was repeated at the first recurrence of the attack in May, 1868, preventing the further development of the attack for that year. — *Scientific American.*

NATURAL SELECTION IN THE CASE OF MAN.

In the "Quarterly Journal of Science" for January, 1869, is a review, from which the following are extracts: —

" A writer in a recent number of 'Fraser's Magazine' endeavors to point out that although there is a struggle for existence of a more or less intense kind, between different races and nations of men, yet that between man and man in a civilized condition there is no such struggle, the weak being protected, and the feeble inheriting wealth which they have not won. Thus the fittest do not survive, contends this writer, and the law of selection is so far interfered with as to fail, and, indeed, we may expect degeneracy rather than improvement in civilized men."

" The 'Spectator' accepts the view propounded by the writer in 'Fraser' in part, but, making use of the mysterious term 'supernatural selection,' asserts that a new source of benefit is opened up to man by the cultivation of his moral nature, which counterbalances any attendant evils. The error in this view of the case arises from a neglect of the fact that civilized man is a social animal, in a truly zoölogical sense. There is no struggle for existence between the various bees of a hive, nor among the polyps of a polypidom; the struggle is between hive and hive, and polypidom and polypidom. So with the communities of civilized men; the struggle is between one society and another, whatever may be the bond uniting such society; and in the far distant future we can see no end to the possible combinations of societies which may arise amongst men, and by their emulation tend to his development. Moral qualities, amongst the others thus developed in the individual, necessarily arise in societies of men, and are naturally selected, being a source of strength to the community which has them most developed; and there is no excuse for speaking of a failure of Darwin's law, or of 'supernatural selection.' We must remember what Alfred Wallace has insisted upon most rightly, that in man development does not affect so much the bodily as the mental characteristics; the brain in him has become much more sensitive to the operation of selection than the body, and hence is almost its sole subject. At the same time it is clear that the struggle between man and man is going on to a much larger extent than the writer in 'Fraser' allowed. The rich fool dissipates his fortune and becomes poor; the large-brained artisan does frequently rise to wealth and position; and it is a well-known law that the poor do not succeed in rearing so large a contribution to the new generation as do the richer. Hence we have a perpetual survival of the fittest. In the most barbarous conditions of mankind, the struggle is almost entirely between individuals; in proportion as civilization has increased among men, it is easy to trace the transference of a great part of the struggle, little by little, from individuals to tribes, nations, leagues, guilds, corporations, societies, and other such combinations; and accompanying this transference has been undeniably the development of the moral qualities and of social virtues."

SOUTH AMERICAN INDIANS AND NEGROES.

The following are extracts from the Appendix of Prof. Agassiz's " Journey in Brazil ": —

" What struck me at first view, in seeing Indians and Negroes together, was the marked difference in the relative proportions of the different parts of the body. Like long-armed monkeys the Negroes are generally slender, with long legs, long arms, and a comparatively short body, while the Indians are short-legged, short-armed, and long-bodied, the trunk being also rather heavy in build. To continue the comparison, I may say that if the Negro by his bearing recalls the slender, active Hylobates, the Indian is more like the slow, inactive, stout Orang. Of course there are exceptions to this rule; short, thick-built Negroes are occasionally to be seen, as well as tall, lean Indians; but, so far as my observation goes, the essential difference between the Indian and Negro races, taken as a whole, consists in the length and square build of the trunk and the shortness of limbs in the Indian, as compared with the lean frame, short trunk, deep-cleft legs, and long arms of the Negro.

" Another feature not less striking, though it does not affect the whole figure so much, is the short neck and great width of the shoulders in the Indian. This peculiarity is quite as marked in the female as in the male, so that, when seen from behind, the Indian woman has a very masculine air, extending indeed more or less to her whole bearing; for even her features have rarely the feminine delicacy of higher womanhood. In the Negro, on the contrary, the narrowness of chest and shoulder, characteristic of woman, is almost as marked in the man; indeed, it may well be said that, while the Indian female is remarkable for her masculine build, the Negro male is equally so for his feminine aspect. Nevertheless, the difference between the sexes in the two races is not equally marked. The female Indian resembles in every respect much more the male than is the case with the Negroes; the females among the latter having generally more delicate features than the males.

" As to the limbs, they are not only much longer in proportion in the Negro than in the Indian; their form and carriage differ also. The legs of the Indian are remarkably straight; in the Negro the knees are bent in, and the hip as well as knee-joint habitually flexed. Similar differences in other parts of the body are visible from behind; in the Indians the interval between the two shoulders, the shoulder-blades being comparatively short in themselves, is much greater than in any other race. In this respect the women do not differ from the men, but share in a feature characteristic of the whole race. This peculiarity is especially noticeable in a profile view of the figure, in which the broad, rounded shoulder marks the outline in the upper part of the trunk, and tapers gradually to a well-shaped arm, terminating usually in a rather small hand; the little finger is remarkably short. In the Negro, on the contrary, the shoulder-blades are long and placed more closely together, the shoulder being rather slim and narrow, and the hand disproportionately slender, though the fingers are more extensively webbed than in any other race. In this respect there is little difference between male and female, the build of the male being more muscular, but hardly stouter; in both a profile view shows the back and breast projected forward and backward of the arm. The proportions between the length and width of the trunk, as compared with each other, and measured from the shoulder to the base of the trunk, hardly differ in the Indian and Negro; this renders the difference in the relative length and strength of the arms and legs the more apparent.

"Like distinct species among animals, different races of men, when crossing, bring forth half-breeds; and the half-breeds between these different races differ greatly. The hybrid between the White and Negro, called Mulatto, is too well known to require further description; his features are handsome, his complexion clear, and his character confiding, but indolent. The hybrid between the Indian and Negro, known under the name of Cafuzo, is quite different; his features have nothing of the delicacy of the Mulatto; his complexion is dark; his hair long, wiry, and curly; and his character exhibits a happy combination between the jolly disposition of the Negro and the energetic enduring powers of the Indian. The hybrid between White and Indian, called Mammeluco in Brazil, is pallid, effeminate, feeble, lazy, and rather obstinate; though it seems as if the Indian influence had only gone so far as to obliterate the higher characteristics of the White, without imparting its own energies to the offspring. It is very remarkable how, in both combinations, with Negroes as well as Whites, the Indian impresses his mark more deeply upon his progeny than the other races, and how readily, also, in further crossings, the pure Indian characteristics are reclaimed, and those of the other races thrown off. I have known the offspring of a hybrid between Indian and Negro with a hybrid between Indian and White resume almost completely the characteristics of the pure Indian."

THE ESQUIMAUX.

Capt. W. S. Hall, at the last meeting of the British Association, read a paper "On the Esquimaux Considered in their Relationship to Man's Antiquity." The Esquimaux inhabit regions within the Arctic Regions, comprising Greenland and the islands to the west of that continent. Ethnologically considered, they are of the Mongolian type, and in this respect allied to the Finns and Laplanders, and the races of Central and Eastern Asia. The question arises, Where and when did this peculiar people originate? That no originating centre of the human species can have occurred within the Arctic Circle, as at present constituted, is self-evident. That the progenitors of the present inhabitants migrated within any recognizable period of history, from southern and more genial latitudes, is equally irreconcilable with ordinary reason, even if their peculiar type did not render such hypothesis untenable. Against the possibility of Greenland having been peopled from Lapland or Finland, the evidence is so strong as to amount almost to a certainty. In the first place, the North Cape of Europe is separated from Cape Farewell, in Greenland, by at least 69½ degrees of longitude. Again, the prevailing winds in these latitudes are from the west, or from Greenland to Lapland; and, lastly, the Gulf Stream, in its north-easterly course, between Iceland and the coast of Norway, would naturally carry any fragile craft from the north rather towards Nova Zembla than to Greenland. He then proceeded to show that a temperate climate prevailed in the Arctic regions during the miocene era, and proved this by giving a list of the fossil plants which had been found in Greenland, and submitted to Prof. Heer. These showed that, at the time they lived within the Arctic Circle, a warmer climate characterized that latitude than that now prevailing in Devonshire. From this, Capt. Hall deduced the conclusion that the miocene was the epoch when man first made his appearance on the earth.

Sir John Lubbock said he had no doubt that ultimately man's advent on the globe would be traced to the miocene epoch, but he differed from the author in holding that man was to be found in his original condition in the Devonshire bone caves, rather than in the temperate fossil forests of the extreme North. The reindeer and the whale had always accompanied pre-historic man, and he did not see why he should be less happy than in more temperate regions.

PAUCITY OF ABORIGINAL MONUMENTS IN CANADA.

Sir Duncan Gibb read a paper on this subject at the last meeting of the British Association. Being familiar with the archæological discoveries in Canada, from long residence there, it seemed to him there must be some reason why monuments of an aboriginal character were wholly absent or exceedingly scarce. Humboldt referred to one found in the Western Prairies, but now lost. The author, in his inquiry, excluded small Indian remains, such as flint implements, pottery, burying-grounds, etc., also mounds or barrows. It referred to monuments of stone, built either as dwellings or temples, as met with in Central America. There were two reasons, he said, why such remains were not found in Canada and other northern nations; the first was the extreme cold and rigor of such a climate as exists in Canada, with its six months of winter. The ground covered with snow was unfavorable for the preservation of architectural monuments or remains of any kind, unless carefully looked after as in modern times. For the same reason, similar remains were scarce in Northern Europe and Asia. Climate was not only the great drawback to their preservation, but if any monuments had existed, some centuries of frost would have completely destroyed them. Secondly, the people who built the American and Canadian mounds, he believed, were the descendants of the Tartars who crossed into America by Behring's Straits, and occupied the whole or greater part of the continent. He considered them a different race from those who built the magnificent temples of Central and South America, and they were not builders of stone, unless as met with in some of the mounds. But, supposing either race to be builders of stone, had any such monuments existed in the colder parts of North America, they would not have held together for any period of time. Although the climate varies somewhat in Canada, being milder in the western part, still no evidence of true aboriginal monuments is to be found. The climates of Egypt and Central America were peculiarly favorable for their preservation, and who could say the builders were not the descendants of the same people? Of rock sculptures and markings, Canada could boast of few, especially in caverns, but there was no reason why some day they might not be discovered, especially in the series of caverns existing between Flamborough and Georgian Bay, and also in a similar series of caverns which the author conjectured would be some day discovered in rocks of a similar formation in the Island of Anticosti.

MAN IN THE QUATERNARY PERIOD.

In the "American Journal of Science" for July, 1869, are quoted some paragraphs by Prof. Paul Broca, on human remains found in the caves of Perigord, which not only furnish satisfactory proofs of the contemporaneity of man and the mammoth, but reveal curious details of the life and manners of these old cave-dwellers, and give the anatomical characters of the race. The carved objects in one cave correspond with the reindeer period, while the human bones found in another belong rather to the period of the mammoth; "and though a considerable time must have elapsed between the two periods, yet there is nothing to hinder the belief of the gradual passage from one to the other, without any ethnic revolution, the same race maintaining itself in the same district uninterruptedly; so that, if the bones from Cro-Magnon are not those of the artists of the reindeer period, they are, at least, those of the ancestors of that people.

"The remains of the men of the quaternary period that we have hitherto been able to study belonged, for the most part, to individuals of short stature, with a rather small cranium, and a more or less prognathous face. Hence it has been concluded that the primitive population of Europe belonged to a Negroid race, according to some, and according to others to a Mongoloid race, whose stature did not much exceed that of the modern Laps.

The facts on which this opinion rests I take as exact; but it rests also on a preconceived idea, which, for my part, I have long combated, namely, that in quaternary Europe there was only one race of men. Starting with the ethnogenic theory, that the diversity of the human race is produced by the influence of time and circumstances, the holders of the above-mentioned opinion admit that the typical differences ought to be less and less as we look back to past ages; and when the polygenists object that the separation of the principal groups of races was already complete in the earliest historical times, they are told that it was not in those times, so close to our own, but in the immense and incalculable preceding periods that the divergencies from the original type were manifested. Reduced to these terms, the question of the unity of the human race is adjourned to the time when palæontology shall have discovered the remains of primitive man, or at least relics of the races of the quaternary epoch. The monogenists suppose that these races, separated from us by thousands of ages perhaps, and for certain infinitely nearer to original man than the most ancient of the historic races, ought to present, if not an absolute uniformity, at least a manifest convergence toward the type of the common mould whence, they believe, all the races came.

"It comes to this, however (and it is usually the case), that facts begin to contradict a preconceived hypothesis. The quaternary race of Dordogne (Cro-Magnon) differs from the quaternary race of the Belgian caves, as much at least as dissimilar modern races differ one from another. The contrast is complete, not only when we look at the conformation and volume of the head, but also if we look at the form and dimensions of the bones of the limbs."

FORMER CONNECTION BETWEEN AUSTRALIA AND ASIA.

In the recently published work of Mr. A. R. Wallace, on the "Malay Archipelago," the author maintains that the Asiatic continent at a former period extended much farther eastward, and Australia farther westward, than at present, and were probably separated by the strait of Lombok, one of the Timor islands, dividing the island of this name, supposed to have formed part of Australia, from Bali, another existing island, believed, with Java and Sumatra, to have formed a part of the Asiatic continent. This theory is strongly supported by data from physical geography, zoölogy, botany, and ethnology. This Indo-Malayan region, including the Malay peninsula, Sumatra, Java, Borneo, and Bali, is surrounded by a shallow sea; another shallow sea surrounds the Papuan region, and a deep one the island of Celebes, the Timor group, and the Moluccas, forming his Austro-Malayan region. The Australian fauna extends to Lombok, the Asiatic to Bali, and in the Timor group the fauna and flora are transition types; as the latter are separated from each other by a deep sea, it is naturally inferred that the islands must at some time have been connected together; without stating that Timor was actually united with Australia in recent geological periods, he thinks they were much nearer than at present. Though Bali is separated from Lombok by a strait only 15 miles wide, the animals are very different, those of the former having an Asiatic, and of the latter an Australian type.

EPIORNIS.

At the time of the discovery of the immense egg of this bird in Madagascar in 1851, M. I. Geoffroy St. Hilaire placed the bird near the brevipinnate or ostrich family; but Valenciennes, from the study of the same specimens, thought it belonged near the penguins; after him Brianconi maintained that it was a rapacious bird near the condors, and probably the " roc " of Marco Polo. Recently the bones of the lower extremity have been found, the examination of which confirms the original opinion of St. Hilaire. The tibia is remarkable for the exceptional enlargement of the articular extremities; the length being 64 centimetres, the circumference of the upper end is 45, of the lower 38, and of the shaft only 15½ in its narrowest part. It has no bony bridge over the groove of the extensor muscle of the toes; this is the case in the brevipinnates, except *Dinornis* and *Palapteryx*; the foot is much more massive than in *D. elephantopus*. The size of the femur is extraordinary, its length, however, being less than one and one-half times that of its lower extremity. Behind and above the condyles is a very deep fossa, in which are the large orifices for the entrance of air into the interior of the bone, not found in *Apteryx* and *Dinornis*. The vertebræ indicate that the body of *Epiornis* was much more bulky than that of *Dinornis*. It resembles *Dinornis* more than any other genus, yet is distinct, especially in its massive form and large feet; its height was less than that of *Dinornis*, not exceeding that of a large ostrich, or about two metres, while the *Dinornis* attained a height of 3 metres; but it was much more bulky. Beside the *E. maximus*, others have been found, one of the size of the cassowary, and another of the size of the large bustard. There were then in Madagascar several species of large terrestrial birds, analogous to the *Dinornis* and its congeners in New Zealand. — *Comptes Rendus*, Oct. 11, 1869.

APHANAPTERYX; AN EXTINCT BIRD OF MAURITIUS.

M. Alph. Milne-Edwards, in " Comptes Rendus," April 12, 1869, describes the bones of this bird, found in the island of Mauritius with the remains of the dodo and the gigantic gallinule. It is not a gallinaceous bird, nor does it belong to the apteryx group; it is neither a rail proper, but comes near the genus *Ocydromus*, of Australia. The bill was pointed, of dense tissue, somewhat like that of the gallinule, but more resembling that of the oyster-catcher, and well suited for breaking the shells and resisting envelopes of the molluscs, on which it probably fed. The

25

feet are strong, and admirably adapted for walking; in going from the gallinules to the rails, to *Tribonyx* and *Ocydromus*, we come by degrees to the form of foot presented by this fossil. It is a transition form, one of the rail family adapted for an essentially terrestrial existence. The wings were rudimentary, and their feathers too little resistant for purposes of flight. The extinction of this bird must be attributed to man and the animal species connected with him. It is interesting to observe that the *Aphanapteryx*, living in Mauritius till recently, shows the close relation between the fauna of these isolated regions and that of the Australian region, and also its complete separation from the fauna of the African continent.

NEW FOSSIL REPTILES.

Prof. O. C. Marsh ("Amer. Journ. Science," Nov., 1869) describes several new Mosasauroid reptiles from the green-sand of New Jersey, and a new fossil serpent from the tertiary of the same State. He states that a striking difference between the reptilian fauna of the cretaceous of Europe and America is the prevalence in the former of remains of Ichthyosaurus and Plesiosaurus, which here appear to be entirely wanting; while the Mosasauroids, a group comparatively rare in the Old World, replace them in this country, and are abundantly represented both in genera and species. He describes many new forms of this peculiar type of reptilian life, ranging in length from 75 to 25 feet; his genus *Halisaurus* has well marked ophidian affinities. He adds, " The earliest remains of *Ophidia* both in Europe and this country have been found in the eocene, and nearly all the species from strata older than the post-pliocene appear to be more or less related to the constricting serpents. Remains of this character are not uncommon in European rocks, but in this country two species only, one founded on a single vertebra, have been described hitherto, and both of these were discovered in the tertiary green-sand of New Jersey. An interesting specimen from the same formation, recently presented to the Museum of Yale College, indicates a third species, much larger than either of the others, in fact superior in size to any known fossil ophidian, and not surpassed by the largest of modern serpents." This species, which he calls *Dinophis grandis*, was probably not less than 30 feet in length, a sea-serpent allied to the boas of the present era. The paper concludes as follows: " The occurrence of closely related species of large serpents in the same geological formation in Europe and America, just after the total disappearance in each country of *Mosasaurus* and its allies, which show such marked ophidian affinities, is a fact of peculiar interest, in view of the not improbable origin of the former type; and the intermediate forms, which recent discoveries have led palæontologists familiar with these groups to confidently anticipate, will doubtless at no distant day reward explorations in the proper geological horizon."

THE EARLY STAGES OF BRACHIOPODS. BY EDWARD S. MORSE.

The writer made a visit to Eastport, Me., early in the summer, for the purpose of discovering the early stages of a species of brachiopod (*Terebratulina septentrionalis*, Couth.) so abundant in those waters. As little has been known regarding the early stages of this class of animals, the facts here presented will be of interest, as settling beyond a doubt their intimate relations with the Polyzoa. In a few individuals, the ovaries were found partially filled with eggs. The eggs were kidney-shaped, and resembled the statoblasts of Fredericella. No intermediate stages were seen between the eggs and a form which recalled in general proportions Megerlia or Argiope, in being transversely oval, in having the hinge-margin wide and straight, and in the large foramen. Between this stage and the next, the shell elongates, until we have a form remarkably like Lingula, having, like Lingula, a peduncle longer than the shell, by which it holds fast to the rock. It suggests, also, in its movements, the nervously acting Pedicellina.

In this and the several succeeding stages, the mouth points directly backward (forward of authors), or away from the peduncular end, and is surrounded by a few ciliated cirri, which forcibly recall certain polyzoa. The stomach and intestine form a simple chamber, alternating in their contractions, and forcing the particles of food from one portion to the other. At this time, also, the brownish appearance of the walls of the stomach resemble the hepatic folds of the Polyzoa. In a more advanced stage, a fold is seen on each side of the stomach; from this fold, the complicated liver of the adult is developed, first, by a few diverticular appendages.

When the animal is about one-eighth of an inch in length, the lophophore begins to assume the horseshoe-shaped form of Pectinatella, and other high Polyzoa. The mouth at this stage begins to turn towards the dorsal valve (ventral of authors); and, as the central lobes of the lophophore begin to develop, the lateral arms are deflected. In these stages an episiome is very marked; and it was noticed that the end of the intestine was held to the mantle by attachment, as in the adult, reminding one of the *funiculus* in *Phylactolæmata*. No trace of an anus was discovered, though many specimens were carefully examined under high powers for this purpose, the intestine of the adult being repeatedly ruptured under the compressor without showing any evidence of an anal aperture. — *American Naturalist, September,* 1869.

PRIMORDIAL FAUNA.

Dr. J. J. Bigsby, in his "Thesaurus Siluricus," remarks, "The primordial stage did not start forth, Pallas-like, at once, in full maturity. The quantity, variety, and high rank of its fauna shut us up from any other conclusion than that it is only part — and a rich part — of an already established flora and fauna lying undetected at present." His tables show that more than half of the known Silurian species have hitherto been found in only one locality, giving force to the assertion of Prof. Edward Forbes, that a large proportion of all known species of fossils are founded on single specimens. The species thus restricted to a small geographical area also attain only a small vertical range or duration in time. As stated by the "Quarterly Journal of Science" (January, 1869), "The general law of the range of species in space and time may be broadly and roughly stated as follows: long life and great range; short life and restricted range. Now, without at all doubting the fact that the lives of species, like those of individuals, may vary in length to a great extent, we think that naturalists who "count heads" should satisfy themselves whether a species which has spread over three-fourths of the globe, and enjoyed an existence extending through several divisions of the Silurian period, is precisely equivalent, in Natural History value, to a species of the same genus which, with scores of others, was both created and destroyed within the limits of one minor subdivision of the same period, and which never extended beyond an area of a few square miles. To put this question in a concrete form, let us ask whether *Orthoceras annulatum* is of an equivalent value to *O. intermixtum?* — the former a species ranging from the Caradoc to the Ludlow rocks inclusive, and from New York, through Northern Europe and Great Britain, to Bohemia, while the latter occurs in only one subdivision of the Silurian system, and in but one small district in Bohemia."

His conclusions are: 1. "We already have materials from almost all parts of the Silurian scale of rocks to show, with some force, that life began earlier and more abundantly in the valleys of the St. Lawrence and Mississippi than in Europe. 2. It would appear that the Silurian system of rocks is universal in extent, and that its component parts were laid down at a proximate time, and in like manner ceased to be laid down, — statements approved by M. Barrande. 3. It is a very striking fact that the great majority of the Silurian fauna made their first appearance on the same horizon; that is, everywhere on, proximately, the same stage or subdivision of the epoch. 4. Silurian life was discontinued everywhere at the same time, proximately. 5. The upper Silurian fossils, which people the Prague colonies in fauna D. d., except as they come from another area, are not recurrents; are not the posterity of Bohemian molluscs. They are the precursors of an identical and larger coming fauna. Signs are not wanting that they come from a country where the Silurian epoch was more advanced than in Bohemia; and they become of great value by indicating local inequality of progress in the act of deposition during this epoch; suggesting, moreover, that any of the Silurian stages may be in process of formation about the same time with another, in different parts of the world.

DEEP-SEA DREDGINGS.

At the last meeting of the British Association, a letter was read from Prof. Wyville Thomson on recent dredging in 2,435 fathoms.

The remarkable extension of knowledge in this direction had removed the idea which, started by the late Prof. Forbes, had prevailed till very recently, that marine life did not exist at depths beyond 300 fathoms. That was a most remarkable illustration of the necessity for caution in coming to conclusions. If Prof. Forbes could fall into such an error, how careful needed every one to be in coming to conclusions! Some interesting results had been obtained by Prof. Percival Wright off the coast of Spain; and H. M. S. "Lightning" had been sent out to dredge in the sea between the Hebrides and the Faroe Islands; and one result was, to find that there were two distinct sets of temperature and two sets of fauna within 50 miles; that difference of temperature was probably caused by the return of the waters of the Gulf Stream, after being cooled at the Pole. The investigations of the "Lightning" had only been carried to the depth of 650 fathoms, and found no life at that depth. Prof. Thomson had, however, dredged in the Bay of Biscay to the depth of 2,800 fathoms; and the letter gave an interesting account of the casting of the dredge at such depth. Above one and one-half cwt. of ooze was the general result of a cast of the dredge, and the thermometric instruments employed showed the temperature to be about 36.4; and life was distributed over the whole area which had been examined before the specimens were of a dwarfed character, owing, probably, to the low temperature. In the course of the discussion which ensued, Prof. Huxley said he hoped it would not be at once assumed that naturalists had assumed Prof. Forbes' inference as to the depth at which life might be expected to exist. No revolution had taken place in science on account of the recent dredgings. Men of science — and even Prof. Forbes himself — were too well aware of the unsatisfactory nature of the merely negative evidence, of which they were always distrustful.

He had recently had the opportunity of examining a quantity of soundings sent him by the Admiralty, which had been dredged in all parts of the world; and it appeared from these that there was a gigantic band of life encircling the globe at the bottom of the sea. It was, too, extremely interesting to reflect that the sea bottom in which these creatures were found was of the same geological formation as that which was millions of years old; and the forms of life found there also resembled those found in the geological formations, called the cretacean period.

THE AMŒBA.

The following extracts on this singular creature are from the "London Quarterly Review":—

"Perhaps the clearest instance of the uselessness of attempting

25*

to make the possession of a stomach a distinctive feature of animal nature is shown by the history of a group of creatures, of which the well-known and common amœba may be taken as a type. In these, there can be no question of definition; for in no sense whatever can they be said to possess a permanent stomach.

"The amœba has a just claim to the title of animal, for its affinities with the foraminifera are clear; and no one would deny that these creatures, with their exquisitely beautiful shells, are animals. Yet the amœba has no stomach, — possesses, indeed, no organs at all, unless we consider its so-called nucleus as one; and there are closely allied forms in which even this is absent. Conceive of a minute drop of transparent jelly, so small as to be invisible without the help of a microscope, — a drop of jelly sprinkled and studded with a dust of opaque granules, sometimes hiding in its midst a more solid rounded body, or kernel, called the nucleus, and perhaps with the outer rind a little different from the internal mass. Conceive, further, of this amœba as of no constant shape, but, like the Empusa, shifting, as we look upon it, from one form into another. At one moment, it is like a star with straggling, unequal limbs; at another, club-shaped: now it is a rounded square; soon it will be the image of an hour-glass. None of these changes can be referred to currents in the water in which it lives, or to any other forces acting directly upon it from without. It seems to have within it some inner spring, an inborn power of flowing, whereby this part of it or that moves in this or that direction. And not only do its parts thus shift and change in form, but through their changes the whole body moves from place to place. As we begin to watch it, for instance, at the moment when it is in what may be called its rounded phase, a little protuberance may be seen starting out on one side. Speedily the little knob swells, lengthens, flows into a long process. The process thickens, faint streams of granules indicating in which way the currents of the unseen molecules are setting. The substance of the body surges into the process; and as the latter widens and grows thick, the former shrinks and grows small. At last the whole body has flowed into the process; where the body was, there is now nothing, and where the process reached to, the whole body now is. The creature has moved, has flowed from one spot into another. Here, then, we have movement without muscles, locomotion without any special organs of locomotion. We have, also, feeling without nerves or organs of sense; for if a process such as we have described, while flowing out, meet with any obnoxious body, it will shrink back, and stop in its work. And the whole body, terrified by some potent shock, will often gather itself up into a ball. As it moves without muscles, so, also, does it eat without a stomach. Meeting, in its sluggish travels, with some morsel (and diatoms are its frequent food), it pours itself over its meal, and, coalescing at all points around it, thus swallows its food by fluxion. To use a homely illustration, it is much as if a piece of living mobile dough were to creep around an apple, and to knead itself together into a continuous envelope, in order to form an apple-dumpling. Watching the food thus enveloped by the gelatinous substance of the amœba, we see it grow fainter and fainter, as its nutritious constituents become dissolved by the corrosive action of the same transparent but chemically active jelly; and, when all the goodness has been got out of the meal, the body of the eater flows away from the indigestible remains, just in the same way that it flowed around the original morsel.

"We have in this a creature, then, eating without a stomach, moving without muscles and without limbs, feeling without nerves, and, we may add, breathing without lungs, and nutrition without blood. The amœba is a being of no constant outline, of no fixed shape, which changes its form according to its moods and its needs, and turns its outside into its inside whenever it pleases, which is without organs, without tissues, without unlike parts, a mere speck of living matter all alike all over. And yet, in the midst of this simplicity, it enjoys all the fundamental powers, and fulfils all the essential duties, of an animal body, and is, moreover, bound by chains of close-joined links with those complicated forms of animal life which are provided with special mechanisms for the most trifling of their wants.

"The dormant capabilities of this organless being are indirectly and interestingly shown by the shells which, in allied forms, are built up by the agency of similar homogeneous living matter, and which are, in many cases, ' structures of extraordinary complexity and most singular beauty.' Prof. Huxley, in his lectures, most justly says: —

"' That this particle of jelly is capable of combining physical forces in such a manner as to give rise to those exquisite and almost mathematically arranged structures — being itself structureless, and without permanent distinction or separation of parts — is, to my mind, a fact of the profoundest significance.'"

GLYCERINE FOR PRESERVING NATURAL COLORS OF MARINE ANIMALS.

While collecting on the coast of Maine last summer, I made numerous experiments with glycerine, most of which were eminently satisfactory. At the present time, I have a large lot of specimens which have the colors perfectly preserved, and nearly as brilliant as in life. Among these are many kinds of crustacea, such as shrimp and prawns, amphipods and entomostraca; also many species of starfishes, worms, sea-anemones. The starfishes and crustacea are particularly satisfactory. The internal parts are as well preserved as the colors; and in these animals the form is not injured by contraction, as it is apt to be in soft-bodied animals, either by alcohol or glycerine. The only precaution taken was to use very heavy glycerine, and to keep up the strength by transferring the specimens to new as soon as they had given out water enough to weaken it much, repeating the transfer two or three times, according to the size or number of specimens, or until the water was all removed. The old can be used again for the first bath. In many cases, the specimens, especially crustacea, were killed by immersing them for a few minutes in strong alcohol, which aids greatly in the extraction of water, but usually turns the delicate kinds to an opaque, dull white color; but this opacity disappears when they are put into glycerine, and the real colors again appear. Many colors, however, quickly fade or turn red in alcohol, so that such specimens must be put at once into glycerine. Green shades usually turn red almost instantly in alcohol. Specimens of various lepidopterous larvæ were also well preserved in the same manner.

The expense is usually regarded as an objection to the use of glycerine. The best and strongest can be bought at about one dollar per pound; but recently I have been able to obtain a very dense and colorless article at 42 cents per pound, which is entirely satisfactory. As there is no loss by evaporation, the specimens will keep, when once well preserved, if merely covered by it. The expense for small and medium-sized specimens is not much more than for alcohol. — *A. E. Verrill, Yale College.*

CHANGE OF COLOR IN AUTUMNAL FOLIAGE.

Mr. Joseph Wharton, in the "American Journal of Science" for March, 1869, makes the following observations: —

"If chorophyl, the green coloring matter of leaves, should be, like many other greens, a compound color, it must have for one of its elements a vegetable blue, capable of being reddened by acids. If the juices of leaves, kept in a neutral condition by the vital force, or by alkaline matter brought in the sap from the earth, should, when circulation ceases, become acidified by the atmospheric oxygen, those juices would then be capable of reddening the vegetable blue of the chorophyl. If, however, that vegetable blue should be thus reddened, it ought to become blue again when exposed to an alkali; or, in other words, if green leaves should be reddened in the autumn in the manner here suggested, by the unresisted action of the oxidizing atmosphere, they ought to return from red to green if immersed in an alkaline atmosphere."

He exposed upon a staging, under a glass receiver with a capsule containing ammonia, a variety of autumnal red leaves, and had the gratification to perceive that in most cases the green color was restored, — the leaves having a thin and porous cuticle undergoing the change most rapidly and completely, the restored green color remaining from some minutes to hours.

"Frost probably plays no other part in causing the autumnal tints, than merely to arrest the circulation by killing the leaves. When a sharp frost occurs early in the fall, while the pulp of the leaves is still full and plump, the red colors come out brilliantly, because there is plenty of the blue substance to be acted upon by the juices, then also abundant. When, on the other hand, the leaves die slowly and are at the same time slowly dessicated in a late and dry autumn, the pulp becomes so meagre, and the skin so dry and hard, that an abundant production of fine red tints is impossible, and brown, the color of decay, predominates."

DIATOMS OR BRITTLEWORTS.

The *Diatomaceæ*, or *Brittleworts*, are unicellular microscopic plants, so numerous that there is hardly a spot on the face of the earth, from Spitzbergen to Victoria Land, where they may not be found. They abound in the ocean, in still running fresh water, and even on the surface of the bare ground.

They extend in latitude beyond the limits of all other plants, and can endure extremes of temperature, being able to exist in thermal springs, and in the pancake ice in the south polar latitudes. Though much too small to be visible to the naked eye, they occur in such countless myriads as to stain the berg and pancake ice wherever they are washed by the swell of the sea; and when enclosed in the congealing surface of the water, they impart to the brash and the pancake ice a pale ochreous color.

Some species of diatoms are so universal that they are found in every region of the globe; others are local; but the same species does not inhabit both fresh and salt water, though some are found in brackish pools. The ocean teems with them. Though invisible as individuals to the naked eye, the living masses of the pelagic diatoms form colored fringes on larger plants, and cover stones and rocks in cushion-like tufts; they spread over the surface as delicate velvet, in filamental strata on the sand, or mixed with the scum of living or decayed vegetable matter, floating on the surface of the sea; and they exist in immense profusion in the open ocean as free forms. The numbers in which they exist in all latitudes, at all seasons, and at all depths, — extending from an inch to the lowest limit to which the most attenuated ray of light can penetrate, or at which the pressure permits, — are immeasurably in excess of what we have been in the habit of assuming. Temperature has little to do with the distribution of diatoms in the tropics; it decreases with the depth at a tolerably fixed rate, till it becomes stationary. It increases in the polar regions with the depth, and approaches the standard, which is probably universal, near the bed of the ocean.

Diatoms are social plants crowded together in vast multitudes. Dr. Wallich met with an enormous assemblage of a filamental species, from 6 to 20 times as long as it is broad, aggregated in tufted yellow masses, which covered the sea to the depth of some feet, and extended with little interruption throughout 6 degrees of longitude in the Indian Ocean. They were mixed with glistening yellow cylindrical species of such comparatively gigantic size as to be visible to the naked eye.

Other genera constitute the only vegetation in the high latitudes of the Antarctic Ocean. Dr. Hooker observes that, without the universal diffusion of diatoms in the south polar ocean, there would neither be food for the aquatic animals, nor would the water be purified from the carbonic acid which animal respiration and the decomposition of matter produce. These small plants afford an abundant supply of food to the herbivorous mollusca and other inhabitants of the sea, for they have been found in the stomaohs of oysters, whelks, crabs, lobsters, scallops, etc. Even the *Noctilucæ*, those luminous specks that make the wake of a boat shine like silver in a warm summer night, live on the floating pelagic diatoms, and countless myriads are devoured by the enormous shoals of Salpæ, and other social marine animals. — *Mrs. Somerville.*

GROWTH OF CEREALS.

At the last meeting of the British Association, Mr. F. F. Hallett read a paper on "The Law of Development of Cereals." His experience showed him several years ago that corn, and especially wheat, was injured by being planted too closely. He found a wheat plant would increase above the ground in proportion as its roots had room to develop, and that the roots might be hindered by being in contact with the roots of another plant. He continued a series of experiments, planting one kernel of wheat only, and succeeded so well in improving the method of cultivation as to raise wheat whose ears contained 123 grains, or more than 60 on each side. In the course of his investigations, Mr. Hallett made other discoveries with regard to the growth of cereals, which he sums up as follows : —

" 1. Every fully developed plant, whether of wheat, oats, or barley, presents an ear superior in productive power to any of the rest on that plant. 2. Every such plant contains one grain which, upon trial, proves more productive than any other. 3. The best grain in a given plant is found in its best ear. 4. The superior vigor of this grain is transmissible in different degress to its progeny. 5. By repeated careful selection the superiority is accumulated. 6. The improvement, which is first raised gradually, after a long series of years is diminished in amount, and eventually so far arrested that, practically speaking, a limit to improvement in the desired quality is reached. 7. By still continuing to select, the improvement is maintained, and practically a fixed type is the result."

AMERICAN FOSSIL BOTANY.

M. Lesquereux says the American continent is "the only part of the world where questions of general significance concerning palæontological distribution can be studied with some chances of satisfactory conclusions." We quote the following from his report : —

" The few vegetable remains obtained from the tertiary of Tennessee and of Mississippi, and from the cretacean formation of Nebraska and California, have demonstrated facts which science was scarcely prepared to admit : —

" First. That the floras of our ancient formations already had peculiar types, which separated them from each other in the different continents. This is even evident in the vegetation of the coal measures. Therefore, the supposition of a continental union of Europe with America, by Atlantides, or other intermediate lands, is proved to be untenable.

"Second. That the essential types of the old floras, of the cretaceous and tertiary formations, have passed into our present vegetation, or are preserved to our time. The cretacean of America, for example, has already the magnolias, which we find still more abundant in our tertiary. This last formation has furnished a number of species of the genus Magnolia, nearly identical with that now existing in the United States, while the genus is totally absent in the corresponding floras of Europe. More than this, we find in our tertiary the same predominating types marked on both sides of the Rocky Mountains. On the Atlantic slope, leaves of magnolias, of oaks, of elms, of maples and poplars, and not a trace of coniferous trees; while in California and Vancouver's Island the redwoods or Sequoia abound in the cretacean and tertiary, as now they still form the predominant vegetation of the country."

BIOLOGICAL SUMMARY.

Identity of Visual Impressions in the Animal Kingdom. — According to the experiments of M. Bert, as reported to the French Academy by Milne Edwards, performed on the *Daphnia*, a minute crustacean inhabiting fresh water, all animals see the so-called luminous rays of the spectrum for the same range and with the same relative intensity as man does, and none other. If we consider the great difference between the structure of the human eye and that of the single composite unfacetted eye of the *Daphnia*, and the distance which separates these zoölogical types, we are authorized, until the contrary be proved, to assume that the animals between this crustacean and man, and perhaps those below the former, see the same rays and with the same relative intensity.—*Comptes Rendus, Aug. 2, 1869.*

Transfusion of Blood. — The chief causes of the discredit into which this operation has fallen, are the employment of fibrinized blood, inability to measure the quantity used, and the imperfection of the instruments. Fibrinized blood coagulates in the tubes of the apparatus; hence either the transfusion becomes impossible, or there is danger of introducing clots, which may cause death, immediate by obstruction of the pulmonary artery, or delayed if the clots arrive at a more distant part of the circulation. The fibrine is not an essential part of the blood, and may be removed without inconvenience; in fact, the process of removing the fibrine by whipping saturates it with oxygen and frees it from carbonic acid. If too much blood, or too much at a time, be used, the heart is overburdened, and paralysis of the organ or dangerous congestions may ensue. An apparatus for performing this operation with success is described in "Comptes Rendus" for October 4, 1869.

Function of the Marrow of the Bones.—According to M. Neumann ("Comptes Rendus," May 10, 1869), this is an important organ in the formation of the blood, continually developing new red blood-cells by the transformation of colorless cells resembling the corpuscles of the lymph.

M. Goujon has also demonstrated in his prize essay ("Comptes Rendus," June 14, 1869), by experiments on rabbits and chickens, that portions of the marrow inserted among the muscles become united to the surrounding tissues, and, like the periosteum, possess the property of reproducing bony matter. This tissue plays an important part also in the formation of callus.

The Ovarian Egg. — In 1864 M. Balbiani showed that the ovarian egg contains, beside the vesicle of Purkinje, a second vesicle, which also concurs in the formation of the embryo. M. Gerbe, in a prize essay for 1868, has demonstrated that, in the primitive ovule of the *Sacculina,* an animal parasite on marine crustaceans, both these vesicles coexist before any other element is developed in it. In following the evolution to complete development he found that one of the vesicles became gradually surrounded by molecular granulations destined to form a cicatricula analogous to that of the egg of most ovipara, while the other was surrounded by materials for the nourishment of the embryo, or the elements analogous to the yolk. This discovery proves that the vesicle pointed out by Purkinje in birds, in 1825, is really, in the egg of such species as have a cicatricula, the centre of its formation, that is, of the germ. Science thus, by direct observation, ascends even to the sources of life. — *Comptes Rendus, June* 14, 1869.

Inoculability of Tubercle. — The experiments of M. Villemin show conclusively that tuberculosis may be produced in certain animals by the insertion under the skin of tuberculous matter from man or any infected animal; a similar effect follows the introduction beneath the skin of the sputa in this disease; and recently it has been shown that the dried and powdered sputa mixed with food will introduce the tubercle through the intestines, and consequently produce a general tuberculosis. From the fact of inoculation follows that of its specific virulence, and from the latter its contagiousness; inoculable from man to animals, it is doubtless so from man to man. The particular conditions of cohabitation which will render this disease transmissible form an important subject for future investigation. — *Comptes Rendus, June* 14, 1869.

Cholesterine. — According to the researches of Dr. Austin Flint, cholesterine is an excrementitious product, formed in great part from the brain and nerves, absorbed by the blood, separated from it by the liver, entering into the composition of the bile, to which it gives its excrementitious character, poured with the bile into the small intestine, where the act of digestion changes it into stercorine or seroline of Boudet, under which form it is evacuated with the fæces. Its retention in the blood constitutes a grave disease, called by him "cholesteremia," in which this substance acts like a poison, bringing on coma and death, as in uræmic poisoning. It is a disease wholly distinct from jaundice, though the two may coexist. — *Comptes Rendus, June,* 1869.

Poison of Batrachicans. — A tree-frog of New Granada, *Phyllobates melanorhinus?* or the *roja,* of a reddish color, shaded with Naples yellow, and sometimes black underneath, secretes a poison from the dorsal region, of the greatest activity when collected at the time of secretion by the living animal. Under the influence of acute pain the upper portion of the body becomes covered with a white, milky, viscid liquid; this is the poison, in which the natives quickly dip the ends of their arrows. The poison is sufficient to kill animals as large as the jaguar, and also man. Experiments on animals show that, as in curare, the poison acts upon the organs of motion, and not on those of sensation. — *Comptes Rendus, June,* 1869.

Influence of Trades on Cholera. — Extensive statistical researches have shown that among 37,000 workmen in copper, there were only 29 cases of cholera, or one in 1,270; among 28,000 workers on iron and steel, 202 cases, or one in 209; among 7,500 workmen on other metals, 42 cases, or one in 278. — *Comptes Rendus, Sept.* 27, 1869.

Fibrine. — MM. Béchamp and Estor announced to the French Academy, in February, 1869, that numerous experiments had led them to the conclusion that what is called the fibrine of the blood is only a false membrane formed by the microzymas or molecular granulations of the blood, associated by a substance which they secrete with the aid of the albuminoid elements of this fluid. — *Comptes Rendus, Sept.* 20, 1869.

Occasional Cause of Sudden Death. — According to M. Bert, ("Comptes Rendus," Aug. 23, 1869), violent excitation of the pneumogastric nerve, and its laryngeal branches, may cause sudden death, without convulsions; respiration and the general movements of the body are immediately arrested, and the animal dies as if killed by lightning. He thus caused death in mammals and birds, especially in ducks; the latter is an important fact, as the suddenness of the death proves that it is not due to asphyxia, these animals resisting asphyxia from 8 to 15 minutes. The death is doubtless due to the immediate cessation of action, from too great peripheral excitation of the respiratory tract of the medulla, often called the "vital knot" (*nœud vital*). However it be explained, certain cases of sudden death after violent excitation of the larynx (as ammoniacal cauterization, small foreign bodies, etc.), and after certain attacks of so-called *angina pectoris*, may perhaps be thus accounted for.

Origin of Bacteriums. — According to M. Béchamp, these organisms may develop themselves and remain equally well in an acid, alkaline, or neutral menstruum. The normal microzymas of plants and of animals may develop into bacteriums; and many forms of both may exist in the same plant. The inoculation of the bacterium in a plant or animal causes their increased number, not by multiplication, but by so-modifying the medium that the normal microzymas more readily develop themselves into bacteriums. Many of the phenomena of spontaneous generation are explained by these molecular granulations. Their natural and universal presence has been alluded to in "Annual of Scientific Discovery" for 1869, pp. 304–306, and for 1868, p. 269.

Singing Mice. — It is stated that the singing or whistling in these rodents is always accompanied by the presence of a parasite, *Cysticercus fasciolaris*, in the liver, and the sounds may be the re-

26

sult of spasmodic breathing caused by its presence. The marmot, another rodent, has been known to produce similar musical sounds.

Organ of Hearing in Molluscs. — In a communication to the French Academy, M. Lacaze Duthiers has shown that the nerve to the otolithic sac of molluscs is not derived from the pedal ganglion, but from the supra-œsophageal or brain ganglion, from which all the organs of sense in this branch of the animal kingdom are derived.

Section of Pneumo-gastric nerves vs. *Respiration.* — It has been generally admitted by physiologists that, after section of this nerve, the amount of carbonic acid exhaled is unaffected. Drs. Voit and Raber, of Munich, from recent experiments, find that this is true only for a few hours after the section ; afterward, when the tissue of the lungs has begun to undergo a change, the quantity of carbonic acid diminishes rapidly, while that of oxygen is increased.

Composition of the Milk of Different Animals. — 1,000 parts contain : —

	Water.	Butter.	Cheesey Matter.	Sugar.	Mineral Matter.
Woman	889.08	26.66	39.30	43.68	1.30
Cow	864.20	31.30	48.80	47.70	6.00
Goat	844.90	66.87	35.14	36.91	6.18
Ewe	832.32	51.37	69.78	39.43	7.16
Mare	904.30	24.36	33.35	32.76	5.23
Ass	890.12	18.53	35.65	50.46	5.24
Sow	818.00	60.00	53.00	60.70	8.30

Proportions of solids and water in different kinds of milk : —

	Woman.	Cow.	Goat.	Ewe.	Mare.	Ass.	Sow.
Water	889.08	864.20	844.90	832.32	904.30	890.12	818.00
Solids	110.92	135.80	155.10	167.68	95.70	109.88	182.00
	1,000.00	1,000.00	1,000.00	1,000.00	1,000.00	1,000.00	1,000.00

Pig's milk is extremely rich, containing, as it does, nearly 50 per cent. more nutritive matter than is found in that of the cow. It is not unlikely that in certain forms of disease where a milk diet is prescribed the use of so concentrated a liquid food might prove serviceable. — *Chemical News.*

Simple Method of Ascertaining Death. — Dr. Carriere, of St. Jean du Gard, in reply to an offer of a premium of twenty thousand francs for a practical method of determining death, furnished the following, which he says he has practised for forty years :   Place the hand, with the fingers closely pressed one against the other, close to a lighted lamp or candle ; if alive, the tissues will be observed to be of a transparent, rosy hue, and the capillary circulation in full play ; if, on the contrary, the hand of a dead person be placed in the same relation to light, none of the phenomena are observed — we see a hand as of marble, without circulation, without life. — *Jour. de Med. et de Chirurg.*

Pepsin. — The strongest pepsin is obtained from young healthy pigs, which are kept hungry and then excited by savory food; while the influence of it is strong upon them, and the secretions are pouring out in expectation of the meal, the animals are pithed.

Pepsin, like diastase, is rendered inert by a temperature of from 120 to 130° F.; and, therefore, very hot drinks are hurtful. — *Chemical News.*

Crime vs. *Cranial Capacity.* — Dr. Wilson, at the last meeting of the British Association, read a paper "On the Moral Imbecility of Habitual Criminals, Exemplified by Cranial Measurements." His theory was that habitual criminals did not possess such an amount of intellect as to enable them to discriminate between right and wrong, and that the majority of them were devoid of moral sense. The habitual criminal was of a low type of intellectual development, and some of them were unable to surmount the rudimentary difficulties of education. The measurements submitted by Dr. Wilson were from 464 separate measurements, and all showed a cranial deficiency, especially in the anterior lobes of the brain. He recommended the adoption of a system of treatment of criminals similar to that in practice in Ireland, — a system of punishment more reformatory than punitive.

Pulsations of Man rendered Audible and Visible. — At the 1869 meeting of the "American Association for the Advancement of Science," Dr. J. B. Upham, after explaining the improvements in the diagnosis of aneurisms which the case of malformation in Dr. Groux had suggested, proceeded, with the aid of the telegraph and magnesium light, to render audible and visible at Salem the pulsations of patients in the City Hospital in Boston, — Mr. Farmer having charge of the telegraph instruments in the lecture-room, Mr. Stearns at the City Hospital, and the internes of the hospital taking the medical direction. The Franklin Telegraph Company placed their entire line between Salem and New York at the disposal of the Association, and every pulse-click of the magnet was heard simultaneously at every station on the entire line. A full report of these interesting and novel experiments will be published in the "Proceedings" of the Association.

The Natives of Vancouver's Island. — The natives are called Flat Heads, of which there are 4 varieties; the elongated head from before backward, the conical head, the square head, and the elongated head from side to side. These artificial heads are produced by pressure on the forehead, and bandaging on the sides (the elongated head from side to side excepted), until the child is a year old. It does not affect the intellect. It is mere displacement of brain.

The native population of Vancouver's Island is estimated by Dr. King at 18,000, but, as in all cases of estimates of the uncivilized races, wandering as they do, this estimate cannot be relied upon. By far the most numerous and powerful tribes live on the west coast or on the outward seaboard of the island, and the white man is respected by them. The natives generally are in a very degraded state; occasionally industrious, trustworthy individuals are to be met with, but, as a body, continuous labor cannot be depended on. They live entirely on fish, and on a small esculent plant, called camass, which they collect and store up for winter, as we do potatoes, and they cook them, as we do, by boiling and baking. The camass digging is a great season of *réunion* for the women of the various tribes, and answers to our haymaking or harvest home.

Westerly Drifting of the Nomades from the 5th to the 19th Century. — According to Mr. H. H. Howarth, the Circassians of modern writers are identified with the White Khazars of the Byzantine and Arabian writers, from the evidence of tradition, language, and historical notices, and also with the White Huns of Priscus. This fills the area north of the Caspian and the Oral with a race of Ugrian affinities, and very high culture; remarkable, too, for being the last nation added to the list of Jewish proselytes. The Turks, in the 8th century, contrary to the opinion of Dr. Latham and others, were confined to the countries east of the Altai Mountains; the previous invaders of Europe, Avares, Huns, etc., having all belonged to the great Ugrian family of races.

Megalithic Monuments. — Mr. A. L. Lewis read a paper on this subject before the British Association. He said there exists a practically unbroken chain of megalithic (Druidic) monuments extending from India to Great Britain. Who were their builders? Circumstances — namely, such an identity of plan as could not be accidental, extending through an unbroken chain of communication, and the existence of common practices and superstitions, and other traces of affinity throughout that chain — lead to the conclusion that there must at least have been a great common influence at work throughout this area, though possibly not an absolute community of race. Judging from the probable social condition of the builders of these monuments, the localities in which they are principally found, the remains found with them, and other circumstances, they were probably constructed under Celtic influences, at least in Europe and Africa. The consideration of a number of facts induces the belief that the single upright stones were used as memorial pillars, the circles and alignments primarily as places of sacrifice, and the dolmens or table stones, of which there are two well-marked varieties, as places of sepulture on the one hand, and places of sacrifice or memorial on the other hand.

Fossil Asiatic Elephant. — In the "Proceedings of the Geological Society" (Oct., 1868), Dr. Adams announces the discovery of the Asiatic elephant in a fossil state, from the examination of a tooth found in Japan, 40 miles from the sea, and at the base of a surface coal bed. Mr. Busk, from the examination of a plaster cast of the specimen, considers it the antepenultimate upper left molar of what, if found in the recent condition, he should unhesitatingly refer to *Elephas Indicus.* The differences, which are unimportant, are the considerable curvature, greater size, and somewhat greater proportionate width, and greater thickness of the plates.

Development in Vertebrates. — In a recently published work, Dr. Wilhelm His, of Basel, specially insists on the presence of two germinal elements, — the principal or primary, and the subordinate or secondary germ. From the first are developed the most essential tissues, as the nervous, muscular, and epithelial; from the second the skeletal and nutrient structures, as cartilage, bone, connective tissues, and the vascular system. The development of these two portions may be distinguished in the early embryo, but afterwards they grow into each other, producing a complex interlacement of parts. The development of the secondary germ is very much affected by mechanical conditions. The perivascular lymph-spaces of the brain, discovered by him, are shown to arise from the intrusion of blood-vessels formed by the secondary germ into spaces excavated in the primary germ.

The Glass-rope Sponge. — Prof. Loven is doubtless right in supposing, from the study of a sponge which he called *Hyalonema boreale* (but which does not belong in this genus), that the long tuft of glassy fibres constituting the so-called axis is the pedicle by which it is fixed in the sea-bottom, and that the sponge grows on the top of this. This is confirmed by Profs. Wright and Thompson, and Dr. Carpenter. Dr. Wright thinks Max Schultze correct as to the parasitic nature of the coral which sometimes encrusts the axis of Hyalonema, which is a true sponge. Dr. Gray, however, retains his opinion that the axis is the work of the coral, and that the sponge on the end of it is parasitic. — *Quart. Journal of Science*, Jan., 1869.

Singular Mode of Reproduction in a Fish. — The species observed was from China. When the season for laying the eggs arrives, the male projects from the mouth little globules of air, which rise to the surface, but do not burst, probably consolidated by mucus as they come out. In this way he forms upon the water a roof of froth, often a centimetre thick; this is the receptacle for the eggs, in which the hatching is completed. Then the sexes come together, the male forming a complete ring in which the female is pressed,— an approach to the sexual congress of the higher animals. The eggs are fecundated as they leave the female, and the male collects the scattered masses and arranges them in proper thickness under the roof of foam; he watches them, taking no food, from 62 to 65 hours, when the young appear; he keeps these within the protecting roof until they can provide for themselves, bringing back any wanderers in his mouth. — *Comptes Rendus, Aug.* 16, 1869.

Extinct Reptiles. — From the investigations of Mr. E. D. Cope ("Trans. of Amer. Phil. Society," Aug., 1869), it is stated, 1. That the *Dinosauria* present a graduated series of approximations to the birds, and possess some peculiarities in common with that class, standing between it and the *Crocodilia*; 2. That serpents exist in the eocene formations of this country; 3. That the *Chelydra* type was greatly developed during the American cretaceous, and that all the supposed marine turtles described from it are really of the first-named group; and, 4. That the reptiles of the American triassic are of the *Belodon* type.

Reproduction by Larval Batrachians. — According to M. Jullien, "Comptes Rendus," April 19, 1869, the *Lissotriton punctatus* may reproduce its species while in the tadpole state. He found in the

26 *

month of April, near Paris, several specimens, of both sexes, in which the generative apparatus was perfectly developed, while the head, branchiæ, limbs, tail, and all the rest of the body showed the development only of the tadpole state.

Stratification of Guano. — Guano has been considered as a simple accumulation of the excrements of birds; but M. Habel, as stated in an abstract of a seven years' journey in tropical America, published in the "Comptes Rendus," for July 26, 1869, found this substance at the Chincha Islands regularly stratified, like all the sedimentary rocks, with layers of different colors, inclination, and extent. Some layers, for instance, in a part of one of the islands he found with an inclination of 5 degrees, and in another part of the same island of 15 degrees. In one part of the southern island he saw layers running from N. to S., with an inclination of 4 degrees, covered by others from S.W. to N.E., with an inclination of 20 degrees. It is very evident that there have been two epochs in the formation of guano; the lower, older, and more extensive mass is stratified, while the upper, more recent, and thinner, is without stratification. Below the guano, there are layers of sand more or less mingled with guano; and in some places it is easy to see that the lower layers contain much less guano than the upper. He found bones of birds, not only in the different layers of guano, but in the underlying sand and sandstone. This would seem to indicate that geological causes were concerned in the deposition or subsequent condition of guano.

Fishes with External Gills. — M. Steindachner, of Vienna, has described a new species of *Polypterus* from Senegal, *P. Lapradei*, which, as well as *P. Sengealus*, has external branchiæ in the young. In the new species they existed in individuals about 19 inches long, as a long flattened band, fringed on the edge, on each side, behind the operculum, and extending beyond the posterior border of the pectoral fin, very like the external branchiæ of the batrachian axolotl, but single instead of triple. In the other species, this transition organ disappears earlier, when the fish is about 4 inches long. It would be interesting to know if the species of the Nile has a similar apparatus when young. The sharks, rays, and African *Protopterus anguilliformis* are not, therefore, the only fishes provided with external branchiæ. Prof. Hyrtl has shown that these organs in the above new ganoid fish perform the function of respiration. — *Comptes Rendus, Oct.* 18, 1869.

Vitality of the Sponge. — According to the experiments of M. Vaillant on the *Tethya lyncurium* (Lam.), a sponge common on the coast of Brittany, the cortical substance, when isolated, will reproduce the medullary substance, and *vice versa*. The vitality of the cortical substance is, however, greater than that of the medullary; it can reproduce the prolongations by which the sponge is attached, and serves to protect the softer interior. Different individuals of this species may be united by grafting, after a sufficient time; but hitherto this union has not been effected with individuals of another genus. — *Comptes Rendus, January*, 1869.

Tusks of the Mammoth. — According to Mr. Woodward, all the tusks of *Elephas primigenius* have, in old individuals, a tendency to curve inward at their extremities.

Bottom of the Sea. — The precise nature of the mud which is formed at the bottom of the sea has been only recently determined. It consists largely of organic matter, more or less decomposed, interspersed with minute round bodies, about sixteen one-hundredths of an inch in diameter. These bodies have been called coccospheres and coccolites, and are so set in the mud as to resemble mosaic work. Some of these look, under the microscope, like thick watch-glasses. Immense numbers of minute shells are also found. The mud is excessively sticky, being rendered so by minute pellets of a jelly-like consistence. These pellets are dotted all over their surfaces, and are found to contain great numbers of granules, from one four-thousandth to one twenty-thousandth of an inch in diameter, which are undoubtedly organic in their character, forming one of the representatives of the common ground between plants and animals, about which there has been so much dispute among naturalists.

Preserving Insects. — Dr. S. P. Knox, of Brownsville, Pa., writes to the "American Naturalist," that, after killing his insect with chloroform, he paints it with a solution of carbolic acid in alcohol — 4 grains to the ounce, — and then dries it in the sun. It keeps fresh and beautiful. In stuffing animals, he uses cotton soaked in the same solution. He does not even think it necessary to skin them, as formerly, but simply removes the contents of the thorax and abdomen.

Velocity of Insects' Wings during Flight. — According to E. J. Marey, in "Comptes Rendus," the numbers per second are as follows: in common fly, 330; drone, 240; bee, 190; wasp, 110; hawk-moth, 72; dragon-fly, 28; cabbage butterfly, 9. He obtains these figures by a very simple and ingenious method, which he fully describes.

Primordial Flora. — The discovery of eozoön in the Laurentian rocks of Canada was of great interest. One of the most important discoveries recently made in palæontological science is analogous with it. It is the detection of what appears to be the remains of a terrestrial flora in certain Swedish rocks of lower Cambrian age, — the supposed equivalents of our Longmynd rocks. A peculiar interest attaches to this discovery, inasmuch as it carries back the appearance of terrestrial vegetation upon the earth's surface through a vast interval of time, no land plants having previously been known older than the upper Ludlow beds. The Swedish fossils now discovered appear to be the stems and long parallel-veined leaves of monocotyledonous plants, somewhat allied to the grasses and rushes of the present day. These plants apparently grew on the margin of shallow waters, and were buried in sand and silt. Although it is probable that several species, and even genera, may occur in the sand-stone blocks which have been examined, they are provisionally included in a single species, to which the name of *Eophyton Linnæaum* has been given. Eophyton, therefore, stands by the side of eozoön, — the one being, in the present state of our knowledge, the earliest land plant, as the other is the earliest animal organism. — *Quart. Journ. of Science,* *Jan.,* 1869.

Fertilization of Flowers by Insects. — According to Mr. T. H. Farrer ("Annals of Natural History," October, 1868), the parts of the flower of the scarlet-runner are so arranged that a bee, alighting on it in search of honey, of necessity shakes any pollen off his proboscis on to the stigma; while, at the same time, his proboscis, as he withdraws it, is covered with the pollen of this flower, and is thus prepared to fertilize another. In Lobelia, the parts are so arranged that the pollen is ejected, in small quantities at a time, on the exact spot of the back of the visiting bee on which it should be placed to be carried to the stigma of another flower, — the stigma being so arranged that, at the next flower visted by the bee, it sweeps off the previously acquired pollen.

Evaporation by Plants. — In a memoir presented to the French Academy by M. Deherain, experiments are given with the view of proving that the evaporation of water by the leaves of plants takes place under conditions entirely different from those which regulate the evaporation of an inert body, as it occurs in a saturated atmosphere; that it is especially effected by light; and that the luminous rays efficacious in causing the decomposition of carbonic acid by the leaves are also those which favor evaporation. The yellow and red rays, which have little action on photographic paper, act with most intensity in causing the reduction of carbonic acid, while the blue and green rays decompose the chloride of silver, and have no action on the leaves. These experiments confirm the old observation of Guettard, that the hard and smooth upper part of the leaves evaporates the most water; Boussingault has shown that the greatest amount of carbonic acid is decomposed by the same portion. It is interesting to observe these intimate relations between the two capital functions of leaves, the decomposition of carbonic acid and evaporation.— *Comptes Rendus, Aug.* 9, 1869.

Organisms in Hot Springs. — Mr. A. M. Edwards has recently drawn attention to the occurrence of diatomaceæ, with the hairs of insects, in some fine sandy deposit obtained from a geyser. Dr. L. Lindsay enumerates 7 genera of confervæ and diatomaceæ from the geysers of Iceland, and observes that the abundance of diatoms in the thermal waters of Europe warrants the expectation of large additions to the Icelandic flora from this source. Dr. Cohn has described oscillatoriæ from hot springs containing sulphates, and ascribes the elimination of sulphuretted hydrogen to the action of these organisms. Mr. Edwards suggests the importance of an examination of the hot sulphureous springs of California for these organisms and for diatoms; it would be very interesting to ascertain by comparison of specimens from sulphureous and neighboring fresh-water springs what modifying effect the thermal conditions have had on the form of the various species; in this way we may hope to arrive at a knowledge of the exact relations of living forms to the conditions of their existence. — *Quart. Journ. of Science.*

Reproduction of Diatoms. — In the "Quarterly Journal of

Microscopical Science" (for Oct. 1868), Count Castracane express-
es the belief that these organisms reproduce by means of germs.
He describes what he considered as zoöspores, having cilia and
containing diatoms. The young germs do not present the brown
endochrome, but are of a bluish-green color.

Diatoms. — Mr. H. L. Smith has given a further proof of the
vegetable nature of diatoms by the application of the spectroscope. The results of more than 50 comparisons of spectra prove
the absolute identity of *chlorophyl* on the green endochrome of
plants with *diatomin,* or the olive yellow endochrome of the
diatomaceæ. — *Amer. Journ. of Science, July,* 1869.

Reproductive organs of Lichens. — According to recent investigations of Famitzin and Boranetsky, not only algæ and fungi, but
also lichens, are provided with zoöspores. As these bodies have
been found in very different genera of lichens, taken at random,
it is probable that they exist in all lichens furnished with chloro-
phyll. The identity of free gonidia with unicellular algæ they
consider as demonstrated; and many described genera of the latter are in reality only the gonidia of lichens in a state of development when separated from the thalli which produced them.

ASTRONOMY AND METEOROLOGY.

THE OBSERVATIONS OF THE MATTOON EXPEDITION ON THE GREAT ECLIPSE OF 1869. COMMUNICATED FROM THE DUDLEY OBSERVATORY, AT ALBANY.

THE night preceding the day of the eclipse was one of unusual anxiety to the observers, from the fact that about 6 o'clock it began to rain, and continued almost without intermission until 11 P.M. In order to learn the worst, we went to the telegraph offices and asked for weather reports from west and east. At nearly all the stations from which reports had been received, extending from Omaha to Cincinnati, it was rainy or cloudy. These reports led us to expect a storm extending over a large area of territory. And it was presumed that it would be a day or two in passing over. But fortunately our prognostics were in error, for at 11 o'clock P.M. the rain ceased, and stars began to make their appearance. The morning of the 7th was perfectly clear, with not a cloud to be seen, and it so continued during the whole day and subsequent night. It was one of those rare days but seldom seen in this climate; the atmospheric disturbance being at a minimum.

One hour before the beginning of the eclipse, observations were made on the solar spots, and their position and magnitude mapped on a diagram prepared for the purpose. As the time drew near for the first contact of the moon's limb, each observer examined carefully the region where the moon was expected, to see whether it would be visible before contact with the solar disc. The closest scrutiny of five observers failed to discover it.

At 10 seconds before the true contact of the limbs, a lunar mountain, distant 8 or 10 degrees north of the contact-point, plunged into the solar disc, and was recorded on the chronograph. The true contact of the limbs was well observed by all, and at nearly the same instant. The moon's limb, instead of appearing round, as it should, was nearly flat and a little notched, showing a mountainous region. As the eclipse advanced, observations were made by means of the micrometer and chronograph for measuring the relative position of the two bodies. When the sun was about one half eclipsed, a red band of light was seen surrounding the limb of the moon over the solar disc. Later, during the progress of the phenomenon, tails of light were seen projecting out tangent to the moon's limb, and extending 15 or 20 degrees along the edge.

As the crescent of solar light grew less and less, every eye was intently watching for an unusual appearance. Nearly a minute

310

before totality, we saw with wonder a red flame suddenly shoot out from the upper edge of the moon, and shortly after the remarkable and beautiful phenomenon of Bailly's beads. The slender crescent of light was suddenly broken up into numerous globules, resembling drops of water flowing together, or a string of beads. One observer compared it to a chain of sausages of unequal lengths.

This peculiar breaking up of the solar crescent was noticed by Bailly in 1836. But during subsequent eclipses it has not generally been seen. This fact has led some of the ablest astronomers to doubt its reality, believing it to be an optical illusion.

At Mattoon, the appearance was distinctly seen by all the observers, and its duration recorded on the chronograph by Mr. Swift and myself. That the phenomenon is real we have no doubt. It is well known that the limb of the moon is exceedingly rough and jagged, with mountains projecting to a great height. Now it is reasonable to suppose that when this mountainous limb of the moon cuts off the slender crescent of light it must be more or less broken up into sections, depending on the irregularities of the surface and the position of the observer. We are more strengthened in this opinion, since previous to the first contact Mr. Swift saw 5 mountain peaks on the moon, and he reported the beads the most conspicuous in the region towards this part of the lunar disc.

The duration of Bailly's beads was accurately recorded on the chronograph by Mr. Swift and myself, and found to be 5½ seconds. This is the first exact record ever made of the duration of the phenomenon.

As the light grew less and less, suddenly the sun seemed to pass under the black disc of the moon, producing a feeling of chilliness. Now was seen in all its splendor the large red protuberance sitting on the edge of the moon, and appearing very much like a great ship under full sail. Farther to the left was another, nearly as large, with two bent rays, somewhat resembling the antlers of a deer. Five others, not quite as large, were seen on different parts of the disc, all of a deep-red color.

After looking with astonishment for a few seconds, we proceeded to measure with the micrometer the height and position of the largest flame. But just at the critical moment, fortunately or unfortunately, one of the hand-rods for moving the telescope came off, and it was necessary to remove the eye from the tube to fix it. On looking up one of the grandest spectacles met the eye of which it is possible to conceive. Surrounding the dark body of the moon was a crown of light with rays shooting out in 5 great sheaths, to a distance equal to the sun's diameter, or nearly a million of miles. For a time everything else was forgotten, and we gazed for 8 or 10 seconds with astonishment, akin to awe, at this magnificent spectacle. No painting can represent it, and no pen can describe it. It is one of those sights which must be seen to be appreciated. But we soon realized that precious moments were slipping away. The telescope was again brought in position, and the height of the large protuberance measured, and found to be 0 2' 45", or more than 70,000 miles, 150,000 at the base.

While still gazing, a ray of light suddenly flashed out, and the total eclipse of Aug. 7th was over.

The duration of totality, according to the chronograph records, was 2 minutes and 42 seconds. The large protuberance, however, remained visible for 5 minutes and 5 seconds after the sun had appeared, or, as Mr. Swift reports, until it was apparently lifted up by the advancing crescent of solar light.

Previous to the beginning of the eclipse, we set up a number of light wooden rods, indicating the direction of stars and planets. Prof. Twining and Mr. Marshall succeeded in seeing Saturn 8 minutes before, and Venus 4 minutes before, totality. During the totality, Mercury, Venus, Mars, Saturn, and a number of bright stars, were visible to the naked eye.

Observations made by Prof. Smith, with a thermometer exposed to the direct rays of the sun, showed a variation of 42 degrees during the progress of the eclipse.

The observations of Mr. House, with a thermometer placed in the shade, showed a variation of 13 degrees.

Prof. David Murray, at my request, prepared the paper on the physical phenomena, which is herewith appended.

The peculiar phenomena which have attracted so much attention in solar eclipses are only visible during the brief period of totality. This, in the present case, only extended through 2 minutes and 43 seconds. The difficulty of observing them lies in this exceeding brevity, and in the fact that, no matter how much the observer may have studied the experiences of others, the phenomena comes upon him as a complete surprise. The moment the last ray of light disappears with the extinguishment of Bailly's Beads, there bursts upon him a vision so marvellously beautiful, so startling by its novelty, that his self-possession and self-control desert him, and leave him, for an instant, a helpless gazer. As soon as he can collect his thoughts, and tries to marshal them into order, he will find especially two phenomena of notable interest.

In immediate contact with the solar disc, it appears as a clear, silvery light, as bright as the brightest part of an aurora, and somewhat resembling it in consistency. Farther out, it appears streaked with pencils radiating in the direction of the centre. These rays are more especially noticeable at 5 points of the circumference, 2 of them pointing upwards and outwards, and 3 having a general downward direction. These prongs could be traced through a distance even exceeding the diameter of the sun, and near one of them was visible a curved mass of light, in shape resembling the petal of a flower. On the upper edge of the disc was plainly seen an arch of light, parallel with the edge, and within the boundary of the corona.

It should be stated that the phenomenon of the corona is best observed with the naked eye, and cannot be included within the field of any ordinary telescope. Our party are indebted to the observations of Mr. Bostwick, of Mattoon, and Gen. Keifer, of Springfield, Ohio, for the best configuration of the corona.

The commonly received explanation of the corona has attributed it to an atmosphere surrounding the sun, which was illuminated by the light of the sun in the same way that our atmosphere is illuminated in twilight. This will undoubtedly explain the luminosity found nearest the disc; but it can hardly be received as satisfactory in regard to the luminous prongs which extend out to such a great distance. It must be remembered that these prongs projected a distance greater than the whole diameter of the sun, and must have reached an altitude, if they belonged to the sun, of at least a million of miles. This is, of course, beyond all possibility; and the idea of the whole phenomena being of a solar-atmospheric origin is untenable. Equally untenable must be the idea that it is a solar aurora, because an aurora supposes an atmospheric medium in which it exhibits itself.

The impression which was firmly made upon my mind by witnessing it was that, in some way, the interstriated part, at least, was formed in the earth's atmosphere.

The second phenomenon attracting attention was that of the sudden appearance of a number of protuberances of various shape and magnitude, which projected beyond the black disc of the moon, and were of a bright rosy-red color. We saw 6 or 8 in all. It must be remembered that these were of immense size. The largest was not less than 70,000 miles in altitude. They seemed to have a cloudy consistency; and the form of some of them forbade the idea that they could have been either solid or liquid. These protuberances are seen in all total eclipses; but in no two are they in the same place, or of the same form. They are thus shown to be of a changeable and transitory character. This was really all that could certainly be known about them, until the application of the spectroscope to celestial bodies gave us a new road to a knowledge of them. By means of this, we are able to distinguish a solid body from a gaseous, a self-luminous from a reflective body; and, even more, to determine with certainty the very elements composing the incandescent body. This mode of investigation, used first in the total eclipse of 1868, and still more in that of the recent eclipse, has revealed to us that the red protuberances are mainly a mass of incandescent hydrogen gas. The thought is overpowering. Here are vast accumulations of blazing matter, reaching to a height of 50,000 to 100,000 miles. What convulsions in the matter of the surface of our sun does this view of it reveal!

That the spots which are seen on the surface of the sun will finally be proved to be identical with the protuberances, I venture to predict.

A few moments before totality, and during that period, nearly all the telescopic observers at our station noticed faint whitish bodies floating past their glasses. Prof. Hough saw 3; Mr. Swift 4 or 5; Mr. Simons 5 or 6; Mr. House as many; and I saw 4, at least. At the time, they made no impression on my mind. I thought of thistle-down, or some other winged seed. Others thought of midges which had been awaked by the darkness; others of swallows. But when we came to compare our observa-

27

tions and our conjectures, we found, to our surprise, that all these floating bodies had one direction, namely, from the north-west downward toward the south-east; and it seemed, therefore, impossible to explain them on any of the hypotheses which had been started.

The idea that they were meteoric is, perhaps, more plausible; and it is strengthened by the fact that the time nearly corresponded to the August period of meteoric showers.

No one who has not seen the phenomena of a total eclipse can appreciate fully the grandeur of the occasion. As the light, ray by ray, is cut off, a strange and ghastly darkness comes down upon us; not like the darkness of night, but a violet-colored darkness, which makes the faces of our neighbors turn ashy pale, and gives to the landscape the hues which it takes in a stereoscopic picture. I cannot better describe the appearances which strike an intelligent eye-observer than in the words of President Hill, who, declining the use of all instruments, devoted himself to noting the external phenomena. He reports the results of his observations as follows: —

"During the total eclipse this afternoon, I was in the open field, near a small barn, about 1,000 feet west, and 550 feet south, of your station. According to your request, I herewith give you a memorandum of what I noticed. This memorandum has been twice read to a party of five gentlemen who were with me; and they agree, after full discussion, in every statement.

"A cow grazing in the field became uneasy at five o'clock, and started for home at 5h. and 6m. Soon after a hen gathered her brood under her wings. Swallows were skimming the ground. About two minutes before the total obscuration about 70 cocks and hens went to roost in the barn. A flock of birds flew southward in a hurried and confused manner after the darkness became total. Soon after the reappearance of the sun the chickens came from under the hen, then the fowls came down from their roosts, and the cocks, which had crowed occasionally all the afternoon, took it up by general consent and crowed vigorously.

"No other animals were near us. No plants sensitive to light were in the field, and it was not until after the eclipse was over that I discovered Cassia in an adjoining field. Some of us thought there was a slight deposit of dew upon the grass, but others failed to perceive it.

"Venus appeared a minute or two before the total obscuration, and remained visible for several minutes after the reappearance of the sun. At the instant of total obscuration, Mercury, Arcturus and Vega appeared. Even Arcturus was of a silvery whiteness. Arcturus remained visible some seconds after the total phase had passed. We looked sharply for Capella, Procyon, Castor and Pollux, Regulus, and Altair, and also looked less carefully for Saturn, Antares, Spica, and Mars, but we had nothing but our general recollection of the stars to guide us as to the direction in which to look, and we saw nothing either with the naked eye or our opera-glasses, beyond the two planets and two stars already mentioned. At the instant of total obscuration one or two of us had a feeling that we were seeing half-a-dozen stars bursting into sight at once, but we could only find the two.

"The approach of the deep violet shadow in the air from the W.N.W., a little to the right of the sun, and its receding in the opposite quarter, was much slower and more majestic and beautiful than we had been led to expect. The gradual diminution of light during the eclipse had revealed the presence of faint cirro-stratus clouds in the horizon of what appeared, both before and after the eclipse, a cloudless sky. The transition from penumbra to umbra, although rapid, did not seem absolutely instantaneous. It was a sweeping upward and eastward of the dense violet shadow. This shadow then stretched from the W.N.W. to the E.S.Eastern horizon, while in the transverse direction it did not reach the horizon by 6 or 8 degrees, and the low arch beneath was full of a deep orange twilight. No difference was observed between the height of these arches. The transition from the orange-yellow of the northern and southern horizon to the dusky violet of the zenith during the total phase was at an altitude of 12 or 15 degrees, and then the violet seemed darker than in the zenith; as though two broad dark arches ran one on each side the zenith from west north-west to east south-east.

"The corona appeared to us a white ring of 4 or 5 min. breadth, with white rings 30 to 35 min. in length, one of which on the right hand upper limb was curved. No change was observed in the corona during the total phase, except that one of us thought there was a tremulous flashing at the instant before the reappearance of the sun.

"A crimson cloud on the lower limb was particularly brilliant. One on the left limb was brilliant at the beginning, and one on the right limb at the end of the total phase."

OBSERVATIONS ON THE ECLIPSE. BY PROF. C. A. YOUNG.

Professor C. A. Young, of Dartmouth College, gave papers on his new method of observing contacts by the spectroscope, and also on the spectrum of the solar prominences and corona, etc. The spectroscope furnishes the means of a very accurate observation of the instant of first contact in the following manner: Let an image of the sun, about two inches in diameter, be thrown upon the slit. Bring to the centre of the slit, and perpendicular to it, the point of the limb where the contact is to take place. The spectrum will then be half bright and half dusky, divided by a longitudinal line of demarcation; most of the dark lines will extend clear across both portions of the spectrum alike, but the spectrum of the chromosphere will be seen in the C line as a *needle of scarlet light* extending a little way into the dusky spectrum from the extremity of the dark line in the brilliant portion. As the moon approaches, this red needle will be gradually shortened, and will finally disappear at the instant of contact, the C line then becoming exactly like its neighbors. The same method of observation of course might be used with the F line, or any other line of the chromosphere spectrum, but the C line is by far the easiest to observe. At Burlington, Iowa, the time of contact determined in this manner was about 5 seconds earlier than that of any of the other observations, but agreed within one-third of a second with that obtained from measurements of the photographs.

Special attention was paid to the question whether the moon has any atmosphere; the results were wholly negative, under circumstances where a refraction of one quarter of a second would have been clearly perceptible.

During the totality the following 9 bright lines were seen in the spectrum of the prominences, — the numbers refer to the scale of Kirchoff, — namely: (1) C, (2) 1017.5, (3) 1250 plus or minus 20, (4) 1,350 plus or minus 20, (5) 1474, (6) F, (7) 2602 plus or minus 2, (8) 2796, and (9) h. Of these all but the 2d, 3d, 4th, 5th, and 7th, are the well-known hydrogen lines; the 2d is the well-known but mysterious line above D.

The line 1474 is just below E, and coincides *exactly* with a small line marked as *iron* on Kirchoff's and Angström's maps. It had been previously discovered by Professor Young, in July. It turns out also to coincide very closely if it is not (as is much more probable) absolutely identical with a line recently discovered by Professor Winlock, of Cambridge, in the spectrum of the aurora borealis. (It is hardly conceivable that *iron* really exists as vapor in the aurora borealis. Can this line indicate some new gaseous element which, occluded in ordinary iron, causes this line to appear in the spectrum of the spark between iron electrodes, and yet exists independently in our higher atmosphere?) The two faint lines Nos. 3 and 4 also coincide closely with two other lines reported by him.

This line, 1474, and probably the two fainter ones, 2 and 3, belong to the spectrum of the *corona*, not that of the prominences.

The corona showed besides these bright lines a faint, continuous spectrum without any dark lines. The light of this was polarized strongly in a plane passing through the sun, but, as suggested by Professor Pickering, this polarization may arise from the refraction of light through the five prisms that produced the dispersion of the colors.

Professor Young's papers were remarked upon by Professor Peirce and by Dr. Gould in a very complimentary manner, especially the first. The new method of observing contacts seems likely to prove of value in the observations of the coming transit of Venus.

PAPERS ON THE ECLIPSE READ AT THE MEETING OF THE AMERICAN ASSOCIATION.

Dr. Baker Edwards, of Montreal, read a paper by Dr. Charles Smallwood, of McGill College, Montreal. There was a slight agitation of the sun's limb a second or two before the first contact, the edge of the sun being lighted up with rose-colored protuberances, shooting out coruscations of the same rose-colored light towards the sun. The contrast between the color of the sun's bright disc and these rose-colored prominences was very distinct, and of surpassing beauty, resembling the strontium light of fireworks. A collodion plate was submitted to the sun, moved forward every five minutes, and also a strip of paper prepared by the chromotype process, with good results, showing the action of the sun's light in producing photographs. No distortion of the cusps was apparent; they appeared at all times sharp and well defined, and no coruscations across the moon were apparent. Of two polariscopes placed one due north and the other south, the latter showed a want of sky polarization during part of the time; the former gave the usual appearance. There was a perceptible increase of moisture in the atmosphere, and ozone was much in excess. The barometer and thermometer both fell during the eclipse, rising afterwards. There were very slight indications of atmospheric electricity; the inclination magnet showed a very slight decrease in dip.

Prof. David Murray, of Rutgers College, N. J., gave the result of the observations of the party at Mattoon, Illinois, on the general phenomena of the eclipse, and a diagram of the corona and protuberances. Of the red protuberances seven were seen, two of them of remarkable size and brilliancy. The largest of these showed large black masses in its centre, arising either from the cloudy mass being open through so as to disclose the space beyond, or from the presence of a dense core or nucleus. The corona was of a soft, bright consistency, and at five points extended out into long rays. The inner part of the corona was bright, but not striated, the projecting prongs, however, being distinctly radiated. There was a curved petal in the corona at one point, near the largest protuberance, and some observers noticed other curved portions of the corona.

Mr. T. Bassnett gave a paper from his observations made at Des Moines. The shape of the corona, as represented by all, was generally of a rhomboidal character. His theory was that there is a physical medium filling all interstellar space, which is driven off by centrifugal force at the equator of the solar system, and drawn in again at the pole.

Professor Peirce gave the results of the observations made by parties connected with the Coast Survey. With these parties precision in noting the times was the great object; all else was only accidental, and will be handed over to the physicists. There were five parties, all of which have made their reports except the one at Sitka. Two of these parties made great use of the photograph, and the professor felt confident that these observations, with those of the spectrum which had been brought to notice to-day, would be the only ones from which we could get observations at all worthy of confidence, surpassing in value the transit of Venus, which must be observed photographically to bring it up to the observations on the eclipse. These photographs will bear to be magnified up to a high power, so that they can be measured up to one-tenth of a second of arc. The photograph will give time more accurately than the chronograph. The measurements for these photographs will be made from the negatives direct, by

27*

the aid of Rutherford's screw, which the professor pronounced the most perfect work of art in the world. The photograph can be taken in one-thirtieth of a second, and we can get the semi-diameter of the moon to one-tenth of a second of arc. Professor Peirce regards the theory that the corona is of the same character as the aurora, as the most plausible one.

OBSERVATIONS OF THE CORONA DURING THE TOTAL ECLIPSE, AUGUST 7, 1869. BY PROFESSOR EDWARD C. PICKERING.

Among other expeditions to observe the recent eclipse was one under the direction of Professor Henry Morton, sent by the Nautical-Almanac Office to photograph the sun. I was attached to this party to make general and physical observations, and from our station at Mt. Pleasant, Iowa, arrived at the following results :—

It is commonly supposed that the light of the corona is polarized in planes passing through the sun's centre, and that it shines by reflected light. Wishing to verify this observation, I prepared an Arago's polariscope (in which the objects are viewed through a plate of quartz), and a double-image prism of Iceland spar. The two images appear of complementary colors when the light is polarized, the tint changing with the plane of polarization. I therefore expected to see two colored coronas, the tint of each portion being complementary to that of the part at right angles to it, and the color revolving with the polariscope. In reality the two images were pure white, without any traces of color; but the sky adjoining one was blue, adjoining the other yellow. As the instrument is of considerable delicacy, we must conclude that little or no polarized light is emitted by the corona. The sky adjoining it, however, is polarized in a plane independent of the position of the sun, since its color (as seen in the polariscope) is the same whether above, below, or on one side of it. The most probable explanation of this curious phenomenon is, that the earth beyond the limits of the shadow, being strongly illuminated, acts as a new source of light, and thus gives rise to a polarization in a plane perpendicular to the horizon.

In hopes of determining the cause of discrepancy between this observation and those previously made, I have endeavored to learn what form of polariscope has heretofore been used ; but unfortunately, in most cases, no description has been published. One observer used a Savart's polariscope, and, holding it with its principal plane vertical, found strong traces of polarization in this plane. This observation, however, agrees with mine if we suppose that the polarization of the sky was taken for that of the corona, a natural mistake with this form of instrument. Another observer, who used a single plate of tourmaline, saw no evidence of polarization, that of the sky being too feeble to be perceived in this way. I verified my results with a simple prism of Iceland-spar, with which two images of the corona were seen precisely alike, and showing no signs of polarization. We cannot infer from this that the corona is self-luminous, since polarization is produced only by specular, and not by diffuse, reflection.

The spectrum of the corona was observed in the following manner: A common chemical spectroscope was used; but instead of attaching it to a telescope, it was merely pointed in the proper direction a short time before totality. As its field of view was 7 or 8 degrees in diameter, the sun remained in it for a considerable time, and the spectrum obtained was that due to the corona, protuberances, and sky near the sun. On looking through the instrument during totality, a continuous spectrum was seen free from dark lines, but containing two or three bright ones, — one near E, and a second near C. At the time, I supposed that these were due to the protuberances; but Professor Young, with a large spectroscope of 5 prisms, found a line near E which remained visible even when the image of the protuberance was moved off the slit, and therefore inferred that it was due to the corona. He also found the continuous spectrum free from dark lines, and that one, perhaps three, of the bright lines coincide with those of the aurora borealis. These results would lead to the belief that the corona is self-luminous, the bright lines rendering its gaseous nature probable. If it is a part of the sun, even the remoter portions are one hundred times as near as the earth, and would receive ten thousand times as much heat, which would be sufficient to raise any known substance to incandescence.

Other observations, however, point to quite a different conclusion. A thermometer with blackened bulb was exposed to the sun's rays, and the temperature recorded every 5 minutes. I found that it began to rise some time before contact, descending again as soon as the moon's limb became visible. It did not reach its former temperature until about a quarter of an hour after the eclipse began, or until a seventh of the sun's disc was obscured. The approach of the moon, therefore, appeared to cause an *increase* in the sun's heat. The amount of the change was only about 1.3° C., the total difference between this thermometer and one in the shade being about 18° C., or in the ratio of 1 to 14. This fraction is but one-half of that given above, owing, perhaps, to the diminution of heat on the borders of the sun. During totality, the difference between the two thermometers was almost nothing. In examining the photographs taken by the party, it was noticed that, while the light diminished near the edge of the sun, the moon's limb was very distinct, and that there was a marked increase in the light of the parts nearest it. It was suggested that this might be a subjective effect; but an examination of the photographs is sufficient to convince any one that the appearance is a real one. The glass positives especially show that this effect extends over a large part of the sun's disc. The exposure was rendered instantaneous by passing a diaphragm with a slit in it in front of the camera, the rapidity of motion being regulated by a series of springs. Any irregularity in the motion would cause variations in shade in the photographs; but these would form bands parallel to the slit, while the shade mentioned above was not parallel to it, and was curved so as to follow the moon's edge. Since, then, there is an increase both of the actinic power and of the heat, it would seem that these effects are real, since the methods of observing them are so totally different that no error in one could be introduced into the other. The only explanation of the phenomenon that seems possible is to assume the presence of a lunar atmosphere. The corona would then be caused by refraction, light reaching the observer from parts of the sun already eclipsed. Although, for various reasons, this hypothesis is unsatisfactory, yet it is strengthened by other observations. The protuberances have often seemed to indent the moon's edge,—an appearance usually ascribed to irradiation. Several of the photographs, however, show this same effect; and in some of them the exposure was so short, and the edges of the protuberances are so well defined, that it cannot be caused by the intensity of their light, but must have its origin outside of the eye of the observer. It is noticeable on all sides of the moon, sometimes in half-a-dozen protuberances in a single photograph. An atmosphere of rapidly increasing density might produce this effect by reflection, and of course would not influence the corona, if it was caused by refraction. On this supposition, reliance could not be placed on measurements of the moon's diameter by occultations, or by contacts during eclipses, and would account for the uncertainty of this constant.

The principal reason for supposing the corona a portion of the sun is, that, during totality, it does not appear to move with the moon, but remains concentric with the sun, or, more properly, is brightest where the sun's edge is nearest. Many of the photographs show this very well, the difference on the two opposite sides of the moon being very marked. Now, this effect would be explained equally well by supposing the corona caused by refraction. For the centres of the sun and moon never differ during totality by more than half a digit, while the breadth of the corona is sometimes several times as much; so that merely covering a small portion of it would not produce a greater diminution of light than would be caused by a slight change in the direction of the sun's rays shining through a lunar atmosphere. On the other hand, it is difficult to conceive of an atmosphere dense enough to produce these effects, and yet so transparent that the edges of the full moon are perfectly distinct, and that the light of the sun, during an eclipse, should be increased rather than diminished. Again, we should expect that such variations would be produced by changes of temperature that they could scarcely fail to be detected.

We, then, conclude that the polariscope gives only negative results, and cannot be regarded as proving that the light is reflected. The evidence of the spectroscope needs confirmation, since the dark lines may have been invisible, owing to the feeble light of the corona. But if the observations with it are correct, the self-luminous character of the corona is established. The thermometric and actinic experiments point towards a lunar atmosphere as the cause of the corona.

In the above, I have endeavored to give the evidence in favor of each view, unbiased by any theory, leaving to those best able to judge to determine whether either explains all the facts observed. The absence of a lunar atmosphere is so generally admitted, that its existence is suggested only with reluctance, and merely as the most natural explanation of the observations.

Note on the Supposed Polarization of the Corona. — The form of the instrument used has been, in one or two cases, misunderstood. It consisted of a sheet-iron tube, closed at one end with a plate of quartz, and at the other with a prism of Rochon. The latter has the property of giving two images of any object seen through it, separated by an angle of nearly 3°. Looking through the tube, we therefore see two images of the quartz touching, but not overlapping. When the light is polarized, these images assume complementary tints, which vary with the plane of polarization and the thickness of the quartz.

The corona appeared white; but the sky surrounding it was colored in one image blue, in the other yellow. The conclusion to be drawn from this is, that the light of the corona is unpolarized, or, more strictly, that the amount of polarized light, if any, is too slight to be perceptible with this instrument. Its delicacy, although not equal to Savart's polariscope, is very great, giving colored images with paper, wood, and other bodies which reflect a small amount of light specularly. The day before the eclipse, it showed, in a very marked manner, the polarization of the wet pavements and roofs. To measure its sensitiveness, I viewed the light reflected by a piece of plate glass, at different angles of incidence, and found that the color ceased to be visible when this angle was about 10°, which, allowing for the reflection from the second face, would give about one part of polarized to 24 of natural light.

Observers heretofore have generally attached their polariscope to a telescope, and thus introduced a source of error, avoided in my instrument. For light passing through the object-glass and field-lens would be polarized by refraction, before reaching the polariscope, by the obliquity of the incidence, caused both by the curvature of the surfaces and the fact that the edge of the field of view receives its light not parallel to the axis. The plane of polarization would be perpendicular to a plane falling through the axis of the instrument. Now, if any part of the corona was brought into the centre of the field of view, the adjoining portions would appear polarized in planes parallel to the edge of the field, or passing through the sun's centre. In sweeping around the sun's edge, the plane of polarization would continually change, as the corona passed through different parts of the field, and the comparative darkness of the moon's disc and the exterior sky prevent the polarization of the other portions of the field from being visible. The degree of polarization by refraction would be very slight, and, perhaps, imperceptible; but the agreement of observation with this hypothesis is certainly a curious coincidence.

The strongest argument against the polarization of the corona is furnished by the spectroscope, the presence of bright lines and absence of dark ones, as observed by Prof. Young, denoting incandescence, — a view strengthened by the consideration that each square centimetre of the surface of the corona would receive several thousand units of heat per minute. I am well aware that my results are at variance with those obtained by previous observers, including some of the most eminent astronomers of the day; but, as far as I can learn, this form of polariscope has not been used for the purpose, and therefore hope that my experiment may be repeated during the next eclipse.

Since writing the above, I learn, from Prof. F. H. Smith, that an excellent Arago's polariscope was used in Eden Ridge, Tenn., in observing the eclipse. The result agreed with mine, namely, that no traces of polarization could be detected in the corona with this instrument.

OBSERVATIONS ON THE PROTUBERANCES OF THE SUN.

Zöllner has communicated to the Royal Society of Sciences of Saxony the results of observations of the solar protuberances made by a new method, the details of which are, however, not given in the paper from which this abstract is taken. The author states that by this method the protuberances can be observed with great sharpness and distinctness, and gives a number of figures of much interest, representing various forms of the red eruptive flames. The method of observation employed gives the same protuberance in three different colors at the same time, corresponding to the three homogeneous lines of the spectrum, red, yellow, and blue. A marked difference is observed between the yellow and the other two images. The yellow image is very intense near to the edge of the sun's disc, where it corresponds with the other images, while at a greater distance the finer details are lost. Zöllner infers from this, either that the rays to which the yellow image is due proceed from a gas specifically heavier than hydrogen, and, therefore, occupying a lower stratum, or that the increase in the temperature and pressure of the hydrogen near the surface of the sun determines the emission of the yellow rays in question. The author remarks that the protuberances, as seen by his method, for the most part strongly resemble the various forms of terrestrial clouds, the cumulus type being most distinctly exhibited. There are, however, some exceptions; in certain cases the phenomena resemble those of eruption of volcanoes or of hot springs. Zöllner suggests that it may hereafter be possible to observe at the same time all the protuberances as in the case of a total eclipse. In conclusion the author mentions another observation of great interest. On the 27th June the slit of the spectroscope was made to approach a part of the sun's disc where the spectral lines of the protuberances were particularly long and bright. At a distance of 3 or 4 minutes above the sun's edge, the whole length of the spectrum was crossed by bright linear flashes. These flashes extended over the whole portion of spectrum in the field of view, and were so abundant at one point of the sun's edge that it seemed as if the whole spectrum were crossed by the straight paths of rapidly following electric discharges. This phenomenon would be explained by the assumption that small intensely ignited bodies are moving near the sun's surface and sending out rays of all refrangibilities. As the images pass rapidly before the slit of the spectroscope they give a spectrum with flashing lines. — *American Journal of Science and Arts*, Nov., 1869.

ZÖLLNER'S REVERSION SPECTROSCOPE.

An important addition to the resources of spectrum analysis has been made by Zöllner's invention of a reversion spectroscope by which extremely small changes in refrangibility, and consequently comparatively slow motions of a star or sun-flame can be detected. It consists of a spectroscope in which by reflection the spectrum of a source of light can be superposed above a reversed spectrum of the same source ; so that if a white flame containing sodium be viewed, there will be seen in the upper part of the field a sodium line with the blue end of the spectrum on the one side, and underneath it a sodium line with the red end of the spectrum on the same side. The two bright lines may be made to coincide exactly by an adjustment; and if any change in refrangibility takes place, the motion of the line is doubled, and is also more exactly measured, because it is referred to itself as a standard.— *Comptes Rendus.*

ASTRONOMY.

Mr. Kincaid suggests an ingenious mode of constructing an automatic transit instrument. The apparatus consists of a plane mirror, and burning-glass, to be adjusted in such a manner that, at the instant the sun reaches the meridian, the rays ignite a thread which burns without smoke or residue ; this releases a detent, and a motion is thereby given to the hands of the clock, bringing it to the correct local mean time. There is a supplementary arrangement by which, if the thread should not ignite in consequence of a passing cloud at the instant of the transit of the first limb, the subsequent ignition of the thread will not affect the clock. Mr. Lockyer, in a note on Mr. Huggins' paper "On a possible Method of viewing Red Flames without an Eclipse," writes to show that he was not aided by the eclipse observations in seeking for the prominence spectrum. Unless Mr. Lockyer claims credit for the discovery of the gaseity of the prominences, apart from the credit due him for his share in the discovery that their spectrum can be seen without an eclipse, we cannot see how Mr. Huggins' mistake (assuming it to be such) at all affects the proper apportionment of recognition in the matter of recent solar discoveries. The eclipse observers clearly deserve all the credit due to the first-mentioned discovery, which had been fully discussed in England for two months before Mr. Lockyer examined the prominence spectra. It is impossible to undiscover the discovered. On the other hand, no one has disputed the claim of Janssen and Lockyer to the discovery that the prominence-spectra can be seen without an eclipse. Professor Brayley supplies an interesting paper on the relation of the luminous prominences to the faculæ of the sun. He shows that there is strong reason for supposing the faculæ and prominences to be identical, or at least that the latter are the superior terminations of the former. Some very singular facts connected with the mean distances of the asteroids, and the commensurability of their periods with that of Jupiter, are pointed out by Prof. Kirkwood. He shows that wherever there is a wider gap than usual between the asteroids (considered in the order of their distances from the sun), that gap invariably corresponds with such values of the mean distance as would give a period having some simple association of commensurability with the period of Jupiter. It is well known that any such association would result in disturbance, and Prof. Kirkwood argues that the particles which, on the nebular hypothesis, would have occupied these vacant zones, must have been so disturbed by Jupiter, as to adopt eccentric orbits, and so come into collision with exterior or interior particles. Even if this did not happen, the disturbance of their orbits would lead to a change of period, and so of mean distance. Either result serves to account for the gaps in the asteroidal zone. He considers that very strong evidence is afforded by these coincidences (which certainly cannot be looked upon as accidental) in favor of the nebular hypothesis. He goes on to examine the Saturnian rings, which he remarks have been quoted in Proctor's Saturn as furnishing strong evidence of the nebular hypothesis of Laplace. He shows that the great division between the rings corresponds exactly with that portion of the width of the system where the particles would move in periods commensurate with those of the four inner satellites. The coincidence is certainly most remarkable. — *Quarterly Journal of Science, April*, 1869.

At a recent meeting of the Royal Astronomical Society, the Astronomer Royal stated that he had obtained from Dr. Miller, of Cambridge, evidence confirmatory of the connection which has been supposed to exist between comets and meteors. It will be remembered that Mr. Huggins' analysis of Comet II, 1868, showed that that object consisted of carbon in the state of incandescent gas. It appears that there are four meteoric stones, at least, which contain carbon. Of these, one fell in the south of France, one at the Cape of Good Hope, one at Debreczin, in Hungary, and the fourth at Orgeuil, in France. The number of discovered asteroids has now reached 106.

Mr. J. Tebbutt, Jr., supplies a series of observations made by him upon the star η Argûs. He compared this singular variable with neighboring stars. It appears from these observations, that η Argûs has not exceeded the sixth magnitude during the past two years. Thus we are compelled to reject the theory of Professor Wolf, who assigned a law of variation according to which the epoch of minimum brilliancy should have occurred in 1861, and the magnitude of the star should have been 3.6. Certainly η Argûs is the most remarkable star in the whole heavens. A quarter of a century ago, it outshone the brilliant Canopus, and rivalled Sirius itself in splendor; now it can only just be detected with the naked eye on a very clear night. — *Chronicles of Science*, *Jan.* 1869.

DISTANCE OF THE SUN.

At the general meeting of the Astronomical Society, on Feb. 12th, it was announced that the gold medal for the year had been awarded to Mr. Stone, of the Greenwich Observatory, for his labors towards the determination of the sun's distance. We have already had occasion to refer at intervals to the various papers which Mr. Stone has written upon this subject; and a reference to the accompanying review of the proceedings of the Astronomical Society will show that he is still engaged on the same interesting work. What he has done may be divided into two sections: first, independent solutions of the problem of determining the sun's distance; and, secondly, the careful re-examination of the observations and calculations of others. He has detected numerical errors in the processes of Leverrier and other mathematicians, besides errors of interpretation in the work of those who investigated the transit observations made in 1769; and he has given a large share of attention to the consideration of the proper means of weighing discordant observations, — a question of great difficulty, which largely enters into the problem of determining the sun's distance. The result of his labors has been to show that the sun's equatorial horizontal parallax is probably about 8.91''; his distance, therefore, about 91,700,000 miles. — *Journal of Science, April*, 1869.

DISCOVERY OF A NEW PLANET,—THE 109TH. BY DR. E. H. F. PETERS, IN A LETTER TO THE EDITORS.

I write to communicate the discovery, made here on Saturday night, of a planet, the 109th of the asteroid group. It is in the constellation of Pisces, more properly in the following position: —
1869, Oct. 9, 13h. 31m. 58s., Hamilton College mean time.
A. R. = 0h. 56m. 2.60'' Decl. = + 9° 37' 10.6''.
Its motion in declination is almost nothing; that in right ascension over a minute per day. In brightness it equals a star of the 10th magnitude. — *American Journal of Science and Arts, Nov.*, 1869.

TEMPEL'S COMET.

I enclose an orbit for the comet discovered by Tempel on Oct. 11, of which no elements have yet been published in the " Astronomische Nachrichten." Indeed, but for an observation kindly sent me by Dr. Winnecke, and not yet printed, it would not have been practicable to work out an orbit.
Elements of the Orbit of Tempel's Comet, Oct. 11, 1869. — Elements calculated from an observation at Bonn, Oct. 12; one by

Dr. Winnecke, at Carlsruhe, Oct. 17; and a third at Leipzig, Oct. 23: —

Perihelion Passage, 1869.

October, ...	. 8.4421 Greenwich M. T.
Longitude of Perihelion, . . .	124° 41′ 1′′ ⎫ From apparent
Longitude of Ascending Node, .	311° 24′ 4′′ ⎬ Equinox.
Inclination to Ecliptic, ...	. 68° 48′ 8′′
Log perihelion distance, ...	.0°08985
Heliocentric motion retrograde.	

The above orbit does not resemble that of any comet previously computed. — *J. R. Hind, Observatory, Twickenham, Nov.* 8.

SPECTRUM OF THE AURORA, ZODIACAL LIGHT, ETC.

In connection with the observation of Prof. Young, during the late eclipse, the following translation from a few paragraphs in the text accompanying Angström's chart of the solar spectrum may be of interest. On page 42, he says, after some introductory remarks: —

"In fact, during the winter of 1867–8, I have been able to observe, repeatedly, the spectrum of the luminous arc bordering the obscure segment, and always seen during the feeble auroras. Its light is almost monochromatic, and consists of a *single brilliant ray*, situated to the left of the well-known group of calcium lines. By measuring the distance from this group, I have determined the wave-length of this ray, which is found equal to $\lambda = 5567$. Beside this ray, of which the intensity is relatively great, I have observed, also, by widening the slit of the spectroscope, traces of three lines extending almost as far as F. On a single occasion, when the luminous arc was agitated by undulations which changed its shape, I saw regions momentarily illuminated by certain feeble spectral rays; but, taking into account the intensity of these rays, I would, nevertheless, say that the light of the luminous arc is sensibly monochromatic. There is a circumstance which gives to this observation of the aurora spectrum a much greater importance, and, indeed, a cosmical character. During one week of March, 1867, I succeeded in observing this same spectral ray in the zodiacal light, which then presented itself with an intensity truly extraordinary for the latitude of Upsal. Finally, when, during a starlight night, all the sky was, in a certain sense, phosphorescent, I found traces of it in the feeble light emitted by all parts of the firmament. A very notable fact is, that this remarkable ray does not correspond with any of the known rays of simple or compound gases, so far, at least, as I have studied them up to this time. It follows, from what I have said, that an intense aurora, such as may be seen above the polar circle, would probably give a more complicated spectrum than that which I have found. Granting this, we may hope that an opportunity will be afforded of explaining the origin of the rays already found, and the nature of the phenomenon itself. Not being able to give this explanation at present, I propose to return to it another time."— *Journal of Franklin Inst., Nov.,* 1869.

THE USE OF THE THERMOMETER TO DETERMINE THE PERIOD OF SOLAR ROTATION. BY PLINY EARLE CHASE.

Professor Henry's experiments on the temperature of the solar disc showed that the spots are cooler than the brighter portions of the photosphere, and the centre is warmer than the rim. These evidences of difference in calorific power have been confirmed by subsequent observers, and Schwabe, Henshall, and Kirkwood, by a study of sun-spots and the variations of solar magnetism, have sought for indications of fixed points, or meridians, on the sun. If the sun is a variable star, any permanent differences in superficial structure, however masked by the irregular disturbances to which the spots are usually attributed, may perhaps be accompanied by regularly recurring differences of temperature, which should be manifested by the thermometer.

The 7 years' hourly thermometric observations at St. Helena (1840–7) were examined in various ways, in order to discover any traces they might furnish of cycles approximating to the supposed period of solar rotation. After testing, by the method of least squares, various assumed intervals between the limits of 25 and 29 days, the pointings were so decided and uniform, that all the observations were arranged in accordance with a hypothetical period of 27 1-14 days. The annual, semi-annual, and quarterly groupings all confirmed the hypothesis that this was a normal interval, and the belief was still further strengthened by various comparisons with observations at Philadelphia, extending over a period of 44 years (1825-69).

If we then assume 27 1-14 days for the synodical rotation of the sun, the time of its sidereal rotation is about 25.065 days. This is somewhat greater than the estimates of Sporer (24.6244) and Carrington (24.9711), but nearly accordant with the more recent estimate of Faye (25.07472.) Mr. Chase proposes to continue the investigation by a discussion of observations at other stations.

PLANETARY INFLUENCE ON RAINFALL AND TEMPERATURE. BY PLINY EARLE CHASE.

The author has recently undertaken, for the Coast Survey, some discussions of the meteorological influences of the moon. An examination of the records which have been kept at the Pennsylvania Hospital, in Philadelphia, for forty-four years, confirmed the conclusions of Loomis and others that cloudiness, rainfall, and temperature, are each, to some degree, controlled by the lunar phases. The "establishments," or local influences which modify the results at different stations, often occasioning an entire opposition of curves, especially on opposite sides of large bodies of water, were also clearly shown. There were marked evidences of such establishments, due not only to position, but also to the season of the year, occasioning contrasts between the summer and winter curves, and resemblances between the vernal and autumnal curves.

These results, together with a certain degree of opposition between the lunar curves of rainfall and temperature, seemed to indicate a partial dependence of the temperature upon the tidal currents in the atmosphere. If this hypothesis was correct, it seemed probable that some of the planets, especially Jupiter, should furnish corroborative indications. The observations, both of rainfall and of temperature, were therefore arranged successively in accordance with the positions of Jupiter, Venus, Neptune, and Mercury. The arrangement resulted in the production of consistent curves, varying with the varying distances of the several planets, and with their positions relative to the sun. In comparing these curves an opposition was apparent between those of rainfall and temperature, which was more strongly marked than that which had been previously noticed in the lunar curves. It seems unreasonable to attribute the temperature fluctuations to varying planetary radiation; but it is easy to understand that any influence which tends so to disturb the atmosphere as to produce a northerly wind, should depress the temperature and increase precipitation, while one which tends to produce a south wind, increases both the temperature and the evaporation.

THE TRANSITS OF VENUS.

The French Astronomer Royal is wisely making arrangements in good time for observing the transits of Venus, which will take place in the year 1874 and 1882. The event is one of considerable interest and value to scientific men, and it is therefore desirable that it should be viewed from those parts of the earth's surface where it can be best observed. The stations fixed upon for 1874 are Oahu (one of the Sandwich islands), Kerguelen Island (in the Indian Ocean), Rodriguez (a dependency of the Mauritius), Auckland (New Zealand), and Alexandria. Both the Admiralty and the Treasury have responded with alacrity to the appeal which has been made to them for funds. Mr. Warren De la Rue is of opinion that photography may be used with the utmost advantage in registering the transit.

DR. TYNDALL'S THEORY OF COMETS.

Prof. Tyndall has developed a cometary theory out of his late researches upon the actinic power of light. It will be remembered that he has found that a beam of light is capable of forming a bright glowing cloud in its course through a space containing a modicum of vapor, the said cloud being first reduced by the chemical action of the light, and then rendered visible by illumination of the condensed particles.

The application of this principle to the explanation of cometary phenomena is as follows: A comet is held to be a mass of vapor decomposable by the solar light, the visible head and tail being an actinic cloud resulting from such decomposition. The tail is not matter projected from the head, but matter precipitated on the solar beams which traverse the cometary atmosphere; nothing being carried from the comet to form the tail, but something being deposited from the interplanetary space through which the body is coursing. But this explanation supposes that the sunlight has a different power when it has passed through a vapory comet to that which it possesses when it has traversed no such medium; otherwise all space would be lit up like a comet's tail. To account for such a peculiar property, Prof. Tyndall assumes that the sun's heating and chemical powers are antagonistic, and that the calorific rays are absorbed more copiously by the head and nucleus than the actinic rays. This augments the relative superiority of the actinic rays behind the head and nucleus, and enables them to bring down the cloud which constitutes the tail. Thus the caudal appendage is in a perpetual state of renovation as the comets move through space; the old tails being dissipated by the solar heat as soon as they cease to be screened by the nucleus. Nearly all the phenomena observed in those mysterious bodies are accounted for by Dr. Tyndall. One, however, he has not mentioned; namely, the peculiar luminous envelopes, familiar to comet-gazers, which surround the nucleus like a series of cloudy glass cases. No theory can be called complete which does not account for those remarkable and evidently important features.

COMETS.

M. Bionne has submitted the following opinion upon the nature of comets to the Academy of Sciences: "Comets are bodies which describe spirals originating in a nebula terminating in the sun; each spiral may be considered as an ellipse. Formed of the incandescent matter of the nebulœ, comets would appear to be the regulators of the grand movement of celestial bodies, the agents of that vast transformation of calorific work into mechanical work, and would come at the end of their course to lose themselves in the atmosphere of the sun, to which they would serve as an aliment."

WINNECKE'S COMET.

Huggins' spectral analysis of this comet is well known, and his conclusion that the light of this comet is produced by incandescent carbon vapor. The experiments of Watts, published in "The Philosophical Magazine," seem to prove that this spectrum is really that of carbon; and, further, that the temperature of the carbon producing it must be between 1,500° C. and 2,500° C. If no other explanation of this comet spectrum can be found, and if the temperature of cosmical space may really reach 1,500° C., important changes must be made in the theories of the universe as at present accepted. — *The Academy, Nov.* 12, 1869.

28*

SUMMARY OF FACTS IN ASTRONOMY AND METEOROLOGY.

Local Attraction. — Colonel Sir Henry James, Director-General of the Ordnance Survey, reports that during the past year inquiry has been prosecuted into this very remarkable phenomenon. He observes that the relative extent to which the plumb line and the levels of our astronomical instruments are affected in a country where there is nothing on the surface of the ground to account for it, may be judged from the fact that it is nearly double the amount of the deflection on Schehallion mountain, 8,547 feet high, with the instrument placed on the sides of the mountain itself, at one-third of its altitude, the position to produce the greatest effect from the mass of the mountain on the plumb lines. He considers that we have very decided indications that the cause is in the granitic rocks which extend in a southwest direction from the Cowhythe through Banffshire, and which are highly impregnated in some parts with magnetic iron in a metallic state. The range of mountains on the south-east of Banffshire culminates in Ben Muich Dhui, 4,305 feet high, which, after Ben Nevis, 4,368 feet high, is the highest mountain in Scotland. The great amount of the attraction at Cowhythe, and along the coast to the east and west of Portsoy, cannot be explained by anything visible on the surface, and obliges us to imagine the existence of some large and very dense mass of matter underneath it. Sir H. James hopes to resume this important inquiry this season; and the geological structure, as well as the mineral character of the rocks, will be carefully investigated by the Director of the Geological Survey of Scotland.

The Captive Balloon. — Mr. Glaisher narrated the results of some meteorological experiments made in the car of the Captive Balloon. The principal fact was, that often, when the air near the ground is quite still, and the smoke from the chimneys of the houses rising vertically, a hard gale is blowing aloft, and that at a height of less than 1,000 feet. — Dr. Mann pointed out that meteorological observations between the surface of the ground and moderate elevations, such as 1,000 feet, are of more practical value than those taken higher up, especially during the rapid motion of a free balloon. Professor Newton said that he thought it important to learn everything possible about the atmosphere, even at the highest altitudes. Observations made in the United States on the motion of the smoke left by meteors had proved in some instances that gales in opposite directions occurred, even so high up as 50 or 60 miles.

M. Janssen, in a letter dated from Darjeeling, Sikim, British India, 22d May last, says that the spectra of some stars, which are rather ruddy colored when not disclosing the presence of hydrogen, do positively disclose the presence of aqueous vapor.

The Light of Uranus. — This planet emits light which differs from that of any other of our system. According to Father Secchi, its spectrum exhibits broad absorption lines. The surface modifies the sun's light which it reflects, in the same manner as do colored bodies.

Mountains in the Moon.— The German astronomer, Maedler, has measured the height of 1,093 mountains in the moon. Twenty-two of these are higher than Mount Blanc, which is within a few feet of being 3 miles high; 6 are above 19,000 feet. The highest observed mountain in the moon is 24,844 feet high.

Chemical Analysis of the Solar Atmosphere. — Rayet announces that he has been for some time aware of the existence of a new bright spectral line from the above source, which has not been before pointed out. It is between G and H of Fraunhofer, and is the fourth of the principal brilliant rays of hydrogen, three of which have already been recognized in the "chromosphere." It is often bulbous or globular in appearance, like F. This makes 6 bright rays now known from the chromosphere, and it is remarkable that 4 of these belong to hydrogen. Nevertheless this atmosphere is not, as Lockyer and others have supposed, composed exclusively of hydrogen. Secchi has observed the third ray of magnesium, and the yellow line near D is not believed to be a ray of hydrogen. Rayet himself, in an article published in the "Comptes Rendus" of the 8th of last February, discussed this yellow ray.

The observations made during the eclipse of the 18th of August last have shown, moreover, that the protuberances or elevated masses of the chromosphere do not always have the same chemical composition. — *Comptes Rendus, June* 7, 1869, p. 1321.

The Spectrum of Lightning. — Lieut. John Herschel has communicated to the Royal Society an account of the spectrum produced by lightning. He says : " The principal features are a more or less bright continuous spectrum, crossed by numerous bright lines,— so numerous as to perplex one as to their identity."

GEOGRAPHY AND ANTIQUITIES.

LIVINGSTONE'S DISCOVERIES.

THE latest discoveries of Dr. Livingstone, communicated at a meeting of the Royal Geographical Society, are of great interest and importance, independently of their supposed connection with the ultimate source of the Nile. He has found, in the first place, that the Chambeze, a considerable stream draining the northern slope of the great wooded humid plateau in 11°–12° S. lat., instead of flowing southward to the Zambesi, as was formerly supposed, turns to the north-west and discharges itself into a large lake, called Bangweolo, upwards of 50 miles in length. The plateau, therefore, which he crossed, as described in one of his former letters about the end of December, 1866, and which the Portuguese expeditions of 1798 and 1831 also traversed, turns out to be the water-shed between the basins of the Zambesi and the lake system of Equatorial Africa. It enhances the interest of this great discovery to find that Bangweolo is only one of a chain of lakes connected by rivers. The first in succession north of Bangweolo is Lake Moero, which is 50 miles in length, and varies in breadth from 20 to 60 miles. The town of Cazembe, visited by the Portuguese, lies on the banks of a much smaller lake called Mofué, to the east of Moero. Continuing down stream is a third lake, Ulenge; but Livingstone had not, when he wrote, pursued his examination further in this direction, and he was not sure whether this chain of lakes drained into Tanganyika, or continued to the west of this lake, and communicated independently with Albert Nyanza far to the north. The latter and their connecting rivers flowed through a deep valley hemmed in by wooded mountains. Another discovery of interest was Lake Liemba, which Livingstone thought to be an arm of Tanganyika near its southern end. He gives the altitude of this sheet of water as 2,800 feet above the level of the sea; a datum which, we venture to remark, will afford much food for geographical speculation until more definite information is received. This elevation, in fact, agrees almost exactly with that of Albert Nyanza as observed by Baker, and with that of the intermediate Lake Tanganyika as deduced by Mr. Findlay from an elaborate examination of the observations of Burton, Speke, and Baker. Thus if Liemba be connected (which is not yet indeed quite determined) both with the Chambeze lakes and with Tanganyika, the connection of the whole with the Nile is extremely probable. But Livingstone reserves his greatest marvel for the postscript to his dispatch. He had heard of a tribe of Troglodytes, a dark-skinned race with oblique eyes, dwelling in caves, some of which extended for many miles under ground. — *The Academy*, Nov. 13, 1869.

ARCTIC RESEARCHES.

Dr. I. I. Hayes continues to commend to public attention the importance of sending out a new American expedition for the survey of the Polar basin, entering by Smith's Sound. The following summary of his project is printed in the " New York Tribune " : —

" *First*, as to design. The design of the expedition which I have proposed is to complete the exploration of the entire region northward of Baffin's Bay ; to trace Greenland and Grinnell Land to their termination ; then ascertain if other lands lie to the northward ; to explore the open Polar Sea ; and, lastly, to reach the North Pole, making upon the course such observations as circumstances will allow. Thus will a field be opened for the most valuable discoveries in geography, geology, in glacier formations, magnetism, countries and currents, and in natural history. *Second*, as to plan. I would set out in May with two vessels, one a small steamer, and would make my course northward, provided with the best chart of Greenland, through the *Middle Ice*, until I reached Smith's Sound, in latitude 78° 17′, where, in my old harbor of 1860–61, I would pass the winter. Here there is abundance of game, and I would found a colony. Walrus, seals, reindeer, and foxes could be caught in great numbers, and not only would the colony be made self-sustaining, in point of food, but a valuable cargo of furs and oil might be collected. Then I would push northward the next summer with the steamer, and would thus strike for the North Pole. In any case, I would secure a harbor and a base of operations much to the north of the colony, and thus would the steamer and the colony become the centres from which the explorations already mentioned would be made. *Third*, as to cost. A public-spirited citizen of New York has offered to supply a suitable steamer ; and there is good reason to suppose that we could obtain from the government the loan of a sailing-vessel, one of the many not in use. These vessels furnished, they could be equipped and maintained in the field for two summers and two winters at a cost of 40,000 dollars. *Fourth*. Let it be remembered that this is the ' American route.' The land extends there further north than in any other quarter so far as known, and Americans have thence explored to within less than 8°, that is to say, within 450 miles of the pole. Independent, therefore, of the value to science of this particular line of discovery above any other in the unexplored parts of the Arctic regions, there is something of national honor involved in the pursuit of it, especially at this time when England, France, Germany, and Sweden are each aiming to reach the North Pole by various other routes ; to which end expeditions are now actually preparing. Shall we let those nations win from us the coveted honor of priority ? I do not believe there is a single person within the sound of my voice who would be indifferent to the matter, and who would not unite to see the American flag first planted at the North Pole. *Fifth,* as to the advantages of the Smith's Sound route over all other routes, for discovery in the unexplored parts of the Arctic regions, they are but the simple enumerations which I have before made to the Society: 1. Land as a base of operations; 2. The opportunity to colonize a party of hunters and natives as the means to a permanent support."

Capt. Silas Bent, late of the U. S. Navy, who rendered important hydrographical services in the Perry expedition to Japan, and who was also attached to the "Preble," under Capt. Glynn, in an earlier visit to Japan, has also published his views on the subject of the best mode of reaching the North Pole. Capt. Bent, while on the coast of Eastern Asia, made important observations on the Kuro-Siroo, or Japanese Gulf Stream, which presents some very interesting analogies to the American Gulf Stream. These observations are contained in the second volume of the Report of the Perry Expedition. In his opinion, every attempt to reach the North Pole should be made by following the continuation of one or the other of these Gulf Streams, that is, through Behring's Straits, or by the Spitzbergen route, which he terms the "Thermometric Gateways to the Pole." He is, therefore, decidedly opposed to the project of Dr. Hayes for an expedition through Smith's Sound. His views, though formed independently and upon his own observations and studies, coincide in many respects with those which are held by the continental geographers in Europe. — *American Journal of Science and Arts, May,* 1869.

SOUTH AMERICAN INDIANS.

Mr. Porter C. Bliss read, at the meeting of the American Association, at Salem, a paper upon a "New Classification of the South American Indians, upon the basis of Philology." Mr. Bliss gave, as one of the results of several years of travel and investigation among the aborigines of the Argentine Republic, Bolivia, Paraguay, Brazil, etc., the discovery that the number of stock languages within those regions has been exaggerated tenfold, and that there are, instead of 150 or more, as has been loosely stated by the Jesuits and other later writers, but 12 or 13 stock languages in the southern half of South America. Of all these he had collected vocabularies, having visited most of them as commissioner on the part of the Argentine government, but had lost them by their seizure, last year, by Lopez, of Paraguay.

Mr. Bliss proceeded to point out, on a large map of South America, the localities of each of the tribes mentioned, beginning with the Fuegians, and passing to the two races of Patagonians, the Araucanians, of Chile, whom he identified with the Pehuenches, Huilliches, and Aucas, of the Pampas of Buenos Ayres, the Abipones, Tobas, Mocobis, Ocoles, Mataguayos, and Machicuys, of the Gran Chaco, or region between Paraguay and Bolivia.

He then described the Guaranis and Payaguas, of Paraguay, the Atacamas, Quichuas, Aymaras, Chiriguanos, and Chiquitians, of

Bolivia, and gave many facts respecting the character of their various languages. He adverted to the extensive area of the Guarani tongue, which extends substantially from the La Plata to the Orinoco, embracing a great portion of Brazil, and most of the basin of the Amazon. He stated that he had found the Quichua language spoken in the centre of the Argentine Republic, in the province of Santiago del Estero, 800 miles from the nearest point in Bolivia where the same language is now spoken. Consequently, Mr. Bliss considered this province to have been an outlying colony of the empire of the Incas.

The languages of the Indians of the Chaco are extremely meagre, and none of them exceeds about a thousand root-words, — a point which was illustrated by anecdotes of some curious experiences in procuring vocabularies.

Mr. Bliss stated that the principle of reduplication was largely concerned in the formation of the language of the Incas, and that he had collected, in Bolivia, more than 300 geographical names formed in this way, as Moco-moco, Coro-coro, Quilli-quilli, and cited, as a double reduplication, the name of the famous lake Ti-ti-ca-ca. He stated that, within 200 years, the Guarani language had undergone an almost complete change; so that, instead of being now, as formerly, made up from monosyllabic radicals, it is quite as polysyllabic as most other Indian tongues.

Mr. Bliss refuted the geographical classification of the naturalist, D'Obigny, as separating the same races, and uniting very dissimilar ones, as the Fuegians, Araucanians, and Quichuans, under the same group. He stated that his own classification, upon a linguistic basis, had been embodied in a report to the Argentine government in 1863, and had since been adopted by the latest European writers upon that subject, such as Dr. Martin de Moussy and Mr. Charles Beck Bernard, in their recent works upon the regions of the La Plata.

NORTH AMERICA.

Prof. Morgan, at the meeting of the American Association, read a paper upon the following topics: 1. Physical Geography of North America, with reference to Natural Highways, and Means of Natural Subsistence afforded by its Areas. 2. Agricultural Subsistence, and the character and extent of Indian Agriculture. 3. Migrations of Roving and partially Village Indians; deduced from languages, traditions, and known migrations. 4. Migration of Village Indians; as deduced from the same sources.

The Indians, he said, were nations of fishermen and hunters; and afterwards, to a limited extent, some of them were supported by the products of agriculture. The migrations of men were not accidental or fortuitous, but deliberate movements, governed by law; and the initial point of migration did not become such by accident. Subsistence was the governing law which controlled the increase and migration of men; and this was manifest in the migration of the aborigines of this country.

In speaking of the geographical features of North America, he divided the country into prairie, mountain, and forest area; the first the least, and the last the most desirable for Indian occupation. He defined the extent of the prairie, which, he said, was over 31 parallels of latitude, and 19 parallels of longitude; the greatest expanse measuring more than 1,700 miles from north to south, and 1,000 from east to west, containing 800,000 square miles. After crossing the Missouri, going westward, the forests decreased and disappeared, except along the margins of the principal water-courses, and the prairies grew less luxurious as one advanced, until they degenerated into barren plains before the Rocky Mountains were reached. As the Indians had to obtain their sustenance by the way, and had no means of transportation, there were only three or four routes by which migration was possible; and over either of these routes 800 miles of prairie must be traversed, which Americans, aided by the advantages of civilization, were, for a long time, barely able to pass. These prairies were never occupied by the Indians, inasmuch as they were fishers and hunters, except to a very limited extent.

The mountain regions were distinguished for their great length, and for their lateral extent. These great ranges furnished as well as suggested the highways of migration, and gave to the movements a general direction from north to south, or the reverse.

The forest areas presented the greatest obstacles and hindrances to the migration of the Indians; yet, notwithstanding this, the finest Indians were found in the strictly forest nations.

Prof. Morgan, after speaking at some length on the different areas, referred to the means of subsistence which the Indians possessed, and said that the abundance or scarcity of food must exercise a great influence over their migration. The different kinds of food on which the Indians subsisted, and their modes of obtaining the same, were stated in detail. He then considered whether the natural or agricultural subsistence held the mastery as time advanced. The art of cultivation, doubtless, sprung up as a happy accident. Where it originated, it was impossible to ascertain; but the reasonable inference was, that it must have been in a hot climate. Without agriculture, the Indians could not have reached the second stage of their development, namely, villages. In Central America, Mexico, and the West Indian Isles, the greatest attention was paid to agriculture; but the implements in use were very rude, and the productions necessarily small. Their efforts were limited to garden spots, where the soil, if dry, was irrigated. The methods of irrigation adopted by the Indians were explained by Prof. Morgan. The great drawback to their advancement was the contracted extent of the areas cultivated, the difficulty of subduing the forests, which was impossible without the use of metallic instruments; and extensive cultivation was impossible without the assistance of the horse, ox, and plough.

THE TRADE ROUTES BETWEEN NORTHERN INDIA AND CENTRAL ASIA.

This was the subject of a lengthy and interesting paper, read at the meeting of the British Association, by T. Douglas Forsyth, C.B., F.R.G.S., of the Indian Civil Service. Mr. Forsyth commenced by observing that he had no geographical discoveries to make known, but he pertinently asked what was to be the practical effect of all our geographical knowledge? There was the work of practically applying the knowledge acquired by scientific men to the purposes of material progress. If it could be found that a knowledge of geography enables us to open out new routes to trade, or to improve old tortuous lines of traffic, those who had devoted their time and energies to the subject trusted that their exertions might receive some share of general approval. There are two great outlets for trade from Northern India. The largest trade, in fact a very large commerce, crosses the Indus at different points between Kurrachee and Peshawur, and threading the various passes of Bolan, Goleri, Kyber, etc., finds its way into Affghanistan, Balkh, Bokhara, Kokan, and Western Turkistan. The other outlet crosses the Himalayan passes, and enters that tract of country known as Eastern Turkistan or Chinese Tartary. Having given the history and description of the country north of the Himalayas, he proceeded to show why we took an interest in it, and why we sought to improve our communication with it. On more than one occasion it had been asserted that the Central Asia trade was a myth, and that therefore all efforts to open communications with Eastern Turkistan were worthless. He then proceeded to prove that from the earliest times trade had been carried on there, and was so at the present time. The Yarkund traders who appeared last year at Palumpoor brought lumps of silver and gold in their bags. Khotan, which is famed for its silk, sent a small quantity of raw produce, as a sample, to the market. Turfan wool, which is grown on the Tiam Shan mountains, and has maintained its character for surpassing excellence for centuries, was for the first time introduced into the Indian market. Precious stones and metals might be imported into India, in return for which our cotton and woollen fabrics and tea would be taken in large quantities. He then referred to the discovery of the new route between India and Turkistan, and said that trade had now been established, and a fair was founded in the heart of the tea-growing valley of Kangra, to which traders from all parts of the world now came. Mr. Forsyth then described the various routes into Central Asia, and, referring to the Himalayas, said that atmospheric influences and deficiency of fuel apart, there would be absolutely less physical difficulty opposed by nature in making the railroad talked of by Mr. Saunders, from Tso Moreri Lake to Yarkund, than there was in making the railway from Suez to St. Michel. The impassable nature of the Himalayas was a myth. He insisted that a valuable trade was to be opened up with Central Asia.

29

RECENT SURVEYS IN THE STRAITS OF MAGELLAN.

Captain R. C. Mayne, R.N., at the meeting of the British Association, gave an interesting account of the recent government survey in the Straits of Magellan. He glanced at the history of the discovery of the straits by the first circumnavigator, Magellan, and to the geographical position of the straits. The straits are 300 miles in length, and the width varied from two miles at the narrowest to 15 or 20 miles at the wider parts. In that distance a complete change of scenery and climate took place. At the entrance they come upon low prairie land, bare of trees, with a bright sky and fresh wind; but further on they come upon mountains, rising almost perpendicular from the sea, covered with antarctic, evergreen leaves; torrents of rain, varied with snow and hail, in their seasons. In some parts the rain never ceased for 24 hours together, and he and his crew had gone for three months without being able to dry their clothes, except at the engine fires. He referred to the great use that was now made of the straits to avoid the troublesome passage around the Horn. He gave the results of the recent survey in which he was engaged, from December, 1866, to the end of May last. He gave a description of the Patagonians, and Fuegans, their manners and customs. The Patagonians were not such giants as represented; he had measured one who was 6 ft. 10½ in. high; but the average height of the men was 5 ft. 10 in. to 5 ft. 11 in., and the women were nearly as large. The Fuegans were small, badly shaped, and ugly. The Patagonians drank very hard, but the Fuegans would not touch wine or spirit of any kind; on the other hand, the Patagonians would not smoke, but the Fuegans would smoke until they were insensible. The information obtained by Fitzroy, as to the Patagonians killing their old people, was true; he never saw anybody above a working age. He thought the inhabitants of the region might be very easily educated.

HUMAN REMAINS.

A recent discovery in the Department de la Dordogne, France, of human skeletons coeval with the mammoths, and undeniably appertaining to the earliest quaternary period, presents features of such unusual interest that the French government has sent M. Larter, the palæontologist, to make a report on the subject. He reports that the bones of five skeletons have been discovered, and that they belong to some gigantic race whose limbs, both in size and form, must have resembled those of the gorilla. But the similar origin of man must not be inferred from these analogies, as the skulls, of which only three are perfect, afford testimony fatal to this theory, having evidently contained very voluminous brains. The skulls are now in the hands of a committee of savants, who are preparing an exhaustive craniological report.

EFFECTS OF THE REMOVAL OF FORESTS UPON CLIMATE.

An interesting letter was recently read before the Geographical Society of London, which shows the effects upon climate resulting from the clearing away of large tracts of forest. The facts given are of universal interest.

The paper was "On the Effects on Climate of Forest Destruction in Coorg, Southern India," by Dr. Bidie. This district is composed of hills and valleys, which were formerly covered with forests. The lower slopes, however, are now denuded, and the rainfall is found to decrease with the arboreal vegetation. As regards the elevated crests of the Ghauts, which intercept the rain-bearing winds of the south-west monsoon, they would cause an abundant precipitation whether they were covered with trees or not, but the water supply and fertility of the lower slopes and plains to the east are seriously diminished by the clearing of forest on the hills, and the result is brought about in the following way: The natural forest acts as a check on the too rapid evaporation, and carrying off by streams, of the rainfall on the surface of the land. As the rain descends, it is gradually conveyed by the leaves of trees to the dense undergrowth of shrubs, and carpet of dead leaves, and below this it encounters a layer of vegetation mould, which absorbs the water like a sponge. By these, aided by the roots of trees, the moisture is transferred to the depths of the earth, and a reservoir of springs is thus formed, which keeps up a perennial supply of water to the lower land. But rain falling on the bare surface of cleared lands runs off at once by the nearest water-courses, and none is retained to keep up the flow during the dry season. Beside which, evaporation is so much more abundant from a surface exposed to the rain than from land screened by a clothing of forest, and the flow of surface water tends to sweep away the clothing of soil and render a district utterly barren. There is no doubt that this is one of the main causes, in hilly countries, of drought and floods. In France, for instance, since the mountains of Auvergne and Forey have been so denuded of forests, the Loire has been constantly flooded, occasioning vast destruction of property. The same cause, in Algeria, has caused frequent droughts, and the French government have lately been considering the proposition of some scientific men to replant these districts with trees.

THE MOUND-BUILDERS.

In Dr. Foster's "Mississippi Valley," the author gives an account of the extent and distribution of the relics of the ancient Mound-Builders, a race which, long antecedent to the North American Indian, once occupied the region of the great lakes and the valley of the Mississippi. The trees which covered the mounds when first discovered by the white settlers differed in no degree, either of size or form, from those of surrounding woods.

Investigations by the geologist and the antiquary have proved, beyond a doubt, that these mounds were formed by human hands. Evidence afforded by the earth-works has also connected their builders with the ancient copper miners of Lake Superior, whose operations represent, probably, the most extensive prehistoric mines in the world. Dr. Foster points out that the number and magnitude of these earth-works not only indicate a vast population, but also a people subsisting by agricultural pursuits; as no mere nomadic race, subsisting by the chase, could have devoted the time necessary for the formation of such extensive national works. The earth-work at Cahokia, Illinois, is 79 feet high, and has a base of 666 feet; while the famous mound at Grave Creek, Virginia, is 70 feet high, with a base of 333 feet; and the next in rank is that of Miamisburgh, Ohio, which is 68 feet high, with a base of 284 feet. Near Newark, Ohio, the circles, squares, parallel roads, and tumuli extend over many leagues of ground, and outrival in cubical contents the great pyramid of Cheops.

Their weapons were spear and arrow-heads, chipped with much skill out of hornstone or schists; hammers, generally of porphyry, grooved near the head for the attachment of a withe; fleshing instruments of the same material, brought down to a blunt edge; pestles for cracking and grinding corn; plates of steatite, or chloride slate, pierced with holes to gauge the size of the thread in spinning; circular discs, like weights, and concave on both sides, ordinarily of porphyry and grooved; ornaments like plum-bobs, double-coned, or egg-shaped, and pierced or grooved at one end for the attachment of a string made of specular iron, like that of Lake Superior; lastly, elaborately wrought pipes, showing that they indulged in the luxury of tobacco. They mined extensively the native copper on the shores of Lake Superior, and wrought it into knives, spear-heads, chisels, bracelets, and other personal ornaments. They were unacquainted with tin, and had no alloy; and there is reason to believe they did not even smelt the copper, but hammered it cold. They had also made considerable advance in the ceramic art. Dr. Foster concludes that the Mound-Builders were an industrious, peaceful, and numerous race, pursuing agriculture as a means of support, maize being their staple article of food; ruled over by a despotic government, under whose direction their great public movements were carried out; and, lastly, that their extermination has resulted from the invasion of a less civilized but more vigorous and warlike people.

THE PERFORATED IMPLEMENTS OF THE STONE PERIOD.

Sir John Lubbock and the other archæologists are inclined to hold that the perforated axes and hammers of stone are coeval with the commencement of the bronze period. That many of them really do belong to this period there can be little doubt, since bronzes and stone are frequently found buried together, and it is well known that stone weapons continued to be made and used after the introduction of bronze. But this by no means proves that all perforated stone implements are to be referred to this period, and the present number of the "Archiv für Anthropologie" contains a paper by Rau, showing the mode in which they might be formed before a knowledge of bronze existed. M. Rau considers that the holes were made in two ways, or perhaps by means of two different borers. The more highly finished holes are of equal diameter throughout, and present a smooth surface, and exhibit at short distances from each other a succession of circular grooves. Such perforations as these, he thinks, were effected by means of a hollow cylinder of bronze. But there is another kind of perforation, the surface of which is more or less smooth, but which is not marked by the lines or grooves above mentioned. These perforations are constricted in the centre, so as to present on section more or less of an hour-glass form, indicating that they have been bored in from opposite sides. These, he thinks, belong exclusively to the stone period. In both methods it is probable that hard sand and water were employed to assist the process. His view is supported by an examination of weapons in which the perforations have not been completed, but carried only through a portion of the thickness of the stone. In the former class of borings the hole on section presented somewhat of the appearance that would be presented by the bottom of a champagne bottle on section, the periphery being more deeply bored than the centre, whilst, in the latter class of borings, the bottom of the depression was simply rounded and rather narrower than the superficial margin. M. Rau has been able to produce borings in a hard stone exactly resembling those on the weapons of the stone period, without the aid of any metallic instrument, but merely by means of the rounded extremity of a piece of hard wood made to rotate with a bow-drill, together with a little sand and water. The stone on which he experimented was a piece of diorite, so hard that a well-tempered knife-blade only marked it with a metallic streak, and of the same kind as that formerly employed, on account of its combining hardness with tenacity, in the construction of various weapons during the stone period, and still used for the same purposes by the North American Indians of the present day. In commencing the perforation, which required infinite patience, M. Rau found it advantageous to attach a piece of wood, with a hole in it, on the stone, which prevented the boring instrument from perpetually slipping off. Two hours' severe work were required to deepen the perforation by the thickness of an ordinary tracing with a lead pencil, and, though with many interruptions, he was fully two years in completing it. It was found requisite to add fresh sand every 5 or 6 minutes. When serpentine rock was experimented on the perforation was accomplished with very much greater rapidity. — *The Academy, Nov.* 13, 1869.

HUMAN REMAINS FROM THE CAVE OF BRUNIQUEL.

This cavern is situated in a limestone cliff on the north side of the valley of the Aveyron, Department Tarne et Garonne. Al-

29*

though this deposit is chiefly rich in remains of the reindeer and wild horse, — both of these animals having been eaten in great numbers by the ancient denizens of the cavern, — there is here a total absence of the remains of the cave lion, cave bear, hyena, and those large extinct pachyderms that have elsewhere been found in ossiferous deposits. Of the existence of early man in Western Europe with the mammoth, rhinoceros, hyena, etc., there can now be little doubt; but at the time when he occupied the caves of Dordogne and the Aveyron, and left behind, in the hearth stuff of these caves, such indubitable evidence of his long-continued residence, the larger pachyderms and more formidable beasts of prey had apparently given place to vast migratory herds of reindeer and wild horses, upon which the cave men subsisted, and of the bones and horns of which their weapons of the chase were made. The mammalian fauna of such caves as Kent's Hole, Torquay or Genisla Cave, Gibraltar, may be more varied and remarkable, but as regards the excellence of the drawings of animals on some of the bones, the fine workmanship of the barbed harpoons and bone needles, no cavern has yielded a better or finer series than Bruniquel. — *Quarterly Science.*

KENT'S CAVERN.

Mr. Pengelly, F.R.S., at the meeting of the British Association, was called on by the President to read the "Fifth Report of the Committee on the Exploration of Kent's Cavern." He said that beneath the floor of the "vestibule" was a layer of black soil, 6 to 9 inches deep, which had yielded 366 flint implements, bones and teeth of recent and extinct animals, charcoal, flint cones, etc. It had been objected that people could never have lived in the caverns, because smoke would have suffocated them. An experiment which had been tried, in burning six fagots of wood, showed the fallacy of the objection. In the exploration of the cavern, a daily journal had been kept, and every circumstance was noted down. 8,948 boxes of fossil bones had been found, and these Professor Boyd Dawkins undertook to examine for the purpose of determining the species to which they belonged. Among other objects a bone needle had been found in the black band beneath the stalagmitic floor. The eye was capable of carrying a thread the thickness of thin twine. A bone harpoon, or fish-spear, forked on one side only, had been met with. Other undoubted evidences of early human art had been found. During the years 1868-9, Mr. Everett, who is engaged by the Rajah of Sarawak to explore the caves of Borneo, visited Kent's Hole for the purpose of familiarizing himself with the mode of operation. Mr. Pengelly then detailed the various layers underlying the stalagmitic floor, in which he was aided by a series of large diagrams. The cave earth, or floor underneath the stalagmite, was full of flint implements, teeth of the mammoth, bear, hyena, etc., and gnawed and split bones. Inscriptions dated 1688 had been found on the stalagmitic walls of that part of the cavern known as the "crypt." The deduction drawn by Mr. Pengelly was that this period of time, although the dripping of water was very copious, had been insufficient to coat over and obliterate the writing. This gives some idea of the immense age of the stalagmite floor, and of the time occupied in its formation. Beneath the earth was a breccia, and up to last year not the slightest traces of man had been found. This year, however, a flint flake was met with, thus carrying the antiquity of man further back. A monthly report had been sent up to Sir Charles Lyell. In some places the stalagmitic floor was as much as 12 feet thick. Associated with the flake were the remains of the cave-lion, the cave-bear, mammoth, etc. In fact, this was the most important anthropological relic which the cavern had yielded. Mr. John Evans, F.R.S., had seen the flint flake, and had declared it to be of undoubted human workmanship.

Professor Boyd Dawkins read a few notes on the mammalian remains mentioned by Mr. Pengelly. He showed that the various strata of the floor of the cavern contained remains of animals of different epochs, from the postglacial upwards. During the time the black or upper band was being formed, a race of cannibals inhabited the cavern. The older deposits contained remains of the glutton, a species of hare larger than the existing type, the beaver, etc. Mr. Dawkins concluded by remarking on the vast antiquity of the human race as indicated by the facts mentioned in the report.

OBITUARY

OF MEN EMINENT IN SCIENCE. 1869.

Buber, Rev. Henry Hervey, M.A.,F.R.S., English Scholar and Bibliographer, March 28, æt. 94.
Berard, J. E., French Physicist, July.
Bergenroth, Gustave N., Prussian Scholar, Feb. 13, æt. 53.
Berlioz, Louis Hector, French Musical Composer, March 4, æt. 65.
Cassin, John, American Ornithologist, Jan. 10, æt. 56.
Cleveland, Chas. Dexter, LL.D., American Scholar, Aug. 18, æt. 67.
Dixon, Joseph, American Inventor, June 14, æt. 71.
Du Noyer, George V., Irish Geologist, Jan. 3.
Erdman, Axel Joachim, Swedish Geologist, Dec. 1, æt. 55.
Erdman, O. L., German Chemist, Oct. 9, æt. 65.
Folson, George, LL.D., American Scholar, March 27, æt. 67.
Forbes, James David, Scotch Physicist, Dec. 31, æt. 60.
Gottschalk, Moreau Louis, Musical Composer, Dec. 18, æt. 41.
Graham, Thomas, English Chemist, Sept. 17, æt. 64.
Grisi, Giula, Italian Singer, Nov. 29, æt. 57.
Hengstenburg, Rev. Ernest Wilhelm, German Theologian, June 3, æt. 67.
Hörnes, Dr. Moriz, Austrian Mineralogist, Nov. 4, 1868, æt. 54.
Huet, Paul, French Artist, January, æt. 65.
Jerdan William, British Critic and Author, July 11, æt. 87.
Jomini, Baron Henri, Swiss General and Military Critic, March 24, æt. 90.
Jukes, Joseph Beek, English Geologist, August, æt. 58.
Lamartine, Alphonse, Marie Louis Prat de, French Poet, March 1, æt. 79.
Leys, Baron Henry, Artist.
Libri, Count, Italian Mathematician, October, æt. 69.
Mitchell, William, American Astronomer, April 2, æt. 76.
Nickles, Prof., French Chemist, 1869, æt. 49.
Overbeck, Friedrich, German Artist, November, æt. 80.
Peabody, George, American Philanthropist and Patron of Science, Nov. 4, æt. 75.
Purkinje, Prof. J. E., German Physiologist, July 28, æt. 82.
Reichenbach, Carl von, Ph.D., German Naturalist, Jan. 19, æt. 81.
Roebling, John A., Prussian Engineer, Resident of the United States, July 22, æt. 63.
Roget, Peter Mark, M.D., English Physiologist, Sept. 17, æt. 90.
Sars, Michael, Norwegian Zoölogist, Oct. 22, æt. 65.
Saint-Beuve, Charles Augustin, French Poet and Critic, Oct. 13, æt. 65.
Sclinitzlein, Adalbert, German Botanist, Oct., 1868.
Shumard, Dr. B. E., American Geologist, April 14, æt. 48.
Strong, Prof. Theodore, American Mathematician, Feb. 1, æt. 79.
Strangford, Viscount, English Philologist, Jan. 9, æt. 43.
Tennent, Sir James Emerson, English Traveller, March 6, æt. 75.
Von Martius, Carl F. P., Bavarian Naturalist and Traveller, Dec. 13, 1868, æt. 74.
Welcker, Friedrich G., German Philologist and Archæologist, January, æt. 84.

AMERICAN SCIENTIFIC BIBLIOGRAPHY.

Alden, Joseph, D.D. The Science of Government in Connection with American Institutions. Sheldon & Co., New York, 1869.

Barnard, F. A. P., LL.D. Machinery and Processes of the Industrial Arts and Apparatus of the Exact Sciences at the Paris Exposition. 8vo, pp. 669. Van Nostrand, New York, 1869.

Barnes, Lieut.-Comm. U. S. N. Submarine Warfare. Van Nostrand, New York, 1869.

Bulletin of the Museum of Comparative Zoölogy. Cambridge, 1869.

Caldwell, Prof. G. C. Agricultural Qualitative and Quantitative Chemical Analysis. Orange Judd & Co., New York, 1869.

Cope, Edward D. Synopsis of the Extinct Batrachia, Reptilia, and Aves of North America. Transactions of the American Phil. Soc. Philadelphia, 1869.

Colbert, E. Astronomy without a Telescope; being a Guide-Book to the Visible Heavens. George & C. W. Sherwood, Chicago, 1869.

Crafts, Prof. J. M. A Short Course in Qualitative Analysis, with the New Notation. 12mo, 133 pp. J. Wiley & Son, New York, 1869.

Gould, B. A., Ph.D. Investigations in the Military and Anthropological Statistics of American Soldiery. 655 pp. 8vo. New York, 1869.

Haven, Joseph, D.D. Studies in Philosophy and Theology. Warren F. Draper, Andover, 1869.

Hayden, Dr. F. V. Geological Report of the Explorations of the Yellowstone and Missouri Rivers. pp. 174. 8vo. 1869.

Kneeland, Samuel, M.D. Annual of Scientific Discovery for 1869. 12mo, pp. 377. Gould & Lincoln, Boston.

Loomis, Prof. E. Elements of Astronomy. Harper & Bros., New York, 1869.

Memoirs Boston Soc. Nat. Hist. Boston.

Osborn, H. S., LL.D. The Metallurgy of Iron and Steel. Henry C. Baird, Philadelphia, 1869.

Whitney, Prof. J. D. Palæontology of the Geological Survey of California. Published by Authority of Legislature of California. pp. 300. 8vo. 1869.

Pope, Frank L. Modern Practice of Electric Telegraph. 128 pp. 8vo. Russell Brothers, New York, 1869.

Lovering, Prof. Joseph. Proceedings of the American Association for the Advancement of Science. Seventeenth Meeting, held at Chicago, Ill., August, 1868. Cambridge, 1869.

Proceedings Portland Soc. Nat. Hist.

Pumpelly, Prof. R. Across America and Asia. Leypoldt & Holt, New York, 1869.

Raymond, Rossiter W. Report on the Mineral Resources of the States and Territories West of the Rocky Mountains. 256 pp. 8vo. Washington, 1869.

Report of the Superintendent of the United States Coast Survey; Showing the Progress of the Survey during the Year 1866. Government Printing Office, Washington.

Rolfe, W. F. and J. A. Gillet. Hand-Book of Chemistry, for School and Home Use. 12mo. pp. viii. 205. Boston, 1869.

Scudder, S. H. Occasional Papers of Boston Society of Natural History. Vol. I. Entomological Correspondence of Thaddeus William Harris, M.D. Boston, 1869.

Smith, J. Lawrence. The Progress and Condition of Several Departments of Industrial Chemistry. Report from the Paris Exposition of 1867. Washington, 1869.

Smithsonian Report for 1868.

Wallen, H. D. Service Manual, for the Instruction of Newly Appointed Commissioned Officers and the Rank and File of an Army. Van Nostrand, New York, 1869.

White, Chas. J., A.M. The Elements of Theoretical and Descriptive Astronomy, for the Use of Colleges and Schools. Claxton, Remsen, & Haffelfinger, Philadelphia, 1859.

Whitney, Prof. J. D. The Yo-Semite Guide-Book. 1869.

Winslow, Chas. F., M.D. Force and Nature, Attraction and Repulsion. J. B. Lippincott & Co., Philadelphia, 1869.

INDEX.

Gould and Lincoln's Publications.

ROGET'S THESAURUS OF ENGLISH WORDS AND PHRASES, so classified and arranged as to facilitate the expression of ideas, and assist in literary composition. New and improved edition. By PETER MARK ROGET, late Secretary of the Royal Society, London, etc. Revised and edited, with a List of Foreign Words defined in English, and other additions, by BARNAS SEARS, D. D., President of Brown University. A NEW AMERICAN Edition, with ADDITIONS AND IMPROVEMENTS. 12mo, cloth, 2.00.

The first American edition having been prepared by Prof. Sears for *strictly educational purposes*, those words and phrases properly termed "vulgar," incorporated in the original work, were omitted. These expurgated portions have, in the present edition, been *restored*, but by such an arrangement of the matter as not to interfere with the educational purposes of the American editor. Besides this it contains important additions not in the English edition, of words and phrases, and also an alphabetical list of "FOREIGN WORDS AND PHRASES"—Latin, French, Italian, Spanish, Greek, etc.—which most frequently occur in works of general literature, defined in English, making it *in all respects more full and perfect than the author's edition.*

GUYOT'S EARTH AND MAN; Lectures on COMPARATIVE PHYSICAL GEOGRAPHY, in its relation to the History of Mankind. By ARNOLD GUYOT. With Illustrations. 12mo, cloth, 1.75.

GUYOT'S MURAL MAPS. A series of elegant Colored Maps, projected on a large scale for the Recitation Room, consisting of a Map of the World, North and South America, Geographical Elements, &c., exhibiting the Physical Phenomena of the Globe. By Professor ARNOLD GUYOT, viz.,

GUYOT'S MAP OF THE WORLD, *mounted,* 12.00.

GUYOT'S MAP OF NORTH AMERICA, *mounted,* 11.00.

GUYOT'S MAP OF SOUTH AMERICA, *mounted,* 11.00.

GUYOT'S GEOGRAPHICAL ELEMENTS, *mounted,* 11.00.

☞ These elegant and entirely original Mural Maps are projected on a large scale, so that when suspended in the recitation room they may be seen from any point, and the delineations without difficulty traced distinctly with the eye. They are beautifully printed in colors, and neatly mounted for use.

BARTON'S EASY LESSONS IN ENGLISH GRAMMAR. for Young Beginners. By W. S. BARTON, A. M. 12mo, half mor., 75 cts.

Designed as a SEQUEL TO THE AUTHOR'S NEW SYSTEM OF ENGLISH GRAMMAR, which forms a gradual introduction to the first principles of composition.

BARTON'S NEW INTERMEDIATE SYSTEM OF ENGLISH GRAMMAR. By W. S. BARTON, A. M. 12mo, half mor., 1.00.

BARTON'S PRACTICAL EXERCISES IN ENGLISH COMPOSITION; or, THE YOUNG COMPOSER'S GUIDE. By W. S. BARTON, A. M. 12mo, half mor., 1.00.

BARTON'S HIGH SCHOOL GRAMMAR; or, an Exposition of Grammatical Structure of the English Language. By W. S. BARTON, A. M. 12mo. half mor., 1.50.

The above works by Prof. Barton, designed as text-books for the use of schools and academies, are the result of long experience, and will be found to possess many and peculiar merits.

Gould and Lincoln's Publications.

MILLER'S CRUISE OF THE BETSEY ; or, a Summer Ramble among the Fossiliferous Deposits of the Hebrides. With Rambles of a Geologist; or, Ten Thousand Miles over the Fossiliferous Deposits of Scotland. 12mo, pp. 524, cloth, 1.75.

MILLER'S ESSAYS, Historical and Biographical, Political and Social, Literary and Scientific. By HUGH MILLER. With Preface by Peter Bayne. 12mo, cloth, 1.75.

MILLER'S FOOT-PRINTS OF THE CREATOR ; or, the Asterolepis of Stromness, with numerous Illustrations. With a Memoir of the Author, by LOUIS AGASSIZ. 12mo, cloth, 1.75.

MILLER'S FIRST IMPRESSIONS OF ENGLAND AND ITS PEOPLE. With a fine Engraving of the Author. 12mo, cloth, 1.50.

MILLER'S HEADSHIP OF CHRIST, and the Rights of the Christian People, a Collection of Personal Portraitures, Historical and Descriptive Sketches and Essays, with the Author's celebrated Letter to Lord Brougham. By HUGH MILLER. Edited, with a Preface, by PETER BAYNE, A. M. 12mo, cloth, 1.75.

MILLER'S OLD RED SANDSTONE ; or, New Walks in an Old Field. Illustrated with Plates and Geological Sections. NEW EDITION, REVISED AND MUCH ENLARGED, by the addition of new matter and new Illustrations &c. 12mo, cloth, 1.75.

MILLER'S POPULAR GEOLOGY ; With Descriptive Sketches from a Geologist's Portfolio. By HUGH MILLER. With a Resume of the Progress of Geological Science during the last two years. By MRS. MILLER. 12mo, cloth, 1.75.

MILLER'S SCHOOLS AND SCHOOLMASTERS ; or, the Story of my Education. AN AUTOBIOGRAPHY. With a full-length Portrait of the Author. 12mo, 1.75.

MILLER'S TALES AND SKETCHES. Edited, with a Preface, &c., by MRS. MILLER. 12mo, 1.50.
Among the subjects are: Recollections of Ferguson — Burns — The Salmon Fisher of Udoll — The Widow of Dunskaith — The Lykewake — Bill Whyte — The Young Surgeon — George Ross, the Scotch Agent — M'Culloch, the Mechanician — A True Story of the Life of a Scotch Merchant of the Eighteenth Century.

MILLER'S TESTIMONY OF THE ROCKS ; or, Geology in its Bearings on the two Theologies, Natural and Revealed. "Thou shalt be in league with the stones of the field." — *Job.* With numerous elegant Illustrations One volume, royal 12mo, cloth, 1.75.

HUGH MILLER'S WORKS. Ten volumes, uniform style, in an elegant box, embossed cloth, 17 ; library sheep, 20 ; half calf, 34; antique, 34.

MACAULAY ON SCOTLAND. A Critique from HUGH MILLER'S "Witness." 16mo, flexible cloth. 37 cts.

CHAMBERS' CYCLOPÆDIA OF ENGLISH LITERATURE. A Selection of the choicest productions of English Authors, from the earliest to the present time. Connected by a Critical and Biographical History. Forming two large imperial octavo volumes of 700 pages each, double-column letter press; with upwards of three hundred elegant Illustrations. Edited by ROBERT CHAMBERS. Embossed cloth, 6.50; sheep, 7.50; cloth, full gilt, 9.00; half calf, 12.00; full calf, 16.00.

This work embraces about *one thousand Authors*, chronologically arranged, and classed as poets, historians, dramatists, philosophers, metaphysicians, divines, &c., with choice selections from their writings, connected by a Biographical, Historical, and Critical Narrative; thus presenting a complete view of English Literature from the earliest to the present time. Let the reader open where he will, he cannot fail to find matter for profit and delight. The selections are gems — infinite riches in a little room; in the language of another, "A WHOLE ENGLISH LIBRARY FUSED DOWN INTO ONE CHEAP BOOK."

☞ THE AMERICAN edition of this valuable work is enriched by the addition of fine steel and mezzotint engravings of the heads of SHAKSPEARE, ADDISON, BYRON; a full-length portrait of DR. JOHNSON; and a beautiful scenic representation of OLIVER GOLDSMITH and DR. JOHNSON. These important and elegant additions, together with superior paper and binding, and other improvements, render the AMERICAN far superior to the English edition.

CHAMBERS' HOME BOOK; or, Pocket Miscellany, containing a Choice Selection of Interesting and Instructive Reading, for the Old and Young. Six volumes. 16mo, cloth, 6.00; library sheep, 7.00.

ARVINE'S CYCLOPÆDIA OF ANECDOTES OF LITERATURE AND THE FINE ARTS. Containing a copious and choice Selection of Anecdotes of the various forms of Literature, of the Arts, of Architecture, Engravings, Music, Poetry, Painting, and Sculpture, and of the most celebrated Literary Characters and Artists of different Countries and Ages, &c. By KAZLITT ARVINE, A. M., author of "Cyclopædia of Moral and Religious Anecdotes." With numerous illustrations. 725 pp. octavo, cloth, 4.00; sheep, 5.00; cloth, gilt, 6.00; half calf, 7.00.

This is unquestionably the choicest collection of *Anecdotes* ever published. It contains *three thousand and forty Anecdotes:* and such is the wonderful variety, that it will be found an almost inexhaustible fund of interest for every class of readers. The elaborate classification and Indexes must commend it especially to public speakers, to the various classes of *literary and scientific men*, to *artists, mechanics*, and *others*, as a DICTIONARY *for reference*, in relation to facts on the numberless subjects and characters introduced. There are also more than *one hundred and fifty fine Illustrations.*

BAYNE'S ESSAYS IN BIOGRAPHY AND CRITICISM. By PETER BAYNE, M. A., author of "The Christian Life, Social and Individual." Arranged in two Series, or Parts. 12mo, cloth, each, 1.75.

These volumes have been prepared and a number of the Essays written by the author expressly for his American publishers.

THE LANDING AT CAPE ANNE; or, THE CHARTER OF THE FIRST PERMANENT COLONY ON THE TERRITORY OF THE MASSACHUSETTS COMPANY. Now discovered, and first published from the ORIGINAL MANUSCRIPT, with an inquiry into its authority, and a HISTORY OF THE COLONY, 1624–1626, Roger Conant, Governor. By J. WINGATE THORNTON. 8vo, cloth. 2.50.

☞ "A rare contribution to the early history of New England." — *Journal.*

5

Gould and Lincoln's Publications.

ANNUAL OF SCIENTIFIC DISCOVERY FOR 1871; or, Year Book of Facts in Science and Art, exhibiting the most important Discoveries and Improvements in Mechanics, Useful Arts, Natural Philosophy, Chemistry, Astronomy, Meteorology, Zoölogy, Botany, Mineralogy, Geology, Geography, Antiquities, &c., together with a list of recent Scientific Publications; a classified list of Patents; Obituaries of eminent Scientific Men; an Index of Important Papers in Scientific Journals, Reports, &c.
12mo. 2.00.

VOLUMES OF THE SAME WORK for years 1850 to 1870 (twenty vols.), with the Likeness of some distinguished Scientific or Literary man in each. 2.00 per volume.

The whole Series bound in uniform style, and put up in an elegant, substantial box, 40.00.

This work, issued annually, contains all important facts discovered or announced during the year. ☞ Each volume is distinct in itself, and contains *entirely new matter.*

THE PLURALITY OF WORLDS. A NEW EDITION. With a SUPPLEMENTARY DIALOGUE, in which the author's Reviewers are reviewed. 12mo, cloth, 1.50.

THE ROMANCE OF NATURAL HISTORY. By PHILIP HENRY GOSSE. With numerous elegant Illustrations. 12mo, cloth, 1.75.

THE NATURAL HISTORY OF THE HUMAN SPECIES; Its Typical Forms and Primeval Distribution. By CHARLES HAMILTON SMITH. With an Introduction containing an Abstract of the views of Blumenbach, Prichard, Bachman, Agassiz, and other writers of repute. By SAMUEL KNEELAND, Jr., M. D. With elegant Illustrations. 12mo, cloth, 1.75.

TREATISE ON THE COMPARATIVE ANATOMY OF THE ANIMAL KINGDOM. By Profs. C. TH. VON SIEBOLD and H. STANNIUS. Translated from the German, with Notes, Additions, &c. By WALDO I. BURNETT, M. D., Boston. One elegant octavo volume, cloth, 3.50.

This is believed to be incomparably the best and most complete work on the subject extant.

THE CAMEL; His Organization, Habits, and Uses, considered with reference to his introduction into the United States. By GEORGE P. MARSH, late U. S. Minister at Constantinople. 12mo, cloth, 75 cts.

INFLUENCE OF THE HISTORY OF SCIENCE UPON INTELLECTUAL EDUCATION. By WILLIAM WHEWELL, D. D., of Trinity College, England, and the alleged author of " Plurality of Worlds." 12mo, cloth, 40 cts.

KNOWLEDGE IS POWER. A view of the Productive Forces of Modern Society, and the Results of Labor, Capital, and Skill. By CHARLES KNIGHT. With numerous Illustrations. American Edition. Revised, with additions, by DAVID A. WELLS, Editor of the "Annual of Scientific Discovery." 12mo, cloth, 1.75.

**LIFE, TIMES, AND CORRESPONDENCE OF JAMES MAN-
NING,** AND THE EARLY HISTORY OF BROWN UNIVERSITY. By REUBEN
ALDRIDGE GUILD. With Likenesses of President Manning and Nicholas
Brown, Views of Brown University, The First Baptist Church, Providence, etc.,
Royal 12mo, cloth, 3.00.

A most important and interesting historical work.

MEMOIR OF GEORGE N. BRIGGS, LL. D., late Governor of Massachusetts. By W. C. RICHARDS. With Illustrations. Royal 12mo. 2.50

THE LIFE OF JOHN MILTON, narrated in connection with the POLIT-
ICAL, ECCLESIASTICAL, AND LITERARY HISTORY OF HIS TIME. By DAVID
MASSON, M. A., Professor of English Literature, University College, London.
Vol. I., embracing the period from 1608 to 1639. With Portraits and specimens
of his handwriting at different periods. Royal octavo, cloth, 3.50.

LIFE AND CORRESPONDENCE OF REV. DANIEL WILSON,
D. D., late Bishop of Calcutta. By Rev. JOSIAH BATEMAN, M. A., Rector
of North Cray, Kent. With Portraits, Map, and numerous Illustrations. One
volume royal octavo, cloth, 3.50.

An interesting life of a great and good man.

THE LIFE AND TIMES OF JOHN HUSS; or, The Bohemian Refor-
mation of the Fifteenth Century. By Rev. E. H. GILLETT. Two vols. royal
octavo, 7.00.

"The author," says the *New York Observer,* "has achieved a great work, performed a valuable
service for Protestantism and the world, made a name for himself among religious historians, and
produced a book that will hold a prominent place in the esteem of every religious scholar."
The *New York Evangelist* speaks of it as "one of the most valuable contributions to ecclesiastical history yet made in this country."

**MEMOIR OF THE CHRISTIAN LABORS, Pastoral and Philan-
thropic, of THOMAS CHALMERS, D. D. L.L. D.** By FRANCIS WAY-
LAND. 16mo, cloth, 1.00.

The moral and intellectual greatness of Chalmers is, we might say, overwhelming to the mind of
the ordinary reader. Dr. Wayland draws the portraiture with a master hand. — Method. Quart. Rev.

LIFE OF JAMES MONTGOMERY. By Mrs. H. C. KNIGHT, author of
"Lady Huntington and her Friends," etc. Likeness, and elegant Illustrated
Title-Page on steel. 12mo, cloth, 1.50.

DIARY AND CORRESPONDENCE OF AMOS LAWRENCE. With
a brief account of some Incidents in his Life. Edited by his son, WM. R. LAW-
RENCE, M. D. With elegant Portraits of Amos and Abbott Lawrence, an En-
graving of their Birthplace, an Autograph page of Handwriting, and a copious
Index. One large octavo volume, cloth, 2.50.
THE SAME WORK. Royal 12mo, cloth, 1.75.

DR. GRANT AND THE MOUNTAIN NESTORIANS. By Rev. THOM-
AS LAURIE, his surviving associate in that Mission. With a Likeness, Map of
the Country, and numerous Illustrations. Third edition. Revised and improved.
12mo, cloth, 1.75. A most valuable memoir of a *remarkable man.*

GOULD AND LINCOLN,

59 WASHINGTON STREET, BOSTON.

Would call particular attention to the following valuable works described in their Catalogue of Publications, viz.:

Hugh Miller's Works.

Bayne's Works. Walker's Works. Miall's Works. Bungener's Work.
Annual of Scientific Discovery. Knight's Knowledge is Power.
Krummacher's Suffering Saviour,
Banvard's American Histories. The Aimwell Stories.
Newcomb's Works. Tweedie's Works. Chambers's Works. Harris' Works.
Kitto's Cyclopædia of Biblical Literature.
Mrs. Knight's Life of Montgomery. Kitto's History of Palestine.
Whewell's Work. Wayland's Works. Agassiz's Works.

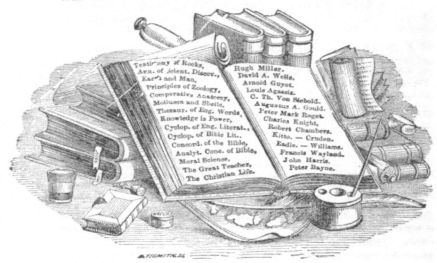

Williams' Works. Guyot's Works.
Thompson's Better Land. Kimball's Heaven. Valuable Works on Missions.
Haven's Mental Philosophy. Buchanan's Modern Atheism.
Cruden's Condensed Concordance. Eadie's Analytical Concordance,
The Psalmist: a Collection of Hymns.
Valuable School Books. Works for Sabbath Schools.
Memoir of Amos Lawrence.
Poetical Works of Milton, Cowper, Scott. Elegant Miniature Volumes,
Arvine's Cyclopædia of Anecdotes.
Ripley's Notes on Gospels, Acts, and Romans.
Sprague's European Celebrities. Marsh's Camel and the Hallig.
Roget's Thesaurus of English Words.
Hackett's Notes on Acts. M'Whorter's Yahveh Christ.
Siebold and Stannius's Comparative Anatomy. Marcou's Geological Map, U. S.
Religious and Miscellaneous Works.
Works in the various Departments of Literature, Science and Art.

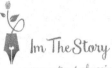

CPSIA information can be obtained
at www.ICGtesting.com
Printed in the USA
BVHW081805220819
556561BV00019B/4356/P

9 781314 985702